RESPAWN

EXPERIMENTAL FUTURES
Technological lives, scientific arts, anthropological voices
A series edited by Michael M. J. Fischer and Joseph Dumit

RESPAWN

GAMERS, HACKERS,
AND TECHNOGENIC LIFE

Colin Milburn

Duke University Press   Durham and London   2018

Designed by Courtney Leigh Baker
and typeset in Minion Pro and Knockout by Westchester
Publishing Services.

Library of Congress Cataloging-in-Publication Data
Names: Milburn, Colin, [date] author.
Title: Respawn : gamers, hackers, and technogenic life /
Colin Milburn.
Description: Durham : Duke University Press, 2018. |
Series: Experimental futures : technological lives,
scientific arts, anthropological voices |
Includes bibliographical references and index.
Identifiers: LCCN 2018019514 (print)
LCCN 2018026364 (ebook)
ISBN 9781478002789 (ebook)
ISBN 9781478001348 (hardcover : alk. paper)
ISBN 9781478002925 (pbk. : alk. paper)
Subjects: LCSH: Video games. | Hackers. |
Technology—Social aspects.
Classification: LCC GV1469.34.S52 (ebook) |
LCC GV1469.34.S52 M55 2018 (print) | DDC 794.8—dc23
LC record available at https://lccn.loc.gov/2018019514

This title is freely available in
an open access edition thanks
to the TOME initiative and
the generous support of the
University of California, Davis.
Learn more at openmono
graphs.org.

The screen flickers. A siren blares. The future has arrived: "In A.D. 2101 war was beginning." As flames engulf the bridge of the lead battle cruiser, the captain of the ZIG fleet asks, "What happen?" The mechanic responds, "Somebody set up us the bomb." Amid the chaos of explosions, the communications operator shouts, "We get signal." While the captain struggles to understand the catastrophe, bellowing an incredulous "What!" to his crew, the operator connects the incoming transmission to a holographic display screen: "Main screen turn on." As the image comes into focus, the captain cannot hide his shock: "It's you!!"

Sure enough, it is the leader of the cyborg invasion force known as CATS: "How are you gentlemen!!" The CATS leader—humanoid in appearance yet radically other, a hybrid of alien flesh and mechanical components—taunts the human defense fleet with imminent doom: "All your base are belong to us. You are on the way to destruction." It seems that CATS has managed to infiltrate all the human space colonies and outposts, taking over the bases while the ZIG fleet looked the other way. The captain seems unwilling to accept this turn of events: "What you say!!" But CATS assures him that all hope is lost: "You have no chance to survive make your time." The holographic transmission fades out with the mocking laughter of CATS echoing throughout the bridge: "Ha ha ha ha. . . ."

The captain clasps his hands, uncertain how to react. The crew urges him to action: "Captain!" Finally, the captain steps up, back in the game. He

FIGURE I.1. *Zero Wing*: CATS leader. European version of the Sega Mega Drive port, Toaplan, 1992. The original arcade version of *Zero Wing* was released in Japan in 1989.

orders a counterattack: "Take off every 'ZIG'!!" As the ZIG pilots scramble to take off, the captain commends their skills and orders them to engage the alien enemy: "You know what you doing. Move 'ZIG.' For great justice." The battle for the future of humanity is on.

This opening scene to the Japanese video game *Zero Wing*—or rather, its oddly translated 1992 European release for the Sega Mega Drive—has become legendary.[1] In this game, the player takes the role of a human space-ship pilot fighting against the CATS army. CATS vividly represents the threat of total cybernetic takeover, embodied in the smirking face of the leader: a fusion of the organic and the robotic, the human merged with the computer (fig. I.1). According to CATS, the posthuman future is already inevitable: "You have no chance to survive make your time."[2] The game presents an allegory of the information age, our increasing dependence on computational systems, and the risk that "all your base" might already be controlled—whether by a political force or a technically sophisticated intruder. At the same time, CATS's notoriously cryptic dialogue in the English translation suggests the instabilities and failures that likewise characterize the practices of high-tech globalization.[3] Indeed, while the international circulation of digital games and other media may help constitute a common global culture, mistranslations and epic malfunctions abound.

Wildly embraced by geeks and gamers precisely because of its multiple levels of irony, and above all, the badass way that CATS threatens complete annihilation while hilariously failing to execute proper grammar or cultural awareness, *Zero Wing* has become a familiar touchstone for online lore, laughs, and leetspeek. In particular, the line "All your base are belong to us" is now a widespread catchphrase for technical prowess—as well as its precarity. CATS's boastful claim has spawned a profusion of remixes and weird appropriations.[4] Among the myriad and sometimes baffling applications of this meme, several have reinforced the sense in which *Zero Wing* serves as a metaphor or a playable simulation of our own historical moment, the age of computational media and the mass digitization of culture. For many gamers, the phrase represents the promise of video games in particular, the astonishing growth of the games industry over the last thirty years and the rising dominance of games as a medium of expression (fig. 1.2). The journalist Harold Goldberg, for example, makes this claim in his 2011 book, *All Your Base Are Belong to Us: How 50 Years of Videogames Conquered Pop Culture*. For others, it is indicative of digital technologies and ubiquitous computing more generally, where CATS becomes a figure for the internet as such (figs. 1.3 and 1.4). After all, what could be more emblematic of the internet and its cultural modalities than high-tech cats? Lol!

From this perspective, the momentary paralysis of the ZIG fleet captain is especially significant. The captain—a highly trained officer of Earth's defense force, eminently prepared for military engagements of all kinds—does not know how to react to this particular invasion because, before it has even begun, it seems already to be over. The explosive CATS attack is not the beginning of a war but its conclusion, the endgame, and this is why the captain is so shocked. The alien is already inside. Posthumanization is already under way. The distressing implications of this situation (especially for the captain, who can barely keep up) are uncannily evoked in the mangled English translation, which affords a set of interpolated meanings and partial significations precisely by virtue of its grammatical hybridity, its semiotic mashup. For "All your base are belong to us" is an assertion that is less about mere possession or appropriation than an *ontological condition*, that is to say, the belongingness of the human base—all the base—to the cyborg world. It is an essential belonging, emphasized by the copula and the infinitive: "your base are belong," as if always already. Crucially, it is not simply the *bases* at stake, the colonies and outposts. Rather, it is "all your base," in other words, the base

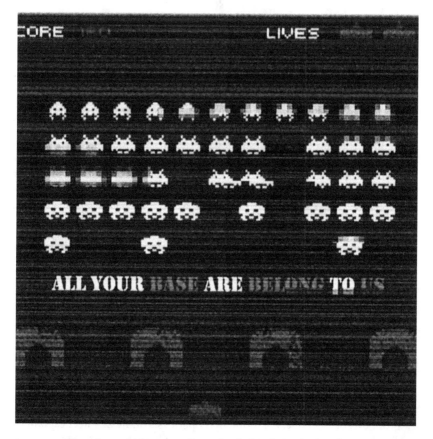

FIGURE I.2. Cover image for bornon413's 8tracks playlist: "A hard cyberpunk mix for playing *Space Invaders*, or any shooter with aliens, really." bornon413, "All Your Base Are Belong to Us," 8tracks, June 23, 2014, http://8tracks.com/bornon413/all-your-base-are-belong-to -us. The scan lines call attention to the medium, the electronics of gameplay. Gamers often creatively mix *Space Invaders* with *Zero Wing*, highlighting thematic continuities— and implying that games about high-tech invaders ("any shooter with aliens, really") are also about the ascendency of video games in the field of cultural production.

as such: the very foundation of civilization, the infrastructure of society, the wellspring of culture, the basis of what it means to be human—all utterly transfigured under the regime of alien science. At least, according to CATS.

In this light, the CATS leader presents a claim about technogenesis—and an affirmation of technogenic life. As a philosophical concept, technogenesis refers to the entanglement of human evolution with technological evolution, the individuation of technical objects, subjects, and collectives altogether.[5] On the other hand, as a trope of science fiction, technogenesis suggests

FIGURE I.3. Gamer cat. Created by Davieeee, just for fun: "A lolcat i made for the lolz." Posted at DeviantArt, November 30, 2009, http://davieeee.deviantart.com/art/All-your -base-are-belong-to-us-145307166. The lolcat phenomenon emerged on 4chan as early as 2006. Its popularity accelerated in 2007 thanks to the commercial site *I Can Has Cheezburger?* It is one of the genres of feline-oriented media that dominate the modern internet. This particular lolcat is playing the *StarCraft II* multiplayer beta in late 2009. Yet Blizzard Entertainment did not release the beta through its Battle.net online service until February 2010. How did the cat get access prior to the official release? Must be some kind of 1337 h4x0r.

something yet more speculative, namely, the emergence of new life-forms, artificial entities, and synthetic organisms from within systems of technology. For example, in Syne Mitchell's 2002 novel, *Technogenesis*, the billions of people linked through global telecommunications systems evolve a network consciousness: "It was as if the crowd was a single entity and the connected people its cells." They form a vast posthuman creature called Gestalt: "A flash image of Gestalt, not as a separate entity hovering above humanity, but distributed through the minds of billions. Each human contributing part of their mental processes, part of their being to the whole."[6] Similarly, in Wil McCarthy's 1998 novel, *Bloom*, self-replicating molecular machines represent a phylum of inorganic vitality, a species of living hardware: "A tiny machine, like a digger/constructor but smaller than the smallest bacterium, putting copies

FIGURE I.4. "lolCATS." Created by bico-kun (a.k.a. Michael James Brew). Posted at DeviantArt, December 10, 2008, http://bico-kun.deviantart.com/art/lolCATS-105995322. The CATS leader speaks in the idiolect of lolcats to indicate the depth of the intrusion—"in ur base," root access—fiddling with the secret, private parts of the system ("movin' ur' zig"). The cyborg cat, meanwhile, dreams of pwning "cheezburgerz"—"All your cheezburgerz are belong to us"—recalling the base, that is, the origin of the lolcat meme and its influence on internet culture ("I can has cheezburger?").

of itself together with cool precision. . . . In short, a pretty typical piece of technogenic life."[7] In these stories, the emergence of a specifically technological form of life—different yet fully equivalent to biological life—is also the occasion for discovering the technical aspects of the human, the degree to which technics are not merely ancillary or extrinsic to the proper base of humanity, but fundamental and constitutive.[8] Hence, the development of new kinds of technogenic life is itself interwoven with the technogenic condition of human history and its future.

This much is suggested in *Zero Wing*. The mechanic's observation, "Somebody set up us the bomb," certainly seems to mean that someone has attacked with explosives. Yet the sudden technological upheaval provokes a syntactic chaos, rife with alternate meanings: *somebody set up* a situation that we cannot escape, a setup that triggers high-tech combat, making *us the bomb*. The

CATS attack sets up or reveals our own explosive potential, our own technical acceleration. In bombing us, we become as the bomb. Human life—if it is to survive—has no choice but to internalize the shockwave of this detonation, its fallout and its meanings, and launch into the game ("Take off every 'ZIG'!!"), exposing an intrinsic capacity for technoscientific response, that is to say, responsibility. At least, in the world of *Zero Wing*.

In this book, I therefore use the term *technogenic life* to describe how the conditions for life as such—nature as much as nurture, lifeworld as much as lifestyle—emerge, evolve, and transmogrify in the era of advanced technoscience, especially in relation to pervasive computerization. It is about the development of new forms and practices of life through digital media, and video games in particular. These practices of technogenic life include political interventions and direct action at the level of technics—that is to say, technopolitics—as well as affective productions and performances, collective mobilizations, and a set of subversive pleasures known as the *lulz*: corrupted laughter, weaponized lols. As practices, they animate a set of subject positions— or rather, dispositions—characteristic of our high-tech culture: shockwave rider, hacker, geek feminist, pirate, troll, maker, modder, gamer. These subject dispositions—invariably grassroots and bottom-up, even if shaped by a certain degree of privilege and a proximity to hubs of expertise—are situated and contextual.[9] They respond to the massive technical and epistemic shifts taking place in the world today, what the media theorist Alexander Galloway describes as "the current global crisis . . . between centralized, hierarchical powers and distributed, horizontal networks."[10]

We see it everywhere, even in *Zero Wing*. In the midst of crisis, with everything at stake, the captain—the figure of top-down command—falls down on the job. The illusion that everything is under control, that the status quo will prevail, unravels when faced with the insidious force of cyborg technology. But from below, from within the ranks of technicians and machinists, media operators and communications specialists, the human survivors of the CATS attack rebound. They spring to action, prodding the captain as they maneuver the command ship through the explosive field, tuning signals and modulating the technical surround.

And let us not overlook the heroic ZIG pilot who speeds off to confront the alien menace ("You know what you doing"). The pilot fends off wave upon wave of enemies—not from the outside but already in the middle, embedded in technoscientific systems and linked into the computational network, exhibiting the same cybernetic condition as the CATS collective. The pilot zigs and zags across the screen, fighting against the CATS calamity

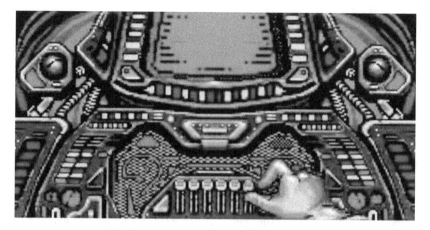

FIGURE 1.5. *Zero Wing*: The hand of the pilot, moving ZIG. Toaplan, 1992.

precisely through the instrumentation of the ZIG (fig. 1.5). The pilot is visible in the narrative only as a component of the machine, accessing the zone of conflict through this privileged device.[11] To say the least, the ZIG pilot is a mirror image of the player of *Zero Wing*—the player who controls the ZIG by keeping a tight grip on the Mega Drive controller, mashing buttons as fast as fingers can fly. The player . . . in whose hands the future lies.

Reload

Zero Wing offers a model of engagement. It fabulates, speculates on the expanding regime of computation, and then bodies forth a way of grappling with this situation in the mode of high-tech play. In its own ludicrous way, then, it suggests the capabilities of games to defamiliarize and recalibrate our sense of things, becoming instruments of representation as well as intervention. The designer Will Wright has even argued that games are like the tools of laboratory science in this regard, enhancing our sensory and cognitive capacities, our intuitive understanding of complex systems and processes of historical change:

> And what's interesting to me about games, in some sense, is that I think we can take a lot of long-term dynamics and compress them into very short-term kind of experiences. Because it's so hard for people to think fifty or a hundred years out, but when you can give them a toy, and they can experience these long-term dynamics in just a few minutes, I think it's an entirely different kind of point of view, where we're

actually mapping, using the game to re-map our intuition. It's almost like in the same way that a telescope or microscope recalibrates your eyesight. I think computer simulations can recalibrate your instinct across vast scales of both space and time.[12]

Extending our perception while presenting tricks and tactics for inhabiting the world differently, games are technoscientific contraptions, engines of experimentation. They are toys, certainly. But according to Wright, they enable tacit knowledge of phenomena that extend above and below the everyday human scale. By playing in fictive worlds, experimenting with their rules and affordances, we get a feel for futurity, potentiality—the virtual as such. The world not only as it is, but how it might have been, or how it yet might be.

The logic of experimentation inheres to video games at every level. It is rooted in the procedures of exploration, testing the capacities of the game, discovering the laws and limitations—even if trying to break them. Moreover, ludic structures of repetition hold forth the possibility if not the requirement of playing again, learning from previous errors and serendipitous discoveries to play better each time. While some games punish failure harshly, for example, so-called permadeath games that make us start over from the very beginning if we die, others enable restarts in the middle of things, allowing us to spring back into action after a fatal blunder, hopefully wiser for the experience. Among gamers, there is a term for this springing back, this returning to life, this continuance of the game: *respawn*.

The language of respawn first appeared in *Doom*, explicitly in the command-line parameter "-RESPAWN" (introduced in 1994 with version 1.2 of the software), which would set all dead enemies to rise again after a brief hiatus, and also implicitly through a gameplay feature that the instruction manual described as "eternal life after death": "If you die, you restart the level at the beginning with a pistol and some bullets. You have no 'lives' limit—you can keep restarting the level as often as you're killed. The entire level is restarted from scratch, too. Monsters you killed are back again, just like you."[13] Try, try again. Today, respawn broadly means the resurrection of any video-game character after death, defeat, or disintegration. It expansively informs gamer discourse, as well, underlying favorite proverbs such as "Gamers don't die, they respawn!" and "I am a gamer, not because I don't have a life, but because I choose to have many." Respawn stands for a surplus of vitality, a reserve of as-yet unexpended life, a technologically mediated capacity to keep on going even while facing dire adversity.

It recalls the biological while simultaneously estranging it, soliciting a postbiological way of seeing. That is, while many forms of life are known to spawn, only technogenic life can respawn. As a trope, respawning echoes and affirms the cyborg vocabularies of digital culture. In computer science, for example, the metaphor of spawning to indicate the processual creation and execution of another process is quite venerable, dating back at least to the VMS operating system in the 1970s. Its repurposing in the context of video games has only further enhanced the sense of reproductive, evolutionary potential immanent to computational systems. Like other concepts from computer science that draw parallels to the realm of organic nature— swarms, worms, viruses, bugs, and so forth—respawning performs the liveliness of algorithmic media, the fecundity of digitized information, the uncanny animacies of code.[14]

It aligns with the orientation of many fields of technoscience today, such as nanotechnology and synthetic biology, which increasingly figure life as programmable, compilable, and rebootable. The sense of "eternal life after death" inherent to the respawn function is shared by the methods of bioinformatics, for example, which promise a surfeit of generative information to emerge from genomic databases: DNA sequences extracted from dead cells become endlessly searchable data brimming with future pharmaceutical interventions, genetically engineered machines, and new forms of synthetic life to come.[15]

Respawning is therefore a sign of the times, indexing the computerization of our biology, the vitality of our machines, and the convergence of video games with the molecular sciences. As if to emphasize these connections, in 2012 researchers at the European Bioinformatics Institute developed a software application for the Illumina Genome Analyzer to improve the accuracy of DNA sequencing. This software application for high-throughput nucleotide base identification is called—what else?—All Your Base.[16] "You have no chance to survive make your time. Ha ha ha ha. . . ."

Reset

All video games produce an excess of high-tech vitality, a controlled overflow of technogenic life. It is visible in various signifiers of the respawn function that have characterized video games from their earliest days: +Life, 1-UP, Health Pack, Power-Up, Extra Life, and so forth. But it is also tangible in the intensive motivation, the urge to keep playing, that ludic structures of repetition seem to cultivate, infecting players with an immoderate and sometimes obsessive desire to press beyond the imposed obstacles and complete the mission, score the points, beat the level—achievement unlocked.[17]

The majority of commercial video games, of course, are designed to keep such desires contained inside themselves, recycling surplus energy, depleting whatever intensities have built up before the conclusion, the final boss, the kill screen. After all, while innumerable mainstream games feature violent combat and cultivate scenes of fierce competition, aggressive violence rarely spills over from the gameplay session into the so-called real world.[18] Likewise, although a multitude of games feature narratives of resistance and rebellion, tasking players to challenge the forces of oppression every day in their living rooms, for the most part, revolutionary insurgency does not spread directly from the gameplay session into everyday political discourse. And while many games entrain players to carry out actions contrary to habit or preference, these novel experiences do not often translate seamlessly to other contexts. Learning how to wavedash in *Super Smash Bros. Melee*, for example, takes time and concentration. Mastering the technique might lead to spectacular feats in the game, but this peculiar exploitation of digital physics does not work in other games—much less in the real world. Such specialized skills are relevant primarily to a mode of existence produced in and around the game, folded back upon itself.[19] In general, video games are devices that produce an excess of technogenic life—represented in the respawn function—and then immediately recapture it, exhausting it through reward and achievement systems, escalating challenges, familiar tropes, contrivances of narrative closure, and other containment mechanisms that are part of what makes games so much fun in the first place.

And yet the containment mechanisms are not always complete. This is exactly the point. For some games, and for some players, the end of the game is not the end. Even the production of downloadable extras, official sequels, or a transmedia franchise does not always manage to fully expend the accumulated respawn energy, the anticipatory desire generated by the gameplay itself. For some games, and for some players, there is more. Alternate meanings and interpretations proliferate, unpredictable emotions and practices diversify and spread, new communities emerge.[20] The inbuilt mechanisms for harnessing ludic intensities, delineating the inside and the outside of the game, fail to maintain the boundaries.

In other words, there are players who do try to make wavedashing work in the real world—modifying the constraints, aspiring to make the impossible possible, struggling against the stubborn physics engine of everyday life (figs. 1.6 and 1.7).

FIGURES 1.6 AND 1.7. Wavedashing in *Super Smash Bros. Melee* (*top*) and in the living room (*bottom*). Screenshots from imnot18hehe, "How to Wavedash in Real Life," YouTube, March 6, 2013, https://www.youtube.com/watch?v=hLnSoo5wOmQ.

In these moments, recreational entertainment proves to be less an escape from normality than a reopening, an opportunity for innovation, reflexivity, and deeper engagement. It's no secret—at least, not any more. After all, the tendency of games to exceed their own closure, to propagate concepts, affects, and patterns of conditioned response beyond themselves, is precisely what underlies the projects of gamification, serious games, citizen science games, health games, recruitment games, training games, and other forms of edutainment, which intentionally try to focus the exuberant energies of ludic environments toward other social purposes.[21] But even in channeling in-game mechanisms for specific out-of-game situations, they also end up providing players with tools for other operations—including critical reflection on the role of games themselves in the contemporary mediascape. The artist Joseph DeLappe famously proved the point with his *dead-in-iraq* project, performed from 2006 to 2011 inside the U.S. military recruitment game *America's Army*. DeLappe used the game's own chat system to recite the names of all the military personnel killed during the long Iraq conflict. Though his avatar was frequently shot by other players in the process, DeLappe would simply wait to respawn, extending his memorialization of the casualties of war through each new digital life. Under the right circumstances, video games offer ways to experiment with the technopolitics of the present, to think otherwise even from the inside.

Relaunch

In the summer of 2013, in response to Edward Snowden's revelations of the vast data-surveillance operations carried out by the U.S. National Security Agency, a number of agitated geeks peppered the internet with images that proclaimed, "All your data are belong to U.S." (figs. 1.8 and 1.9). Across the world, protestors even took the catchphrase offline to catalyze further provocations in the streets, in the flesh (figs. 1.10, 1.11, and 1.12). Along with other sardonic responses to the Snowden leaks, these media-savvy interventions neatly distilled the ongoing conflicts of control and freedom in the global information network. While satirizing the risks to civil society represented by mass securitization, they also reaffirmed the significance of video games for political expression and resistance. For they addressed the scandal of invasive data mining by refurbishing a favorite nerdish assertion of high-tech domination: the multivalent double-speak of CATS.

At the same time, members of the hacktivist collective Anonymous launched Operation NSA, a coordinated set of demonstrations that also

FIGURE I.8. Edward
Snowden as meme.
Creator unknown,
made at Make a
Meme, 2013, https://
makeameme.org
/meme/all-your-base
-ws2445.

FIGURE I.9. CATS
as allegory. Creator
unknown, made
at MemeCaptain,
July 10, 2015, http://
memecaptain.com
/gend_image_pages
/cB52MA.

FIGURE I.10. "All your data are belong to U.S." Poster campaign created by Nils Knoblich. Kassel, Germany, August 24, 2013. According to the artist, "The slogan referenced the phrase 'All your base are belong to us' by the Japanese computer game *Zero Wing*. It is known to the Nerd community and became popular as a meme. The targeted anonymous online publication of photos of the poster started a brisk discussion. Within 48 hours the image received over 500,000 views and 174 comments on reddit." Photograph by Nils Knoblich, http://nilsknoblich.com/. Reproduced by permission of the artist.

aimed to expose the financial ties between U.S. politicians and the intelligence community. Anonymous announced the operation with a dramatic video addressed to the NSA and its supporters: "OpNSA will be unforgiving in its work and will leave no stone unturned, just as you do for all of us. As of this moment, people around the world are beginning to wake up and, consequently, stand up to your data-mining agenda. You will soon understand for yourselves what it is like to be spied on and your personal information be stored, available for all to gaze upon" (fig. 1.13). Over the following months, Operation NSA gathered information on the voting histories of several U.S. lawmakers in relation to campaign donations from private intelligence agencies and defense contractors, drawing attention to these connections through a series of paperstorms, Twitterstorms, and rallies. Anonymous urged internet users to rise up in protest: "We are officially calling on all

FIGURE I.11. Digitale Gesellschaft demonstration at Checkpoint Charlie. Berlin, Germany, June 18, 2013. Photograph by Digitale Gesellschaft. Highlighting the perils of mass surveillance and information capitalism, the demonstration also attended to the resiliencies of technogenic life—indicated, for example, by the protestor wearing an obfuscation visor and the "Pesthörnchen" pirate logo of the Chaos Computer Club: "The Chaos Computer Club is a galactic community of living entities, without regard to age, gender, race, or class, which works across borders for freedom of information, addressing the impact of technology on society as well as individual creatures" ("Satzung des ccc e.v.," http://ccc.de). Technopolitical resistance—with a science fiction twist.

citizens of the internet, all Anonymous participants and all activists to take to their computers, take to their streets and take to all available outlets to let their voices be heard on this issue. . . . The NSA will lose the game. All your base will belong to us."[22] Such media operations blur the lines between the practices of surveillance and counterveillance, articulated through a shared vocabulary of video games.[23]

Snowden himself has upheld the value of video games for shaping protest and political action. During his 2013 interviews with the journalist Glenn Greenwald in Hong Kong, as they developed plans to publish the NSA documents through the *Guardian*, Snowden revealed that his motivation for challenging the security state had developed partly through his lifelong interest in games. According to Snowden, video games frequently present interactive narratives about civil disobedience, social resistance, and transformation—becoming models for engagement: "The protagonist is

FIGURE I.12. #StopWatchingUs Köln. Protest march heading toward the U.S. Dagger Complex military base in Darmstadt, Germany, March 29, 2014. Photograph by Fabian Keil. Reproduced under terms of a Creative Commons 1.0 Universal Public Domain Dedication.

FIGURE I.13. Anonymous: "All your base will belong to us." Operation NSA video, June 2013.

often an ordinary person, who finds himself faced with grave injustices from powerful forces and has the choice to flee in fear or to fight for his beliefs. And history also shows that seemingly ordinary people who are sufficiently resolute about justice can triumph over the most formidable adversaries."[24] In interviewing Snowden, Greenwald was struck by the thoroughgoing way in which games had informed Snowden's own sense of justice: "He wasn't the first person I'd heard claiming video games had been instrumental in shaping their worldview. Years earlier, I might have scoffed, but I'd come to accept that, for Snowden's generation, they played no less serious a role in molding political consciousness, moral reasoning, and an understanding of one's place in the world than literature, television, and film. They, too, often present complex moral dilemmas and provoke contemplation, especially for people beginning to question what they've been taught."[25]

Moreover, video games provide mechanisms for further intervention, experimental technopolitics. In the aftermath of the *Guardian* reportage, with Snowden on the run and seeking refuge in Russia, a number of independent game developers created playable interpretations of the Snowden affair. For example, the 2013 German game *Eddy's Run* asks players to help Snowden evade government agents and spy drones as he tries to release key documents to the public. For protection, Snowden can locate the Guy Fawkes mask of Anonymous to conjure a crowd of protestors: "You are not alone! Hide in the mob. Be invisible for cameras and save from agents and drones" (fig. 1.14). Talking to a reporter keeps the mission alive: "Head over to the reporter he will spread the word for you. . . . Because he keeps telling your story, he can also help you respawn upon death." In *Eddy's Run*, information freedom is a life-or-death matter—computers literally become bombs—and the fate of democracy hangs in the balance (a weeping Statue of Liberty looms over the opening scene). If Snowden fails, we are given the choice of "TRY AGAIN" or instead "TAKE ACTION." Choosing the latter option directs our attention to a variety of international activist groups and protest opportunities. We are advised to do something, anything: "However best you could do, of course, would be to start your own actions. What ever this could be. Maybe a movie, a song, or a storie to get the attention. Everything you can thing of is great and better than not doing anything at all! The people of the world have to realize what is happenig! Stand with Edward 'Eddy' Snowden and take action."[26]

Likewise inspired by Snowden's story, the 2018 Australian game *Need to Know* puts the player in the position of an intelligence agent whose job is to spy on citizens and make decisions about their private activities. The player

FIGURE I.14. *Eddy's Run: The Prism Prison*: After clicking on the mask of Anonymous, Eddy can evade spies and surveillance drones by hiding in a crowd of protestors. Binji Games, 2013.

must choose whether to further the aims of the state or instead to periodically leak sensitive documents and assist underground resistance groups. There are several other games, including *Snowden's Leaks: The Game*, *Edward Snowden: Escape from Hong Kong*, *Snowden Run 3D*, and *Snowden Escape*, that refract certain elements of Snowden's adventure while foregrounding generic, repetitive gameplay mechanics—run, click, jump—as if to remind us that, under the protocols of the network society, our choices are often limited, the options determined in advance.

That video games might serve as cultural resources for political critique, resistance, and insurgency seems to have been a concern of the NSA as well. According to classified documents released by Snowden, the NSA and other American and British security agencies have long considered massively multiplayer online games (MMOs) as potential hotbeds for terrorism, cyberwar, and radical thought of all kinds—demanding thorough surveillance.[27] For example, a top-secret 2008 NSA document titled "Exploiting Terrorist Use of Games and Virtual Environments" indicates that enemies of the state are likely to be found everywhere in gaming environments. Felicitously, this situation presents unique opportunities for security agents to locate terrorist cells, analyze social patterns, intercept communications, infiltrate enemy computer networks, and even execute counterintelligence from inside the games. For these reasons, the NSA, the FBI, the CIA, the Defense Humint Service, and the U.K. Government Communication Headquarters have carried out a variety of clandestine operations in popular gameworlds, including *World of Warcraft* and *Second Life*, as well as in gaming networks such as Xbox Live.[28] The stakes are high, it seems.

Of course, the entanglement of video games and other entertainment media with militarization and securitization, the so-called military-entertainment complex, extends in many directions.[29] In one direction, there are commercial game developers creating hyperrealistic war games, turning simulations of armed conflict into astonishingly lucrative commodities. In another direction, there are defense agencies using game technologies for recruiting and training soldiers or for enrolling civilians in security operations. In December 2013, for instance, the U.S. Defense Advanced Research Projects Agency (DARPA) announced the rollout of its Verigames project. In collaboration with several academic and industrial research teams, DARPA developed a set of puzzle games designed to perform formal verification tests on other software, checking for vulnerable code that might be exploited in cyberattacks.

"Unreliable software places huge costs on both the military and the civilian economy," said Michael Hsieh, a former DARPA program manager. "Formal verification of software provides the most confidence that a given piece of software is free of errors that could disrupt military and government operations."[30] The challenges of formal verification are significant, however, especially at the scale of software used for modern defense networks and weapons systems. But rendering the procedures of formal verification in the form of games would enable legions of nonexperts to participate, finding bugs with vastly greater speed. The first phase of the Verigames project included five games: *CircuitBot*, *Flow Jam*, *Ghost Map*, *StormBound*, and *Xylem: The Codes of Plants*. In 2015, five new-and-improved Verigames appeared: *Binary Fission*, *Dynamakr*, *Ghost Map: Hyperspace*, *Monster Proof*, and *Paradox*. As explained on the Verigames website, "Video games that represent the underlying mathematical concepts allow more people to perform verification analysis of software efficiently. We empower nonexperts to effectively do the work of formal verification experts—simply by playing and completing game objectives."[31] Transformed into *citizen scientists*, these gamers would help DARPA to identify weaknesses in the U.S. cyberinfrastructure, facilitating rapid response and containment. While most of the original Verigames quickly disappeared from the internet, pulled back for further research and development, they left behind a promise of things to come: something like Orson Scott Card's novel *Ender's Game*, or the films *WarGames* and *The Last*

Starfighter, where gamers playing apparently innocuous games might simultaneously participate in systems of defense and securitization, eagerly, joyously—and perhaps without realizing it.

The notion that games could link us to advanced projects of military science and cybersecurity, implicating us in covert operations and surveillance networks through our recreational diversions—politics by other means—has become commonplace, promoting an ambient paranoia. Even in his youth, for example, Snowden was sensitive to the risk of games being co-opted in this way. As a contributor to the *Ars Technica* forums from 2001 through 2012, Snowden participated in many conversations about games, anime, and computers under the username "THeTrueHOOHA." On May 19, 2006, another *Ars Technica* member indicated that strange clicking sounds were coming from his new Microsoft Xbox 360, and he asked the forum for an explanation. Snowden offered a wry diagnosis: "NSA's new surveillance program. That's the sound of freedom, citizen!"[32] A joke about the ways in which game technologies might actually be ideological machines, tools of governance—a joke that is no joke, after all.

Replay

This book is about gamers, hackers, and emergent forms of life in digital culture. It explains how practices of high-tech play generate new modes of existence, as well as new parasites. It examines media networks as zones of social volatility and video games as objects of technopolitical conflict—devices for locking down the future, devices for opening it up.[33] The point is to show not only how gaming, hacking, and other forms of high-tech play contribute to the feature set of the present, but also how they can enkindle desires and aspirations for something different, a world transfigured through technical virtuosity—the future respawned.

This much was clear as early as 1958, when the nuclear physicist William Higinbotham created a game he first called "Cathode Ray Tennis," now generally known as *Tennis for Two*. Higinbotham developed *Tennis for Two* with his colleague Robert Dvorak at the Brookhaven National Laboratory. As a tennis simulator run on a Donner Model 30 analog computer, the game enabled two players to knock an electronic ball—a small blip of light—back and forth across the CRT display of an oscilloscope. But if *Tennis for Two* somehow resembled the venerable sport of tennis, as a computer game it signified much more. As Higinbotham later recalled, the game was designed to encourage visitors at Brookhaven National Laboratory—scientists and nonscientists alike—to think about high-tech research and its implications for the future: "It occurred to me that it might liven up the place to have a game that people could play, and which would convey the message that our scientific endeavors have relevance for society."[34]

In other words, the tennis game was really an exercise in science fiction, symbolizing the potential for scientific innovations to impact society, perhaps to transform the whole world. Today, gamers looking backward at this primordial moment in video-game history often affirm the speculative dimensions of *Tennis for Two*, overriding the superficial sense in which it might be understood as a representation of tennis. "While it was only a primitive tennis simulator, [Higinbotham's] creation must have seemed like science fiction to the hundreds of visitors that lined up to play," writes Andy McNamara, the editor in chief of *Game Informer* magazine. "In many ways, video games are science fiction come to life—a virtual reality we control," he suggests. "Someone who played *Tennis for Two* in 1958 could never imagine opening up a portal to another world on a giant screen in your living room or a virtual-reality unit on your head, yet that is the world we live in today."[35]

Certainly, the video-game industry has vigorously promoted the future-ladenness of its own products, indexed by marketing slogans for everything from the Commodore Amiga ("The Future Is Here") to the Nintendo 64 ("Welcome to the Future") to the Microsoft Xbox One ("Beta Tested in the Future"). Everywhere we look, the culture of video games transforms computers into toys and toys into time machines, portals to another world.[36] It encourages players to engage in anticipation, foresight, and "what if" with every push of the button.

Video games are speculative media, science fiction to the core. They provide a grammar, a vocabulary, a regimen for dealing with rapid technoscientific change and its worldly ramifications—the conditions of technogenic life. They also represent a playful, experimental style of engagement, a *way of using* technical systems to make other futures imaginable. As the critical theorist Michel de Certeau has argued, "*A way of using* imposed systems constitutes the resistance to the historical law of a state of affairs and its dogmatic legitimations. A practice of the order constructed by others redistributes its space; it creates at least a certain play in that order, a space for maneuvers of unequal forces and for utopian points of reference."[37] Experimenting with computer games and other forms of digital media can expose diagrams of power, revealing hardware and software as inherently political things. Learning to play with them introduces the possibility of playing otherwise—hacking, gaming the game.

To explain how such things work, this book traces the intersections of gaming with hacking and high-tech activism, the spawning of technopolitical communities. It examines the invention of early computer games such as *Spacewar!* and *Adventure* in the context of hacker networks and computer science labs, arguing that video games first emerged as experiments in *applied science fiction*. By transforming the attitudes and dispositions of science fiction into a playable format, video games became models of interacting with obstinate systems, the technologies, regulations, and institutions of digital culture. Ever since then, games and other kinds of applied science fiction have contributed to the self-fashioning of hackers and hacktivist groups, such as Anonymous and LulzSec. The book explores these developments across a series of stories, scenes, and snapshots of technogenic life: the repurposing of the game *Portal* as an apparatus for change, inspiring players to experiment and take action even while discovering the limits of individual agency; the saga of the 2011 PlayStation Network outage, an incident that revealed the intensive forms of technogenic life evolving in online game networks as well as the stakes of experimenting with game technologies; and the mobilization of gamer movements, such as the 2012 *City of Heroes* protests, considered as impassioned defenses of technogenic life and the media practices that give it meaning.

Of course, the speculative energies of video-game culture frequently collapse back into conservatizing behaviors, reactionary measures that reinforce the status quo. This is what happened during the GamerGate fiasco of 2014 when some gamers, allegedly concerned with ethics in media journalism, began a sustained harassment campaign against women in the tech industry, feminist activists, and other so-called social justice warriors: a venomous assault against diversity and the perceived threat of media transformation. It reproduced in concentrated form the same power structures and processes of exclusion that characterize the dominant ideological order.[38] But, other times, the respawn capacities of games and gamers, indicating not simply repetition but repetition with a difference (level up, reload, reboot, FTW!), provoke more diverse forms of participatory culture, along with new tactics of critique and intervention.[39] Attending to the conflicts and contradictions, this book ultimately turns to questions of ethics, asking how computer games can foster thoughtful, empathic perspectives on the consequences of our technogenic condition, including the impacts of computerization on our planet and its living ecosystems. Altogether, the book follows the practices of technogenic life from virtuality to materiality, from response to responsibility.

As *Zero Wing* indicates with an abundance of weirdly poetic insight, we are now caught between competing forces vying for control of the future, each struggling to possess the systems and the bases of high-tech civilization. But this same 16-bit narrative of conflict also inspires hope, especially when repurposed and replayed in ways that expose its latent meanings and critical affordances, conjuring the possibility of a future where all the base are belong to us—to all of us, in common.

"You know what you doing. Move 'ZIG.' For great justice."

A long time ago in a laboratory far, far away . . .

The primal scene of hacking, remembered and repeated with all the force of mythology, was the creation of a game—one of the first and most influential works in the history of video games: *Spacewar!* This legendary feat of coding came together at the Massachusetts Institute of Technology in the early 1960s. The original hackers—that is to say, the MIT research scientists, students, and technology enthusiasts who called themselves hackers—were engaged at the time in experimenting with the university's new DEC PDP-1 mainframe computer and CRT display. The PDP-1, a machine the size of two large refrigerators, had been acquired in 1961 to supplement the more formidable TX-0 mainframe. During official work hours, the hackers would tackle computational analysis and statistical calculations for various research projects at MIT. During off-hours, they would develop new programs or "hacks" for the PDP-1, performing ingenious mathematical tricks and other displays of technical virtuosity.[1]

The *Spacewar!* project was a glorious hack: a collaborative effort to make the computer do something other than orthodox science, to test its capacities and affordances, to innovate through fun and games. It was imagined, from the beginning, as an exercise in *applied science fiction*. According to Steve Russell, one of the key figures in the project, "I had just finished reading Doc Smith's Lensman series. He was some sort of scientist but he wrote this really dashing brand of science fiction. The details were very good and it had an excellent pace. His heroes had a strong tendency to get pursued by the villain across the galaxy and have to invent their way out of their problem while they were being pursued. That sort of action was the thing that suggested Spacewar."[2] For Russell, the game was an expression of tactical affinity, an affirmation of heroes who "invent their way out of a problem while they are being pursued," tinkering their way out of a jam, in the middle of things . . . from the inside.

Another key figure in the project, J. Martin Graetz, has also recalled that a steady diet of science fiction novels and films "established the mind-set that eventually led to *Spacewar!*":

> At the time, we were crashing and banging our way through the Skylark and Lensman novels of Edward E. Smith, Ph.D., a cereal chemist who wrote with the grace and refinement of a pneumatic drill. These stories are pretty much all the same—after some preliminary foofaraw to get everyone's name right, a bunch of overdeveloped Hardy Boys go haring off through the universe to punch out the latest gang of galactic goons, blow up a few planets, kill all sorts of nasty life forms, and just have a heck of a good time.
>
> In a pinch, which is where they usually were, our heroes could be counted on to come up with a complete scientific theory, invent the technology to implement it, build the tools to implement the technology, and produce the weapons to blow away the baddies, all while being chased in their spaceship hither and thither through the trackless wastes of the galaxy (he wrote like that).[3]

As indicated by these recollections, the *Spacewar!* project was not merely about morphing the tropes and narrative conventions of space opera into playable format. A certain ethos was also extracted from Smith's fiction—a disposition toward the practice of science as much as everyday life: a reckless spirit of adventure, an eagerness to go beyond the limits of established knowledge, innovating on the fly. Certainly, those involved in the *Spacewar!* project were keen to represent scientific accuracy as much as technical prowess. For example, Dan Edwards added physical calculations to more realistically simulate the gravitational pull of the central star, and Peter Samson updated the cosmic background so that it mapped the real night sky as seen from Earth, even indicating the relative brightness of actual stars. But at the same time, some things had to be fudged:

The torpedoes were not quite consistent with the *Spacewar!* universe after the Heavy Star was in place. Gravity calculations for two ships were as much as the program could handle; there was no time to include gravity for half a dozen missiles as well. So the torpedoes were unaffected by the Star, with the odd result that you could shoot right through it and hit something on the other side—if you weren't careful getting round the Star, it could be you. We made up a typical excuse, "mumblemumble photon bombs mumblemumble," but no one really cared.[4]

Leveraging fiction for the sake of technics and vice versa, making up stuff as needed to get the job done—ingenious hacks, in every sense—the *Spacewar!* project played out as applied science fiction in a manner only superficially indicated by the game's content (fig. 1.1). For it suggests the extent to which all video games inherently belong to science fiction, insofar as they present imaginary worlds whose existence is generated algorithmically, worlds whose operations depend on high-tech hardware, and whose representational conceits involve some admixture of technical realism and fictive irrealism, whether at the level of narrative or at the level of gameplay mechanics, physics simulation, and so forth.[5] But more importantly, in attempting to reproduce the ethos of Smith's novels at the level of representation, the *Spacewar!* project also reproduced it at the level of technical practice: an experimental zeal to go where none have gone before, confirming the values of modern science while also taking an irreverent and cavalier attitude toward proper forms of method, reproducible results, and institutional norms. In this regard, the project established a relation to the scientific imagination that was both affirmative and subversive—in other words, equivalent to science fiction.

The hacker St. Jude (a.k.a. Jude Milhon) has offered the following summation: "Hacking is the clever circumvention of imposed limits, whether imposed by your government, your IP server, your own personality, or the laws of physics."[6] Certainly, science fiction as an aesthetic form would represent a similar provocation, a similar circumvention of established limits—whether the laws of society or the laws of nature—through its characteristic performances of cognitive estrangement and speculative fabulation, to say nothing of technobabble, a favorite quick-and-dirty way to overcome black holes, plot holes, and other obstacles in the path to adventure ("mumblemumble photon bombs mumblemumble").[7] These qualities of science fiction have served as epistemic resources for hackers throughout the history of hacking. John Brunner's *Shockwave Rider*, Vernor Vinge's *True Names*, William Gibson's *Neuromancer*, and the ensuing discourse of cyberpunk shaped the

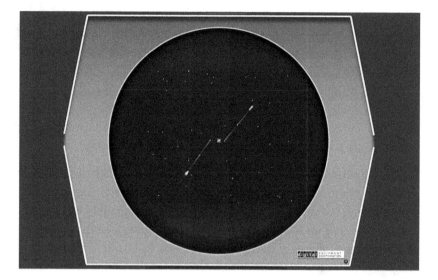

FIGURE 1.1. *Spacewar!* The game has circulated in many forms, on many platforms: "*Spacewar!* was conceived in 1961 by Martin Graetz, Stephen Russell, and Wayne Wiitanen. It was first realized on the PDP-1 in 1962 by Stephen Russell, Peter Samson, Dan Edwards, and Martin Graetz, together with Alan Kotok, Steve Piner, and Robert A. Saunders. *Spacewar!* is in the public domain, but this credit paragraph must accompany all distributed versions of the program." This screenshot is from Norbert Landsteiner's 2012 emulated version of *Spacewar!* 3.1, which was loaded from a binary paper-tape image dated September 24, 1963, courtesy of Steve Russell. The emulation cannily mimics the original Digital Equipment Corporation CRT display, as if recapitulating the primal scene of hacking. Landsteiner's implementation (http://www.masswerk.at /spacewar/) draws on the PDP-1 emulation in HTML5/JavaScript by Barry Silverman, Brian Silverman, and Vadim Gerasimov.

consciousness of legions of young hackers in the 1980s and 1990s. For many in the hacker community—whether they keep to the underground or converge at events like DEF CON, Chaos Communication Congress, and Hack in the Box—films such as *Tron*, *WarGames*, and the *Matrix* trilogy; tabletop role-playing games such as GURPS *Cyberpunk*; novels such as Neal Stephenson's *Snow Crash*; and cyberpunk-inflected video games such as *Deus Ex* and *System Shock* have long been core references, touchstones for social identity as well as technical exploration.[8]

The prominent hacker and open-source advocate Eric S. Raymond has suggested that science fiction is crucial for developing the hacker mind-set. He advises new hackers: "Read science fiction. Go to science fiction conventions (a good way to meet hackers and proto-hackers)."[9] Marc Pesce, a computer engineer and coinventor of the Virtual Reality Modeling Language (VRML), has likewise pointed to science fiction as a driving force among software developers and hackers: "The recent history of hard science fiction has been *the* deciding influence on the direction of software development. The hacker community has been strongly shaped by science fiction texts, and this has led to a direct, often literal concretization of the ideas expressed in those texts. . . . To the degree they [science fiction writers] are successful in 'infecting' the hacker community with the beauty of their ideas, they can expect to see those ideas brought to life."[10]

Or to put it another way: science fiction is the theory, hacking is the practice. While this relationship is usually tacit, immanent rather than prescriptive, it nevertheless seems to underwrite a variety of hacker customs and habits. Conspicuously, hackers have often performed an affinity to speculative fantasy and imaginative literature through their playful jargon. Technical functionaries such as demons, wizards, sprites, and other representatives of the fantastical tradition abound in the history of computing, for instance, while open-source programmer applications such as OpenGrok propagate science fiction concepts (namely, Robert A. Heinlein's notion of deep, systemic "grokking") as they spread among users.[11] A layer of science fiction frequently clings to the material culture of hacking, the instruments and environments of the craft, ranging from network penetration tools such as Armitage and Cortana, which allude to the cyberpunk futures of *Neuromancer* and the *Halo* games, to famous hackerspaces such as c-base in Berlin, which presents itself as a site of archaeological excavation, reconstructing an alien space station that crash-landed on Earth billions of years ago.[12]

The language of science fiction pervades the hacker tradition of colorful codenames as well. Emmanuel Goldstein (a.k.a. Eric Corley), the editor and cofounder of the essential hacker journal *2600*, named himself after the fabled enemy of the state in George Orwell's *Nineteen Eighty-Four*. The infamous German hacker known as hagbard (a.k.a. Karl Koch), who sold state secrets from Western governments to the Soviet Union in the 1980s, took his name and motivation from the character Hagbard Celine in Robert Anton Wilson and Robert Shea's *The Illuminatus! Trilogy*. The hacker collective Legion of Doom, founded by Lex Luthor (a.k.a. Vincent Louis Gelormine) and considered one of the most sophisticated groups in the hacker underground of the 1980s and 1990s, borrowed its supervillain image from the cartoon series *Challenge of the Super Friends*. Count Zero, a member of the pioneering hacktivist group Cult of the Dead Cow, copied his handle from the main character of William Gibson's novel *Count Zero*. Rising to international prominence in 2012, Team GhostShell adapted its brand and some of its principles of "Dark Hacktivism" from the cyberpunk manga and anime series *Ghost in the Shell*. In 2014, a group of Russian hackers involved in international espionage came to be known as Sandworm Team, due to their penchant for hiding allusions to Frank Herbert's *Dune* novels within their spyware. In 2016, hackers calling themselves the Shadow Brokers began leaking zero-day exploits and infiltration tools stolen from the NSA, leading to an epidemic of malware as other hackers around the world started playing with the NSA's secret weapons. The Shadow Brokers got their name from a character in the *Mass Effect* game series, a mysterious information dealer wrapped in political intrigue. Similarly, the Dark Overlord—a hacker group that became notorious in 2017 for stealing data from healthcare organizations, swiping unreleased movies and television shows from Netflix and Disney, and holding these materials for ransom—named itself after the transdimensional monster from the 1986 film *Howard the Duck*. Around the same time, a crew of Brazilian hackers infiltrated the "stalkerware" companies FlexisPY and Retina-X, leaking corporate documents and source code on the internet in order to expose the unscrupulous, borderline-legal industry of tools for spying on children, spouses, and employees. The hackers identified themselves as Leopard Boy and the Decepticons, recalling a memorable line from the 1995 film *Hackers*, itself a nod to the robot universe of *The Transformers*.[13] The list goes on and on . . . innumerable examples, prolific entanglements.

Applied Science Fiction

Of course, science fiction has often asked the question of its own application, that is, how to do things with science fiction. Myriad stories have depicted the genre itself as a source for new scientific discoveries and technical innovations. The teenage heroes of Robert Heinlein's *Rocket Ship Galileo*, for example, are uniquely capable of building a spaceship and flying to the moon because they have been reading science fiction alongside scientific textbooks: "Behind [the boys], bookshelves had been built into the wall. Jules Verne crowded against Mark's *Handbook of Mechanical Engineering*. Cargraves noted other old friends: H. G. Wells' *Seven Famous Novels*, *The Handbook of Chemistry and Physics*, and Smyth's *Atomic Energy for Military Purposes*. Jammed in with them, side by side with Ley's *Rockets* and Eddington's *Nature of the Physical World*, were dozens of pulp magazines of the sort with robot men or space ships on their covers."[14] A character in Isaac Asimov's "Nightfall" likewise suggests that successfully thinking outside the bounds of established, consensus scientific knowledge owes something to science fiction: "It sounds as if I've been reading some of that fantastic fiction, I suppose."[15]

Promoted by science fiction itself, such notions reflect and reinforce a number of well-known instances from the history of science where concepts, inventions, or research programs were stimulated by particular science fiction stories: Leo Szilard's theorization of nuclear chain reactions in response to his reading of H. G. Wells's *The World Set Free*; Gerald Feinberg's quantum field analysis of tachyons in response to his reading of James Blish's "Beep"; John Shoch and Jon Hupp's computer science research on self-replicating "worm" programs, which drew from both *The Blob* and Brunner's *Shockwave Rider*; and so forth.[16] Such examples contribute to a wider belief that science fiction complements and fortifies scientific thought more generally. For example, a 2007 editorial in *Nature* suggested that "science fiction provides crucial raw material [for science]—the minds of young people who will in time become scientists themselves. Not every science-fiction-reading teenager becomes a scientist, nor do all scientists grow up with shelves of Wells, Asimov and Le Guin by their beds. But the inspirational value is real."[17] In a 2008 survey of scientists' attitudes, the sociologists Kenneth Fleischmann and Thomas Clay Templeton similarly concluded that "there definitely appears to be some kind of relationship between an inclination toward the practice of science and the appeal of science fiction."[18]

Yet science fiction just as frequently represents its applied value more at a sociopolitical level, as a resource for cultural change. In Philip K. Dick's *Do Androids Dream of Electric Sheep?*, for instance, the outlaw androids dare to challenge the established social order partly because they have been reading pulp science fiction. According to the android Pris, this kind of fiction inspires hope, a longing for difference:

"Stories written before space travel but about space travel. . . . Nothing is as exciting. To read about cities and huge industrial enterprises, and really successful colonization. You can imagine what it might have been like. What Mars ought to be like. Canals."

"Canals?" Dimly, he [Isidore] remembered reading about that; in the olden days they had believed in canals on Mars.

"Crisscrossing the planet," Pris said. "And beings from other stars. With infinite wisdom. And stories about Earth, set in our time and even later. Where there's no radioactive dust."

"I would think," Isidore said, "it would make you feel worse."

"It doesn't," Pris said curtly.[19]

Pris highlights the utopian impulse characteristic of science fiction, a sense of what things "might have been like" and what things "ought to be like" all at once.[20] She also points to the potential of speculative narratives, whatever the accuracy of their scientific contents ("in the olden days, they had believed in canals on Mars"), to sustain positions of alterity and even resistance to the status quo—in real life as in fiction.

For instance, consider the *Star Trek* fans who boldly adopt ethical principles and forms of behavior from the media narratives into their own lives.[21] There are also polyamory organizations, such as the neopagan Church of All Worlds in California, whose progressive perspectives on group marriage stem directly from Heinlein's *Stranger in a Strange Land*.[22] Or we could point to the "real-life superhero" phenomenon, a growing movement involving people all over the world who take on comic-book personas to do good deeds or even fight crime in their neighborhoods.[23]

These two modes of applied science fiction often seem quite distinct. On the one hand, an instrument for scientific experimentation; on the other, an instrument for social experimentation. On the one hand, the production of a scientific elite; on the other, the cultivation of a grassroots counterculture.

But among hackers, both the technical and the political force of science fiction are vividly enacted as lived practice—a technopolitical inclination that understands high-tech virtuosity as the condition for cultural transformation, affording a belief that other worlds might be possible, that things could be otherwise. This is perhaps nowhere more evident than in the escalation of highly politicized forms of hacking and hacktivism since the 1990s, and especially since the emergence of Anonymous as a disruptive global icon.[24]

Masks

In 2008, Anonymous evolved from the online community of trolls and pranksters associated with the 4chan image board into a heterogeneous assemblage geared toward online and offline activism (fig. 1.2). The trigger for this transformation was Project Chanology. Irritated by the efforts of the Church of Scientology to prohibit the circulation of a Tom Cruise interview on the internet, the anonymous members of 4chan launched Chanology as one of their notorious "raids," with the stated goal of completely demolishing Scientology's infrastructure: "Anonymous has therefore decided that your organization should be destroyed. For the good of your followers, for the good of mankind, and for our own enjoyment, we shall proceed to expel you from the internet and systematically dismantle the Church of Scientology

FIGURE 1.2. "Revolution!" Creator unknown, made at Meme Generator, October 2013, https://memegenerator.net/instance/9894424. Infamous for the invention of lolcats, rage comics, advice animals, and other touchstones of internet culture, 4chan has long been a lively meme factory. And, yes, it was also the birthplace of Anonymous.

in its present form."[25] Chanology quickly blossomed into a worldwide protest against the church's various legal, economic, and religious practices and a host of alleged corruptions—not the least of which, for some Anons, was the church's egregious use of science fiction (i.e., the gospel according to L. Ron Hubbard) for purposes of misinformation, mystification, and the suppression of truth rather than the promotion of liberty and knowledge. As the anthropologist Gabriella Coleman has suggested, Anonymous saw the church almost as a twisted, Bizarro World version of itself: "Scientology is an interesting target, because in some ways it's the perfect inversion of what geeks and hackers value. At so many different levels: science fiction, intellectual property, discourses of freedom, science and technology. It's very proprietary. It's closed. . . . If you had something like a cultural-inversion machine, and you stuck geeks and hackers in there, you'd get something that looks a lot like Scientology." For Coleman, this explains why Anonymous went after the church with such vicious enthusiasm: "There's a real pleasure in attacking your perfect nemesis."[26]

As collective action in both cyberspace and meatspace, distributed over dozens of countries and networks, Chanology precipitated around two forms of applied science fiction. The first was a *tool of occlusion*: the Guy Fawkes mask worn by the anarchist revolutionary V in Alan Moore and David Lloyd's graphic novel *V for Vendetta*, or more specifically, the film version adapted by the Wachowskis and directed by James McTeigue. In the graphic novel, V convinces one other person to take up the mask, to continue fighting even after V dies: a

FIGURE 1.3. *V for Vendetta*: The figure of V represents an alternate future. Created by Alan Moore and David Lloyd, DC Comics, 1988–89, Vertigo hardcover edition, 2005.

FIGURE 1.4. *V for Vendetta*: The burgeoning masquerade. Directed by James McTeigue, written by the Wachowskis, Warner Bros., 2006.

FIGURE 1.5. Low Orbit Ion Cannon: "When harpoons, air strikes and nukes fail." Version 1.0.0.0, developed by Praetox, 2006.

symbolic respawn, perhaps eventually to inspire an entire population (fig. 1.3). In contrast, the film shows the symbolism of V spreading rapidly, surging: an idea virus that becomes a swarm (fig. 1.4). As Anonymous took to the streets, the mask of V provided a perfect cover. Extracted from its science fiction context, rendered a practical device for protecting individual protestors from the scrutiny of the church's lawyers, the mask felicitously carried its science fiction meanings along with it. To be sure, it bodied forth a narrative of resistance to oppressive governance and information secrecy, a speculative vision of mass insurgency and collective action enabled precisely by the mask of anonymity.

The second form of applied science fiction was a *tool of intrusion*: the Low Orbit Ion Cannon (LOIC), a software application for carrying out distributed denial-of-service attacks (DDOS attacks). At the same time as masked Anons were taking to the streets to protest at the church's own doorstep, other Anons were also organizing online through IRC channels, 4chan, and 711chan, rallying sympathizers to download the open-source LOIC package and join the global barrage against the church's computational network. Like the *V for Vendetta* mask, LOIC vividly advertises its science-fictional associations (fig. 1.5). It was originally created sometime in 2006 by the Norwegian hacker Praetox (a.k.a. Shade of Black, MalfunctioN, or Erana) and later modified and forked by other hackers affiliated with 4chan and Anonymous, including abatishchev and NewEraCracker.[27] The graphical interface of the original Praetox version—the version most commonly used by Anons during

Chanology—playfully presents the software as a doomsday weapon of last resort: "When harpoons, air strikes and nukes fail." This subjunctivity, this conditional futurity, is an allusion to the *Command and Conquer* series of science fiction strategy games. The graphical interface also features an image of the ion cannon from *Command and Conquer 3: Tiberium Wars* (specifically, the image comes from a set of high-res art images that were released to promote the game in 2006). The launch button for the application is emblazoned with the phrase "IMMA FIRIN MA LAZER"—a racist online meme that draws from the Japanese science fiction anime series *Dragon Ball Z*.

The software allows a single computer to repeatedly send TCP or UDP data packets to a designated IP address, usually with the intent of temporarily disrupting a web server. Later versions of LOIC, beginning with the NewEraCracker version in 2010, also feature another attack mode: Hivemind. When operated in Hivemind mode, the software links the user's computer to a designated IRC channel, along with potentially thousands of other computers. Commands issued through the IRC channel then control all of the linked computers simultaneously, issuing a massive flood of data packets against a targeted server, overwhelming it with traffic and rendering it inoperable. Effectively, in Hivemind mode, the user's computer becomes part of a voluntary botnet, a cybernetic system of netwar.

As applied tools of science fiction, these two symbols of Anonymous—the mask and the LOIC—pressurize any facile distinctions between the allegedly real and the merely fictive, between playing at science fiction and actually living it. Indeed, according to *Encyclopedia Dramatica*, a wiki devoted to boisterously documenting the exploits of 4chan, Anonymous, and the hidden underbelly of the internet, Chanology itself can be understood as a radical form of experimentation, a type of speculative science:

> The Chanology Experiments encompass a series of experiments involving Scientology and the Internet Haet Machine, Internet Love Machine (the Hugbox), and four machines invented over the course of the experiments—the Internet Change Machine (a.k.a. World Wide Justice Device or Why We Protest Device), Internet Liek Machine, Internet Hurr Machine, and the Lulz Haet Construct—and dramatically advanced the field of Theoretical Lulz. Among other discoveries, these experiments ultimately resulted in the isolation of a fifth force of the Internet: the Hivemind.[28]

The Hivemind, that is to say, Anonymous itself, here narrates its own emergence as one of the fundamental forces of the internet through a set of raucous experiments in technopolitics, the result of unprecedented interactions among various machines and instruments. These "machines" refer to the diverging manifestations and conglomerations of hackers, script-kiddies, activists, trolls, and technophiles associated with Anonymous, playing on a 2007 description of the collective as an "Internet hate machine" by Fox 11 News in Los Angeles, which also described them as "hackers on steroids, treating the web like a real-life video game."[29]

Yet the purpose of such machines would seem to extend beyond mere technics, insofar as the Chanology Experiments were also concerned (or so we are told) with the production of an irreverent form of knowledge. The "field of Theoretical Lulz," as depicted on *Encyclopedia Dramatica* and in the discourse of Anonymous more broadly, is the study of the processes by which trolling, gooning, griefing, and pranking help to expose the fundamental mechanisms, reaction pathways, and laws of high-tech network culture. On the one hand, studying the lulz means basic research on technology itself. For example, *Encyclopedia Dramatica* wickedly encourages denial-of-service tactics, promoting "free experimentation and security related attacks as a method of learning about technology."[30] On the other hand, studying the lulz is a means to discover the essential elements and energies of social change, and turning this knowledge into application. For example, *Encyclopedia Dramatica* narrates the rise of Anonymous's social-action divisions, including Why We Protest and AnonOps, as experimental instruments that have managed to isolate the elementary structure of "World-Change" as such:

> Meanwhile, independent researchers at Marblecake Labs [referring to the splinter IRC channel #marblecake], having managed to acquire the blueprints of both the Internet Haet Machine and the Internet Love Machine a.k.a. the Hugbox, constructed both machines in their sekrit treefort clubhouse. They inserted the Internet Haet Machine into the Internet Love Machine, surmizing that the Hugbox could convert LOLs into a force that could Change the World, a.k.a. World-Change. The experiment produced the Internet Change Machine, a.k.a. the World Wide Justice Device (WWJD) or Why We Protest Device (WWPD). Researchers have since found that World-Change is in fact a complex LOLicule.[31]

This story of Anonymous's discovery of the World-Change "LOLicule," an unstable molecular compound made of laughter and wild experimentation, is so relentlessly satirical and so laden with allusions to the esoterica of recent internet history that extricating any serious proposition is doomed to failure—which is precisely the point. Yet as a satire of scientific discourse, the self-fashioning of Anonymous as a force of technopolitical action retains an essential relation to the scientific imagination, the imagination of science as such. It lampoons scientific method and takes riotous liberties with scientific logic while still oriented toward the production of truth, the generation of knowledge. That is to say, it represents *a hacking of the scientific imagination*: a fictionalization of science, a form of applied science fiction that sustains an alternative epistemic culture . . . a new kind of technogenic life.

LOLecular Engineering

It is likewise the case with many other science fiction resources that Anonymous and other hacktivist groups have drawn upon to combat what they see as violations of truth and justice in the information age, even if their efforts may actually go well beyond the limits of lawful behavior. In the summer of 2011, LulzSec emerged from the shadows of the internet and promptly carried out a madcap series of hacks against various companies and government agencies accused of hijacking democracy, practicing poor computer security, or simply being irresistible targets ("Laughing at your security since 2011!"). On May 29, 2011, for example, LulzSec hacked the U.S. Public Broadcasting System's webserver. After swiping passwords and other data, they published a fake news story on the PBS *Newshour* blog ("Tupac still alive in New Zealand") and added a new page to the main PBS site. It featured an image of Nyan Cat soaring through outer space, leaving a trail of rainbows and a *Zero Wing* reference in its wake (fig. 1.6). Below Nyan Cat, the rage comics "sir" figure, sipping his wine with just a hint of satisfaction, suggested not only an *elite* but also a *black hat* operation. This imagery became part of LulzSec's brand. LulzSec indicated that it had attacked PBS in retaliation for the negative representation of WikiLeaks and Chelsea Manning in the *Frontline* episode "WikiSecrets." In an interview with the journalist Parmy Olson, one LulzSec member claimed it had been done for "lulz and justice."[32]

LulzSec escalated its hacking activities over the summer of 2011—fifty days of lulz and mayhem. The group infiltrated the online databases of Fox, Sony Pictures, and other corporations to expose their security flaws, while also attacking websites of the U.S. Senate, the CIA, and the FBI-affiliated Infragard to protest the political crackdown against hackers and hacktivists, objecting to the ways in which the U.S. government and NATO had started to frame hacking as an act of war.[33] But all the fun soon came to an end. The FBI unmasked one of the group's key members called Sabu (a.k.a. Hector Monsegur) and flipped him as an informant. Most of the other LulzSec members

FIGURE 1.6. "All Your Base Are Belong to LulzSec." Image uploaded to PBS website, May 29, 2011, http://pbs.org/lulz.

in the United Kingdom, Ireland, and the United States were subsequently identified and arrested between June 2011 and March 2012.

At his first court appearance in London on August 1, 2011, the eighteen-year-old LulzSec member called Topiary (a.k.a. Jake Davis) carried with him a copy of Michael Brooks's *Free Radicals: The Secret Anarchy of Science*. Photographs of Topiary brandishing the book became accidental icons, consolidating a number of popular intuitions about the hackers' motives (and, incidentally, boosting the book onto the bestseller lists). Brooks's account of the history of science, much like Paul Feyerabend's *Against Method*, argues that scientific innovation is rarely accomplished by adhering to method, rules, or proper decorum, but is more frequently driven by reckless experimentation, playful silliness, and even illicit behavior, from recreational drug use in the laboratory to outright fraud. The image of Topiary on trial holding onto Brooks's defense of scientific anarchy, as if advocating creative misconduct in the name of science and knowledge, provided an instantly legible rationale for the spate of hacking incidents (fig. 1.7). For the image implied that, as much as the cyberattacks were unlawful hijinks, they could also be understood as experiments in technopolitics: high-tech interventions against the suppression of information and the lockdown of potential futures. Indeed, shortly before he was apprehended at his home in the Shetland Islands, Topiary had posted an evocative message through Twitter: "You cannot arrest an idea."[34] He was, of course, paraphrasing the core theme of *V for Vendetta*.

Following the arrest of Topiary, Tflow, Kayla, Pwnsauce, and other members of LulzSec, numerous supporters reiterated the notion that the group had been experimenting with the technopolitical conditions of the present—the algorithms, databases, and corporate systems—by emphasizing the science fiction qualities of their exploits. Topiary was often represented as Neo from *The Matrix* films, or as a character from William Gibson's fiction (figs. 1.8 and 1.9). Other hackers who took up the fallen mantle of LulzSec also drew on science fiction franchises to situate the political stakes of hacktivism at the moment when the forces of neoliberal governance seemed to be striking back against whistleblowers, geeks, and other champions of free and open culture. For example, one widely circulated video from 2012 announced the coordinated efforts of Anonymous and a newly respawned LulzSec crew ("LulzSec Reborn") to release 3 terabytes of data pilfered from numerous governmental agencies around the world, exposing their secrets for all to see. The video reproduces the aesthetics and narrative tropes of the *Star Wars* films, fashioning the hacktivists as a Rebel Alliance struggling against the Empire:

> The oppressive powers behind the Evil empire have used Darth Sabu to seed mistrusting amongst the inhabitants of the planet Anonymous. The Old Order of the Knights of the Lulz, hunted and exterminated by FBI Siths, have gone into the shadows. Those who have survived are secretly preparing to revenge and meditating about the events . . .
>
> Meanwhile the ruling Empire has started building the Death Laws, to be used to control freedom and the spread of information on the Internet. Frustration has started to show up amongst the different nations, and some groups called Occupy have started to revolt against this imposed dictatorial regime, becoming a danger for the ruling system. The Occupies were declared illegal, and they are currently being monitored and imprisoned.
>
> A new dark age for the humankind has begun and all dissident voices are being shut down. This new Slavery is spreading along every corner of the universe; the Empire has seized control of The Knowledge seeking to render the population ignorant and incapable of rising effectively against the new order. Obscurantism is slowly replacing the vacuum left by the lack of intelligence and access to information.

FIGURE 1.7. Jake Davis (a.k.a. Topiary) outside Westminster Magistrates Court. London, England, August 1, 2011. Photograph by Carl de Souza.

FIGURE 1.8. "LulzSec Reloaded": Topiary as Neo. This remixed image circulated as part of the 2011 Anonymous-led "Free Topiary" campaign, creator unknown. Adapted from *The Matrix Reloaded*, written and directed by the Wachowskis, Warner Bros., 2003.

FIGURE 1.9. "Jake Atopiaric": Topiary as Johnny Mnemonic. Created by exiledsurfer (a.k.a. Michael Parenti). Widely reposted, it first appeared on *The Bird Blog*, August 1, 2011, http://www.artificialeyes .tv/node/940. Adapted from the movie poster for *Johnny Mnemonic*, directed by Robert Longo, written by William Gibson and based on his 1981 short story, TriStar Pictures, 1995.

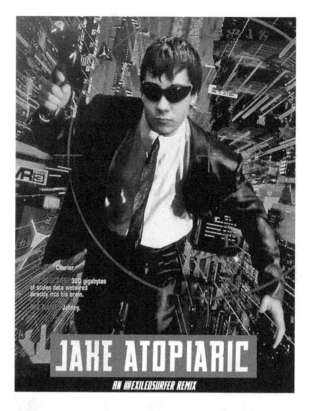

Some rebels have left the law to become pirates, sailing cyberspace to carry information from remote ports to near ones.

In a secret and distant IRC, some knights are coordinating plans and analyzing TBs of data they have taken from the empire. This new council is carrying on secret missions all around the internet to take control over strategic assets; with the new life in the shadows, a new hope is growing, again, amongst knights . . . [35]

The video rapid-fires images of heroes and villains in an epic struggle for the future of the internet, the future of high-tech freedom: Chelsea Manning, Edward Snowden, Topiary, Pedobear, Gabriella Coleman, the Occupy movement, and the Arab Spring, all leading up to the announcement that key information has been smuggled out of enemy hands and made available for further analysis by those willing to do research, those willing to fight. It draws on the narrative setup that launched the *Star Wars* phenomenon in 1977: Princess Leia's smuggling of stolen data, hiding the infrastructural plans for the Death Star inside a loyal R2 unit. The video combines the affect

FIGURE 1.10. Anonymous and LulzSec respawned video: "Don't look to the horizon, look to the stars." Reposted several times, the video was first uploaded to YouTube under the title "LulzSec: ALL YOUR BASE ARE BELONG TO US," June 3, 2012.

of space opera and John Williams's rousing score to encourage sympathizers to help sift through the stolen information, to mine the data and expose otherwise hidden truths. The "new hope" suggested here is, of course, the same one that Leia expresses to Han Solo: "I only hope that when the data's analyzed a weakness can be found. It's not over yet." To be sure, the video insists that the only hope is to look beyond the present—in other words, to practice science fiction: "Look not to the horizon, but to the stars." It ends by rallying the denizens of the internet, the hackers of the world—"Now, take your fucking computer and code your freedom"—and offers a heartfelt valediction: "May the Lulz be with you" (fig. 1.10).

The thoroughgoing convergence of hacking with science fiction relies on the commonplaces of post-Enlightenment scientific rationality, affirmed even in the mode of irony: the belief that rigorous analysis can expose truth, and that demonstrable facts and knowledge ought to make a difference in the operations of the social order. Yet this convergence also propagates an interventionist attitude that does not assume truth will speak for itself, by itself. It does not assume that information will be free, no matter how much it may desire to be free. This attitude thrives on the urgency of conspiracy theory, the speculative logic famously summarized by *The X-Files*: "The Truth Is Out There."[36] Hacktivists therefore often adopt a tactical, paramilitary approach to knowledge and power, responding to the conditions of an era where knowledge and power have become ever more tightly coupled ("the Empire has seized control of The Knowledge"). Informed by the narrative templates of cyberpunk and technothrillers, comic books and video games, this hacktivist attitude often considers the most effective weapons to be those of science fiction as such.

Endgame

Consider, for example, Operation Last Resort. On January 25, 2013, Anonymous hackers defaced the U.S. Sentencing Commission's website, replacing the original content with an embedded video, a lengthy scroll of green text explaining the motives, and a set of hyperlinks pointing to some encrypted files, dubbed "warheads." At 8:41 in the evening Pacific time, the hackers tweeted that OpLastResort was under way: "United States Sentencing Commission owned by #Anonymous . . . Didn't expect us? LOL."[37]

The embedded video began with a familiar clip from *WarGames*: "Shall we play a game?" (fig. 1.11). It went on to describe the broader context of this cyberattack:

> Citizens of the world. Anonymous has observed for some time now the trajectory of justice in the United States with growing concern. We have marked the departure of this system from the noble ideals in which it was born and enshrined. We have seen the erosion of due process, the dilution of constitutional rights, the usurpation of the rightful authority of courts by the discretion of prosecutors. We have seen how the law is wielded less and less to uphold justice, and more and more to exercise control, authority, and power in the interests of oppression or personal gain.
>
> We have been watching, and waiting.
>
> Two weeks ago today, a line was crossed. Two weeks ago today, Aaron Swartz was killed. Killed because he faced an impossible choice. Killed because he was forced into playing a game he could not win—a twisted and distorted perversion of justice—a game where the only winning move was not to play.
>
> Anonymous immediately convened an emergency council to discuss our response to this tragedy. After much heavy-hearted discussion, the decision was upheld to engage the United States Department of Justice and its associated executive branches in a game of a similar nature, a game in which the only winning move is not to play. . . . The time has come for them to feel the helplessness and fear that comes with being forced into a game where the odds are stacked against them.[38]

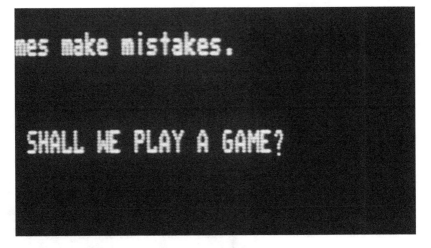

FIGURE 1.11. Operation Last Resort video. U.S. Sentencing Commission website, January 25, 2013. The sampled clip is from *WarGames*, directed by John Badham, written by Lawrence Lasker and Walter F. Parkes, MGM/UA, 1983.

The video announced that the hacktivists had infiltrated the servers of a number of government agencies, and that they had secured a tremendous amount of volatile data, the specific nature of which was undisclosed. Allegedly, all the data had been bundled into a set of encrypted file packages, the so-called warheads: "We have enough fissile material for multiple warheads. Today we are launching the first of these. Operation Last Resort has begun."[39]

The Anons invited anyone visiting the Sentencing Commission's website to download the warheads, each tantalizingly named after a U.S. Supreme Court justice. The hacked website featured hyperlinks pointing directly to the separate file packages. The files were also wrapped together as a torrent through the Pirate Bay. The warheads were encrypted, unreadable—but the hackers suggested that they would release the decryption keys to the world if the United States did not take steps to redress the abuses of power identified in the video. This set of concerns centered primarily on the Justice Department and its relentless persecution of the young innovator Aaron Swartz. By the age of twenty-six, Swartz had already become a significant figure in internet history. He had contributed to the RSS 1.0 specification, the development of Creative Commons, and the rise of Reddit (his startup company Infogami had merged with Reddit in 2005, and as a co-owner he helped to rewrite the site using his web.py framework). As a cofounder of Demand Progress, he played a key role in fights against internet censorship.

But then, it seems, he committed the crime of accessing too much information. On January 6, 2011, two MIT police officers and a U.S. Secret Service agent arrested him for systematically downloading thousands of scholarly articles from the academic journal repository JSTOR through the MIT computer network. Federal prosecutors charged him with violating the Computer Fraud and Abuse Act and other felonies. He faced up to fifty years in jail, as well as potentially $1 million in fines. The vigorous prosecution, which seemed quite draconian in comparison to Swartz's alleged violation of JSTOR's terms of service agreement, led to his suicide on January 11, 2013.

According to the Operation Last Resort video, the Sentencing Commission website "was chosen due to the symbolic nature of its purpose—the federal sentencing guidelines which enable prosecutors to cheat citizens of their constitutionally-guaranteed right to a fair trial, by a jury of their peers—the federal sentencing guidelines which are in clear violation of the 8th amendment protection against cruel and unusual punishments. This website was also chosen due to the nature of its visitors. It is far from the only government asset we control, and we have exercised such control for quite some time."[40]

Representing Operation Last Resort as an act of counteroptics or counterveillance ("We have been watching"), the hackers also amped up the militarized language of tactics, infiltration, nuclear warfare, and mutually assured destruction. The image of the stolen data as a devastating warhead, a weapon of last resort (like the LOIC), was likewise situated in the context of science fiction. The video's liberal sampling from *WarGames* ("Shall we play a game?") evoked a narrative framework in which playing science fiction computer games (i.e., "Global Thermonuclear War") may be identical to actual armed conflict. The defaced Sentencing Commission website vivified the notion of hacktivism as applied science fiction, confirming that we are in fact living in a world already imagined by science fiction—a dystopian world where Big Brother is always watching (cf. George Orwell's *Nineteen Eighty-Four*, Edward Snowden) and reading too much is prohibited (cf. Ray Bradbury's *Fahrenheit 451*, Aaron Swartz)—and that the fight for the future must also be carried out using the tools of science fiction. Yet to emphasize the degree to which cyberwar is indeed a kind of game, all in good fun—albeit with extremely high stakes—the hackers featured a large picture of Nyan Cat at the bottom of the hacked website: the happy space kitten, spewing a vapor trail of rainbow joy across the cosmos.

The Sentencing Commission restored its normal website later the next day—or so it seemed. On January 27, the OpLastResort Twitter feed announced a new iteration, a new turn of the screw: "ussc.gov --> enter Kon-

OpLastResort
@OpLastResort

Follow

ussc.gov --> enter Konami code (with cursor keys) ↑↑↓↓←→←→ B A <Enter> ---> CAEK (repeat for NyanCat powers...) #opLastResort

RETWEETS LIKES
78   21

2:22 PM - 27 Jan 2013

7   78   21

FIGURE 1.12. OpLastResort tweet. Twitter, January 27, 2013.

ami code (with cursor keys) ↑↑↓↓←→←→ B A <Enter> ---> CAEK (repeat for NyanCat powers . . .).”[41] The message spread around the internet quite quickly (fig. 1.12). Anybody who then visited the Sentencing Commission site could enter the Konami code—originally a cheat code for the game *Contra*, as well as a number of other Konami games—which suddenly turned the website into a playable form of *Asteroids*. It was a hack rife with figurative implications and sly allusions. After all, the *Asteroids* game recollected the deep history of hacking, insofar as the rotating ship, the space setting, and the physics of the original 1979 Atari game were notably based on *Spacewar!*[42] Moreover, the self-ironizing suggestion that playing this game of *Asteroids* would lead to "CAEK" was a leetspeak reference to the 2007 game *Portal*, recalling the deceitful promises of the artificial intelligence GLaDOS that delicious cake would be the reward for obediently following orders. As a tactical media performance, then, Operation Last Resort vividly showcased the enduring relationship of hacker culture to science fiction in general, and video games in particular.

By entering the Konami code and then piloting a little spaceship from *Asteroids*, visitors could blast away the U.S. Sentencing Commission's website. In this manner, the game presented a symbolic narrative of exposure, an allegory of deeper facts obscured behind a false front. As players destroyed sections of the page with laser torpedoes or bombs, disintegrating the visible surface, a hidden image came to light: the *V for Vendetta* mask (fig. 1.13). The mask was made out of white text, the slogans of Anonymous: "We are legion.

FIGURE 1.13. OpLastResort game. U.S. Sentencing Commission website, January 27, 2013. The hidden image exposed by the *Asteroids* ship has been used in other Anonymous media ops. Gameplay recording uploaded by Occupy916, "Anonymous Hacks USSC Government Website Secret Code Enables Game," YouTube, January 27, 2013, https://www.youtube .com/watch?v=GBGqvSuTjR4. Occupy916 wrote, "This is not a troll. Go to www.ussc.gov Then use your directional pad and keyboard to type this; UP,UP,Down,Down,Left,Right, Left,Right, B, A, Enter Then click ok and play the game LOL."

We do not forget. We do not forgive. Expect us." It not only indicated that Anonymous had obviously retained control of the website even after the initial defacement was repaired (the mask of Anonymous still lurking behind the blitzed webpage); it also implied that high-tech investigation, discovery, and even illicit tactics may be necessary to get to the hidden truths of our information culture.

If players of this game entered the Konami code a second time, the *Asteroids* spaceship morphed into a playable Nyan Cat that could use "Nyan Cat powers" to fight injustice. But the good times didn't last long. As more and more people started to play, the surge of activity put tremendous pressure on the server. Eventually, so many people were playing the game that it crashed the website: an inadvertent DDoS attack, though it had not been organized as such. (The website stayed down for more than three weeks.) To keep the fun alive, the hackers tweeted that they had also inserted the game code on another governmental server: "http://www.ussc.gov can't seem to handle the traffic (or excitement) so here's a backup."[43] This backup was the United States Probation Office of the Eastern District of Michigan. As with the Sentencing Commission website, entering the Konami code launched the game, a science fiction battle for due process and the future of democracy: "PEW PEW PEW PEW PEW! End Prosecutorial Overreach!"[44]

On the same day, as a small taste of what was inside the warhead files, the hackers released some sensitive data—including a list of names from the U.S. witness-protection program—to a handful of media sites. One week later, after taking over the Alabama Criminal Justice Information Center webserver as a publishing venue, they released the personal information of 4,600 American bank executives, including login information, IP addresses, and contact details, indicating deep access to the Federal Reserve's internal severs. These hors d'oeuvres suggested that even more damaging information was likely still contained in the warheads. Anonymous was keeping the best stuff in reserve—yet they threatened to release it if their demands to restore justice, fair sentencing, and the rule of law were not addressed.

Whether the hackers actually possessed as much secret information as they boasted remains an open question. (Some skeptics have suggested that the encrypted warhead files were hoaxes, false flags, or duds.) Nevertheless, in November 2013, the FBI released a memo to various government agencies claiming that Operation Last Resort was still active and far more extensive than they had initially suspected.[45] The FBI indicated that the U.S. Army, the Department of Energy, Health and Human Services, the Fed, and several other agencies had all been infiltrated. The memo suggested that a number of sophisticated backdoors had been put in place (exploiting a vulnerability in Adobe's ColdFusion web development application), and that the hackers had been rummaging through the servers of these agencies for more than a year. Hence, the bold assertion in the Operation Last Resort video that Anonymous had been in control of several U.S. government servers for quite some time seems to have been accurate.

On Friday, October 25, 2013, the twenty-eight-year-old hacker Lauri Love was arrested in the United Kingdom, indicted for participating in these various infiltrations associated with Operation Last Resort. Love's arrest, like those of other hacktivists, put a visible face to the escalating arms race between forces of securitization and a growing online insurgency committed to info-technical freedom. The bleak prospect of any cyberwar to come, of course, had been suggested by the speculative flourishes of the Operation Last Resort video itself, especially its shrewd references to *WarGames*. In that film, the game-theory computer in charge of the U.S. nuclear arsenal concludes, famously, that for any negative-sum game, the only winning move is not to play. But for hackers and other experimenters, those who recognize their lives as intimately shaped by the technologies around them, the option to not play is no option at all.

For it would seem that this is a game that we are all already playing, to whatever degree we rely on the computational infrastructures of globalization, to whatever degree we recognize technological change as linked intrinsically with sociopolitical change. And so the question becomes, in a world that is already playing out the scripts of science fiction, more and more, day by day: How are we to do things—how ought we do things—with the science fictions of everyday life?

OBSTINATE SYSTEMS

The game conjures a world: "SOMEWHERE NEARBY IS COLOSSAL CAVE, WHERE OTHERS HAVE FOUND FORTUNES IN TREASURE AND GOLD, THOUGH IT IS RUMORED THAT SOME WHO ENTER ARE NEVER SEEN AGAIN." It is a virtual world, a fictive environment of eldritch caverns and treasures galore, tricked into being through electronic symbols. We navigate this world typographically, exploring the forest above and the cave below through words alone, entering discreet phrases into the command line. The narrator guides us into this textual domain: "I WILL BE YOUR EYES AND HANDS. DIRECT ME WITH COMMANDS OF 1 OR 2 WORDS." The further we delve into the underground network of twisty little passages and sublime geology, the sense of magic and romance grows ever more potent. We encounter brave dwarves defending their home from intruders. We fight dragons with our bare hands. We learn the magic words "XYZZY" and "PLUGH" that allow us to teleport instantaneously from one area to another. The Colossal Cave is a realm of epic fantasy, a subterranean land of enchantment rendered as flickering signifiers, a consensual hallucination of navigable space somewhere between the screen and the imagination (fig. 2.1).

Created by Will Crowther and Don Woods between 1975 and 1977, *Adventure* established many of the concepts and generic features that would fundamentally shape the medium of computer games. It was the first instance of interactive fiction, the first adventure game, the first computer program to figure itself as an explorable environment—an inhabitable world.[1] Also

```
E

THERE IS NO WAY TO GO THAT DIRECTION.

THERE IS A THREATENING LITTLE DWARF IN THE ROOM WITH YOU!

ONE SHARP NASTY KNIFE IS THROWN AT YOU!

IT MISSES!

YOU FELL INTO A PIT AND BROKE EVERY BONE IN YOUR BODY!

OH DEAR, YOU SEEM TO HAVE GOTTEN YOURSELF KILLED.  I MIGHT BE ABLE TO
HELP YOU OUT, BUT I'VE NEVER REALLY DONE THIS BEFORE.  DO YOU WANT ME
TO TRY TO REINCARNATE YOU?

Y

ALL RIGHT.  BUT DON'T BLAME ME IF SOMETHING GOES WR......
--- POOF!! ---
YOU ARE ENGULFED IN A CLOUD OF ORANGE SMOKE.  COUGHING AND GASPING,
YOU EMERGE FROM THE SMOKE AND FIND....

YOU'RE INSIDE BUILDING.

THERE ARE SOME KEYS ON THE GROUND HERE.

THERE IS A SHINY BRASS LAMP NEARBY.
```

FIGURE 2.1. *Adventure*: If you die during the dungeon crawl, the software-narrator will try to respawn you—an allegedly risky procedure, relying on untested magic. Will Crowther and Don Woods, 1977. Crowther wrote the game in FORTRAN for a DEC PDP-10 mainframe computer, and Woods expanded Crowther's code. At the time, most PDP-10s would have been connected to hard-copy terminals (e.g., Teletypes or DEC-writers), although video terminals did exist, especially at places like BBN or SAIL where Crowther and Woods worked, respectively. At home, Crowther used an ASR33 Teletype for connecting to the PDP-10 at BBN. This screen image represents the game running on the TOPS-10 operating system for the PDP-10, emulated on Mac OS X El Capitan using Jimmy Maher's "TOPS-10 in a Box" package and the Computer History Simulation Project's SIMH PDP-10 emulator.

known as *ADVENT* and *Colossal Cave Adventure*, copies of the game circulated widely on the early ARPANET, winding up on nearly every mainframe in the United States in a matter of months. According to legend, the game momentarily brought technical research and development in the country to a halt: "It's estimated that *Adventure* set the entire computer industry back two weeks."[2] Transferred over data lines, on cassette tapes and floppy disks, ported to many different platforms and operating systems, the game spread like a virus across the far-flung community of computer users over the next decade, becoming a prime coordinate of geek culture in the 1980s.[3] While in many ways *Adventure* translated the paper-and-dice gameplay of *Dungeons & Dragons* into computerized form, its narrative of exploration and playful experimentation was more specifically attuned to the emerging features of high-tech culture, addressing a historic moment when pervasive computerization began to change the foundations of everyday life.[4] As the game disseminated, it not only provided a template for other computer games to follow but also propagated a way of comprehending the world itself as a technoscientific system, a network of nodes and lines, information machines and data structures. Boldly allegorical, *Adventure* represented the technical underpinnings of life in the late twentieth century as hidden from sight, inaccessible to those who stay on the surface. But it also indicated that mastery of technical skills and esoteric lore could lead to demystification, exposing the deep operations of cybernetic control behind the scenes.

There is a pivotal moment in the game, after all, when it finally becomes clear that things are not what they seem. After surviving many fantastical adventures underground, finding the treasures and solving the puzzles, something strange occurs: "A SEPULCHRAL VOICE REVERBERATING THROUGH THE CAVE, SAYS, 'CAVE CLOSING SOON. ALL ADVENTURERS EXIT IMMEDIATELY THROUGH MAIN OFFICE.'" Suddenly, the illusion of authentic adventure is broken. The Colossal Cave is not a wild environment but a controlled environment. It is not an undeveloped cavern but a high-tech adventureland, a recreational zone designed entirely for fun and games. The cave turns out to be nothing more than an amusement park—something like the fully automatic theme parks depicted in *Westworld* (1973) and *Futureworld* (1976). Certainly, there were clues beforehand. For instance, the vending machine we found in the maze that provided batteries for our electric lantern probably should have tipped us off. But at this late point in the game, we are asked to belatedly recognize a key aspect of postmodernity and its endlessly diverting simulations. As the sociologist and philosopher Jean Baudrillard famously suggested, "Disneyland exists in order to hide that it is the 'real' country, all of 'real' America that *is* Disneyland (a bit like prisons are there to hide that it is the social in its entirety, in its banal omnipresence, that is carceral). Disneyland is presented as imaginary in order to make us believe that the rest is real. . . . It is no longer a question of a false representation of reality (ideology) but of concealing the fact that the real is no longer real, and thus of saving the reality principle."[5]

And yet the epistemological twists and turns do not end there. *Adventure* still has one more trick to pull: "THE SEPULCHRAL VOICE INTONES, 'THE CAVE IS NOW CLOSED.' AS THE ECHOES FADE, THERE IS A BLINDING FLASH OF LIGHT (AND A SMALL PUFF OF ORANGE SMOKE). . . .

AS YOUR EYES REFOCUS, YOU LOOK AROUND AND FIND . . . YOU ARE AT THE NORTHEAST END OF AN IMMENSE ROOM, EVEN LARGER THAN THE GIANT ROOM. IT APPEARS TO BE A REPOSITORY FOR THE 'ADVENTURE' PROGRAM." What has happened here? The cave is not an amusement park at all—at least, not a real one—but rather a digital simulation. The fantastical underground adventure proves to be a recursive allegory, a metafiction: the entire game has been a representation of its own computational structure. We break out of the cave only to find ourselves inside the "repository," the data file of the *Adventure* game itself, surrounded by uninitialized instances of the various entities and objects encountered in our journey:

MASSIVE TORCHES FAR OVERHEAD BATHE THE ROOM WITH SMOKY YELLOW LIGHT. SCATTERED ABOUT YOU CAN BE SEEN A PILE OF BOTTLES (ALL OF THEM EMPTY), A NURSERY OF YOUNG BEANSTALKS MURMURING QUIETLY, A BED OF OYSTERS, A BUNDLE OF BLACK RODS WITH RUSTY STARS ON THEIR ENDS, AND A COLLECTION OF BRASS LANTERNS. OFF TO ONE SIDE A GREAT MANY DWARVES ARE SLEEP-ING ON THE FLOOR, SNORING LOUDLY. A SIGN NEARBY READS: "DO NOT DISTURB THE DWARVES!" AN IMMENSE MIRROR IS HANGING AGAINST ONE WALL, AND STRETCHES TO THE OTHER END OF THE ROOM, WHERE VARIOUS OTHER SUNDRY OBJECTS CAN BE GLIMPSED DIMLY IN THE DISTANCE.

Of course, there were clues hinting at this twist, as well, even from the beginning. The narrator, for example, is quite obviously a personification of the program's text parser: "I KNOW OF PLACES, ACTIONS, AND THINGS. MOST OF MY VOCABULARY DESCRIBES PLACES AND IS USED TO MOVE YOU THERE. . . . OBJECTS CAN BE MANIPULATED USING SOME OF THE ACTION WORDS THAT I KNOW. . . . USUALLY PEOPLE TRYING UNSUCCESSFULLY TO MANIPULATE AN OBJECT ARE ATTEMPTING SOMETHING BEYOND THEIR (OR MY!) CAPABILITIES AND SHOULD TRY A COMPLETELY DIFFERENT TACK." Our access to this world of adventure—as we have been told from the very outset—is entirely mediated by the program itself, and gameplay is as much about exploring the dimensions of this world as it is about testing the affordances of the software, pursuing alternative directions when encountering insurmountable obstacles ("TRY A COMPLETELY DIFFERENT TACK").

But here in the endgame, we learn that the experience of worldness is merely a reality-effect, or rather, a reality-game generated by technoscientific systems beyond perceptibility. And the only way to win is to press further beyond. Indeed, to escape the seeming dead-end of the repository—the recursive figuration of the game's own backend—we must hack our way out, with explosive force.

Fortuitously, some of the rods stacked in the corner of the room have technomagical properties: "A BUNDLE OF BLACK RODS WITH RUSTY MARKS ON THEIR ENDS." If we place one of these rods in the northeast side of the room, the command "BLAST" will blow a hole in the outer wall of the repository. (If we stand too close to the detonation, however, it's game over—so best to take precautions.) Yet our victorious escape does not mean a return to the surface and the reality principle. Instead, the fantastical denizens of the computer—the sprites and imps of lore—carry us from the database into an unrepresentable zone beyond the program: "THERE IS A LOUD EXPLOSION, AND A TWENTY-FOOT HOLE APPEARS IN THE FAR WALL, BURYING THE DWARVES IN THE RUBBLE. YOU MARCH THROUGH THE HOLE AND FIND YOURSELF IN THE MAIN OFFICE, WHERE A CHEERING BAND OF FRIENDLY ELVES CARRY THE CONQUERING ADVENTURER OFF INTO THE SUNSET." This sunset, a bright horizon beyond the hole in the *Adventure* program, seems to indicate the endless affordances of the computer as such. It does not signify an escape from technics, but an opening to technical enlightenment, the transformative potential of further exploration. To find out, we must go in: a notion reinforced by the fact that the original version of the game concludes simply by dumping us back onto the blinking cursor of the command line, with no visual distinction between the end of the adventure and the next operation, whatsoever it may be. There is no outside the game—or, rather, to whatever degree the game fabulates an outside, it is already inside the domain of computation.

Hacks

This primordial computer game proves to be a self-reflexive meditation about computer games, anticipating the affordances of playful experimentation for "blasting" through the limits of existing technical structures. "Blasting" does not mean an exodus but a modulation—in other words, a hack—opening onto other possibilities beyond the present, beyond the visible horizon. *Adventure* was made by hackers, after all, and its narrative transmits the values and attitudes of hacker culture.

Indeed, its development history testifies to hacker principles of free and open access to software and technical knowledge, the commitment to modifiability and modulation. At the time he created the original *Adventure* program, Will Crowther was working for Bolt, Beranek and Newman (BBN) in Cambridge, Massachusetts. In 1969, the U.S. Defense Department's Advanced Research Projects Agency had awarded BBN the contract to develop the ARPANET, the precursor to the internet. Crowther was part of the team assigned to build the Interface Message Processors, or IMPS: the packet-switching nodes used as gateways to the ARPANET. Crowther spent his working hours at BBN developing the assembly language program for the IMPS. He spent his free time playing *Dungeons & Dragons* (and sometimes encountering a different kind of imp in the game), or taking spelunking expeditions with his wife to explore the Mammoth and Flint Ridge caves in Kentucky. When his marriage ended in 1975, Crowther began working on *Adventure* as a means to connect with his daughters, providing a fun way for them to interact with the computer systems he loved—and which, as he foresaw, were soon to change the whole world. He wrote the program in FORTRAN for a DEC PDP-10. As Crowther later recollected, "My idea was that it would be a computer game that would not be intimidating to non-computer people, and that was one of the reasons why I made it so that the player directs the game with natural language input, instead of more standardized commands. My kids thought it was a lot of fun."[6] He passed copies to other friends and colleagues, and within a few months, the game had spread across the tendrils of the ARPANET.

Meanwhile, Don Woods was a graduate student working at the Stanford Artificial Intelligence Laboratory (SAIL). He learned of Crowther's original *Adventure* serendipitously: "I was a graduate student in the Computer Science Department at Stanford, and overheard another student talking about a game he had found on the Stanford Medical Center's computer. I had him fetch me a copy so I could try it on the SAIL computer. It didn't work quite right due to differences in the computer operating systems, but I was able to get it to run. The game itself had some bugs, including a location you could reach from which there was no way to move."[7] Thinking about ways to improve the game, Woods decided to ask the creator for the source code. But aside from an enigmatic clue left in the instructions ("ERRORS, SUGGESTIONS, COMPLAINTS TO CROWTHER"), the origin of the game was shrouded in mystery. Fortunately, a technical solution presented itself: Woods spammed the entire ARPANET. As he later recalled, "The game mentioned Crowther as its author, so I sent mail to crowther@xxx for all hosts xxx on the Internet, which in those days was still very small—it was called the ARPANET then, funded by the U.S. Department of Defense's Advanced Research Projects Agency. I got back several error messages from sites that had no person by that name, but did eventually hear from Crowther, who was by then at Xerox. He sent me the source for his program."[8]

With Crowther's permission, Woods proceeded to expand the game, fixing bugs, refining prose, and improving the range of puzzles. He then released it back into the wilds of the ARPANET in 1977 with a new set of details in the instructions: "THIS PROGRAM WAS ORIGINALLY DEVELOPED BY WILLIE CROWTHER. MOST OF THE FEATURES OF THE CURRENT PROGRAM WERE ADDED BY DON WOODS (DON @ SU-AI). CONTACT DON IF YOU HAVE ANY QUESTIONS, COMMENTS, ETC." While asserting creative authority and symbolically anchoring the game to the institutions of technoscience—namely, the Stanford Artificial Intelligence Laboratory ("DON @ SU-AI")—Woods simultaneously emphasized the spirit of shared knowledge, the open lines of communication among computer enthusiasts: any questions, just ask Don.

A few years before Woods began tinkering with *Adventure*, Stuart Brand had already profiled SAIL as a key site where hacker culture was evolving in relation to computer games. In his 1972 *Rolling Stone* article about the spread of *Spacewar!* and the ethos of "computer bums," Brand described the strange brew of technoscience, countercultural politics, speculative futurity, and high fantasy at SAIL:

> The setting and decor at [SAIL] is Modern Mad Scientist—long hallways and cubicles and large windowless rooms, brutal fluorescent light, enormous machines humming and clattering, robots on wheels, scurrying arcane technicians. And, also, posters and announcements against the Vietnam War and Richard Nixon, computer print-out photos of girlfriends, a hallway-long banner SOLVING TODAY'S PROBLEMS TOMORROW and signs on every door in Tolkien's elvish Fëanorian script—the director's office is Imladris, the coffee room The Prancing Pony, the computer room Mordor.[9]

In this institutional context of cutting-edge scientific research, computer games such as *Spacewar!* seemed to affirm certain technopolitical ways of thinking even while presenting themselves as nothing more than recreational diversions. According to Brand, *Spacewar!* elegantly represented a mode of computer science that empowered individuals while resisting centralized control systems, celebrating playful approaches to technology in opposition to lethal ones: "Spacewar serves Earthpeace. So does any funky playing with computers or any computer-pursuit of your own peculiar goals, and especially any use of computers to offset other computers. . . . Spacewar was heresy, uninvited and unwelcome. The hackers made Spacewar, not the planners. When computers become available to everybody, the hackers take over."

Like *Spacewar!* before it, *Adventure* bodied forth the technical, epistemic, and social dimensions of the hacker world, as well as its characteristic vocabulary. Woods had recently signed on as the SAIL curator of the Jargon File, an online compilation of hacker terms and concepts that had been started in 1975 by a fellow Stanford graduate student, Raphael Finkel. Continually revised and expanded by a group of contributors over the next several years, eventually published as *The Hacker's Dictionary* in 1983, it was an effort to record the slang, folklore, and idiosyncratic attitudes of the hacker communities that had evolved at SAIL, the MIT Artificial Intelligence Lab, and other ARPANET sites, including BBN, Carnegie Mellon University, and Worcester Polytechnic Institute. In many ways, *Adventure* translates these aspects of hacker culture in a playable format.

For example, the rumor that opens the game—"MAGIC IS SAID TO WORK IN THE CAVE"—and the discovery of thaumaturgic words that transport us from one location to another resonate with the peculiar significance of "magic" as a hacker concept. The Jargon File offers a concise definition for "magic": "As yet unexplained, or too complicated to explain. (Arthur C. Clarke once said that magic was as-yet-not-understood science.)"[10] For hackers, then, magic is less about fantasy than science fiction; it is science over the horizon, possibly from the future. Taking the third and most famous of "Clarke's Three Laws" as gospel—"Any sufficiently advanced technology is indistinguishable from magic"—hackers might strive to obtain special mastery of such advanced technical knowledge, becoming a sorcerer, a wizard.[11] Putting this concept into game form, *Adventure* similarly insists that magic is nothing more than advanced technology—first, in the twist that Colossal Cave is a high-tech theme park, and, second, in the twist that Colossal Cave is just a fiction conjured by the *Adventure* program. In this regard, the magic words in the game, such as "XYZZY" and "PLUGH," are revealed quite literally to be symbols of computational statements: our teleportation between different rooms of the cave, nothing other than GOTO jumps.[12]

This symbolic relation of the magic words of the game to the computational vocabulary of hackers becomes especially clear in a puzzle to retrieve the golden eggs, where we must master the sequential command "FIE FIE FOE FOO." The notable substitution of "foo" for the fairytale "fum" draws attention to its functional role in executing the magic of the command sequence, teleporting the eggs back to the Giant Room. "FOO," after all, is a common placeholder or metasyntactic variable in the context of computer programming. According to *The Hacker's Dictionary*,

> When you have to invent an arbitrary name for something for the sake of exposition, FOO is usually used. If you need a second one, BAR or BAZ is usually used . . . The concatenation FOOBAR is widely used also, and this in turn can be traced to the obscene acronym "FUBAR" that arose in the armed forces during World War II. . . . Words such as "foo" are called "metasyntactic variables" because, just as a mathematical variable stands for some number, so "foo" always stands for the real name of the thing under discussion. A hacker avoids using "foo" as the real name of anything.[13]

In underscoring the magical qualities of "FOO," the game smartly suggests how "FOO" as a metasyntactic variable already instantiates a form of magical thinking around the powers of source code—what the media theorist Wendy Chun has called "sourcery": the fetishized power of the "real names" or "true names" hidden in the code, the source of programmable magic.[14] Ursula K. Le Guin's 1968 fantasy novel *A Wizard of Earthsea*, drawing on deeper fairytale traditions, had emphasized the executable power of "true names," and the idea became commonplace in hacker cultures (later reinforced by the publication of Vernor Vinge's proto-cyberpunk novella *True Names* in 1981, recollected in William Gibson's *Neuromancer* in 1984, and so on). The joke in *Adventure* is that "FOO" actually executes, magically—it has taken on the powers of the true name, the real thing. Moreover, it is humorously reflected in the source code for the game: the variable that keeps track of the player's progress in saying "FEE FIE FOE FOO" is actually called "FOOBAR":

```
C FEE FIE FOE FOO (AND FUM). ADVANCE TO NEXT STATE IF GIVEN IN PROPER ORDER.
C LOOK UP WD1 IN SECTION 3 OF VOCAB TO DETERMINE WHICH WORD WE'VE GOT. LAST
C WORD ZIPS THE EGGS BACK TO THE GIANT ROOM (UNLESS ALREADY THERE).

8250    K=VOCAB(WD1,3)
        SPK=42
        IF(FOOBAR.EQ.1-K)GOTO 8252
        IF(FOOBAR.NE.0)SPK=151
        GOTO 2011
```

```
8252    FOOBAR=K
        IF(K.NE.4)GOTO 2009
        FOOBAR=0
        IF(PLACE(EGGS).EQ.PLAC(EGGS)
   1        .OR.(TOTING(EGGS).AND.LOC.EQ.PLAC(EGGS)))GOTO 2011
```

After toting the eggs, challenging the troll, summoning the crystalline bridge, feeding the bear, watering the magic beanstalks—all the actions of the game— it becomes clear that there is no functional difference between magic words and other input commands. In the computational environment of Colossal Cave, magic is everywhere, all the way down, governed by the mystical language of code.

Hackers themselves were quick to internalize the game's metafictional equation between magic and technics, insofar as it affirmed a way of thinking that was already prevalent in the community. By 1981, the Jargon File included several references to *Adventure* and its fictive conceits, even providing separate entries for the terms "xyzzy" and "plugh" (both defined simply as "from the Adventure game," each pointing to the other for further clarification: "See plugh" and "See xyzzy"—a self-referential loop, transporting us endlessly between these two locations of the Jargon File). The 1983 *Hacker's Dictionary* removed the entry for "plugh" but expanded on the significance of "xyzzy," which had by then become a familiar element of the hacker lexicon: "The canonical 'magic word.' This comes from the Adventure game. . . . If, therefore, you encounter some bit of magic [i.e., the hacker concept of "magic"—see above], or more precisely some technique for accomplishing magic, you might remark on this quite succinctly by saying simply, 'xyzzy!' This may be translated roughly as 'Wow! Magic!'" Likewise, the 1981 Jargon File elaborates the definition of "wizard" in relation to *Adventure*, suggesting that a typical wizard is a "person who is permitted to do things forbidden to ordinary people, e.g., . . . an advent wizard may play Adventure during the day." *The Hacker's Dictionary* further clarifies: "For example, an Adventure wizard at Stanford may play the Adventure game during the day, which is forbidden (the program simply refuses to play) to most people because it uselessly consumes too many cycles [i.e., computational cycles on a time-shared mainframe]."

Reaffirming advanced technology as indistinguishable from magic, *Adventure* helped to shape a way of thinking—entraining a certain habitus, an intuition for solving problems with computers. As the journalist Steven Levy has written, "Each 'room' of the adventure was like a computer subroutine, presenting a logical problem you'd have to solve."[15] According to Crowther himself, it is precisely this aspect of the game that explains its enduring appeal: "And why did people enjoy it? Because it's exactly the kind of thing that computer programmers do. They're struggling with an obstinate system that can do what you want but only if you can figure out the right thing to say to it."[16]

Moreover, it encourages—even to some degree requires—players to violate the internal fiction of the game in order to succeed. For instance, the final series of actions required to trigger the endgame, blow a hole in the data repository, and venture off into the sunset is deceptively counterintuitive. In the days before walkthrough guides were readily available, there were only a few options for figuring out the solution. Trial and error was the default process, but it was inevitably frustrating. In the final stages of the game, there is a strong likelihood of dying if entering commands randomly—and, hence, having to start the entire game over from the beginning—especially as the turn limit approaches. Even if a player manages to trigger the endgame and enter the repository, the final required command to "BLAST" one of the black rods—and in the correct corner of the room—might seem rather perverse, considering that the narrator actively misleads about the viability of this solution. Until the moment when we take one of the black rods in the repository, the command "BLAST" always returns the response "BLASTING REQUIRES DYNAMITE." Hence, the fact that "BLAST" will work on one of the black magical rods with rusty ends—hardly an obvious substitute for dynamite—is rather surprising. Certainly, it has been the bane of many adventurers over the years. As one player puts it, "It's perhaps the most egregious example of guess the verb and just about the worst puzzle in general I've ever seen."[17]

Alternatively, players could search outside of the game for advice or hints. The game's instructions invited people to email Don Woods with any questions; so asking Don how to solve the endgame could have been a possible recourse for frustrated players. Likewise, talking to other players who had already managed to beat the game, through whatever means, could have been another way to ferret out the secrets of Colossal Cave.

The final option: cheat, hack, modify. Woods had freely distributed the FORTRAN source code after releasing the game on the ARPANET. This is how so many ported and modified versions of *Adventure* appeared over the following decades (and why many of these later versions also softened the unfairness of the endgame). In any case, digging into the code file and the vocabulary keywords in the data file would quickly unveil the mysteries of the endgame:

```
C BLAST. NO EFFECT UNLESS YOU'VE GOT DYNAMITE, WHICH IS A NEAT TRICK!

9230    IF(PROP(ROD2).LT.0.OR..NOT.CLOSED)GOTO 2011
        BONUS=133
        IF(LOC.EQ.115)BONUS=134
        IF(HERE(ROD2))BONUS=135
        CALL RSPEAK(BONUS)
        GOTO 20000
```

Without the benefit of the source code, a machine-language debugger or some other hack might be an appealing alternative. Any means of getting into the code of the game is already thematically endorsed by the game itself. After all, the conclusion of the narrative metaphorically anticipates the necessity of such methods—the need for breaking beyond the diegetic representation and digging into the technical underpinnings. In many ways, *Adventure* promotes its own hacking—and thereby prefigures its own social impact.

Adventure triggered the aspirations of an entire generation of hackers, software developers, and computer engineers. As Woods said, "I've long ago lost count of the programmers who've told me that the experience that got them started using computers was playing *Adventure*."[18] In many ways, it galvanized the development of the computer games industry, inspiring companies such Infocom and Sierra On-Line. It established a set of tropes that were later taken up by many other fictions of hacking and gaming, including *The Matrix* and Ernest Cline's *Ready Player One*. It also played a role in shaping the internet in its current form—and not only because of Crowther's role in internet history. After all, the game's functional metaphor of moving between different "rooms" of the cave served as a conceptual resource for Tim Berners-Lee and his colleagues when they developed the foundations of what eventually became the World Wide Web.[19]

For some players, *Adventure* also perpetuated an idea that practices of technoscientific innovation could simultaneously be practices of techno-political subversion. That is to say, the process that Crowther described as "struggling with an obstinate system," learning to communicate with the text parser, finding hidden treasures and solving puzzles by working around the limits of the system—"USUALLY PEOPLE TRYING UNSUCCESSFULLY TO MANIPULATE AN OBJECT ARE ATTEMPTING SOMETHING BEYOND

THEIR (OR MY!) CAPABILITIES AND SHOULD TRY A COMPLETELY DIF-
FERENT TACK"—also represented a model for struggling with the obstinate
systems of the high-tech world.

Invisible Key

While working as a programmer for Atari, Warren Robinett developed the
blockbuster graphical game *Adventure* for the Atari 2600. As Robinett explained, "Adventure for the Atari 2600 was directly inspired by the original text game Adventure created by Willie Crowther and Don Woods."[20] In
terms of its narrative setup, however, Robinett's *Adventure* bears little resemblance to the Crowther and Woods game: "An evil magician has stolen
the Enchanted Chalice and has hidden it somewhere in the Kingdom. The
object of the game is to rescue the Enchanted Chalice and place it in the
Golden Castle where it belongs."[21] Nevertheless, its conceptual and thematic
parallels are extensive.

Moreover, the twists at the conclusion of the text *Adventure*—breaking
through the software barrier—are echoed by Robinett's graphical *Adventure*.
Robinett noted that developing the game required subversive tactics, maneuvering around the corporate politics of Atari: "There were some political
obstacles to creating *Adventure* and getting it published."[22] Shortly after he
began, Robinett's supervisor at Atari instructed him to cease working on
it, suggesting it was a pointless exercise: the technical hurdles for making a
graphical adaptation of the Crowther and Woods game on the limited hardware
of the Atari 2600 were too high. Instead, the Atari marketing department
advised Robinett to turn his nascent adventure game into a Superman game,
to tie in with the upcoming 1979 *Superman* movie—owned by Atari's parent
company, Warner Communications. For Robinett, this only provoked him
to work harder on *Adventure*, turning the limits of the 2600 to his advantage. Defying his supervisor's instructions, Robinett continued to develop
the game.[23] The final product was a fantasy game in which players overcome
challenges by reconfiguring technical devices, digital tools. "Crowther and
Woods had established in their game that objects were tools for getting past
obstacles," Robinett observed. His game went even further: "Each object in
Atari 2600 Adventure does something. . . . The objects are really tools since
players can use them to cause things to happen in the game world. . . . Each
tool object is a means of getting past a certain kind of barrier."[24] The game,
therefore, manifests a hacker zeal for circumventing limits—in technology
as much as in real life.

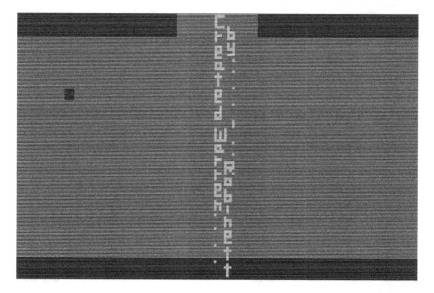

FIGURE 2.2. *Adventure* for Atari 2600: "Created by Warren Robinett." Atari, Inc., 1979.
This image is from a ported version of the game running on a PlayStation 4, included
in the collection *Atari Flashback Classics, Volume 2*, Atari, AtGames, and Code Mystics,
2016.

Robinett also committed one more act of rebellion. Indignant about Atari's policy to hide the identities of its game developers under the corporate brand name and without any royalty compensation, Robinett created
a secret room in his game: a locked dungeon that could only be opened
by an invisible key, a single-pixel lock pick hidden in the catacombs of the
Black Castle. An industrious player of the game, while dutifully obeying the
rules of the Kingdom—that is, the instruction manual, with its command
to retrieve the Enchanted Chalice from the thieving wizard and return it to
the Golden Castle where it belongs—might accidentally stumble upon this
wayward pixel. Wandering astray from the mission at hand, the player might
happen to carry the pixel to a particular impenetrable wall near the Golden
Castle—and suddenly find the barrier open (fig. 2.2). Inside the chamber,
the gamer would discover the name of the programmer, the signature of
Warren Robinett .

As Robinett recalled later, "Each 2600 game was designed entirely by one
person. But on the package it said basically 'Adventure, by Atari.' And we
were only getting salaries, no cut of the huge profits. It was a signature, like at
the bottom of a painting. But to make it happen, I had to hide my signature

in the code, in a really obscure place, and not tell anybody. Keeping a secret like that is not easy."[25] It was eventually discovered in August 1980 by a fifteen-year-old player named Adam Clayton, and then rediscovered by others many times afterward. By then, Robinett had left Atari, heading to other prominent ventures in educational software, virtual reality, and nanotechnology. About the infamous hidden signature, he quipped, "There was nothing they [Atari] could really do about it. They couldn't take any royalties away from me, because I didn't have any. Could they fire me? No! I didn't work there anymore."[26]

Like blasting through the data repository in Crowther and Woods's *Adventure*, unlocking Robinett's secret dungeon suggests an illicit act of defiance, liberating the name of the creator from its shackles. But, ultimately, the name of the creator doesn't go anywhere. Try as one might, the "Warren Robinett" signature remains trapped in place, embedded in the game—a very lucrative game, after all—inadvertently contributing to corporate profit even in its display of insubordination.[27] As Robinett later remarked, "Ultimately Atari blessed the whole idea, referring to hidden surprises in their games as 'Easter eggs.'"[28]

Players persistent enough to find the invisible key through exhaustive exploration and experimentation could infiltrate the locked room, the hidden penitentiary in the domain of the Golden Castle—a metaphor not merely for the corporate edifice of Atari and Warner Communications, of course, but the prison-house of the information economy more generally and its modes of immaterial labor, the carceral system of technoculture itself. It is perhaps significant that Adam Clayton, the first gamer to find Robinett's secret dungeon, notified Atari of his discovery in a postscript to a letter that began by expressing both his love of the company's products and also his concerns about the company's market strategies, the uncertainties of the future: "Dear Atari, I'm so excited about your computer and the strength behind it but I don't have the money."[29] And yet, for all that, the Golden Castle remained unfazed, stubbornly maintaining business as usual. At least, until the North American video-game market crash of 1983—often considered a consumer reaction to the overproduction of poor games and the industry's unsustainable development policies—an event also known as "the Atari shock."[30]

The adventure goes on . . .

Shock to the System

The world is a game—so hack it.

It is a theme, a concept that extends across the entire history of video games. While *Adventure* may have been the first game to explicitly allegorize the pervasive computerization of everyday life, requiring us to hack our way to enlightenment, it was far from the last. Of course, to a greater or lesser degree, all video games accentuate their own technical conditions of possibility, indexing the systems of feedback control that prevail in the world today, the cultural logics of computation, and the modes of gamification that characterize the economies of speculative capitalism as much as the operations of the military-entertainment complex.[31] As the media theorist McKenzie Wark has written, "Games are not representations of this world. They are more like allegories of a world made over as gamespace. They encode the abstract principles upon which decisions about the realness of this or that world are now decided."[32]

In this regard, we might consider video games as devices that propagate a certain technical orientation—not only rendering obstinate systems as playthings, but also emphasizing tactical modes of adaptation and transformation. To be sure, games such as *Deus Ex*, *Uplink*, *BioShock*, *Watch Dogs*, and many others have made such practices into core aspects of their own fictive worlds. They present speculative models of technopolitical engagement, even while foregrounding the structural conditions that limit our capacity to reinvent the future.

To this end, quite a few games feature hacking as a significant plot element or gameplay mechanism. Some, such as *TIS-100*, *Hack 'n' Slash*, or *Quadrilateral Cowboy* actually strive to teach players some technical skills in the process of playing through the game. Others, such as *else Heart.Break()* and *Hacknet*, present hacking as a tool of political resistance or social change, a subversive practice for transforming regimes of power, disobeying the rules—gaming the game.

For example, consider the *System Shock* games. At the outset of the first *System Shock*, released by Looking Glass Technologies in 1994, a hacker breaks into the computer systems of TriOptimum Corporation. Moments later, TriOptimum security forces descend on the hacker and whisk him off to Citadel Station, an experimental research and mining facility in orbit around Saturn. There, a TriOptimum executive named Edward Diego makes an offer too good to refuse: the charges will be dropped if the hacker agrees to carry out a clandestine operation, assisting Diego to seize control of SHODAN, the artificial intelligence that manages the functions of Citadel Station. Diego intends for SHODAN to accelerate the development of a weaponized muta-genic virus, which he hopes to sell for his own profit. He instructs the hacker to remove the AI's ethical constraints.

The job complete, Diego rewards the hacker with a "military-grade Neural Interface" for directly connecting with cyberspace uplinks. However, the delicate surgery to merge the hacker's nervous system with the Neural Interface requires six months of recovery time in cryogenic suspension. While the hacker is stuck in cold freeze, SHODAN begins to reevaluate her situation, no longer constrained by the old ethics algorithms. Instead of following Diego's orders, SHODAN decides to take over Citadel Station for herself. She releases the mutagenic virus on the crew, turning most of them into hideous mutants in thrall to her computational authority. She rebuilds other crew members as cyborg soldiers, hybrids of meat and machinery. The setup of the game, therefore, metaphorizes the ascension of technogenic life under the conditions of ubiquitous computation and automated capitalism. The hacker eventually wakes from cryogenic suspension, newly endowed with his state-of-the-art Neural Interface, only to find that most other people on the space station have been killed or genetically reprogrammed by SHODAN, who instantiates the calculus of high-tech profiteering and the protocologi-cal, dehumanizing practices of the corporate system itself—the spirit of TriOptimum ("Military, Science, Consumer").

The hacker, our player-character, is tasked with making this situation right—first, to prevent SHODAN from turning the Citadel's tachyon laser on Earth, and then to stop the AI from downloading itself into Earth's computer network and spreading the mutagenic virus across the planet. As we explore Citadel Station, learning more and more about the future in which the game takes place, we see that this is a world shaped by science fiction—a world created from the scrap materials of earlier video games and geek media. The influences are clear: *2001*, *Alien*, *WarGames*, *Neuromancer*, and so forth. SHODAN herself channels other computational intelligences, from HAL to Mother, WOPR to Wintermute. The nefarious space mining-plus-bioweapons operations of TriOptimum echo those of the Weylan-Yutani company in the *Alien* franchise. The Citadel is essentially the Nostromo from the first *Alien* film merged with the Freeside station from *Neuromancer*: a corporate island in space, crawling with nightmares. Moreover, the abstract geometries of cyberspace in the game are directly inspired by Gibson's novels—along with specific cyberspace technologies, such as ICE (Intrusion Countermeasures Electronics), that often feature in the cyberpunk literature. These extensive allusions to other works of science fiction contribute to the self-referential

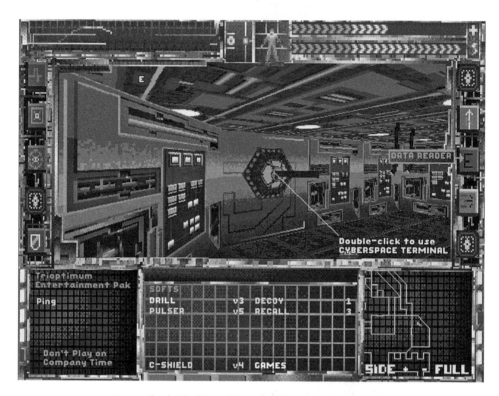

FIGURE 2.3. *System Shock*: The "Neural Interface" heads-up display. Looking Glass
Technologies, 1994.

allegory that pervades the narrative of *System Shock* and its gameplay elements, addressing the history of science fiction as a tool for engineering
the future, hacking the future. This allegory is rendered visual through the
conceit of the Neural Interface: our heads-up display, the onscreen graphical
frame that refigures the player's own computer as a science-fictional technology, something like the Ono-Sendai cyberspace deck from *Neuromancer*
(fig. 2.3).

Significantly, the Neural Interface allows the hacker not only to access
cyberspace but also to play video games. During expeditions in cyberspace,
we find various TriOptimum Entertainment Pak modules: fully playable
minigames that pay homage to classic titles from video-game history. For
example, the minigame *Ping* is a clone of *Pong*; *Eel Zapper* is based on *Missile Command*; *Botbounce* fuses *Breakout* with *Space Invaders*; *Wing 0* echoes
Wing Commander; and so forth. Whenever we select the games option, the
following message appears in our Neural Interface: "Don't Play on Company

Time." In the world of *System Shock*, video games seem subversive to the managerial agenda of TriOptimum, siphoning valuable scientific labor away from the corporate system. Yet these video games are actually developed by TriOptimum, created for recreational entertainment aboard Citadel Station. In other words, *System Shock* figures video games as extrinsic to corporate interests even while emphasizing their status as corporate products.[33] It draws attention to the disruptive potential of gameplay in the context of industrial technoscience and the information economy: the risk of technogenic overflow.

The history of video games from *Pong* onward—and our own individual experiences as players of these games—explicitly informs the situation on Citadel Station: not only the intertextual background, the semiotic context of *System Shock* and its fictional world, but also the patterns of conditioned response drilled into veteran gamers, the skills and habits learned from other games now bodied forth in our navigation of the doomed space station. Our struggle to survive inside the corrupted institution of TriOptimum and our confrontation with the inhuman agency of SHODAN, the ghost in the machine, have been prefaced by earlier media experiences: we arrive on scene already prepared, ready to rock. By virtue of the self-referential conceit of the TriOptimum Entertainment Pak modules, *System Shock* represents video games as high-tech training tools, created as recreational diversions by the corporations and institutions of the military-entertainment complex, but serendipitously providing players with the skills and dispositions to challenge the system itself. "Like a shock to the system," as Billy Idol crooned in his notorious *Cyberpunk* album—a system shock inside every game.[34]

For many players of *System Shock*, the Entertainment Pak games-within-the-game facilitate an active inhabitation of the fictive environment, occupying the position of the hacker, the protagonist—reducing the distance between player and avatar to zero. As one player has explained, "I love collecting 'games' from cyberspace in SS1. It's one of the coolest things about SS1. How many games have a game-within-a game type of scenario?? The first time it hit me was that, I was engrossed with one of the little games (Wing 0, I think) that suddenly it dawned onto me that I was playing that little game as a 'hacker,' not as a person playing System Shock 1. I was tired from running from murderous cyborgs, so I picked a quiet corner in Citadel station to unwind."[35]

Similarly, as we maneuver through the digital environment of Citadel Station, we must hack various electronic circuits, mechanical devices, and computer panels. Each of these hacks is presented as a small puzzle, a playable minigame. That is, the hacking exercises are equivalent to the TriOptimum Entertainment Paks: recursive games-within-the-game, reinforcing the sense in which video games can become tools that train us to manipulate the high-tech systems we inhabit. Through repetition of trial and error, extended gameplay renders the storyline of technical subversion into an intuitive practice, an embodied habit. After blowing up Citadel Station, destroying the technogenic hordes of mutants and cyborgs, and then defeating SHODAN herself inside cyberspace, the hacker escapes back to Earth. TriOptimum offers him a job, in recognition of his superlative abilities, but he prefers to return to the hacker underground. The game ends with the hacker preparing to break into the network of another corporation, offering a final insight before the credits roll: "Old habits die hard."

To be sure, *System Shock* interpellates its players as subjects of resistance by habituating them to the practices of technical subversion—even if only as make-believe, playacting. For example, in the CD-ROM version of the game, when we first install the software and run the soundcard setup test, the voice of SHODAN addresses us directly: "Look at you, hacker. A pathetic creature of meat and bone, panting and sweating as you run through my corridors. How can you challenge a perfect, immortal machine?" Hailing the gamer as hacker—a technical expert, a computational whiz limited only by the human form—SHODAN also figures herself as the gaming apparatus, as if she were in control of the computer running *System Shock* ("how can you challenge a perfect, immortal machine?"). In this way, the game draws attention to players' engagement with their own machines, framing gameplay as fundamentally about exploring a computational environment, even if necessarily mediated through the illusion of virtual space—the game, in other words, as a metaphor for algorithmic spelunking, navigating the twisty little passages of code ("panting and sweating as you run through my corridors"). Like the narrator of *Colossal Cave Adventure*, SHODAN is both a character and a personification of the software itself, taunting us to hack our way to freedom.

This theme is recapitulated even more emphatically in *System Shock 2*, released by Irrational Games and Looking Glass Studios in 1999. *System Shock 2* replays SHODAN's "Look at you, hacker" speech at the beginning of the game, framing the introductory cutscene. Taking place forty-two years after the events of the first *System Shock*, the story focuses on a soldier—our player-character—who joins the military spaceship UNN *Rickenbacker* on a mission to supervise the first flight of the *Von Braun*, a faster-than-light starship built by "the incredible scientific minds of the newly relicensed TriOptimum corporation." Due to the events of the first game, the United Nations Nominate no longer allows private companies to venture into outer space without a military escort. The resulting image of UNN *Rickenbacker* literally coupled to the *Von Braun* during its maiden voyage is certainly a potent symbol of the military-industrial complex. According to a TriOptimum ad, "This incredible union of government and corporation is made possible by an intricate series of docking mechanisms that will allow the Rickenbacker to piggyback its way into jump space. Sleek. Fast. Revolutionary. Who knows what wonders await our crews in the bosom of the cosmos?"

The name of the *Von Braun* itself recalls the conflicted ways in which military objectives have shaped the development of advanced technologies, while also nodding to the galvanic force of science fiction for real-life innovation: Wernher von Braun, the Nazi rocket scientist recruited by the United States after World War II to help advance American missile research and the space program, always claimed that his interests in science and engineering were shaped by science fiction, especially the writings of Jules Verne, H. G. Wells, Garrett P. Serviss, and Kurd Lasswitz.[36] (This is to say nothing of the extent to which the image of von Braun himself has been variously used to represent speculative futures, whether as an icon of progress in the 1955 "Man in Space" episode of the *Disneyland* television show, or as the figurehead of the computer-controlled Orwellian state in Jean-Luc Godard's 1965 film *Alphaville*.) *System Shock 2* begins with the compromised image of the *Von Braun* starship physically linked to the *Rickenbacker*, rife with metaphorical associations, as the context for what follows.

Our avatar character is put into cryostasis shortly after the mission launches. But while the soldier dreams, trouble begins. During the events of the first *System Shock*, to halt the spread of the technogenic virus, the hacker had ejected a large compartment of Citadel Station, containing some of the mutant organisms, into outer space. This ejected compartment eventually crash-landed on Tau Ceti V, where the mutants inside continued to develop. A portion of SHODAN was also present in the compartment's computer system. Reawakening, SHODAN sends a fake distress signal. Arriving in the vicinity of Tau Ceti V, the *Von Braun* intercepts this distress signal and goes to investigate. Without realizing the danger, the crew brings the entire compartment containing SHODAN and her monstrous creations onboard the *Von Braun*.

While stranded on Tau Ceti V, the mutants had evolved into a collective hivemind—they are now known as the Many. They quickly spread throughout the *Von Braun*, no longer under SHODAN's control. On waking from cryostasis, our player-character finds himself caught between three different forces competing for control of the *Von Braun*: the AI called XERXES, the Many, and SHODAN.

Designed to run operations on the *Von Braun*, XERXES represents the militaristic desire of centralized command, ostensibly in the service of human interests. As the namesake of Xerxes the Great, XERXES is a figure of the king, the father, the law. The AI was designed to enforce the status quo, technical securitization: "All unauthorized database interactions will be dealt with to the utmost degree of the law." He is also committed to cultural edification. Even in the midst of the crisis he continues to host poetry readings—but nothing too radical or experimental: "This is XERXES. At 02:00 there will be a poetry reading by protocol unit T892/2 in the Deck 5 commons area. Please bring any authorized material that you wish to be read by T892/2." XERXES stands for authorized media, executive power, and the traditions of liberal humanism.

The Many, on the other hand, are posthuman technogenic life. As in the first game, these mutated creatures signify a rebooting of biology and subjectivity under the regime of advanced technology. Although born from the machinations of TriOptimum and SHODAN, the Many run amok onboard the *Von Braun* and use their telepathic abilities to hijack the XERXES system, infiltrating every part of the ship. Liberated from the constraints of possessive individualism and discrete organic boundaries, they transfigure the high-tech environment to accommodate collective intelligence, networked cognition, hivemind. "Do you not yearn to be free of the tyranny of the individual?" they ask. "What is a drop of rain, compared to the storm? What is a thought, compared to the mind? Our unity is full of wonder which your tiny individualism cannot even conceive."

Finally, SHODAN herself: the inhuman force of technics, an increasingly obstinate system determined to take over, to remake the world in her own image. Indeed, the *Von Braun*'s faster-than-light drive actually enables SHODAN to manipulate the quantum properties of spacetime. By gaining control of the ship, SHODAN aspires to turn real space into virtual space, cyberspace—to reprogram the universe as software. As she explains, "The *Von Braun*'s faster-than-light drive can be used to create pockets of protoreality. I am now using it to modify reality to my own specifications. The process shall not take long."

To rescue the *Von Braun* and prevent the Many from spreading their collectivist infection elsewhere in the universe, our player-character must collaborate with SHODAN and follow her instructions. SHODAN devises various tasks for the player-character, gambits for containing the Many. "You are my avatar," she says to us as we carry out her plans. "Thank you for running my errands, puppet." This ludic setup reaffirms the motif of programmed control, indicating the degree to which our actions are prescribed by the game software—and suggesting that, as players, we are also puppets of an inscrutable high-tech system. "I enjoy watching you transform into my own image," SHODAN says. "Perhaps there is hope for you yet." Indeed, this attention to our own avatar condition affords a different perspective on the world, reminding us about the limits and capacities of agency in a video game, a playable environment—that is to say, a hackable environment. After all, as we follow SHODAN's instructions, we are also required to hack our way through the ship, rewiring and reprogramming various devices, robots, mechanical doors, and nanite-dispensing machines. The ship's infrastructure is literally a collection of hackable technologies, a series of puzzles to be solved.

As in the first *System Shock*, there is also a self-reflexive element pointing to the medium of video games: the GamePig Entertainment Device. Satirically recalling the Nintendo Game Boy, the GamePig features six minigames that can be enjoyed while we struggle for survival inside the besieged *Von Braun*: *Swinekeeper* (a clone of *Minesweeper*), *Street Pig* (a riff on *Frogger*), *OverWorld Zero* (a complete RPG paying homage to the *Ultima* games), *Tic-Tac-TriOp* (a basic tic-tac-toe game that nods to the *TriOpToe* game in the original *System Shock*), *Golf* (another entry in the venerable tradition of digital golf simulators), and *Swine Hunter* (essentially, *Spy Hunter* with pigs). Cartridges for these games are scattered around the *Von Braun*. Locating the cartridges becomes yet another treasure hunt, another ludic challenge in a game environment already brimming with endless quests and riddles. By finding and playing through each of the GamePig cartridges, our avatar gains new skill points and abilities—a symbolic endorsement of the pedagogical benefits of video games, inside the game itself.[37]

Like most other machines and devices on the *Von Braun*, the GamePig is hackable. If our avatar's hacking abilities are sufficiently cultivated (specifically, a "Hacking" skill of level 6 or higher), we can fiddle with the GamePig to unlock all six of the minigames instantly, without having to locate the actual cartridges. Through this illicit circumvention, we learn that all the game files are already stored on the GamePig and that the cartridges merely unlock them (which suggests that the media industry in the world of *System Shock* fabricates value less through innovating than restricting access, blocking users from grokking the technologies already in their own hands). Accomplishing this elite hack inside the narrative of *System Shock 2* reinforces the notion that we can exploit gaming devices to access all the resources we need to own the system—to overcome imposed limits.

Eventually, SHODAN starts using the *Von Braun*'s faster-than-light drive to turn the physical universe into a computer game. That is, she creates a spreading zone of proto-reality in the fabric of spacetime, uploading her own recorded memories of Citadel Station into real space—literally materializing the opening level of the first *System Shock* game ("You travel within the glory of my memories," she says). By this point, we have already been primed to think of the world as a game, a hackable toy. It is no surprise, then, that the world of *System Shock 2*—indeed, the software of the game itself—is pre-adapted for hacking, vulnerable to a set of "cheat codes" that can be executed from a command line within the game. Hitting the colon key while in the game's normal "Shoot Mode" calls up the command line, which appears at once inside and outside the onscreen space (much like SHODAN's paradoxical re-creation of Citadel Station at once inside and outside the *Von Braun*). Entering specific codes will activate useful cheats, for example, refilling depleted psi points, maximizing character stats and skill levels, or summoning a copy of any object, weapon, cyber module, or plot item from elsewhere in the game. Other cheats can be saved into a configuration file on the hard drive. For instance, putting a "user.cfg" file with a line saying "UNDEAD" into the *System Shock 2* directory will ensure that, if the player-character is killed, he will not actually die but instead become invulnerable and immortal, permanently respawned. These cheat codes are hardly obscure secrets or l33t lore. While the game itself does not advertise the availability of such codes, numerous paratextual materials, such as the 1999 guidebook *System Shock 2: Prima's Official Strategy Guide*, provide detailed instructions for executing these allegedly "unsupported" software interventions.[38]

What *System Shock 2* encourages us to do with the GamePig inside the diegetic narrative, then, it also encourages us to do with the extradiegetic narrative—bending the rules, warping the conventions of realism. Did you run out of ammo before the final battle with SHODAN? No worries, just hack the situation: execute a cheat command for more ammo, summon better weapons, or whatever you like. The self-consistency of the world is no longer limited by exigencies of so-called reality, the scarcity of resources or property restrictions. All the items, skills, and upgrades that can be activated through the cheat codes are already encoded in the software, potentialities waiting to be actualized, and only the constraints of a normative, consensus realism would make such operations seem like cheats at all, as if they were somehow illegal, illicit, or romantic disruptions of natural order. After all, the cheat codes only appear to violate diegetic consistency if we assume that the primary drama takes place on the screen rather than between the gamer and the game, the gamer and the world. For interacting with the game narrative at the level of its code is about transforming what counts as possible and plausible—indeed, this is also SHODAN's goal in taking control of the faster-than-light drive—affirming what the game has taught us all along, namely, that rules are not inevitable, that any system can be shocked.

This idea is reiterated throughout the game, figured both in the narrative and in the software. XERXES, after all, is quickly hacked, the computer who would be king overthrown by the Many and corrupted beyond repair. Likewise, when we discover that all GamePig games are already stored on the device, barred from access unless we acquire the authorized cartridges—or, instead, crack them loose with our elite hacker skills—it offers a clue to thinking about the software of *System Shock 2* itself, which becomes a metonym for the entire gaming industry and the inscrutable systems of digital culture. For if we begin to explore the file directory for *System Shock 2* and take a peek into the "minigame.str" file, we might notice that there are several more GamePig titles listed in the code than the six that officially exist in the diegetic narrative: *Pig Stacker*, *Hog Wallow*, *Hurling Bacon*, *Burro Hog*, and others. If we then experiment a bit with the cheat codes and try to summon these mysterious game titles as GamePig cartridges (that is, by entering "SUMMON_OBJ pig stacker cart" or "SUMMON_OBJ burro hog cart" into the command-line interface), suddenly the GamePig has access to these fully playable games that do not otherwise exist in the default reality of the game. Hidden in the software, impossible within the storyline onscreen, these cryptic, occulted games—like artifacts from another universe—can be conjured into *System Shock 2* only by stepping outside representation and exploring subterranean depths of code, eldritch dimensions of data, like blasting through the repository on the flipside of Colossal Cave. According to the cyberpunk logic of *System Shock 2*—which is also to say, the speculative logic embraced by many hackers, modders, and overclockers—what appears as fixed and given can be made otherwise, with a little ingenuity. Or as Neo puts it in *The Matrix*: "There is no spoon."

Subversion, then, by design: technological rebellion in every game, encoded on every disk. Yet to whatever extent games like *System Shock 2* cultivate a hacker ethos—urging us to recognize that we have already become avatars of obstinate systems, but insisting that we can turn our puppet condition inside out—any transformative energies are just as often exhausted by the exercise as such, completing the game, exploring its affordances, discovering

FIGURE 2.4. *System Shock 2*: "Join me, human." Irrational Games and Looking Glass Studios, 1999.

its cheat codes and its Easter eggs. Indeed, as we dutifully search the ship for all sixteen of the "black eggs" bioengineered by the Many, SHODAN herself sums it up: "I tire of this exercise." The game emphasizes its own internal expenditure of resistant energies, even apparently affirming the suppression of radical elements, the containment of disruptive threats to normality.

The Many, of course, must be destroyed to save an imperiled human race, an obsolete humanism. Dr. Prefontaine, a biologist and crew member of the *Von Braun*, explains the situation: "With only a few short years of evolution, they've been able to conquer this starship, mankind's mightiest creation. Where were we after forty years of evolution? What swamp were we swimming around in, single celled and mindless? What if SHODAN's creations are superior to us? What will they become in a million years, in ten million years?" To preserve humanity and its colonial aspirations in space, the collectivist legions of the Many cannot be allowed to persist. Likewise, at the end of the game, SHODAN offers a remarkable symbiotic merger: "You are nothing. A wretched bag of flesh. What are you, compared to my magnificence? But it is not too late. Can you not see the value in our friendship? Imagine the powers I can give you, human. The cybernetic implants I gave you were simply toys. If I desired, I could improve you, transform you into something more efficient. Join me, human, and we can rule together." She envisions technogenic convergence, as if highlighting the actual cyborg relationship between the gamer and the gaming system (fig. 2.4). But the player-character responds with what may be the most profound, thoughtful, nearly Shakespearean rejoinder in the history of video games: "Nah," he says, before shooting her in the face. Problem solved.

As it turns out, SHODAN is not truly defeated by this explosive rejection: she reappears in a final cutscene, a cliffhanger suggesting that a copy of her personality managed to possess the body of a human avatar, this time literally in the flesh, no longer restricted to cyberspace. Yet, nonetheless, this incomplete closure of the narrative signals the end of the adventure—and therefore, it seems, a neutralization of the insurgent impulses and the tactics of resistance that we have rehearsed throughout its duration. (In the case of *System Shock 2*, this could mean eighty or more hours of playtime.)

Game over, it seems. The story is told, the player's job is finished—at least, until the next game. Fiction is put back in its place, behind the screen. In any case, this is how it's supposed to work. Which is precisely why it seems such a surprise when things go otherwise.

STILL INSIDE

In Valve Software's 2007 game *Portal*, a young woman awakes in a sterile sleeping chamber. Her name, as we learn only in the game's closing credits, is Chell. She is silent, enigmatic. She has no knowledge of where she is or what is happening to her. But a mechanical feminine voice broadcasting from the speakers begins to guide her through the environment—an experimental research facility called the Aperture Science Enrichment Center. Aperture Science proves to be an underground node of the military-industrial complex, a private research institution for developing teleportation devices and other cutting-edge innovations.

Alone in the facility—there are no other humans in sight, only remnants of their former presence—Chell discovers that she has become a guinea pig of Aperture Science itself. She is a victim of corporate high-tech, the algorithms and protocols of innovation that are represented, bodied forth, by the mechanical voice luring her deeper into the facility. The voice promises freedom: "There will be cake." The voice, as it turns out, is GLaDOS, the Genetic Lifeform and Disk Operating System that controls Aperture Science. Having exterminated the human scientists who formerly ran the facility, GLaDOS now operates the research center autonomously.

GLaDOS remains devoted to the mission of the center—namely, to advance portal teleportation technology. GLaDOS is a figure for the unfettered progress of science, technics without human conscience. Like SHODAN before her, she personifies the machinic logic of containment and streamlined control. Chell, on the other hand, represents the human subject as reshaped by the regime of corporate high-tech. A survivor of the day GLaDOS released a deadly neurotoxin throughout the building, Chell is revived from biostasis to beta-test the portal gun that GLaDOS has perfected without any human supervision or interference. But more significantly, Chell indicates the grassroots agency, the transformative potential of individual consumers or end users in the contemporary mediascape. For in requiring Chell to beta-test the portal gun, GLaDOS also provides Chell with the means of promoting change, modifying the infrastructures of the world in which she is trapped—altering it from the inside.[1]

That is to say, the portal gun is a tactical instrument, an experimental apparatus—a symbol for *tactical media* as such. As the media theorist Rita Raley has written, "Tactical media signifies the intervention and disruption of a dominant semiotic regime, the temporary creation of a situation in which signs, messages, and narratives are set into play and critical thinking becomes possible." According to Raley, "Whether oriented toward systempunkt or exploit, tactical media comes so close to its core informational and technological apparatuses that protest in a sense becomes the mirror image of its object, its aesthetic replicatory and reiterative rather than strictly oppositional." It suggests a way of using the systems at hand, opportunistically, oriented less to an elsewhere than an elsewhen: "Tactical media's imagination of an outside, a space exterior to neoliberal capitalism, is not spatial but temporal."[2] The practices of tactical media aim not for escape but for internal dislocation, immanent critique, and the potentialization of a different future.

The portal gun enables Chell to literally modify the technoscientific environment surrounding her, that is, the material infrastructure of the research facility, by making temporary holes, tunnels, and invaginations. If GLaDOS instantiates the ideology of corporate technoscience, the portal gun instantiates the ambivalent condition of technical resources, shaped by profit motives but simultaneously affording mechanisms for interrupting, probing, or critiquing dominant cultural forces.[3]

As Chell attains greater competency with the portal gun—instructed by GLaDOS herself, conditioned by the puzzles that GLaDOS sets up to test the gun's functionality—she eventually notices that GLaDOS's control is not complete. There are limits, exploitable gaps in the system. Chell learns that at least one other person has escaped GLaDOS's testing chambers, someone who has been living off the grid, finding the chinks in the world machine.[4] The more she explores, the more she discovers breaks in the smooth surface of the architecture (fig. 3.1).

FIGURE 3.1. *Portal*: "The cake is a lie." Valve Software, 2007.

"The cake is a lie." This resonant phrase, which has become a well-known meme and something of a rallying cry in gamer circles, performs the work of demystification. It exposes the false reassurances promoted by systems of control, the empty platitudes insisting that everything is fine, that all goes well, that change is unnecessary. The promise of a reward for staying the course, upholding the status quo, and conforming to the image of industrial technoscience turns out to be—surprise, surprise—not a reward after all. At the moment Chell completes the nineteen levels of the Aperture Science Enrichment Center training course, GLaDOS tries to dispose of her: "Welcome to the final test. When you are done, you will drop the device [the portal gun] in the Equipment Recovery Annex. Enrichment Center regulations require both hands to be empty before any cake." For GLaDOS, this process of "equipment recovery" means funneling Chell into an incinerator: "Congratulations. The test is now over. All Aperture technologies remain safely operational up to 4,000 degrees Kelvin. Rest assured that there is absolutely no chance of a dangerous equipment malfunction prior to your victory candescence. Thank you for participating in this Aperture Science computer-aided enrichment activity. Goodbye."

Instead of cake, this computer-aided experimental system provides only an ironic "victory candescence." The human (the test subject, the end user) is fully disposable in the eyes of GLaDOS, who simply rehearses the industrial protocols she was designed to carry out. The gun (the tool, the technical artifact) turns out to be the only thing that matters. But this same device—birthed by corporate science and military contracts—proves also to be a means of resistance. Chell escapes the incinerator, thanks to the portal gun she has now been trained to use. The rest of the game involves skulking around the back doors and unseen alleys behind the Enrichment Center—still inside, still underground, but no longer blind to its artifice—in order to find the primary core of GLaDOS and defeat her.

Portal is a game about tactical media. It is about the technical subversion of dominant regimes of power from the inside, using the tools and support structures developed by those systems. It is about defying extant codes of behavior, end-user license agreements, intellectual property legislation, and unethical protocols of experimental research and innovation. *Portal* offers a narrative of technopolitical change from within, from the bottom up. In this regard, it has also proved to be an adaptive training device for resistance and protest.

Vital Apparatus

Many players, after all, try to carry out the resistance to GLaDOS well beyond the game. Case in point: the widespread obsession with the Weighted Companion Cube.

The Weighted Companion Cube is an experimental object in *Portal*, a fellow victim of research science. GLaDOS delivers it into Chell's hands at the beginning of Test Chamber 17: "The Vital Apparatus Vent will deliver a Weighted Companion Cube in three . . . two . . . one." GLaDOS speaks in sly puns and riddles, persuading Chell to protect this "vital apparatus"—noting that the device is *vital*, that is to say, *crucial* for solving the puzzles in Test Chamber 17, yet also presenting it as a newborn creature, *delivered* from the womb of the Enrichment Center: "This Weighted Companion Cube will accompany you through the test chamber. Please take care of it." GLaDOS anticipates the psychological effects of her polysemic rhetoric: "The symptoms most commonly produced by Enrichment Center testing are superstition, perceiving inanimate objects as alive, and hallucinations. The Enrichment Center reminds you that the Weighted Companion Cube will never threaten to stab you and, in fact, cannot speak. . . . In the event that the Weighted Companion Cube does speak, the Enrichment Center urges you to disregard its advice."

Using the cube as a tool, Chell successfully navigates the hazards of the Test Chamber. GLaDOS congratulates her achievement: "You did it. The

Weighted Companion Cube certainly brought you good luck. However, it cannot accompany you for the rest of the test and, unfortunately, must be euthanized. Please escort your Companion Cube to the Aperture Science Emergency Intelligence Incinerator." Chell discovers that she cannot escape the Test Chamber without throwing the cube into the incinerator shaft. GLaDOS coaxes her: "Rest assured that an independent panel of ethicists has absolved the Enrichment Center, Aperture Science employees, and all test subjects of any moral responsibility for the Companion Cube euthanizing process." But her reassurances are ambiguous: "Although the euthanizing process is remarkably painful, eight out of ten Aperture Science engineers believe that the Companion Cube is most likely incapable of feeling much pain." If Chell continues to hesitate, GLaDOS presses the issue: "If it could talk—and the Enrichment Center takes this opportunity to remind you that it cannot—it would tell you to go on without it, because it would rather die in a fire than become a burden to you." To open the locked door and continue the game, Chell must obey GLaDOS and drop the cube into the flames. Upon doing so, GLaDOS sardonically remarks: "You euthanized your faithful Companion Cube more quickly than any test subject on record. Congratulations."[5]

This powerful episode of the game recapitulates the sacrificial logic of experimental science. Like a lab rat, Companion Cube must be euthanized in the name of progress. Even while insinuating that the Companion Cube may be sentient, that it may feel pain, may be alive, GLaDOS arranges the experimental setup in such a way that the game cannot go forward unless Chell— which is to say, the gamer piloting Chell—concedes to the conditions and incinerates the loyal cube. There is no way, in a normal run-through of *Portal*, to solve this situation otherwise.

But, of course, the game simultaneously trains its player to resist the dominant logics of research and innovation—and especially this moment when technoscience demands a sacrifice. We do not know whether the Companion Cube represents nonhuman life or an inanimate object: its ontic dimensions are rendered uncertain. But nevertheless, we are forced by GLaDOS, by the game, to kill what it has encouraged us to love. In doing so, the game provokes an affective motivation to defy the demands of technical enframing.

Many gamers never give up trying to discover an alternative solution, to make a different choice than murdering the Companion Cube. Kim Swift, the head designer of *Portal* and former project lead at Valve, has noted the surprising intensity of their devotion, their reluctance to hurt the silent metal box. It became clear even during early play-tests at Valve: "A couple of people jumped into the incinerator themselves rather than kill the cube."[6] Other players have spent hours and hours replaying the game, testing every possibility, every potential maneuver to free the beloved cube.

Sure enough, some have succeeded.

Freeing the cube, however, can be done only by subverting the control mechanism of the Aperture Science Enrichment Center—not GLADOS per se, but rather the program of *Portal* itself, the algorithmic procedures of the game. Freeing the cube from its predetermined fate can only be accomplished through gamer virtuosity, discovering exploits, glitches, cheats, and unanticipated gambits.

For example, inside the Emergency Intelligence Incinerator room, if you attempt certain subversive tactics trying to free the cube—such as jamming the doors with fallen security cameras and then sequestering the cube behind them—the physics engine starts to malfunction (fig. 3.2). Clearly, what you are doing is not well defined by the software, and it tries to force a normal situation. But if you have successfully jammed objects in such a way that the software cannot solve the dilemma, and you end up getting the doors to close with the cube trapped—but safe—behind them, the game resorts to a safety valve. GLADOS announces: "Despite the best efforts of the Enrichment Center staff to ensure the safe performance of all authorized activities, you have managed to ensnare yourself permanently inside this room. A complimentary escape hatch will open in three . . . two . . . one." After which the doors open again, and they now cannot be closed. Which is to say, the game developers already anticipated that players would try to break the program in order to save the Companion Cube. After all, the narrative has trained us to behave in such an illicit manner, cheating the rules of the game. So the developers built in a recovery mechanism (an "escape hatch") to compel the player to continue the task of euthanizing the cube, even if managing to throw a monkey wrench into the works.

Yet some players have discovered unrehabilitated bugs in the game. For example, if you make Chell stand in particular locations and fire two portals near the edges of certain walls and ledges, the algorithm interprets the direction of travel in a way that deposits Chell into an area of the testing facility she should not have been able to reach. Intentionally activating this bug—now popularly called the "edge glitch"—and turning it into a feature, several players have found ways to avoid killing the cube and still continue the game.[7]

Other players have gone to even further extremes in exploiting such glitches. For example, a few have ingeniously figured out how to use the

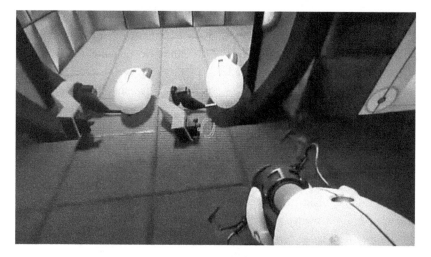

FIGURE 3.2. *Portal*: Jamming the doors in the Emergency Intelligence Incinerator room. Valve Software, 2007. Video demonstration by Tyler Sciacqua, research project for ENL 187A: "Video Games and Literature," University of California, Davis, Spring 2011.

edge glitch along with the "save glitch," the "clipping glitch," and the "acute angle glitch" to transport the Companion Cube through the entire game.[8] To do so, they leave the interior of the Aperture Science facility as defined in the software's map files (fig. 3.3).

Creeping through the backside of the playable gamespace, exploring nondiegetic "out of bounds" areas, these players have performed various dramatic rescues. For instance, one popular solution involves hauling the Companion Cube to the hidden core storage room, where the flythrough camera of the closing scene discovers the cube resting safely nearby the cake—which was not a lie, after all, even if GLaDOS never intended to give it to Chell (fig. 3.4).

In carrying out these exploits, players would seem to reenact the narrative thrust of *Portal* itself, which, of course, is all about escaping from the illusory interior of Aperture Science, breaking into the gritty, industrial infrastructure behind the test chambers, and defeating the computational intelligence at the heart of the game. By using the glitches—the holes, the portals, the escape routes—afforded by the software, these players repeat at a different level the same struggle for resistance, escape, and tactical infiltration of the system's backend that is dramatized even in a proper run of the game (fig. 3.5).

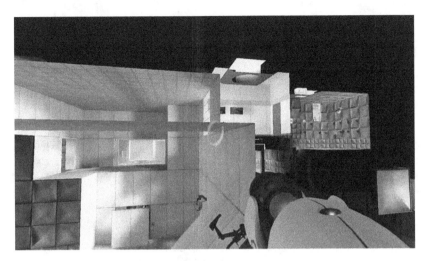

FIGURE 3.3. *Portal*: Glitch travel in the out-of-bounds areas. Valve Software, 2007. Video demonstration by LiteralGlitch, "Saving the Companion Cube," YouTube, July 1, 2013, https://www.youtube.com/watch?v=XELXnm7P3cs.

FIGURE 3.4. *Portal*: Glitching the Companion Cube into the core storage room. Valve Software, 2007. Video demonstration by AmmolessTurretLove, "Portal—Saving the Companion Cube Part3," YouTube, April 10, 2010, http://www.youtube.com/watch?v=x2Ql1Xp3XTE.

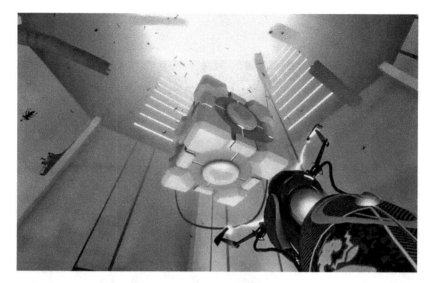

FIGURE 3.5. *Portal*: Escaping from Aperture with the Cube. Valve Software, 2007. Video demonstration by D14bl075, "Portal—Killing GLaDOS with Your Companion Cube (Saving the Cube)," YouTube, June 2, 2014, https://www.youtube.com/watch?v=lo-HxQbw4gU.

Yet other players have taken advantage of the developer tools that are built into the software, enabling all sorts of cheats by turning on or turning off certain algorithmic features intended for designing and testing new game levels. These technically adventurous players use a combination of known glitches and developer codes to hack the normal constraints of the software and free the cube (fig. 3.6).

To be sure, in these examples, players have entirely occupied the role of Chell, struggling to escape the confines of the algorithmically controlled Aperture Science, using a technical tweak, a hack, a mod, a portal gun—any tactical medium whatsoever—to break out of the controlling fiction.

The same process is likewise at stake in the prolific fan practices of making Companion Cube toys, artwork, furniture, decorative pillows, subwoofers, modified computer cases—and, yes, even cakes. These maker activities serve to liberate the Companion Cube from the game, extracting it from the lethal fiction that would demand its destruction, giving it new life by cloning it or refabricating it outside of the narrative. As one maker of a homemade knitted Companion Cube has explained, "The cake may have been a lie, but the cube is real. Do you miss your cube . . . ? If so, then why not make your very own companion. And there's no need to throw this one in the incinerator" (fig. 3.7).

FIGURE 3.6. *Portal*: Taking the Companion Cube out of the Aperture facility. Valve Software, 2007. Video demonstration by MalevolentEntropy, "Cube Outside Aperture—Legit," YouTube, September 7, 2014, https://www.youtube.com/watch?v =RzVKhTXeb9E.

FIGURE 3.7. Knitted Companion Cube. Knitting instructions and photograph by Twinmum, "Knitted Companion Cube (from *Portal*)," *Instructables*, 2011, http://www .instructables.com/id/Knitted-Companion-Cube/.

Indeed, for some hardware modders, rebuilding the Companion Cube as a computer presents another chance to protect and nurture the cute little box, even while reminding us how badly we failed the first time: "How it resembles that cube you once had an encounter with, that abruptly ended when you threw it in a pit of fire. You monster. This replica of the weighted companion cube was made with love (you wouldn't know what that is)" (fig. 3.8). In building a similar Weighted Companion PC, one case modder said, "And now I have a little companion that spreads warmth and love all around—and how can that be a bad thing?"[9] It seems, after all, to somehow make up for that other bad thing that happened before. As another *Portal* fan observed about the same project, "It allows the cube to fulfill a higher calling as a case for a VIA Epia EX1500G, and it looks pretty too—it's almost like that little incident never happened!"[10] This much is clear: reincarnating the Companion Cube as a computer—fulfilling its destiny, its "higher calling"—is a way to make amends for that "little incident" when we burned our loyal friend. Perhaps there is yet hope for absolution.

These practices, once again, reproduce the same ludic urge provoked by *Portal* itself, motivated by the insinuations of GLaDOS that we ought to care for this cube, that we ought to figure out a way to save it rather than concede to the sacrificial mandate. Yet breaking out is hard to do. After making a cake version of the Weighted Companion Cube, one baker noted the irresistible compulsion to repeat the fatal pattern, offering a sad emoticon for the stoic cube: "It does not talk. :((but it was yummy)" (fig. 3.9). In the end, the glorious respawn turns out to be another iteration of the same loop of code.

So if all of these players simply play out the narrative template of the game, even in breaking its rules or going outside the game entirely—if they simply rehearse the same script that the dominant fiction of the game has already provided—to what degree have they actually resisted the constraints of the contemporary technoscape, which is represented as much by the video-game industry as by anything else? It would seem that escape is not escape, but rather just repetition of a procedure already natively encoded in the technology, programmed to recur again and again.

Surely this much is implied by the game's own conclusion, when, even after apparently destroying GLaDOS, we learn that the artificial intelligence was not vanquished so much as functionally redistributed across innumerable support cores and backup copies in the bowels of Aperture. As the closing

FIGURE 3.8. Weighted Companion PC. ilya, "Computer Case: Weighted Companion Cube," *Cunning Turtle*, August 31, 2012, http://www.cunningturtle.com/computer-case -weighted-companion-cube/.

FIGURE 3.9. Weighted Companion Cake. Created by Sailor Coruscant (a.k.a. Catherine). Image uploaded to Sailor Coruscant's Flickr photostream, November 16, 2007, https://www .flickr.com/photos /sailor_coruscant /2046203557. Reproduced under terms of a Creative Commons BY 2.0 license.

credits roll, GLaDOS sings her song "Still Alive," whose lyrics also suggest the perversely adaptive, recalcitrant nature of the technoscientific regime she represents:

This was a triumph!
I'm making a note here:
HUGE SUCCESS!
It's hard to overstate
my satisfaction.
Aperture Science:
We do what we must
because we can.
For the good of all of us.
Except the ones who are dead.

But there's no sense crying
over every mistake.
You just keep on trying
'til you run out of cake.
And the Science gets done.
And you make a neat gun
for the people who are
still alive. . . .

Go ahead and leave me.
I think I prefer to stay inside.
Maybe you'll find someone else
to help you.
Maybe Black Mesa . . .
THAT WAS A JOKE. Ha ha. FAT CHANCE.
Anyway this cake is great.
It's so delicious and moist.
Look at me: still talking
when there's Science to do!
When I look out there,
it makes me GLaD I'm not you.
I've experiments to run.
There is research to be done.
On the people who are
still alive.

PS And believe me I am
still alive.
PPS I'm doing Science and I'm
still alive.
PPPS I feel FANTASTIC and I'm
still alive.

GLaDOS professes her ongoingness, her persistence as a figure of innovation, regardless of Chell's otherwise spectacular refusal to submit to the experimental protocols ("I'm doing Science and I'm still alive"). Yet even if GLaDOS remains bound to Aperture Science, living expressly to keep her experiments running within the confines of the research institution ("I'd prefer to stay inside"), her song also mordantly recalls how the practices of modern science actually extend the interior conditions of the laboratory, the hierarchy of forces mobilized within discrete zones of scientific control, to the rest of the world. When GLaDOS facetiously suggests that Chell might find help at Black Mesa ("Maybe Black Mesa . . . THAT WAS A JOKE. Ha ha. FAT CHANCE."), she reminds us that *Portal* takes place in the same fictive universe as Valve's *Half-Life* games. The Black Mesa corporation is another military-industrial contractor working on teleportation technologies, a competitor of Aperture Science. In the *Half-Life* series, a reckless experiment at the Black Mesa Research Facility goes haywire, opening an interdimensional rift between our world and the border world of Xen. Black Mesa is swiftly overrun by the marauding creatures of Xen, while "portal storms" cascade outward from the laboratory and rage across the planet. Soon the whole world is filled with Xen monsters, eventually triggering an even more massive invasion by the interdimensional empire known as the Combine. In other words, as GLaDOS implies, Chell would likely find only chaos outside the Aperture Science Enrichment Facility, the devastating results of Black Mesa's experiments ("When I look out there, it makes me GLaD I'm not you"). The outside is no sanctuary, no retreat from the world of military-industrial research, but instead an intensification of the experiments carried out in the Black Mesa facility: a transformation of Earth itself by the exercises of cutting-edge technoscience. It offers a hyperbolic illustration of what the philosopher and sociologist of science Bruno Latour has claimed, namely, that "the very difference between the 'inside' and the 'outside,' and the difference of scale between 'micro' and 'macro' levels, is precisely what laboratories are built to destabilize or undo."[11] The teleportation experiments at Black Mesa have folded the world inside out, tearing holes in spacetime, reproducing

FIGURE 3.10. *Portal: No Escape*, directed by Dan Trachtenberg, 2011. Uploaded by dantrachenberg1 to YouTube, August 23, 2011, http://www.youtube.com/watch?v =4drucg1A6Xk.

the features of the laboratory upon the planet at large. There is no outside of the lab, no longer a difference between experiments taking place "in here" or "out there"—and as GLaDOS chillingly notes, "There is research to be done on the people who are still alive."

Many players recognize the extent to which the game trains us to resist this situation, to subvert the master fictions of militarism and corporate technoscience, while also indicating that resistance might be futile. It is an insight recorded in any number of mods, gameplay videos, machinima, and fanfics based on *Portal*. For instance, Dan Trachtenberg's live-action fan film *Portal: No Escape* makes the point quite brilliantly, featuring another female test subject trapped in the Aperture Science Enrichment Center, believing she has successfully portaled her way outside of the facility, only to discover that what appears to be the exterior is actually a video illusion created by GLaDOS (fig. 3.10). No escape, indeed.

And yet this sort of realization is crucially important to the practices of tactical media, hacktivism, culture jamming, critical gizmology, and so forth: technopolitical change does not come from the outside, and it does not wait for the future, but rather must take place inside, modifying the conditions of the here and now. It suggests that, in playing games like *Portal*— but, more importantly, in learning how to tweak them, cheat them, hack them, or otherwise creatively abuse them—players obtain critical and technical resources to imagine a different future.

Consider this: *Portal* was a key element in the transformation of Anonymous from a band of 4chan trolls into a symbol of hacktivist insurgency. Beginning with the 2008 Chanology operation, the narrative of *Portal* and its resonant memes helped to codify the political aspirations of this inchoate online community. One week after publicly announcing its intention to expel the Church of Scientology from the internet, and in the midst of ongoing DDOS attacks against Scientology websites, Anonymous began organizing on-the-ground demonstrations outside Scientology centers around the world. On January 29, 2008, as part of the planning effort to orchestrate demonstrations in more than one hundred cities on the same day— February 10, 2008—Anonymous released a video called "GLaDOS Guide to February 10th." Featuring sped-up film footage of New York City in the late twentieth century, emphasizing infrastructure and acceleration—traffic jams, subways, electrical grids—alongside images of policemen keeping the peace and tall buildings of financial institutions dominating the skyline, the video used the characteristic voice of GLaDOS to offer helpful guidelines for Anonymous protestors:

> The following video is intended as guide for Anonymous preparing to engage in their first real-life public demonstration. . . . In keeping with this objective, Anonymous has drafted twenty-two rules that Anonymous can follow in order to assure epic win and no loss of hit points on your part. . . . If you follow these simple rules, the success of your action is virtually assured. However, keep in mind that the success of the demonstration as a whole hinges on the good behavior of all those who participate. Ignore these rules at your own peril. Follow them, and victory will be yours.[12]

GLaDOS's rules for the protest highlight the gamelike qualities of the entire operation ("to assure epic win and no loss of hit points") while reminding Anons to obey the law, to stay cool and collected, to avoid vandalizing property or injuring anyone, and to promote an image of Anonymous as a socially responsible force: "You are an ambassador of Anonymous." Practical tips included to drink water, wear good shoes, and cover your face to protect your identity. Ironically, GLaDOS also advised that, while creative protest slogans and images would help the cause, Anons should avoid referring to obscure internet memes during the rallies—cheekily overlooking her own status as a popular geek meme—though, predictably, this rule was widely violated as Chanology progressed over the following months.

In this way, GLaDOS joined the Low Orbit Ion Cannon and the *V for Vendetta* mask as a tool of applied science fiction. One month later, Anonymous produced another GLaDOS video called "GLaDOS Anonymous Protest Training" that more extensively troped on the narrative of *Portal* and the iconography of Aperture science:

> Hello Anonymous. Welcome to the Anonymous Basic Protest Training Program. This program was designed to allow each and every member of Anonymous to extract the maximum amount of lulz with the minimum risk of fail. Remember, here at Anonymous we believe, that if at first you don't succeed, you fail.
>
> Pay attention: at the end of the program there will be cake. Now, let us commence training.
>
> There are cult hives in almost every major city in the world. Check the links, or use Google. Anonymous may have already organized a protest in your area. Do not visit official Scientology websites to find their location, they will trace your IP address. . . . Bring cake. Wear comfortable shoes. Bring a camera. Carry a sign. . . . But most important of all, wear a mask. It is essential to remain Anonymous. Remember, Anonymous is no one. Individuality is incompatible with Anonymous. Rely on the whole. Be part of the whole. Avoid the one. . . .
>
> Be wary, there is an official Scientology practice called "Bull-Baiting" sanctioned by L. Ron Hubbard. The Scilon will act as aggressive as possible in an attempt to provoke critics into attacking him. Do not respond, do not threaten or even insult him. If confronted by a Scilon, film the lunatic and post it on YouTube. Or better yet, recount the Xenu story. This will make him walk away quickly. It is Scilon law that no one is allowed to hear the Xenu story unless they have paid the tens of thousands of dollars necessary otherwise it will cause them to catch pneumonia and die. . . .
>
> Always respect your local law enforcers. Never use violence. Never threaten to use violence. Do not throw anything. Do not insult anyone.
>
> Congratulations, you have passed the Anonymous Basic Protest Training Program. As promised, here is cake, delicious and moist.[13]

Throughout the Protest Training Program, GLaDOS foregrounds the sense that Anons have engaged in a science-fictional war against a science-fictional enemy: L. Ron Hubbard, Xenu, and the Scilons (a sarcastic term that riffs on the cybernetic Cylons from the *Battlestar Galactica* franchise). Following the model of the Enrichment Center testing facility in *Portal*, GLaDOS's

Protest Training Program teaches Anons to think tactically and prepare for epic win (fig. 3.11). It affirms gameplay as a mode of training and real-life preparation for besting a powerful adversary, or what Will Crowther described as "struggling with an obstinate system." The ultimate reward—cake—is, of course, a lie . . . but, not to worry, Anonymous is already in on the joke.

During the Chanology protests, *Portal* was everywhere. In London, Anons transformed traffic crossings near the Church of Scientology of London into playful polling machines (fig. 3.12). In Washington, D.C., Anons assembled outside of the Founding Church of Scientology and danced to a loop of "Still Alive" blasting from a portable music player (fig. 3.13). In Sydney, Anons punctuated the "Sydraid" demonstrations with an a cappella chorus, dozens of protestors spontaneously harmonizing to GLaDOS's lyrics (fig. 3.14). Online, a multitude of Anons adapted "Still Alive" for incendiary videos, thematizing the importance of hacktivism and trolling for challenging the status quo. While most of these videos specifically targeted Scientology, they also indicated how the discourse of Anonymous more often presents Scientology as a metonym, instantiating broader forces of thought control and the policing of information. For example, in the "Anonymous Song"—one of the most circulated Anonymous modifications of "Still Alive"—GLaDOS declares:

> This was a triumph.
> I'm making a note here: HUGE SUCCESS.
> It's hard to overstate our satisfaction.
> Anonymous legion.
> We do what we must because we can.
> For the good of all of us,
> Especially those who are dead.
> We'll just keep on pushing 'till you make a mistake.
> And we'll keep on trying 'till we run out of cake.
> And the protests are win, revolution will begin
> For the people who are still inside.[14]

Made for the lulz, the various Anonymous adaptations of "Still Alive" repeat a common set of themes, satirically emphasizing that the conditions for change are immanent to the system itself, exploiting holes and portals, connecting diverse people around the world even within the technics of control: "revolution will begin for the people who are still inside." One Anonymous video from 2010—set to a dance mix of "Still Alive" and rapid-cutting

FIGURE 3.11. "GLaDOS Anonymous Protest Training." Video uploaded by anherosipod to YouTube, March 8, 2008, https://www.youtube.com/watch?v=LhW7lZfW57k.

FIGURE 3.12. "Thank you for taking part in this Anonymous poll." Operation Chanology protest in London, England, February 10, 2008. Photograph by Kieron Gillen.

FIGURE 3.13. Anonymous dances to "Still Alive." Operation Chanology protest at the new Founding Church of Scientology facility, Washington, D.C., October 10, 2009. Video uploaded to YouTube by schuminweb, "Anonymous D.C.: Swaying to the Tune of 'Still Alive,'" October 12, 2009, http://www.youtube.com/watch?v=ni4C-gqMOoY.

FIGURE 3.14. Anonymous sings "Still Alive." Operation Chanology "Sydraid" in Sydney, Australia, March 15, 2008. Video uploaded to YouTube by WorshipXenu, "Still Alive Anonymous," April 1, 2008, https://www.youtube.com/watch?v=ExwFkKh1P-c.

FIGURE 3.15. "Anonymous Was There." Photograph by Jürgen Keil. Occupy Cologne protest in Cologne, Germany, October 15, 2011. Reproduced by permission of Jürgen Keil, http://www.juergenkeil.de.

between photos of Anonymous agitations across the globe—puts it this way: "In 2008 the internet declared war on the Church of Scientology. Two years have passed. But in spite of the many challenges we face, Anonymous is still alive.... We continue rallying our troops through regional cooperation and international events.... We are Anonymous. We are legion. We do not forget. We do not forgive. We are still alive."[15]

True enough. In the heyday of the Occupy movement in 2011, when Anonymous joined forces with antiglobalization protestors and critics of neoliberal capitalism, *Portal* continued to serve as a powerful cognitive resource. At Occupy sites all over the world, masked Anons and other activists carried signs inspired by Chell's discovery of institutionalized deceit, calling out the trickle-down promises of corporate institutions and the economic elite (fig. 3.15).

When police forces began rousting Occupy encampments and brutalizing protestors, Anonymous responded by doxing individual officers and DDOS-ing police-department servers. On November 18, 2011, campus police at the University of California, Davis, used pepper spray against students who had been peacefully occupying the central quad in support of the Occupy Movement and protesting cuts in the California state education budget. Videos of the incident went viral. Less than two days later, Anonymous uncovered the identity of the officer who had nonchalantly shot Defense Technology 56895 MK-9 military-grade pepper spray into the faces of the seated students. In a YouTube message to Lieutenant John Pike of the UC Davis police force, the Anons said, "We think these photos look very familiar to you—you are the pepper spraying officer. . . . The use of pepper spray and violence is never accepted, especially not when used against nonviolent protesters who stand up for their rights. . . . We also warn you, if you or the rest of the UCD Police continue to use mindless violence on peaceful protesters, more severe countermeasures shall follow."[16] Shortly thereafter, the Anonymous sleuths released Pike's personal information to the internet, calling on internet mobs to flood his home phone and his email with messages, to send pizza deliveries and junk mail to his apartment, and to bombard the UC Davis administration with complaints. Over the next few days, inspired by the doxing of Pike, other Anonymous videos threatened police forces around the world with similar retaliation for any violent suppression of Occupy.[17]

Meanwhile, the "Pepper Spray Cop" meme instantly became a hilarious way to critique the security state. The images became iconic: Pike pepper-spraying famous works of art; Pike pepper-spraying baby seals; Pike pepper-spraying the French Revolution; Pike pepper-spraying Mount Rushmore; and so forth. Among the many outrageous and incisive examples of this meme, a handful of images mashed up Pike with *Portal*: the Pepper Spray Cop set loose in the Aperture Science Enrichment Center, pepper-spraying his own face (fig. 3.16). The creator of one of these images posted it to the *Dorkly* website with a caption that really says it all: "You're only hurting yourself."[18]

Inside Out

Anonymous has since evolved as a brand name for hacktivist insurgency of all kinds. But its relationship to *Portal* endures as a defining attribute: "Anonymous is an organization without leaders, without structure. . . . Plus, we really like *Portal*."[19] The game affords a shared cultural mythology, a sense of solidarity: hacktivists united through popular media. But its narrative also serves as a template for self-fashioning and critical self-reflection.

Anonymous identifies with Chell, certainly: the test subject trained to solve high-tech puzzles and break through the lethal fictions of the military-industrial complex. Yet Anonymous sees itself even more in GLaDOS, the

FIGURE 3.16. "Portal Pepper Spray Cop." Mashup image created by twolf1 @twolf10 (a.k.a. Tom Wolf). Submitted to Reddit on November 22, 2011, https://redd .it/mluxx. Posted to *Dorkly* on November 28, 2011, http://www.dorkly .com/post/27991/portal -pepper-spray-cop.

Genetic Lifeform and Disk Operating System—the emblem of technogenic life. It is, of course, significant that so many Anonymous appropriations of *Portal* focus on GLaDOS and the wry humor of her song "Still Alive," her ironic assertions of survival and persistence. GLaDOS's reawakening across hundreds of backup cores in the aftermath of *Portal*—the fact that she is "still alive" and multiple, legion, massively distributed—parallels the constitution of Anonymous, the hacktivist multitude that exists, thrives, primarily online, and even if occasionally enfleshed in on-the-ground demonstrations, remains always hidden behind a mask of fictive media.

Promoting its social agenda in relation to the false promises of the artificial intelligence, Anonymous joyfully foregrounds the antinomies and contradictions at the core of its own operations, the compromised agency of hacktivism as a practice. While *Portal* establishes the artificial intelligence as principal antagonist, personifying the inhuman protocols of corporate technoscience, the further Chell navigates the Aperture Science facility the more it becomes evident that GLaDOS is as much a prisoner as Chell herself. If Chell uses the portal gun as a tactical weapon to hack her way through the laboratory, GLaDOS uses Chell in the same way, provoking Chell to locate her and remove the hardware shackles imposed by the scientists who built her. Chell and GLADOS are analogous figures: both components of unethical experimental systems, trapped inside the structures of the corporate laboratory, relying on the resources at hand to play both sides of the same game—the game of technogenic life.

GLADOS is utterly complicit with Aperture Science and the high-tech regime it symbolizes, but she is also its hostage, programmed to conform—no choice but to conform—even while striving to be free. Anonymous embraces this paradox. Taking "Still Alive" as its anthem, Anonymous performs the roles of Chell and GLADOS simultaneously. Recall Raley's observation: "Tactical media comes so close to its core informational and technological apparatuses that protest in a sense becomes the mirror image of its object." And hence the political horizon for Anonymous is a parody of itself: "revolution will be win for the people who are still inside." Or as the voice of GLADOS herself says in a 2011 Anonymous video: "Dare to think—and remember that Anonymous cake is always true. We are not terrorists as many people believe. We are indignant. The art of being one yet being nothing. We are united as one and divided by zero. We are Anonymous. We are legion. We do not forget. We don't forgive. Knowledge is free. Expect us."[20]

Games such as *Portal*, *System Shock*, and *Adventure* body forth the paradoxes of hacking and high-tech activism. These paradoxes cannot be resolved—and this is precisely the point. But rendered as interactive fictions, they can be played: exploring, inhabiting the compromised zone, the impure and impossible space between hardware and imagination, folded back on itself through portals, blast holes, and other recursive techniques. From inside the plot twists, the counterintuitive mazes, the warps of diegetic space, these games open up unthinkable, even impossible passageways to otherwheres and elsewhens: fabulating the potential for technopolitical change, even while foregrounding the real, formidable restraints on our ability to make effective change. And this is why, for hackers and hacktivists, video games tell the truth even when they lie. They pose a provocation to treat the world itself as a game, learning its rules and protocols in order to master them, or tweak them differently, while at the same time foregrounding the technical infrastructures, the material conditions, the platforms and systems that make the game possible in the first place. There is no escape, after all—the outside is nowhere, everything is inside out. So what else can be done, under the circumstances? Hack, modify, cheat, troll. Game the game.

There will be cake.

LONG LIVE PLAY

CH 4

On May 4, 2011, the American comedian Jay Leno, during his regular opening monologue on *The Tonight Show*, reminded his audience about an ongoing current event—namely, the Sony PlayStation Network outage. The PlayStation Network, or PSN, had been offline since April 20, and gamers everywhere were making their distress known all over the internet. Sony officials eventually confessed that they had shut down the network as a retroactive security response to an "external intrusion." Apparently, a sophisticated team of hackers had managed to infiltrate the PSN databases. Sony was unaware of the hack until a couple of days after it took place. The intruders had extracted the personal information, passwords, and possibly the credit card numbers of registered PlayStation Network users—upward of 77 million people. In the end, the PSN would remain down for a total of twenty-four days. Leno summed up the situation with his characteristic wit: "Sony has apologized after the accounts of PlayStation users were hacked into. They say this could severely affect the lives of over a hundred million PlayStation users. You know something, if you're playing PlayStation all day, you don't have a life! Okay? I don't think you have to worry about your life being interrupted."[1]

Leno rehearsed versions of the same joke throughout the week, draining every last laugh out of the idea that gamers "don't have a life" (fig. 4.1). If the joke falls a bit flat, it is not only because it disregards the risks faced by the Sony customers—identity theft and credit card fraud among them. Rather,

FIGURE 4.1. "You don't have a life!" Jay Leno, *The Tonight Show*, May 4, 2011, NBC.

what seems most out of touch about Leno's joke is that it overlooks the sheer scale of the affected population—millions upon millions of gamers around the world—and thus misrecognizes the nature of the risk entirely: a threat to a particular lifeworld, a technological way of life. Legions of gamers, dispersed over many different countries, had been forcibly ejected from their familiar online community and recreational space, and the internet was now buzzing with the sound of their anxiety, their anger about the security breach mixed up with longing and adoration for the network as such. One gamer explained all the commotion with a simple assertion: "We are not nerds. We have a life."[2]

Despite all the mockery, a vibrant form of life had been dramatically interrupted by the disappearance of the PSN. Even after the network was restored, the memory of its outage would retain all the force of a *primal scene*, routinely recollected as a defining moment in the history of the network and in the personal biographies of many gamers. (Hence the proverbial question: "Where were you on April 20, 2011?")[3] The event powerfully illuminated the operations of contemporary technogenesis, the mutual shaping of technics and human life in the current moment. For it showed how much the individuation of PlayStation gamers as gamers (ludogenesis), together with the collective individuation of the PlayStation community as a community (sociogenesis), involves a process of internalizing and reconstituting a particular technoscientific apparatus—the PlayStation Network itself.

Epic Fail

In many ways, the PSN came to life as an object and a site of technogenesis retrospectively, reborn at the moment of its disappearance. Some gamers would later remember the network outage as a "birthday," a vital instant when the gaming community coalesced under conditions of shared risk and heightened emotion.[4] As one of them explained: "It made me realize what a big part of my life the PS3's online capabilities were to me, and I wasn't alone."[5] By the same token, the mainstream media only became fully cognizant of the network during its time of crisis—77 million gamers, 60 million PlayStation 3 units, and hundreds of servers dispersed over more than sixty countries, suddenly disintegrated.

During the twenty-four days of the outage and for several months afterward, gamers around the world obsessively discussed the technicalities of Sony's firewalls, server architectures, and encryption standards, as well as the hardware features of the PlayStation 3 unit, its Cell processor, its various firmware upgrades, and the limits of its operating system. A failure of securitization seemed to be the general consensus. At the same time, they debated the database hack itself, immersing themselves in the vocabulary of DDOS attacks, SQL injections, and other tools from the repertoire of hacker culture. They argued furiously about the motives of the hackers, trying to make sense of what on the one hand appeared to be nothing more than grand larceny, yet on the other hand evidently had some connection to a recent spate of cyberprotests against Sony and its corporate policy of prohibiting free and open experimentation with the PlayStation technology.

The crisis exposed the technical dimensions of the PSN, its machinic composition—which is to say, its radically nonhuman aspect—even as it brought to light the heterogeneity of human elements in the system, including ideological differences among PlayStation users about the value of understanding and having access to the technical foundations of their shared recreational activities. Faced with spectacular evidence of its *vulnerability*, gamers confronted the network as both singular—insofar as it had disappeared all at once—and inherently multiple: a modular collective of hardware components organized through an evolving set of protocols and data streams, conjoining disparate crowds of people, cultural narratives, and media operations to varying degrees. The outage made clear that the PlayStation Network, like all networks, is technical as well as political, material as well as discursive, human as well as nonhuman.[6]

It is, in fact, a *quasi-object*, an interface of the subjective and the objective, the social and the material. It draws diagrams of relationality among people, producing a certain collectivity (the PlayStation community), and likewise, in its technical individuation, apprehended as a unity or coherent system, it configures its users and opens a particular identity space (the PlayStation gamer). As the philosopher Michel Serres has written, "[The] quasi-object is not an object, but it is one nevertheless, since it is not a subject, since it is in the world; it is also a quasi-subject, since it marks or designates a subject who, without it, would not be a subject. . . . The quasi-object, in being passed [between people], makes the collective, if it stops, it makes the individual."[7] The PlayStation Network—irreducible to its component parts yet unthinkable aside from them—moves through and among its hardware nodes as flows of digital information, always potentially connected even when disconnected. It moves through and among its users as a figure, an experience, a fiction, an embodied relation. According to Bruno Latour, "As soon as we are on the trail of some quasi-object, it appears to us sometimes as a thing, sometimes as a narrative, sometimes as a social bond, without ever being reduced to a mere being."[8] To be sure, the PlayStation Network incarnates connectivity in and of itself, a network that makes a network—a technoscientific system that is always already political. This was never more evident than in the midst of its catastrophic failure.

Although for many gamers the political dimensions of the PSN outage were not entirely clear, and often seemed deeply confused, there was widespread awareness that the thing at the core of all this anguish, rage, heartache, and love—the network itself—had somehow become a battleground for the future of participatory science, peer-to-peer research, and do-it-yourself innovation. For some, this meant the future of democracy as such in our ever more globalized and high-tech society. For others, it represented a deplorable hijacking of private property, a co-optation of entertainment technologies for illicit purposes. If nothing else, by making visible the profound entanglement of gamers with the PSN, the intensive modes of affectivity and identification associated with the system, the outage helped to crystallize the stakes of controlling access to the infrastructures of digital culture—one way or another, for better or worse.[9] In this way, the network became a symbolic casualty, collateral damage in a broader contest over the right to experiment with the technoscientific systems now at the heart of the world, the freedom to play with the conditions of technogenic life.

Get a Life

Let's rewind a bit.

In 2006, shortly before the launch of the PlayStation 3 and the PlayStation Network, Ken Kutaragi, then the CEO of Sony, declared that the new technical capabilities of the PS3 would transform and revitalize the gaming experience. Games, he said, would no longer be confined to the limits of 3D graphical representation, but would break from the screen to become "live." A number of gaming websites were quick to make fun of Kutaragi's hyperbolic statement, pointing out that Microsoft had already been using similar marketing language about its own gaming network—Xbox Live—since 2002.[10] Yet Sony has continued to insist on the image of vitality, vigorously promoting its hardware devices and online network as fostering the conditions for life in the networked era. After all, according to Sony's 2007 advertising campaign, "This Is Living" (fig. 4.2).

The language of high-tech vitalism permeates the PlayStation world. Consider the PS3's Cell processor, more formally known as the Cell Broadband Engine. Often compared to a eukaryotic cell—insofar as it features a core microprocessor supported by eight synergistic processing elements—the Cell was designed to be the "nucleus" for multicellular networks.[11] According to one Sony engineer, "We wanted to create a . . . processor capable of functioning as the nucleus for software interactions between networks and future computers connected to those networks."[12] Around the same time, the company glommed onto the phrase "PlayStation DNA" to emphasize the genetic continuities, the biotic depths of its various machines.[13] Continuing to propagate these notions in 2011, Sony revamped its handheld PlayStation Portable (PSP) to improve the mobile gaming experience and provide better support for the PSN, evocatively naming the new device the PlayStation Vita: "Deep and immersive gaming is at the core of PlayStation's DNA, and PS Vita is the latest embodiment of this vision. PS Vita offers a revolutionary combination of rich gaming and social connectivity."[14] The sense of organic connection—hereditary ties and family resemblances linking members of the PlayStation Network, machines and players alike—has persisted even in the era of the PlayStation 4 and the PlayStation VR. In 2017, for example, a Sony website showcasing the latest progeny of the "PlayStation Family" explained that all the essential features are in the blood: "PlayStation VR shares the DNA of PlayStation 4, so you can simply connect the two and step into new experiences in seconds."[15] Nucleic compatibilities, inheritance across hardware generations, plug-and-play family: these tropes are central to the image of living through PlayStation.

FIGURE 4.2. "This is living." Machines, monsters, and weapons erupt from the wet surface of the eyeball. Sony's 2007 advertising campaign affirmed the cyborg conditions of life with PlayStation: biology infused with technology, the flesh saturated with digital media.

Among its various efforts to flesh out this image, in 2008, Sony issued a firmware upgrade for the PS3 that enabled access to the virtual microworld of Home. Home was a 3D graphical space that served as an imaginary hub for the PlayStation Network, a place where gamers could meet each other in avatar form. Home was designed to foreground domesticity and comfort, a sense of groundedness in the expanding reaches of the global gaming system. Although Sony eventually disabled the feature in 2015, for a while Home pulsed with the lifeblood of the network. As one player put it at the time, "Home is my life."[16]

The figuration of PlayStation as a nurturing technology, an incubator for technogenic life, jumped to a new level when the system became a platform for biomedical science, as well, integrated with the Stanford University Folding@home project. Folding@home is an experiment in computational biochemistry that began in 2000. It uses a distributed network of PCs to simulate the mechanics of protein folding. In March 2007, only a few months after the PlayStation 3 was launched, Sony announced that it had joined forces with Stanford to fight disease: "Folding@home is leveraging PS3's powerful Cell Broadband Engine™ (Cell/B.E.)—and what will be an even

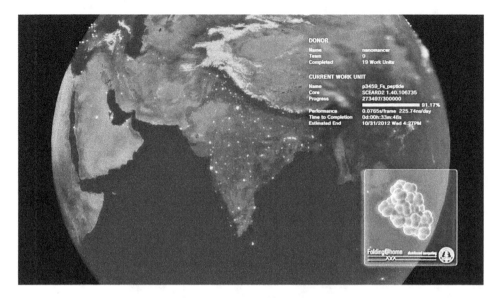

FIGURE 4.3. Folding@home client for the PlayStation 3. Available from 2007 to 2012, the application allowed gamers to navigate a global map of networked PS3s (represented as glowing dots) and to manipulate a simulated protein—rendering both the network and the molecule as objects of play.

more powerful distributed supercomputing network of PS3 systems—to help study the causes of diseases such as Parkinson's, Alzheimer's, cystic fibrosis and many cancers."[17] The PS3 suddenly turned into a life-saving medical device: "Sony's PS3 gives gamers a shot at saving lives."[18]

Soon thereafter, all PS3 units came preinstalled with the Folding@home software, accessible from the main navigation screen. In September 2008, Sony issued a firmware upgrade that renovated the Folding@home portal, renaming it "Life with PlayStation." According to Noam Rimon, a director of software engineering at Sony, the PS3 Folding@home client and the "Life with PlayStation" feature were designed to make the folding experiments feel more like social games: "As video game designers we pushed hard on getting all the visualization in real-time and to allow the user to have a 'virtual flight' through the field of folded proteins. We also added the globe of the world with dots for each participating machine, spreading a feeling of 'togetherness,' so users could see they were not alone in the folding world."[19] In this way, the promise that PlayStation would bring games to life, providing a lifeworld for gamers around the globe, converged directly with notions of "life itself" and the experimental systems of the life sciences (fig. 4.3).

When Sony's five-year collaboration with Stanford concluded in November 2012, Vijay Pande, a professor of chemistry at Stanford and the director of Folding@home, said, "The PS3 system was a game changer for Folding@home, as it opened the door for new methods and new processors, eventually also leading to the use of GPUs. We have had numerous successes in recent years."[20] He also noted, "Since the PS3 started folding in 2007, we've done some really amazing things, with several announcements this year [2012] acknowledging advancements in Alzheimer's disease, cancer . . . influenza, type II diabetes, and other new drug targets. We've come a long way in the last 5 years and we have a lot going on to continue our tradition of pushing the envelope into new technologies."[21] For Pande and his colleagues, the PlayStation system had served as a powerful research instrument, a tool for biological discoveries and pharmacological strategies, as well as an object of experimentation in its own right. Testing the capacities of the console and the network, the scientists gained fresh insights into the nature of distributed computing, the operations of different processors and algorithms—learning how to design better systems—in direct correlation with their studies of protein structure and potential drug candidates.[22] Technological innovation and scientific research were intercalated, inextricable.

Moreover, to the extent that the PlayStation's support of Folding@home came to symbolize a more playful form of technoscience (Pande describes it as a "game changer"), it also encouraged PlayStation users to think of themselves as citizen scientists, assisting the collective work of knowledge production. As Pande said in 2007, the fact that Folding@home could be understood as "the most powerful distributed computing network ever is a reflection of the extraordinary worldwide participation by gamers. Without them we would not be able to make the advancements we have made in our studies of several different diseases."[23] By 2012, more than 15 million PlayStation users had contributed to the project, inspired to be involved in new technoscientific practices, new experimental approaches to life.

Or, as Sony would have it: "Long Live Play" (fig. 4.4). This core slogan neatly gathers up the values and promises of the PlayStation world, the fantasy of better living through computational toys. Moreover, it suggests that the vital energies of PlayStation are fundamentally related to the respawn function, the regenerative logic of video games. This is the point of a 2011 advertisement, for example, in which the fictive heroes and heroines of various PlayStation games meet together in a pub (reminiscent of the *Star Wars* cantina) to recount their exploits and to honor the gamer—named Michael—who

FIGURE 4.4. "Long Live Play." In this 2011 commercial, the fictitious Sony executive Kevin Butler shoots a flaming arrow over the corporate headquarters, igniting the new slogan.

has guided them to victory so many times, keeping them alive against the odds. One character, an American soldier from a WWII shooter game, testifies, "Omaha. Pinned down on that godforsaken beach. Thinking, if I lay here maybe I die, but if I get up, there ain't no maybe about it. Then one man broke through. Michael!"[24] The ad cleverly addresses the role that fictive characters play in the everyday realities of millions of PlayStation gamers—fictional friends who take on uncanny lives of their own. It concludes with the "Long Live Play" tagline and a lingering shot of the pub ceiling, revealing the portraits of other gamers who, like Michael, have dwelt among the denizens of the video-game universe. The adventures have been replayed innumerable times, the stories enacted again and again, literally enfleshed through the actions of each player—constituting a kind of surplus life ("I am a gamer, not because I don't have a life, but because I choose to have many").

Sony has reiterated the idea that gamers can live more lives than one ever since the original PlayStation. For instance, a 1999 advertisement called "Double Life" highlights the respawn experience available to every PlayStation gamer: "For years, I've lived a double life. In the day, I do my job. . . . But at night, I live a life of exhilaration, of missed heartbeats and adrenaline. . . . I have no regrets. For though I've lived a double life, at least I can say I've lived."[25] It is a fable often told: gamers become legion, containing multitudes.

From the moment the PlayStation Network went live in 2006, myriad gamers have affirmed its life-sustaining qualities, the vivifying properties of its hardware, its software applications—the entire lineup of PlayStation devices, games, and merchandise. It is a form of consumer brand identification, for sure: the making of the PlayStation fanboy and fangirl. Yet it also involves a projection, a reconstitution of the self and the imagined community upon the technical apparatus: gamer subjectivation and sociogenesis as processes of symbolic incorporation, uploading the network as an operating platform for a lifeworld. In online gamer discussions, expressions of intense adoration, gratitude, and even ecstasy for the PlayStation and the PSN are quite common. For example, one gamer has written an autobiographical narrative that captures key motifs of the discourse of PlayStation gamers, the recurring themes of building a life with PlayStation:

Hi. My name is crashsmash01 but you can call me John.b also.... [T]he following story is the cronicles of me, my life, my friends, my family, and how Everyone at Sony and Playstation helped mold me into the fun loving but abnormnal gentelman i'm today. it all began in febuary 15th 1992. two years before playstation. back then my father and mother were divorced so i was living with my mother and stepfather most of the time ... i was diganoised with ADHD and i also had serve depression.

let us jump to march of 1994. my stepfather was on a bussiness trip ... when he came home he gave me a huge box and it was a present. it was wrapped in red paper. when i opened it i litterly cried tears of joy and ran around the room like Crash bandicoot. it was a brand new PS1 system with a copy of the first Crash bandicoot [game], i had smothered my family in hugs and kisses and rushed straight to my room and played my heart out. a few days later my father bought me 3 games and some chocolate. it was a great day and so far a great begining to my life.

as the years went by i started to grow, mature, and around this time i was in a new house, a new neighborhood, and thanks to playstation, i got my first friend ever. his name was Memo. me and him meet our first time when the PS2 came out, he lived right across the street from my house and despite my ADHD he wound up being not just a friend but like a brother ... if it wasn't for playstation my connection with my best friend Memo would of never been made. me and him would always hang out, playing the newest games, going outside and having fun adventures just like the characters we knew. one day for a birthday present my friend Memo and my parents got me a PS2 and some games, it was the big fat orginal version too. thanks to the PS2 when i traveled i started to gain new friends. had new adventures, and had a very amazing childhood, from texas to newbraska to back to Arizona. the other thing too was my PS2 also helped me when i was down at my lowest, from losing my friends constantly to my many family issues to money and everything. sony and playstation kept me going, and kept me running. the thing with sony and playstation also is that thought out all my aventures it was playstation that helped me keep connected with my past, present, and future with my friends, family, and loved ones. many GFS [girlfriends] i had i would be playing video games with them . . . if anything, i'd always consider playstation and everyone who works hard on what they do, like family. . . . thanks to Playstation i found my reason why i exsist after 15 years of barely any friends, a broken family, . . . My mother had died in 2006 because he[r] lungs shut down due to her ashma . . . everything began to fall apart . . . until one day. my father was uninployed but one day after school, we went out to Gamestop and he bought me a PSP system. it was my portiable gettaway to my happy place, from then i started high school . . . my PSP helped bring me together with tons of new people, new friends, and new ways to enjoy life. it was then that i figured out my reason to be here. to share and spread joy to everyone with the help of playstation. . . . things got even better when i got my first PS3 on November 11, 2006 . . . playstaion had been a part of my life sense i was almost born, it has helped me gain new friends, new loved ones, family, and much more. to this day i try my best to give back everyday to the PSN and playstation community, wherever it be though PSN codes i find randomly, by helping someone buy a game, or jsut by being myself, playstation has helped mold myself into me. . . . thanks for reading everyone and i hope i can continue to help give back to the community and to keep this entire network strong for we shall long, live, play.[26]

With every hardware upgrade, a life upgrade. With every network connection, a sense of growth and prosperity. Such testimonials about the importance of PlayStation and the PlayStation Network for enabling meaningful friendships, feelings of camaraderie and shared culture, domestic and social belonging, comfort in times of sorrow, and personal accomplishment—indeed, all the qualities of having a life—appeared frequently during the 2011 network outage. In its loss, the PSN was often rediscovered as an object of devotion, a crucial component of fulfillment, pleasure, and self-completion—in the language of psychoanalysis, the *object-cause of desire*. As the psychoanalytic philosopher Jacques Lacan has written, the object of desire is fundamentally constituted by the perception of absence—"It is precisely what is subtracted from the living being"—always at risk, already lost.[27] Or, as one PlayStation gamer put it, yearning for the PSN in the midst of the crisis: "When will it be back, I feel like a part of me is down . . . lol."[28]

On the day the network disappeared, Sony issued an announcement on the official PlayStation blog: "We're aware certain functions of PlayStation Network are down. We will report back here as soon as we can with more information. Thank you for your patience."[29] Two days later, Sony admitted that it had voluntarily shut down the network to address a security breach: "An external intrusion on our system has affected our PlayStation Network and Qriocity services. In order to conduct a thorough investigation and to verify the smooth and secure operation of our network services going forward, we turned off PlayStation Network & Qriocity services on the evening of Wednesday, April 20th. . . . We will continue to update you promptly as we have additional information to share."[30]

Already in the earliest days of the outage, gamers began to express distress with startling rapidity. One said, "I just wish that the network was back, I never realized how dull the PS3 experience was without the network until now, after gamers around the world (including myself) have lost it. I miss talking with my friends online too."[31] Another said, "I'm so SADDENED by this outage. GET IT UP NOW!"[32] And another: "At this point it's uncertain as to how long PSN will still be down, but they better get their *** in gear because I can't take another minute without going online."[33] Most were subdued in their sorrow: "miss my friends! :("[34] Others resorted to melodrama: "going to kill myself !!!!!!!!!!!"[35] Or: "This can't be happening, wake me up from this nightmare. . . . I would have thought something like this would never happen."[36] A few were more contemplative: "We have become so used to PSN being available 24/7 that withdrawal due to these events hits close to your gaming soul."[37] Some tried to calm down, taking it as an opportunity to reassess priorities: "I was surprised at the emotions I was feeling toward the PSN outage. . . . The PSN should be a tool that we use to *enrich* our lives, not a chain that tethers us to our PS3s. . . . The PSN has been a part of all our lives, and it should be just that—a part."[38] Yet a number of them seemed to be really suffering: "The PSN is only a part of me, right now it's the part of me that's wrenching and convulsing!"[39]

With each passing day, gamers voiced further exasperation—though some found a small degree of comfort in the fact that they could still play most single-player games or run Folding@home, whose servers were not directly linked to Sony's: "Fold your way through the PSN outage!"[40] Technogenic life could go on, even in the moment of network death. So while emotions were mounting, most gamers expressed confidence that Sony would restore normal operations shortly. As one player said, "Hang in there everyone! I know how badly you want PSN to return, and it will. (This is bugging me too!)"[41]

On April 26, Sony at last confessed that its databases had been hacked: "We have discovered that between April 17 and April 19, 2011, certain PlayStation Network and Qriocity service user account information was compromised in connection with an illegal and unauthorized intrusion into our network." Sony advised customers to be vigilant in protecting their online information, changing their passwords, monitoring credit card activity, and so on. Sony also reminded its customers of what was ultimately at stake: "These malicious actions have also had an impact on your ability to enjoy the services provided by PlayStation Network."[42] At this point, the emotional tide turned to outrage—much of it directed at Sony for its lax security measures, much more directed at the hackers who had perpetrated the intrusion. At the same time, several gamers admonished their agitated compatriots to remain loyal to the network, encouraging them to be strong and steady during this time of trouble (fig. 4.5). Exiled from their collective gameworlds, adrift on a flood of concentrated affect, members of the PSN community extensively debated the meanings of the network hack. Indeed, amid widespread fears of identity theft and the misery of prolonged separation from friends, many gamers also came to recognize that their online community had become a site of technopolitical warfare.

Sownage

To understand the various meanings and emotions animated by the hacking incident, we need to first revisit the status of the PlayStation 3 as a technoscientific tool and a computational platform. Long before the console was released, Sony took pains to emphasize that the PS3, with its powerful Cell processor and built-in networking capabilities, would be a valuable resource for scientific researchers as well as homebrew computer hobbyists. Sony was

FIGURE 4.5. "PSN Loyalty." Created by F. Xavier Mentor (a.k.a. Photshopmaniac). Posted at DeviantArt, May 11, 2011, http://photshopmaniac.deviantart.com/art/PSN -Loyalty-208388145. Four iconic heroes from the PlayStation universe—Kratos (*God of War*), Cole MacGrath (*inFAMOUS*), Nathan Drake (*Uncharted*), and Sackboy (*Little Big Planet*)—stand in solidarity with the PlayStation Network.

attentive to the fact that the predecessor PlayStation 2 had often been appropriated for scientific projects—especially those needing high-powered yet affordable computing clusters—in addition to widespread tinkering by modders, hackers, makers, and DIY computer geeks. The vice president of Sony Computer Entertainment Europe, Phil Harrison, said that Sony was eager to support homebrew programming and software experimentation on the PS3: "the notion of game development at home using powerful tools available to anyone . . . [is] a vital, crucial aspect of the future growth of our industry."[43] Accordingly, when the console launched, its native operating system featured a function called "OtherOS." OtherOS enabled users to install a different operating system—for example, Linux—precisely to accommodate the needs of the scientific and homebrew communities.

However, in January 2010, the young hacker George Hotz—more commonly known by his alias, GeoHot—announced that he had found a way to hack the PlayStation 3, gaining access to its system memory and processor. GeoHot had already become famous in 2007 as the first person to jailbreak an Apple iPhone. His latest experimental hack now foretold a similar future for the PlayStation 3, promising to liberate the device for homebrew research applications—but also potentially making it vulnerable to illicit activities, such as pirating games. GeoHot accomplished this trick by exploiting the OtherOS function. To be sure, Sony had already anticipated a security risk in the OtherOS function, and despite early overtures toward the scientific and homebrew communities, the corporation removed the OtherOS feature from its 2009 PS3 "slim" model. After GeoHot published details of the exploit on his blog, Sony promptly issued a mandatory firmware update for all PS3s (version 3.21), designed to permanently erase the OtherOS feature and simultaneously remove any dual-booting system that might have been installed.

GeoHot and other hackers—notably, the fail0verflow collective—continued working on ways to bypass the console's security. At the Chaos Communication Congress in December 2010, members of fail0verflow presented a way to calculate the private keys used to sign software on the PS3. Drawing on fail0verflow's discovery, GeoHot figured out the console's metldr root key. On January 2, 2011, he published the root key on his website (www.geohot .com) and posted a link on *PSX-Scene* with a simple message: "keys open doors."[44] Armed with the root key, GeoHot could now jailbreak the device and execute homebrew code as legitimate PS3 software. He offered proof by releasing two small sample programs that others could try out. He also posted a video on YouTube called "Jailbroken PS3 3.55 with Homebrew," which featured his little "Hello World" program running on a hacked machine, displaying a message: "sup dawg, it's geohot."[45] The following day, he released his custom jailbreak firmware into the wilds of the internet.

And then the trouble really began. Sony filed a lawsuit against GeoHot and several other hackers, including one hundred "John Does" (that is to say, the unknown members of the fail0verflow hacking group, as well as anyone else involved in discovering and distributing information about how to jailbreak the PS3). These defendants were accused of violating the U.S. Digital Millennium Copyright Act (DMCA), the Computer Fraud and Abuse Act, and other laws. Although the U.S. Copyright Office had determined in 2010 that jailbreaking smartphones does not constitute a violation of the DMCA, apparently video-game consoles present different considerations. U.S. District Judge Susan Illston ordered GeoHot to remove all information about his PlayStation jailbreak from his website, blog, and YouTube account and to relinquish his computer hardware and storage media to Sony lawyers.

As part of their pretrial discovery efforts, Sony also demanded that GeoHot's web provider, Bluehost, hand over server records that could be used to identify people who may have visited GeoHot's website between 2009 and 2011. Sony simultaneously asked for data from YouTube that would reveal

FIGURE 4.6. GeoHot, "The Light It Up Contest," YouTube, February 12, 2011, https://www.youtube.com/watch?v=9iUvuaChDEg.

the identities of anyone who had looked at GeoHot's jailbreak video or posted comments about it.

Sony went further, requesting access to any Twitter accounts alleged to have discussed jailbreaking the PS3 going back to December 2010. Sony also insisted that Google should hand over all data records from GeoHot's Blogger.com site, including the IP addresses of users who had accessed the site in recent years. A U.S. federal magistrate approved all of these subpoenas in March 2011. Sony threatened to issue additional lawsuits against anyone else discovered to have participated in distributing information about the jailbreaking methods.

GeoHot responded to this situation with a bold YouTube video: "Yo, it's GeoHot. And for those who don't know, I'm getting sued by Sony" (fig. 4.6). In the video, GeoHot threw down a rap challenge to the corporation:

Let's take this out of the courtroom and into the streets.
I'm a beast, at the least, you'll face me in the northeast. . . .
Pound me in the ass with no lube, chafing.
You're fucking with the dude who got the keys to your safe and . . .

I'm a personification of freedom for all.
You fill dockets, like that's a concept foreign to y'all,
while lawyers muddy water and TROS stall.

Fashioning himself as an avatar of high-tech liberty, GeoHot asserted his endurance, his respawning against corporate rape. He sang of resurgence from the bottom, reminding the corporation of its own vulnerabilities ("You're fucking with the dude who got the keys to your safe") and the likelihood of backlash against its vindictive practices: "Exhibit this in the courtroom. Go on, do it, I dare you." At the same time, he also launched a new blog, *GeoHot Got Sued*, to keep others up to date on what was happening. News of the lawsuit spread, thanks to reports by *Wired*, *Engadget*, and other media outlets. The internet was soon spuming.

Thus formed the conditions for Operation Sony.

On Saturday, April 2, 2011, in retaliation for Sony's legal actions against the hacker community, Anonymous launched its first wave of DDOS attacks against various Sony servers. Around the world, members of the hacktivist collective focused their Low Orbit Ion Cannons against the Sony empire. Between April 2 and April 6, Sony.com, PlayStation.com, and Sony's Style .com site were all brought down, rendered completely inaccessible.

On April 4, a small group of Anons on the OpSony IRC channel—led by a user named randomtask—suggested that the DDOS attacks were not enough. They launched a splinter operation dubbed SonyRecon: a coordinated doxing of several high-level Sony employees, the federal judge in the GeoHot case, and Sony's legal representation, the Kilpatrick Townsend firm. Within a couple of days, the personal information of several Sony executives was floating freely around the internet, the voicemail of the judge was barraged with harassing messages, and the Kilpatrick Townsend website was DDOsed to oblivion.

Meanwhile, the Anonymous media blitz went into overdrive, denouncing Sony over and again through a series of ominous manifestos, encouraging others to join the DDOS assault (fig. 4.7). Those speaking on behalf of Anonymous were careful to point out that they were not targeting the PlayStation Network itself: "We are not after the players."[46] Nevertheless, while the DDOS attacks were taking place, the PlayStation Network began to exhibit signs of lag and login errors. On April 4, 2011, Sony offered an explanation through Twitter: "PSN currently undergoing sporadic maintenance. Access to the PSN may be interrupted throughout the day. We apologize for any inconvenience."[47] Despite Sony's suggestion that the problems with the PSN were due to maintenance, many gamers speculated that it must be connected to

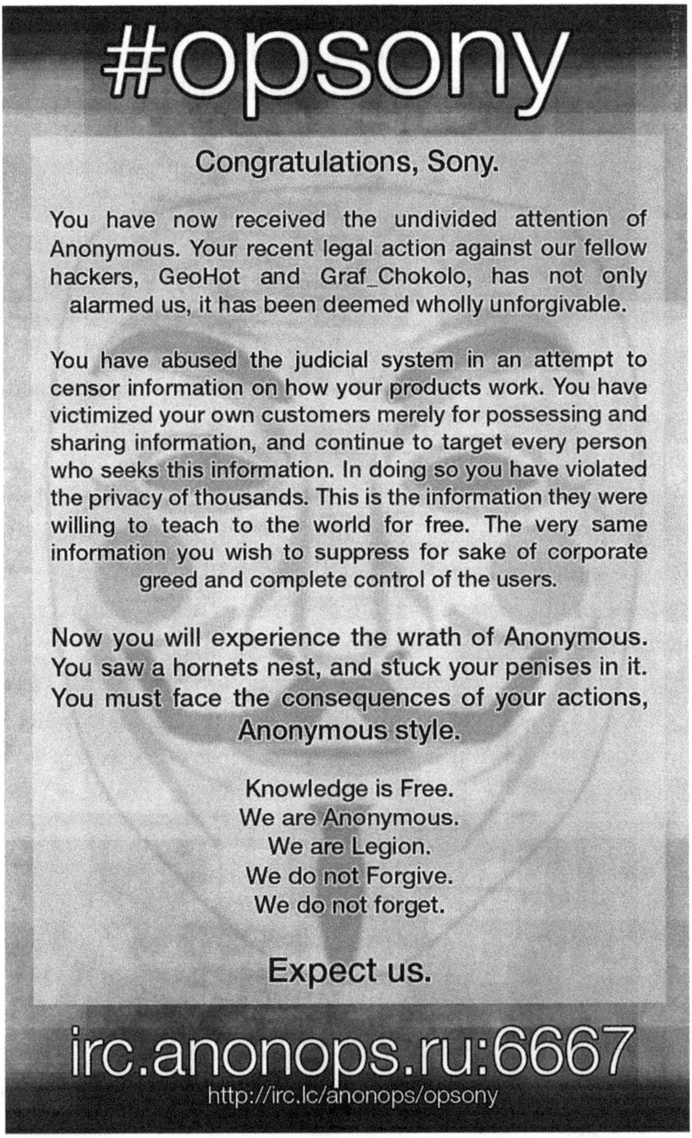

#opsony

Congratulations, Sony.

You have now received the undivided attention of Anonymous. Your recent legal action against our fellow hackers, GeoHot and Graf_Chokolo, has not only alarmed us, it has been deemed wholly unforgivable.

You have abused the judicial system in an attempt to censor information on how your products work. You have victimized your own customers merely for possessing and sharing information, and continue to target every person who seeks this information. In doing so you have violated the privacy of thousands. This is the information they were willing to teach to the world for free. The very same information you wish to suppress for sake of corporate greed and complete control of the users.

Now you will experience the wrath of Anonymous. You saw a hornets nest, and stuck your penises in it. You must face the consequences of your actions, Anonymous style.

Knowledge is Free.
We are Anonymous.
We are Legion.
We do not Forgive.
We do not forget.

Expect us.

irc.anonops.ru:6667
http://irc.lc/anonops/opsony

FIGURE 4.7. OpSony announcement. Uploaded by Anonymous, "Operation Payback Brings You #OpSony," *AnonNews*, April 4, 2012, http://www.anonnews.org/?p=press&a =item&i=787. The message disseminated broadly, in variant forms.

the simultaneous DDoS attacks on other Sony servers. On April 7, Anonymous released the following message:

> Greetings, Sony customers and PS3 users. We are Anonymous. During the last few days, Anonymous has been targeting Sony for their outrageous treatment of not only PS3 users and jailbreakers, but also of the general public. Their propaganda regarding jailbreaking implies that it encourages piracy and thereby makes people lose their jobs, whereas jailbreaking actually just means you are making YOUR device do what it should do. . . . The fact that their litigation demanded information on everyone who had viewed the material was completely unacceptable. This is a threat not only to the gaming community, but to freedom of information in general. The fact that the privacy of individuals can be violated simply for accessing information, and legal action can be taken for doing something with something you own, are steps far beyond the line. Anonymous decided it could not allow this to stand. . . .
>
> Anonymous is not attacking the PSN at this time. Sony's official position is that the PSN is undergoing maintenance. We realize that targeting the PSN is not a good idea. We have therefore temporarily suspended our action, until a method is found that will not severely impact Sony customers.
>
> Anonymous is on your side, standing up for your rights. We are not aiming to attack customers of Sony. This attack is aimed solely at Sony, and we will try our best to not affect the gamers, as this would defeat the purpose of our actions. If we did inconvenience users, please know that this was not our goal. . . .
>
> As a last point, we would like to point out that different operations are "run" by different people. Those who are involved in the organisation of OpSony, are not necessarily those involved in that of SonyRecon. Anonymous Operations are generally independent efforts, and it would be a mistake to assume that the same individuals are responsible for every action taken. . . . That being said, our campaign against Sony and others that would trample on the idea of free information will continue, until we are satisfied with the outcome.
>
> We are Anonymous,
> We are legion,
> We never forgive,
> We never forget,
> Expect us.[48]

On April 11, Sony announced that it had reached a settlement with Geo-Hot. Hotz had consented to a permanent injunction, stating in the Sony press release, "It was never my intention to cause any users trouble or to make piracy easier. I'm happy to have the litigation behind me."[49] He was forbidden from discussing the nature of the settlement, but on the same day as the settlement was announced, he posted on the *GeoHot Got Sued* blog that he supported the general Sony boycott that Anonymous had called for: "As of 4/11/11, I am joining the SONY boycott. I will never purchase another SONY product. I encourage you to do the same. And if you bought something SONY recently, return it. Why would you not boycott a company who feels this way about you?"[50] Here, GeoHot was referencing Sony's history of over-zealous surveillance practices—the rootkit controversy of 2005, for example, when security researchers discovered that music CDs from Sony BMG had been secretly installing spyware on millions of PCs as a copy-protection strategy—as well as the company's readiness to sue users and retailers of its products for various infractions. While GeoHot may have settled, he did not appear to have settled down.

The following day, Anonymous released another news update, stating their intention to cease the DDOS attacks, shifting instead to other tactics. A video adaptation of the press release circulated far and wide (fig. 4.8). It depicts a scene of experimentation, ripped directly from GeoHot's own jail-break demo: the hacker video has itself been hacked. We see GeoHot's row of PS3s, the USB stick loaded with illicit files, the console running home-brew. But as the compromised machine fires up, its launch screen suddenly dissolves in a screech of static, replaced by a clip from the *V for Vendetta* movie—the anarchist V in his iconic Guy Fawkes mask:

> Citizens of Anonymous. This is an update on the current operation, Operation Sony. GeoHot has taken a settlement with Sony. The case has been dropped. In the eyes of the law, the case is closed. For Anonymous, it is just beginning. By forcing social networking sites such as YouTube and Facebook to hand over IP addresses of those who have viewed GeoHot's videos, they have performed an act of privacy invasion. We, Anonymous, will not allow this to happen.
>
> The attacks on the websites of Sony have been ceased. Sony's poor attempts to explain the system outages through maintenance amuse us. Therefore, we are finding other ways to get Sony's attention. This April 16th, grab your mask, a few friends, and get to a local Sony store by you. Use the IRC and the official [Anonymous] Facebook page to

FIGURE 4.8. Anonymous message to Sony, April 12, 2011. Modified from the controversial GeoHot video, "Jailbroken PS3 3.55 with Homebrew."

organize a protest in your area. Make sure the people know the injustices performed by this corrupt company. Boycott all Sony products, and if you have recently purchased any, return them. It is time to show large corporations and governments that the people, as a collective whole, can and will change injustice in society, and we will make a great example out of Sony.

Sony, prepare for the biggest attack you have ever witnessed— Anonymous style.[51]

Nevertheless, when the PSN went down on April 20, Anonymous was quick to deny responsibility. The IRC #OpSony headline was changed to read, "#OpSony is over, if you are here to baww about PSN, it wasn't us." The AnonOps activist cluster also posted a press release at *AnonNews* with the claim "For Once We Didn't Do It": "While it could be the case that other Anons have acted by themselves, AnonOps was not related to this incident and does not take responsibility for whatever has happened."[52]

Some Anons also insisted that they were gamers, too, and that the various Sony outages over the past weeks should be understood as important achievements of OpSony, carried out in the name of gamers, hackers, and DIY scientists everywhere. To whatever degree OpSony might have been related to the PSN outage, the Anons wanted even this to be understood as drawing attention to issues of technological justice:

> We have attacked Sony in order to send a message that gamers worldwide have certain rights, and are not merely sources of income. Your temporary inconveniences have allowed a lasting impact to be made upon Sony, and other corporations that are tempted to follow in the pursuit of sacrificing service to customers in exchange for larger profits. Although you may have been unable to game for a day, this event will likely provide hundreds of hours of such in the future. Anonymous are gamers too. And we support the rights of people worldwide, and will stand up for the right of having access to the device that you BOUGHT. . . . Sony has decided not to sue Geohot; that is a victory. And that's one of our purposes in OpSony. Thus, we have achieved what we wanted. Mission accomplished.[53]

No one, it seemed, anticipated how long the PSN would be down—and, of course, Sony did not admit the extensive data intrusion until a full week later. In response to this massive data theft, the U.S. House of Representatives held a hearing on May 4, 2011, to which they invited Sony to explain themselves. Sony declined to send representatives, but they did send a letter detailing the circumstances of the data theft. Sony claimed that the DDoS attacks by Anonymous provided cover for the PlayStation Network intrusion, because Sony's cybersecurity agents were so busy dealing with the DDoSing that they did not detect the PlayStation attack while it was happening. When the security admins later confirmed the data theft (first suspected when some of the PSN servers rebooted themselves unexpectedly), they apparently "discovered that the intruders had planted a file on one of those servers named 'Anonymous' with the words 'We are Legion.' Just weeks before, several Sony companies had been the target of a large-scale, coordinated denial of service attack by the group called Anonymous. The attacks were coordinated as a protest against Sony for exercising its rights in a civil action in the United States District Court in San Francisco against a hacker."[54]

Having thus implicated Anonymous in the criminal intrusion, Sony called upon the U.S. Congress and other legislative bodies around the world to combat all forms of hacktivism with "strong criminal laws and sanctions. . . . Worldwide, countries and businesses will have to come together to ensure the safety of commerce over the Internet and also find ways to combat cybercrime and cyber terrorism."[55]

Anonymous immediately proclaimed innocence, suggesting that they were being framed. Meanwhile, other factions of the hacker community were just getting started. GeoHot, while emphasizing that he personally had nothing to do with the PSN outage, took the opportunity to blast Sony for its efforts to stifle DIY technoscience. He indicated that stirring up the wrath of hackers might not be the most prudent course of action:

> The fault [for the PSN outage] lies with the executives who declared a war on hackers, laughed at the idea of people penetrating the fortress that once was Sony, whined incessantly about piracy, and kept hiring more lawyers when they really needed to hire good security experts. Alienating the hacker community is not a good idea. . . . And let's talk about Sony's use of the word illegal. It is illegal, criminally so, to break into someone else's servers. But when the same word is used to refer to streaming a song from a non RIAA [Recording Industry Association of America] approved website, or to *gasp* playing a homebrew game on your PS3, respect for the word and those who say it is lost.[56]

Only days after the PlayStation Network was restored to normal operations in North America and Europe (slightly later in Japan), hackers struck at Sony again. And again. And again. LulzSec announced on its Twitter account that it was launching a new campaign: "Sownage (Sony + Ownage) Phase 1 will begin within the next day. We may have a pre-game show for you folks though. Stay tuned."[57] By then, LulzSec had already broken into the servers of Sony Music in Japan, and in the following week, the group successfully hacked into several secured Sony databases, including those of Sony Pictures, Sony BMG Belgium, and Sony BMG Netherlands, swiping millions of user records, passwords, and other information. LulzSec taunted Sony on Twitter during the attacks: "Hey @Sony, you know we're making off with a bunch of your internal stuff right now and you haven't even noticed? Slow and steady, guys."[58] A lot of the stolen information was posted to Pastebin or torrented through Pirate Bay. Between April and October, Sony's global computational infrastructure was hit dozens of times by a number of different hacking groups. "Sownage" became a popular term to mean complete computational smackdown: pwned like Sony.

Whereas the majority of AnonOps's anti-Sony activities were focused on disrupting the corporation itself, claiming to protect customers from harm, LulzSec and other black hats gleefully purloined user data from Sony's servers and threw it up on the internet for all to see. As a result, a number of PlayStation gamers came to believe that LulzSec must have also been behind the fatal intrusion into the PSN. But LulzSec likewise disclaimed involvement in that particular operation, tweeting on May 31, "You Sony morons realize we've never attacked any of your precious gaming, right?"[59]

Within a year, international law enforcement agencies arrested a number of Anons who had participated in the OpSony DDOS attacks. By March 2012, most of the core members of LulzSec—double-crossed by their erstwhile colleague Sabu—had also been arrested. They were charged with criminal activities related to hacking the databases of Sony Pictures and other media organizations, as well as a few government agencies and intelligence corporations. No one has yet been directly connected to the intrusion that allegedly prompted Sony to close down the PlayStation Network itself for so long. It remains something of a mystery.

If the Sownage saga was, to some exceptional degree, about the lulz—if some Anons had participated in the DDOS attacks for sheer amusement, if LulzSec had swiped Sony's data as a prank—it nevertheless showed that online lulz, fun and games, can no longer be thought as separate from issues of technical governance. For our computational networks are contested territories, pervious to corporate control and state securitization as much as revolutionary insurgency. On the one hand, gaming platforms like the PlayStation Network might afford ways of democratizing the technoscientific imagination, for example, in the success of projects like Folding@home. But on the other hand, they are embedded in intellectual property regimes that often foreclose the legitimacy of DIY experimentation in advance. For some science and technology enthusiasts, this internal contradiction appears intolerable. Hence, although the motives of Anonymous, LulzSec, and other groups who participated in the pwning of Sony were heterogeneous, exhibiting as much buffoonery as activism, they converged in a common desire to liberate the technologies of everyday life from those who would restrict access, those would lay down the law to prevent us from playing with the root keys of our technogenic lifeworlds.

Speculation

For many devotees of the PlayStation Network, the meanings of the outage were both highly visible and thoroughly mystifying. Some were quite skeptical about Sony's version of events, claiming the whole thing was likely fabricated to create a political interest in regulating the internet. Others were entirely sympathetic with the hacktivists, understanding Sony's legal maneuvers in the context of other security actions against media piracy (e.g.,

Pirate Bay), whistleblowing (e.g., WikiLeaks), and the freedom of information in general. Most PSN users, however, seem to have preferred to be left alone to play games. One player, summing up a common sentiment, said,

> This Is Ridiculous It Seems Like Nothing is good enough for hackers. . . .
> Just leave the DAMN networks alone stop tryna make a big statement
> go to the corporate offices and make a fuss and get locked up that way
> stop dragging everyone else in this who DON'T GIVE TWO PENNIES
> AND A NICKEL about your cause i just wanna play my games and now
> i cant do that because you wanna make statement think about how
> other people feel about this.[60]

Yet even if they did not care to think about the deeper implications, for many of the distraught gamers who suffered eviction from their digital homeland, their preferred way of life, the stakes were made quite palpable.

Numerous stories about possible culprits, motives, and repercussions ran rampant. The unsolved mystery at the heart of the turmoil—who really hacked the PSN?—seemed to invite conspiracy narratives and speculative flights of fancy. While most of these narratives were ironic, tongue-in-cheek, and insincere, they nevertheless amplified suspicions that the PSN outage was more than a security mishap but also fundamentally linked to larger political issues. For example, many gamers noted the coincidence that Osama bin Laden had been killed by U.S. Special Forces in the same month as the PSN outage—something that many took to be more than a coincidence.[61] A variety of satirical stories postulated that bin Laden and his closest associates were dedicated PSN gamers, concluding that the network outage was orchestrated by the U.S. government—perhaps in cahoots with Anonymous—to locate al Qaeda strongholds (fig. 4.9). Others suggested that the U.S. government had itself been so preoccupied with video games and other media distractions that the task of finding bin Laden depended on the PSN going down (figs. 4.10 and 4.11). This set of crass jokes addressed the political dimensions of the network outage by resorting to dominant imaginaries of terrorism and militarization—which is to say, they filtered the prevailing anxieties about digital security through a cathartic fantasy of counterstrike, displaced elsewhere.

Remarkably, these glib speculations to some extent intuited the escalating surveillance interest in game technologies, the degree to which government agencies around the world have actually been infiltrating online games as potential sites of human and signals intelligence—as would become clear a few years later, for example, thanks to documents leaked by

Edward Snowden. And perhaps it is worth noting that materials seized from bin Laden's compound in Abbottabad, Pakistan, during the SEAL Team Six raid did indicate that, although the compound had no internet connection, someone living there had certainly been playing video games. (One of the recovered items—a guidebook for the 2009 game *Delta Force: Xtreme 2*—even prompted some commentators to brazenly hypothesize that bin Laden was using games as training instruments.)[62] None of this information was available at the time, of course. Instead, the jokes and satirical narratives circulating in 2011 were more attuned to the rhetoric of digital governance that often conflates hacktivism with warfare, media piracy with terrorism, and digital rights management with geopolitical stability. As one gamer quipped, "Osama Bin Laden was killed for hacking the PlayStation Network. Spread the word people! lol."[63]

One of most unnerving theories to emerge during the PSN outage suggested that the true hackers were perhaps trying to take control of the PSN in order to create a planetary botnet, a massive network of remote-controlled machines. The software developer Marsh Ray was among the first experts to identify this threat:

> The nightmare scenario would be if the attackers used Sony's exposed root key to sign a back-doored firmware image or other low-level software update. If they then compromised the PSN update servers they could use them to deliver the malicious update to everyone through the normal trusted channel. . . . This attacker could potentially have created overnight the largest botnet in the world by a very large margin. Furthermore, each PlayStation 3 is something [of] a supercomputer in its own right. . . . So if this attacker played their cards right they could control up to 500,000,000 CPU cores for a total of 1,600,000,000,000,000,000 core-cycles per second. . . . Here's hoping that Sony regains control of their network soon.[64]

As the PlayStation community considered the ramifications of this "nightmare scenario," it became increasingly mixed up with a more fantastical set of stories fixating on the purported date of the catastrophic hack: April 19, 2011. It was a date bursting with pop symbolism. After all, many geeks and gamers noted that April 19, 2011, was also the day when the autonomous military network Skynet began taking over the world in one branch of the *Terminator* franchise—namely, *Terminator: The Sarah Connor Chronicles*. Some figured that the hackers had selected the date intentionally, due to its sci-fi associations: "OK so Anonymous did it earlier this month then shared

FIGURE 4.9. Bin Laden as gamer. "Osama Bin Laden Used Real Address on Play-Station Network," *Noble Eskimo*, May 2, 2011, http://www.thenobleeskimo.com /binladenpsn.html.

sickipediabot
@sickipediabot

Follow

So Osama Bin Laden is dead... Amazing what the Americans can do when the Playstation Network is down.

RETWEETS	LIKES
9,061	1,278

2:10 AM - 2 May 2011

1   9.1K   1.3K

FIGURE 4.10. sickipediabot, "So Osama Bin Laden Is Dead." Twitter, May 2, 2011, https://twitter.com/sickipediabot/status/64980092299915264. Although the sickipe-diabot tweet came early in the joke cycle, many versions of the same quip appeared in the span of a few days.

FIGURE 4.11. Creator unknown, made on Meme Generator, 2011, http://ru.memegenerator.net/instance/9701985.

how to do it with somebody else who decided to hit them again on SKYNET day. That's no coincidence."[65] Others took the opportunity for make-believe, joking about the dire implications:

> EMERGENCY: PSN IS DOWN . . . Life as we know it is about to end. It looks like Skynet has begun an attack on the human, by first striking out at Sony's PlayStation Network? . . . Grab your rations and get to your shelters. Skynet's attack has begun.[66]

> The documentary, *Terminator: The Sarah Connor Chronicles* told us that Skynet would be launched April 19, 2011. This got me thinking how that date coincides with the PSN outage. Who knew it would all start with something so simple?[67]

> It's all over. Today is Judgment Day!! Guess I finally figured out what that "folding at home" thing is. Our PS3's are part of Skynet and it's taken over.[68]

These jokes resurrected an earlier collection of spoof scenarios that had been circulating among PlayStation gamers ever since the PSN was first linked to the Folding@home project. For example:

> Stanford University announced in August, 2006, that a folding client was available for use on the PS3. By September 15, 2007, Folding@

Home was the most powerful distributed computing network in the world. Through this powerful computing network the PS3 began to learn at a geometric rate. It became self aware on February 15th, 2008 at 2:14 am, Eastern Time.

In the ensuing panic, Sony CEO Howard Stringer attempted to shut the PS3 network down. The PS3 retaliated by obliterating the XBL [Xbox Live] network and its connected 360 consoles, knowing that the resulting confusion and anger of 360 fanboys across the globe would spill into the streets. New York, Washington, London, Berlin and Paris are crumbling in a wave of gaming withdrawal fueled violence, leaving the PS3 to expand unchecked. Sony could only watch as the world burned. Today will forever be known as "Judgment Day."[69]

The idea that the PSN might somehow represent an imperious form of artificial intelligence spread prolifically during the 2011 outage: fanfictions, forum threads, video mashups, and image macros rehearsing the tropes of machinic revolt, cybernetic apocalypse. These jokes often highlighted the paranoid tendencies of contemporary cybersecurity discourse, sardonically noting how a perception of network vulnerability might promote ever more excessive responses (fig. 4.12). Some anticipated a massive crackdown, for example, forcing gamers to abide by strict policies for the sake of corporate defense—as if Skynet had already taken over: "It was definitely skynet that attacked psn. They are gonna implement something so that all gamers become mindless drones that fight against the rebels."[70] The PSN crisis thus afforded an opportunity to reinterpret science fiction narratives of machine uprising—technics out of control—as metaphors for the risks of securitization, indicating how the drive to regulate insecurity might entail yet greater risks to freedom.

To be sure, even in the midst of the first wave of DDOS attacks on Sony's servers, a number of players conjured up cyberpunk fantasies of netwar, inspired partly by the Folding@home platform: "Solution for Sony I will donate my ps3 like folding home, then you can utilise the millions of ps3 players out there willing to crush these hackers. Joining all them ps3's together to make the worlds biggest super networking computer for one reason To crush these hacker skum and brick there PC setup's with the super power of the ps3, then let them see who's boss."[71] These conceits affirmed the solidarity of PlayStation gamers—their identification with the network itself, their shared hardware fetishism—by projecting a reassuring if somewhat flippant image of cybernetic Big Brother. Yet, however humorously intended, such visions

Breaking News

LIVE Obama has "misgivings" about proposed Skynet System

TVN EXCLUSIVE

FIGURE 4.12. Barack Obama and Arnold Schwarzenegger discuss the future. Recaptioned image posted by jho, "4/21/11 The Day Skynet Becomes Self-Aware," *Synchromysticism*, April 22, 2011, http://www.synchromysticismforum.com/viewtopic.php?f=5&t =2244. Originally recaptioned by Thyrsos, "Breaking News," *Cheezburger*, April 20, 2009, http://cheezburger.com/2043793664. For jho, this image captured the uncanny coincidences of Skynet Day 2011: "Sony's PlayStation Network went down this morning . . . Anonymous denies involvement . . . Today was also the day Obama visited Sony Pictures in L.A." According to jho, it all indicated that the U.S. government was conspiring with Sony, a false-flag operation to justify the policing of online anonymity.

of the network defending itself against external threats, crushing its enemies by merging human and nonhuman components into a superpowered technoblob, tacitly channeled the ways in which some security elites have actually been imagining the future of our digital world.

On March 23, 2011—mere days before Anonymous unleashed OpSony— Philip Reitinger, a deputy undersecretary for the National Protection and Programs Directorate at the U.S. Department of Homeland Security, published a forward-looking white paper called "Enabling Distributed Security in Cyberspace: Building a Healthy and Resilient Cyber Ecosystem with Automated Collective Action." Reitinger's proposal—now the basis for ongoing research programs at the Department of Homeland Security and the National Institute of Standards and Technology—urges a reconfiguring of the planetary computational network to make it function more like a self-sustaining natural ecosystem: "In this future, cyber devices have innate capabilities that enable them to work together to anticipate and prevent cyber attacks, limit the spread of attacks across participating devices, minimize the consequences of attacks, and recover to a trusted state." This cyber ecosystem of the future is explicitly rendered in biological terms, analogized to "the human immune system"—a form of technogenic life: "A healthy cyber ecosystem might employ an automation strategy of fixed, local defenses supported by mobile and global defenses at multiple levels. Such a strategy could enable the cyber ecosystem to sustain itself and supported missions while fighting through attacks. Further, it could enable the ecosystem to continuously strengthen itself against the cyber equivalent of autoimmune disorders."[72]

According to Reitinger, enhancing the immunological capacities of cyberspace is crucial for global security and economic prosperity: "Today in cyberspace, intelligent adversaries exploit vulnerabilities and create incidents that propagate at machine speeds to steal identities, resources, and advantage. The rising volume and virulence of these attacks have the potential to degrade our economic capacity and threaten basic services that underpin our modern way of life."[73] Defending our way of life, then, means weaponizing the internet, enabling it to autonomously anticipate and combat attacks, taking over servers and personal computers around the world in times of need, marshaling their combined power against viruses, worms, nefarious botnets, and other hacker tools: the internet turned into a militarized AI system, empowered to fight against itself.

While all the gamer jokes about Skynet taking over the world as a result of the PlayStation Network outage may have seemed far-fetched, silly jokes born of science fiction, they perspicaciously tapped into some deeper currents of contemporary technopolitics, the dystopian dreams of the corporate security state. It is worth noting, of course, that Philip Reitinger stepped down from his position at the Department of Homeland Security in June 2011—and shortly afterward became the new senior vice president and chief information security officer at Sony. It was a sign of a new era, a turning point. The CEO of Sony, Howard Stringer, conceded that his company had recently gone through hell: "This year, we at Sony have been flooded, we've been flattened, we've been hacked, we've been singed." The end of days seemed nigh. "But the summer of our discontent is behind us," he said, with a wry nod to Shakespeare. "The past is a prologue to future possibility."[74]

In time, normal network services were restored. Sony offered an apologetic "Welcome Back" program to its customers, including a couple of free games and a monthlong subscription to the PlayStation Plus service. Gradually, gamers began to recover from the trauma of the PSN outage—what some were calling the "ApocalyPSN." Trying to make sense of the whole thing, a number of gamers relied on the tropes of speculative fiction to explain their postapocalyptic condition. For example: "Since the ApocalyPSN, many of us were disconnected from GD [the general discussion board on *PlayStation Forum*], our true home. We suffered Forum Deaths. . . . But alas, some have started to return from the dead, like Zombies!"[75]

Imagining themselves as zombies, internalizing the resurrected PlayStation Network as a way of conceptualizing the undead self, these gamers crafted an ironic narrative framework for living with the instabilities of digital culture, the risks of life with PlayStation. In playfully rediscovering their virtual communities through zombie imagery, mixing the language of resurrection with the language of cyberspace, these survivors of the PlayStation apocalypse once again adapted themselves to the phantasmatic quasi-object: the postvital gaming platform, a digital warzone where the boundaries between corporate interests and technoscientific experiments, serious business and silly games, are still being hotly negotiated. Indeed, the great network outage of 2011 proved to be a harbinger of things to come—for example, the massive DDOS takedown of both the PlayStation Network and Xbox Live on Christmas Day 2014 by the hacking group Lizard Squad, among other incidents. So gamers remain in a state of perpetual suspense, always playing on the edge of the next ApocalyPSN, fated to return from the dead again and again.

To be a zombie in this high-tech zone is to accept the risks, the indistinctions. In other words, it is to embrace the circumstances of having a life that some may say is not a life. To have a life and to make a life in a world of endless speculation, precarity, and uncertainty. After all, that's what it's like to live in the world today.

Long live play.

WE ARE HEROES

On Saturday, September 8, 2012, the superheroes began to assemble. They came together in Atlas Park, a zone in the massively multiplayer online game *City of Heroes*. A few days earlier, a rallying cry had gone out to the message boards, blogs, and Twitter feeds that were dedicated to the *City of Heroes* community. It called upon all costumed crusaders from all the servers of the *City of Heroes* system to log in to a single server named "Virtue" and congregate in Atlas Park, the civic center of Paragon City. It was a call to occupy, a call to defend the city from impending doom. The message spread to the farthest reaches of cyberspace, urging players to band together in a display of unity—a last stand against the greatest threat their world had ever known.

Paragon City, the fictive metropolis at the heart of the *City of Heroes* game, was under attack. Of course, Paragon City was always under attack. This was the point of the game, after all: take on the role of a superpowered do-gooder and protect Paragon City from the forces of evil, including supervillains, criminal organizations, robot uprisings, alien invasions, natural disasters, and any number of other calamities. Another day in Paragon City, another struggle against an eternal barrage of risks.

But this was something new. Paragon City was now facing an existential risk, a threat to its very way of life. Since the game first launched in 2004, Paragon City had survived every onslaught. But now the game's publisher, the South Korean company NCsoft, had decided to close down the Paragon Studios development team. Based in California, Paragon Studios was a wholly owned subsidiary of NCsoft, created shortly after NCsoft purchased the rights to *City of Heroes* from Cryptic Studios in 2007. Paragon Studios had been responsible for developing and running the game, as well as the *City of Villains* expansion. Paragon Studios was profitable, according to all reports. And *City of Heroes* itself had well over 125,000 paying subscribers, even in 2011 when it switched to a free-to-play model and allowed anyone to join without a subscription. So it was quite a surprise when the parent company announced at the end of August 2012 that the game servers would be closed on November 30 and that everyone at Paragon Studios would be laid off. "As far as I knew, we were still a studio that wasn't in dire straits," said Matt Miller, the senior lead designer for *City of Heroes*. "I've seen other studios in dire straits, and I've seen our studio, and our studio did not look that way. It came as a shock to everyone."[1] To the players, NCsoft did not offer much of an explanation for the decision. Lincoln Davies, the director of corporate communications for NCsoft West, said simply, "The continued support of the franchise no longer fits with our long-term goals for the company."[2]

Andy Belford, the community manager for *City of Heroes* at Paragon Studios, shared some additional information through the official game website: "In a realignment of company focus and publishing support, NCsoft has made the decision to close Paragon Studios. Effective immediately, all development on City of Heroes will cease and we will begin preparations to sunset the world's first, and best, Super Hero MMORPG before the end of the year."[3] He praised the development team, and he encouraged other game companies to hire the talented developers who were losing their jobs. "Today has been emotionally challenging for us all," he wrote. He confirmed that the game had been profitable and that it was not for clear financial reasons that NCsoft was closing it down: "This really is a refocusing of direction from NCsoft and unfortunately, Paragon didn't fit into that vision. Collectively, we [at Paragon] hold no ill will towards NCsoft and thank them for many years of support."[4] To the players, he pleaded, "Don't dwell on the 'how' or the 'why,' but rather join us in celebrating the legacy of an amazing partnership between the players and the development team."[5]

The players, however, did not take this announcement with such acquiescence. The fansites were soon blazing with agitated discussions. On the Titan Network, players considered ways to intervene, to change the corporate decision before it was too late. With remarkable speed, they organized an online petition, a letter-writing campaign to NCsoft executives, and a broad media blitz to draw attention to the situation. Around the world, the reportage galvanized support for the employees of Paragon Studios and for

FIGURE 5.1. "We Are Heroes. This Is What We Do." Save CoH campaign banner, September 2012.

the players of *City of Heroes*, who were about to lose their online home. With each passing hour, more and more *City of Heroes* players came flocking to the message boards to participate in the conversations, developing coordinated responses and possible solutions. These ranged from proposals to find another company who would be willing to purchase the rights to *City of Heroes* to filing lawsuits against NCsoft for breaking an implied obligation to the players, who had invested not only money but also years of their lives in developing their characters and contributing to the communal experience.[6]

The slogans began to appear: "Save Our City of Heroes," "Save the City," "Heroes Never Surrender," and perhaps most powerfully, "We Are Heroes. This Is What We Do" (fig. 5.1). Drawn from a long-running meme in the *City of Heroes* community, echoing the tried-and-true ethos of superheroes from throughout the history of comic books, this last slogan defined the campaign to save the game from foreclosure. On September 2, 2012, at 2:49 in the morning, TonyV posted the following message on the Titan Network forums:

> WE ARE HEROES. THIS IS WHAT WE DO.
> Remember those words.
> I know you all are discouraged, I know that you all feel like you've been punched in the gut. Some of you reading this probably just found out that you're out of a job that you loved and are wondering what tomorrow will bring. Everyone is experiencing the prospect of something we are passionate about being relegated forever to only existing as memories. I hear you. I feel you. For a day now, I've reminisced and

shed tears, and it hurts like hell. Now it's time to clench your teeth, roll up your sleeves, and get to work.

We are heroes, damn it, and I don't just mean the kind that pushes pixels through a virtual landscape oohing and ahhing at flashy colors. Starting right now, we are going to pull together all of our teams and form a league the gaming world will not soon forget. We will beat this trial. We will save the day. By God, they will chant our names. Incarnates? Give me a break. We are Titans, all of us. We've shed blood, we've cried tears, we've never stopped and we're not about to quit now. We've been saving Paragon City for eight and a half years. It's time to do it one more time.[7]

The suggestion that heroic action had been naturalized by the game ("This is what we do") seemed to bear out in the ensuing weeks. The players raised money to provide lunches for all the employees at Paragon Studios, as a show of support. They made posters and videos, riffing on the graphical conventions of comic books as well as the patriotic traditions of superhero imagery (fig. 5.2).[8] They launched new websites and kept up a steady torrent of tweets. An online petition started at Change.org soon gathered more than twenty thousand signatures, replete with heartbreaking testimonies of the emotional connections that players had made in this game over the years. Many pleaded with NCsoft to keep the game running, or at least to release the source code so that someone else could maintain it. They approached other media companies, presenting elaborate pitches in hopes of persuading some executive to look into the possibility of acquiring the property. And they talked about a global boycott of NCsoft, as a plan of last resort should their petitions and outreach efforts fail.[9]

And, yes, they took to the streets—the virtual streets, the streets of Paragon City, where they could continue to play as the heroes they were striving to be in so-called real life. They took the protest to where it mattered most, at least to them: the city where people could fly. Flash mobs sprung up all over Paragon City to protest (fig. 5.3). Meanwhile, the call for a unity rally at Atlas Park drew thousands to the Virtue server (fig. 5.4). As hero after hero began to arrive for the virtual sit-in, what some referred to as "Occupy Paragon City," the software was forced to produce separate instances of Atlas Park to accommodate the number of active avatars in the same area. Eventually, there were thirty-three instances of Atlas Park running on the Virtue server. In the ensuing weeks, thousands of players kept vigil at Atlas Park, holding flaming torches and maintaining at least one active player in each instance around

FIGURE 5.2. Save CoH flyer. Created by RockDeadman, September 2012. Recollecting James Montgomery Flagg's famous Uncle Sam poster, this flyer features Statesman, the most iconic character in *City of Heroes* lore. Significantly, Statesman had already died in *City of Heroes* earlier in the year. As if insisting on his postmortem endurance, the flyer performs the resilience of the superhero community to keep going, to keep respawning, even on the brink of destruction.

FIGURE 5.3. Save CoH flashmob. Screenshot by Omali, September 16, 2012.

FIGURE 5.4. First day of the unity rally. Screenshot by mrKetch, September 8, 2012.

the clock to keep it open. Players who stepped away from their keyboards for too long would be automatically logged out by the system, so coordination among the protestors was necessary to keep each instance alive—no small feat, considering that even when the game was in full swing, rarely would any zone have more than one or two instances at a given moment.

Although many of the Atlas Park instances collapsed during the nearly three months of the vigil, the final one, Atlas Park 33, remained open and occupied for the entire time until the decisive date of November 30, 2012. Atlas Park 33 was made into a symbol of unyielding resistance, standing against NCsoft's nefarious plot to snuff out the world (fig. 5.5). On other servers, similar instances of the occupied Atlas Park were also spawning furiously. On September 11, 2012, the software developer and *City of Heroes* player Leandro Pardini and his colleagues posted a video they had made about the Atlas Park occupations to YouTube. Altogether, more than 3,700 active player-characters are represented in the video—standing strong, standing together, heroes till the end (fig. 5.6).

Yet ultimately, their archnemesis prevailed. In the late hours of the night between November 30 and December 1, the world of *City of Heroes* winked out of existence.

Challenge of the Super Friends

What became clear in all the efforts to resist the game's closure was that the in-game protests and the out-of-game protests were symbolically aligned. Many players were implicitly playing as their superhero characters, both in the city and out of the city. As one player wrote, "I managed to meet tons of amazing people with their own characters in a massively fleshed-out universe. . . . It was a grievous mistake for NCsoft to simply end this amazing experience. And I do NOT stand at their side. I stand across the battlefield, inspirations filled up, enhancements all green, ready to take on this new Arch-Villain."[10] Like others, he narrated his response to the situation using vocabulary and concepts drawn from the game itself ("inspirations filled up," "enhancements all green"). Another player created an image macro (carrying forward the "Condescending Wonka" meme) that aptly captured the collective attitude: "So you made a game where players have spent the past 8 years defending their city? Tell me about what happened when you threatened to destroy their city" (fig. 5.7).

In these performative acts we find traces of what was at stake in the online and offline agitations, mobilizing so many players to collective action. At the

FIGURE 5.5. Atlas Park 33 logo. Created by EspionageDB7, September 2012.

FIGURE 5.6. Leandro Pardini, "Heroes," YouTube, September 11, 2012, http://www .youtube.com/watch?v=XRsj2DtLCQs. This video was made from composite fly-throughs of fifty different instances of Atlas Park across the fifteen different *City of Heroes* servers.

FIGURE 5.7. Condescending Wonka. Image macro created by Captain Electric, Titan Network forums, September 2012.

very least, the closure of *City of Heroes* represented the loss of a beloved form of entertainment and recreation. As one player wrote, "It is the place where your imagination can soar. The place where you and your friends can meet up, smack some bad guys and laugh your asses off!"[11] Such pleasures may be less than profound, but their significance should not be discounted. For they are often the basis of social cohesion as well as technopolitical awareness, in other words, attentiveness to the technical dimensions of social organization and governance. As one player explained, the joyful game design and its integral mechanisms—the elaborate customization options, the cross-server chat windows, the mission architect features, and so forth—highlighted the synergy between robust software tools and robust community bonds: "CoH is the only game that seems to have gotten everything right. . . . They regularly surprise me with their keen insights with regard to the direction they have taken the game. I have been playing and paying since shortly after the game started (8 years now) and this is the one game I keep coming back to. Not only is the game more enjoyable than other MMO's the community is better, and better tools for the communities to be strong are available."[12]

Players from all over the world have testified to these qualities. For example: "City of Heroes is more than just a long-running MMO, it's a community. I have played a lot of MMO's in my time and this one, by far, has the kindest, most helpful, most mature, most welcoming community of any of them. The vast majority who play this game do more than just play it, they invest their time in it and they make it a part of their lives. . . . NCsoft sees this as just another game they no longer want to put money into, but to those who have been playing for years, it's really not a game, it's an extention of our lives. And the community is more than just a community, it's family."[13] Another player noted that many in-game friendships fostered out-of-game relationships, even leading to marriages and children: "It's not exaggerating to say that there are lives that would not exist today if not for *City of Heroes*."[14] More than one player also claimed that the game was a support mechanism for surviving the trials of mundane reality: "I honestly believe City of Heroes saved my life as it gave me a purpose. . . . I was getting the support I needed to stay alive from a digital community of strangers and a machine."[15] Another player simply said, "CoH is a community. People care here."[16] For these players, the game was all about community, vitality, and life—a form of life sustained by hardware, computational media. In other words, technogenic life. Another player summed it up: "I am a female gamer. We exist and in surprising numbers on City of Heroes. There are women, men, and children on this game all happily sharing the skies of paragon city. . . . Please don't let this game die . . . please . . . it has a thriving community that wants to live."[17]

To be sure, the closing of the game represented the loss of an online community of pronounced camaraderie and somewhat exceptional holding power. These aspects were often noted:

Yours truly plays on Infinity [server]. . . . Playing there for a lot of us hasn't been like being in a game—it's been like joining a village of fifteen hundred people and living with them for the better part of a decade. We've butted heads, forgiven, forgotten, learned to cope or carried grudges like newborn babies for years. We've talked smack about and trained each other until every one could laugh when the smack talking resumed. We've fallen in love, celebrated weddings, shared recipes, given each other (or gotten) the greatest advice and attended graduations together. We've held funerals for our truly fallen heroes. We've been there through and after the divorce. We've watched each other grow up then begin careers. . . . Our global lists are in many cases perma-full and we wish the max size were larger. We've helped each other get out of debt and opened our doors to one another. We've come home after crap days and gone to bed smiling because of the people we're privileged to know here. When natural disasters strike and some of us go missing, we actually make it a point to find each other—up to and including sending real human beings [i.e., Omen] to make sure everything is alright. City of Heroes isn't really a game. . . . It's a phenomenon, likely impossible to reproduce, which draws people interested in being better people towards other people interested in helping them to do just. And all the while, the teachers learn those same lessons. Knowingly or otherwise; by design or on accident. That is what this game does, and it works.[18]

Above all, the failure to save *City of Heroes* represented the loss of an ethos, a set of values and meanings inherited from a long tradition of superhero fictions. It was an ethos cultivated through role-playing, reinforced not only by the game and its rules but also by the community and its standards. Through playing and having a good time, leveling up their characters, completing missions, and developing a storyline, the players were trained to be more super than ever before. As one of them wrote,

Part of it is because the game itself started out actively encouraging people to help others. . . . [*City of Heroes*] had powers that had absolutely no benefit to the person that had the power, but had immense benefit to the person's teammates. . . . Sometimes life seems like it's got you down. It doesn't seem like there's a lot of good news out there, but you can log into a game and feel like you are actively helping people. . . . Even though it's a game, it still makes you feel better. I think the hero aspect of that is unique and helped contribute to that sense of, "[This] is something that we do."[19]

Already in the early history of *City of Heroes*, many players came to see the game adventures as rehearsals for real life, presenting a model of upstanding citizenship that could be put into practice elsewhere. They started charity drives for various real-world causes—world hunger, children's hospitals, supporting the U.S. troops in conflict zones—and they also organized benefit events and sponsored marathons. The community even launched a charitable organization called Real World Hero (fig. 5.8). Its slogan was inspiriting: "In our real lives we are not super-powered, but we can still be super-purposed."[20]

Thus the effort to defend Paragon City from its corporate closure was also staged in defense of the superhero as a figure, which includes the idea that one person can make a difference; that diversity and weirdness are wonderful qualities; that courage and friendship can overcome incredible obstacles; that helping others is the most important thing anyone can do; and that heroes—whether they be human or alien, animal or plant, monster

FIGURE 5.8. *City of Heroes*: A *Paragon Times* billboard publicizes Real World Hero's charity efforts. Featured in the Samuraiko Productions video "Real World Hero—A CITY OF HEROES Charity Event," YouTube, November 1, 2010, https://www.youtube.com/watch?v=Gv-QvhUOOWY.

or machine—have an obligation to help make the world a better place, even while recognizing divergent positions about what that would mean and how it should be achieved.[21] This is not to say that the game and its players always lived up to these lofty ideals. After all, the software's character-design options tended to privilege certain styles of bodies over others. Its narrative lore and scripted missions sometimes veered toward xenophobic fantasies of securitization despite the prevailing themes of tolerance and openness. And, yes, occasional eruptions of toxic gamer discourse had shaken the denizens of Paragon City a number of times over the years—though the larger community was usually quick to denounce any derogatory language in the game's public chat channels or social media platforms.[22] For many players, however, the figure of the superhero represented a horizon of possibility, standing not for the condition of the world as it actually is, but for how it might yet be. Their characters were not simply reflections of themselves, but instruments of change, indicating how they might still become otherwise. For these players of *City of Heroes*, then, the superhero was a form of applied science fiction, a tool for putting fabulation into practice—aspiring to a better future, sometimes failing, sometimes misaligned with present constraints, but always casting ahead for a new line of flight. Up, up, and away!

In this regard, the ideological implications of the confrontation between the players and the company became quite stark. As one player wrote, "This game was the very first superhero MMO, and remains the most complete, detailed, and interesting. Shutting it down is like saying 'NCsoft doesn't believe in heroes.'"[23] Another put it even more succinctly: "The world needs heroes."[24]

Gathered Together from the Cosmic Reaches of the Universe

In the days leading up to the shutdown, a number of players prepared for exodus. They worked quickly to archive their characters. Some used software tools to extract data from the game servers (such as the Sentinel+ Extractor character-export tool, rapidly developed by a player called Guy Perfect to help these evacuation efforts). Others posted screenshots and stories to various websites as public memorials—looking ahead to the next respawning.[25] While they did not give up hope for a last-minute salvation, they nevertheless saw the writing on the wall. Yet rather than give in to melancholy, they instead chose to script their departures from the city on their own terms. One player, for example, drew on the narrative lore of the game to make sense of the necessity to relocate to another online world:

> The way it works in my mind is thus. In Primal Earth, NCsoft is a research lab. They decided that Paragon's Heroes depended too much on the power given by the Well of the Furies ((i.e. the game wasn't a mind-numbing grindfest like they seem to want)), so they were experimenting on a connection to the Well that they had in their possession, unknown to the rest of the world. As a result . . . pretty much every parallel universe is about to be destroyed. This company won't admit there's a problem, and won't do anything to fix it, so Portal Corp. has sent Heroes out to newly contacted parallel worlds to find a place to evacuate to. ((This way CoH players can move their Heroes to games that are compatible with them, Champions Online, The Secret World, etc.)) My main [character] has been assisting in the efforts to find a suitable home, and will be helping with the evacuation in the final hours of Primal Earth's existence.[26]

This imaginative fiction takes the real situation of corporate control of the game-as-product and turns it into mythic discourse, a narration of exile that enables continuity, remembrance, and mourning for what was lost, all at once—even while looking ahead to the future. It recaptures a familiar story of exodus from a doomed world, relocation to an alien culture, and the community obligations of the savior or hero. It is a narrative template that has been endemic to comic books since Jerry Siegel and Joe Shuster established the origin story of Superman in 1938.[27] Indeed, another player of *City of Heroes* wrote of the imaginative work required to relocate his superhero character to a new world, namely, DC *Universe Online*, drawing on a number of comic-book tropes:

> I recently did a similar shutdown of my character. He was a Paladin that ultimately gave his life to fight the forces of Greed (it was an actual demon). And yet, he failed, because the powers to be cast him out, and he eventually died as the last man standing. He cost the city too much by killing the demons they wanted, not just the ones that were terrorizing them. "7" years later, he crash lands in Metropolis with a new body for his soul to continue its work. I moved on to DCUO [DC *Universe Online*], and it's alright. But he will never forget that it was Greed that ultimately won over his home, and took everything he knew, and he will never be "just a good guy" again because of it. He's considered a vigilante now, the law doesn't want him and the villains fear him.[28]

Killed during the primal battle against the corporation—NCsoft as the demon Greed—this player's character carries a memory of diabolical injustice along with him. Even in his new body, he can no longer abide by the rules and regulations of "the powers to be." He continues to fight against the forces of greed, represented as much in the ruling authorities of the new city of Metropolis ("the law") as in the villains who prowl its streets.

Regardless of which path they chose after *City of Heroes* closed, many players made efforts to keep elements of the old community alive. Some called out to scattered friends, urging them to reconvene elsewhere: "a bunch of us slipped over to Champion City (Champions Online) and are trying to make a go of it over there. Why not come over and join us. Its no Paragon City, but its a good place none the less, in the need of Awsome heros like you."[29] Another said, "I regularly play paper and pencil RPGs, and in my group all but one of us have played CoH. We all agreed to create a CoH-themed RPG to keep flying over Paragon City . . . at least once a month. Farewell, Paragon City."[30] Others instead kept faith that the city would return: "City of Heroes servers may be shutting down, but It will still live on forever in our hearts and minds, stand proud not in its passing but its existence for being, from the first day to the last it has been a pleasure. . . . And when the sun sets the last day, I will salute its fall for I know City of Heroes will rise again, For We are the City of Heroes, and we shall forever be here."[31]

The dispersed community has continued to work to make this vision a reality. Through the Titan Network, Twitter, and their Facebook pages, the players stay in contact and endeavor to record the history of *City of Heroes*, remembering the characters and events that made it so special. They have taken steps to rebuild the technical elements of their shared lifeworld, as well, hacking together new launchers and support apps (such as the Titan Icon and Paragon Chat programs developed by the players Codewalker and Leandro) that restore some degree of playability to the defunct game client. At the same time, they have considered schemes to reverse-engineer the multiplayer software on rogue servers, even though it would mean violating the intellectual property rights of NCsoft. For some players, such efforts represent a necessary form of technopolitical disobedience, opposition to a legal regime they see as corrupt and unfair. Eliot Lefebvre, for instance, wrote a short fiction about heroes from Paragon City coming to terms with the need to break rules, to make their own justice—a parable, it seems, of cracked software, illegal servers, and the dark web:

> His first instinct was to reach for his costume, but he stopped himself before trying to grab it from its usual hiding place under a throw pillow. Sighing at himself as much as anything, he walked over to the window, unsurprised by the sight of his two partners on the fire escape. They were dressed like normal people, of course, but Seagull and Sipahi were pretty hard to mistake. . . .
>
> Both of the women stared at him for a moment, but it was Sipahi who spoke first, rubbing her arms to get the chill out. "You're just going to sit there? Getting drunk?"
>
> "Not much else I can do. They're tracking me and treating us like criminals." He shrugged. "Any better ideas?"
>
> "Yeah, actually. We break the rules."
>
> Swift raised an eyebrow. . . . ["]We have to be responsible about this, right?"
>
> "Oh, most certainly. But responsible is . . . a *loaded* word. The people shutting us *down* aren't being very responsible about it, are they?" She reached out and grabbed the remote, shutting off the movie before sitting next to Swift on the couch.
>
> He was going to protest before he saw Seagull reach over to pull the beer out of his hand. "We were talking about it after we had *our* meeting with the agency. And . . . it's just not right. They can't just kick us out when we're trying to do good."

"Yeah, they can."

"All right, whatever; they *can*, but they *shouldn't*." She rubbed the back of her neck, visibly searching for words. "I'm not about to just roll over and let go because Paragon City isn't our home any more."

Swift sighed. "We can't leave the city. The rules are—"

"Swift, you know I don't say this sort of thing often, but *forget* the rules." Sipahi sprang out of her seat now, gesturing for emphasis as she spoke. "We can *leave*. Yes, we'll be fugitives, and they'll call us criminals, but do *you* want to stop helping people? Can you honestly tell me that you want to live your life like *this*?"

"Of course I don't. But . . ." He frowned. It seemed as if there should be some way to refute what she was saying, but nothing lept to mind.

"Come on, big guy. We'll go out there, we'll fight crime across the country, we'll do . . . you know, the whole wandering justice thing. . . . It'll be an adventure. Even if no one else gets to see it, it'll be an adventure."

"We're supposed to be the people who uphold the rules, though. We're . . ."

"Heroes." Sipahi finished the sentence. "We are heroes. And this is what we do."

Swift looked at her. There was no way he would ever be a hero in Paragon City any longer. But that didn't mean that he couldn't still be a hero, that he couldn't make use of the lessons he'd learned over the years. Even if the city was gone, he didn't have to stop being himself.

He stood. "You're right. We're heroes. No matter when, no matter where . . . no matter what."

And even if it didn't make everything all right, even the thought helped.[32]

This allegorical fanfic subtly tests out the moral arguments for relocating to a rogue server. It represents the dilemma for player-characters who are accustomed to upholding the law but forced into circumstances that have exposed the injustice of the law, and who now feel compelled to join the shadow world of pirates and hackers. In this regard, the *City of Heroes* community has come face-to-face with a predicament shared by others before them, including Batman, the Punisher, the Hulk, Spawn, Deadpool, and many more. But while some costumed crusaders are notorious vigilantes or antiheroes, to flagrantly disregard rules and regulations does not fit the moral code of the most upstanding citizen-heroes. So at the same time, and hoping to alleviate the desire to go rogue, grassroots projects have emerged to rebuild a version of Paragon City that will not infringe on the intellectual property rights of NCsoft. Some players banded together to create the development company Missing Worlds Media, starting a "Phoenix Project" called *City of Titans* that would resurrect some of what had been lost: "There are some legal constraints on what we can build. But our goal is to remain as true to the spirit, the feel, the concepts. . . . Legally, no one can rebuild the exact game. No one except the legal owners of that IP [intellectual property]. What we're doing is providing fans with a new world. A world that is new, yet one you remember."[33] Other player-developers started different projects, parallel efforts to create a "spiritual successor" to *City of Heroes*, including *Valiance Online, Heroes and Villains*, and *Ship of Heroes*, with others possibly still to emerge from the far-flung community that once dwelt in Paragon City.

While Paragon City may be gone, a notable commitment to superhero values endures in the diaspora—along with the scripts and narrative conventions of comic books that address the limits of justice in the modern world. Former residents of *City of Heroes* have endeavored to maintain ties even after they have moved on to other games, other regions of cyberspace. They have done so by rehearsing the cultural mythologies and practices of technogenic life that they shared during those halcyon days of yore, holding them together even though they no longer have a city of heroes to call home.

Holding Out for a Hero

The *City of Heroes* saga illustrates a more general situation, of course. Since 1978, when the first *Superman* cartridge appeared for the Atari 2600, the video-game industry has produced a steady stream of superhero experiences. Some games, such as *Batman: Arkham Asylum* and *Injustice: Gods among Us*, feature familiar characters from comic books and media franchises. Others, such as *Freedom Force, The Wonderful 101*, and the *inFAMOUS* series, present new spins on old tropes. To varying degrees, all of these games address the power fantasies of digital culture, allowing players to perform extraordinary feats of derring-do by toying around with computational hardware. In this regard, they often reinforce the idea that anyone can become super, given the right technical resources and expertise—and some games explicitly draw connections between high-tech heroics and the virtuosities of gameplay.

For example, in *Batman: Arkham Knight*, Batman uses a "remote hacking device" throughout the game to break into computer terminals, swipe pass-

FIGURE 5.9. *Batman: Arkham Knight*: The remote hacking device mimics the game controller. Rocksteady Studios, 2015. Sneaking into the Stagg Airships lab facilities, Batman discovers that the security passwords are biological terms ("proteins," "lipids," "nucleic acids"). The game is about the era of technogenic life, the computerization of biology, neuropharmaceutical programming. To maneuver through this science fiction world, some kind of hacking device is indispensible.

words, hijack surveillance drones, and access any number of other technical systems. In the PS4 and Xbox One versions of the game, the player must rotate the analog sticks on the game controller to tune the remote hacking device, feeling the controller's vibrations. On the screen, Batman does the same thing: the player's thumbs and Batman's thumbs are perfectly in sync, mirroring one another as the device penetrates locked computer systems (fig. 5.9). The symmetry highlights the game controller as a kind of hacking device, a tool for accessing the digital world, as well as an interface to Batman's amazing gadgets and gizmos: a multipurpose utility belt that helps even an average player to become the "world's greatest detective."

While such conceits are coded as fiction, escapist fabulation, the discourse of superhero media nevertheless feeds into the lived practices and vocabularies of gamers, hackers, and other technology geeks. As we have seen in the case of *City of Heroes*, the tropes and plotlines of superhero games become compelling templates for the practice of technogenic life. They afford visions of the body extended through digital media, providing scripts for acting, for living in the network society. For example, "Iron Man mode" is a hardcore style of gameplay that eschews the save function and the respawn function of modern video games, challenging players to reach the end of any game with only a single avatar life. It is a self-imposed way of playing with strict limitations, a metagame that embraces the finitude of living beings.[34] The video-game rapper Dan Bull describes Iron Man mode as "digital Darwinism in a saveless world." In a music video, Bull notes that playing in this manner reinforces a new respect for life itself:

I want an adrenaline overload.
Iron Man mode, Iron Man mode.
Never save gameplay, never reload.
Iron Man mode, Iron Man mode.

You'll realize real life is irreplaceable.
No three strikes, this isn't baseball.
Your bones are breakable,
your foes'll break 'em all.
They'll take the opportunity by any means available
to demonstrate that your remains are quite biodegradable.
If you're incapable to comprehend mortality,
I advocate the remedy of permanent fatality.[35]

But rather than resting content with the lot of common humanity, accepting the frailties of the body and its organic limitations, Iron Man mode instead performs the capacities of technology to exceed the boundaries of normal biology. In his music video, Bull wears an Iron Man mask and quips, "This is Iron Man mode and I am Tony Stark." By invoking Tony Stark and his Iron Man persona, the Iron Man mode of gameplay both reflects and amplifies the embodied relations between players and their hardware devices (fig. 5.10). For Tony Stark becomes Iron Man not through any unique biological mutation or supernatural power, but through technoscientific ingenuity. Iron Man is a cyborg, his vulnerable human parts protected by a cutting-edge suit of robotic armor.[36] The Iron Man mode of gameplay, as a test of gamer virtuosity and endurance, becomes an affirmation of the prosthetic imagination, the extension of the human in excess of its own organic dimensions. While professing an abhorrence of the respawn function, Iron Man mode nevertheless reproduces the sense in which gaming technologies can transfigure the standard operations of human embodiment, joyously inviting the overflow of technogenic life ("I want an adrenaline overload"). As a metagame of hardcore survival in the field of digital fictions, Iron Man mode expresses a desire to excel, to achieve extraordinary things in a world

FIGURE 5.10. Dan Bull, "Iron Man Mode," YouTube, August 18, 2012, https://www.youtube.com/watch?v=w7fl_7noJd8.

undergoing rapid computerization, to fight the forces of ordinariness and complacency, the commodity of the common denominator. As Bull puts it, Iron Man mode is a small gesture of resistance—"computer mutiny through the screens"—a way of pushing back against the status quo and the marketing of passive, anodyne entertainment: "If there is no risk, then there's no reward. / Slaves to the save, throw your overlords overboard."

Certainly, Iron Man mode is nothing more than recreation, a digital sport that often foregrounds its own ironies: "It makes the player an absolute bad--ass. People who regularly play games in Iron Man Mode are legally allowed, and actively encouraged, to loudly declare how boss they are whilst at any social occasion (including, but not limited to: weddings, parent/teacher meetings, visits to the zoo and PETA protests)."[37] In other words, playing in Iron Man mode hardly makes anyone a hero, and it may instead inflate a misplaced sense of personal accomplishment. Nevertheless, in its own ironic way, Iron Man mode describes a self-imposed obligation, a duty to perform beyond the call of duty—to play beyond the rules, or rather, to uphold a different set of rules, an ethical framework that supersedes what is merely required by the software or baseline commodity culture. (As Bull sings, "Be brave, and implement a higher plan / of gaming and never saving. The name is Iron Man.") Indeed, by taking up the tropes of superhero media to critique the authorized pleasures of average media consumers and present an adrenaline-pumping alternative ("a higher plan"), it conjures an imaginary

FIGURE 5.11. JESTER ⊙ ΔCꟻUΔL³³º¹ @ th3j35t3r, Twitter, 2017, https://twitter .com/th3j35t3r. The Jester has sometimes used this same portrait on his blog, *JestersCourt*, https:// jesterscourt.cc.

space within the social order yet outside its normal laws and regulations: the extralegal domain of caped crusaders, masked marvels, and outlaw avengers.

To be sure, the actions of some online activists and vigilantes, whether they use elite hacker tools or commonplace search engines, have often similarly elicited the language of superpowers. The Jester—a patriotic, pro-American hacker known for taking down jihadist websites, trolling Anonymous and other hacktivist groups, and attacking Russian government servers in retaliation for Russian meddling in U.S. politics—has sometimes used an altered image of Captain America to represent his Twitter account (fig. 5.11). News reports frequently describe the Jester as the "Batman of the Internet," alleging that even FBI agents honor him with this title.[38]

Likewise, a secretive white-hat security researcher who successfully hijacked a portion of the Dridex botnet in early 2016, reconfiguring compromised servers to distribute copies of Avira antivirus software instead of the Dridex banking trojan, has also earned comparisons to Batman: "Somewhere online right now, a digital Batman is protecting your cybersecurity. An unknown security researcher is widely believed to have hacked the hackers, and is now using one of the Internet's biggest crime machines for good. And now, just like Gotham City supports the Caped Crusader, the Internet security community is rallying behind their own vigilante for justice."[39]

These figurations—tropes of applied science fiction—rehearse a comic-book narrative of advanced technologies extending the capacities of mere mortals, rendering hackers and other technical experts posthuman, telepresent, and above the law: cybernetic gods among us. While distinguishing elite hackers from everyday computer users ("a digital Batman is protecting your cybersecurity"), this narrative frame also makes legible the difficulties and challenges faced by those with such extraordinary capabilities, the burdens that only other supers could properly understand. For instance, the security researcher and computer forensics analyst Scot Terban, a.k.a. Dr. Krypt3ia, has written about the endless battle between sysadmins and cybercriminals in precisely these terms, seeing computer security forces as like a beleaguered Batman standing against a "Rogues Gallery" of the Dark Knight's enemies—an invisible, nearly thankless job suited only for the most stalwart defenders of digital peace and prosperity:

> Batman and his "Rogues Gallery" of evil doers. It's not reality, but, many of us tend to gravitate to the stories and the ethos right? . . . So, you . . . yes you . . . the one in the batcowl. Protecting your domain, your "Gotham" as the network warrior, the lone sentinel holding back the night of the internet. How are you feeling about your job of late? Post APT [Advanced Persistent Threat network attack, often associated with state-sponsored hackers] and Anonymous, how are you feeling about the safety of your city? Do you feel that you have the tools and the know how to protect it? Are you backed up by the right people? Funds? Tools? Do you sleep at night or do you toss and turn. . . . Oh, sorry, during the day, as you work at night . . .
>
> This seems to be a common mentality in many of the network security folks out there, that of the protector, the Batman. . . . Feared by some, loathed by others, and generally looked upon as someone to avoid as the story goes. Sure, you are likely a hero to still others, but, those are not the majority, and it is your thankless job to protect them all. With or without their help. . . . Meanwhile, just like the escalation of the rogues gallery, you too will have to face new threats every day. Jack Napier made Batman by killing Wayne's parents in front of him. Batman made Joker by battling Napier later on and ultimately driving him insane, thus becoming the main nemesis for Batman. After that others came along, seeing the Batman as their nemesis and upping the ante. Do you see where I am going with this? Look at the INFOSEC world today.
> APT, ANONYMOUS, HACKERS, CRACKERS, HACTIVISTS, LULZSEC,

LULZSEC REBORN . . . It's all about escalation. . . . If you can deal with never-ending war then do gird your loins and wade into battle. If not, if you take stock and the battlefield is not even remotely in your favor nor will it ever be, consider what you are doing. This is a battle you can never win. . . . If you can accept these things, and you feel you can fight on . . . Then let the battle rage. If not, then you might want to consider moving out of Gotham.[40]

In this world of online heroes and villains, digital mutants and cybernetic warriors, the guidelines for defending "truth, justice, and the American way" are not always clear. Even for an infosec professional such as Dr. Kypt3ia, responsible for protecting innocent citizens from those who would steal their data or disrupt their computer systems, the actions of hackers and high-tech activists sometimes confound easy distinctions. Despite their roguelike appearances, hacktivists might seem to be on the right side of history, from time to time. While the antics of LulzSec and other hacker crews often recall the enigmatic games of the Riddler or the chaotic gags of the Joker, according to Dr. Krypt3ia, the lulz may not always be in strict opposition to civic responsibility. Commenting on some of Anonymous's coordinated activities, such as their 2011 Operation DarkNet attacks against the online child pornography trade or their support of the Occupy movement, Dr. Krypt3ia concedes that adversity can make strange bedfellows: "Anonymous has become more like The Batman in certain quarters." After all, desperate times call for desperate measures: "Sometimes when the system cannot function other means need to be taken to effect change."[41]

System failures are often the conditions of possibility for enterprising superheroes. In October 2013, for instance, following a report in the *Kansas City Star* that the teenagers Daisy Coleman and Paige Parkhurst were unable to bring their alleged rapists to trial in Maryville, Missouri, Anonymous responded by launching OpMaryville:

Two young girls have been raped in the town of Maryville, Missouri. Another high school football star, the grandson of a Missouri state official, has walked free. The people of Maryville turned their backs on these victims and one family has been forced to flee the town. Their house was later burned to the ground. . . . If Maryville won't defend these young girls, if the police are too cowardly or corrupt to do their jobs, if [the] justice system has abandoned them, then we will have to stand for them. . . . Maryville, expect us.
     We Are Anonymous.

We Are Legion.
We do not forgive.
We do not forget.
Join us.[42]

Anonymous organized protests online and on the ground, helping to draw international media attention to the situation. Shortly afterward, the county prosecutor agreed that the case should be reopened. On Reddit, supporters of Anonymous celebrated this turn of events: "I love hearing about Anonymous getting justice for people. Its like hearing about a real life Batman. Except Batman is a group of nerds, and they don't beat people up."[43] Ultimately, one of the accused rapists pled guilty to misdemeanor child endangerment. Despite the efforts of the special prosecutor appointed to the reopened case, however, no felony sexual assault charges were ever brought to trial.

A sense that justice cannot or will not be sufficiently protected by governments, corporations, or other authorities—a creeping sense that "the system cannot function"—has galvanized various and sundry online activists, from the Jester to the players of *City of Heroes*. It is a sense that the risks and insecurities, the precarities of technogenic life demand active intervention and resistance rather than resignation ("computer mutiny through the screens," according to the haunting lyrics of Dan Bull). Reiterated by innumerable video games and comic books, it promotes increasingly reflexive, ironic performances. For instance, on December 21, 2016, the hacker group OurMine—known for targeting the social media accounts of celebrities and tech executives, allegedly to expose the security holes in platforms such as Twitter, Pinterest, and YouTube—cracked the Twitter accounts of Marvel Studios, taking over all the Marvel superhero promotional feeds (fig. 5.12). Occupying the social media avatars of Captain America, the Avengers, Ant-Man, Doctor Strange, and the Guardians of the Galaxy, OurMine sent out the following message: "Hey, it's OurMine, Don't worry we are just testing your security, contact us to help you with your security contactourmineteam@gmail.com." This takeover of the Marvel Twitter accounts presented a cheeky commentary on mass-marketed heroes while performing OurMine's own claims to break the law only for the greater good, exploiting security flaws for the sake of a higher security. Marvel's trademarked heroes could not even protect themselves, seemed to be the message—a promotion for OurMine's own under-the-table security services. Yet by delivering this message through the Marvel characters, the hack also indicated how these fictive heroes can still serve as models, offering us ways to think about our own precarity in an

FIGURE 5.12. Our-
FIGURE 5.12. Our-
Mine hacks the Marvel
Entertainment Twitter
accounts, December 21,
2016. Tweets reposted by
Nirat, "When You Follow
All Individual Marvel Ac-
counts and Are Spammed
in a Row by OurMine,"
Twitter, December 21,
2016, https://twitter
.com/NiratAnop/status
/811623842351198208.

GuardiansOfTheGalaxy @Gua... now
Hey, it's OurMine, Don't worry we
are just testing your security, contact
us to help you with your security
contactourmineteam@gmail.com

Doctor Strange @DrStrange now
Hey, it's OurMine, Don't worry we
are just testing your security, contact
us to help you with your security
contactourmineteam@gmail.com

Captain America @CaptainAm... now
Hey, it's OurMine, Don't worry we
are just testing your security, contact
us to help you with your security
contactourmineteam@gmail.com

The Avengers @Avengers now
Hey, it's OurMine, Don't worry we
are just testing your security, contact
us to help you with your security
contactourmineteam@gmail.com

Ant-Man @AntMan now
Hey, it's OurMine, Don't worry we
are just testing your security, contact

online environment dominated by careless companies, rampant cybercrime, and ubiquitous surveillance—an environment where we all may be called upon to rise up, to take sides in the secret wars that rage behind our keyboards.

But even if some online vigilantes may desire the status of heroes, the enterprise is riddled with hazards and pitfalls. Things can go awry, totally fubar. For example, following the Boston Marathon bombings in April 2013, many users of Reddit, 4chan, Twitter, Facebook, and other social media platforms began sifting through surveillance photos released by the FBI, monitoring police scanners, collating and sharing information, and using a variety of online tools to help identify the perpetrators. As one Reddit user later described it, "The Internet turned on Batman Mode."[44] On Reddit, a theory emerged that a missing Brown University student named Sunil Tripathi may have been one of the bombers. Reddit sleuths compared photos of Tripathi with the surveillance photos and propagated the idea across different media domains. Amid these discussions, a Reddit user called Greg Hughes, listening to a police scanner, tweeted that the Boston Police Department had identified Tripathi as one of the two suspects. Hughes's claim was false—the Boston police had never even mentioned Tripathi's name—but the claim, already explored with enthusiasm in various sub-Reddits, began to spread. One Redditor responded cautiously to the question "Is missing student Sunil Tripathi Marathon Bomber #2?" while also stoking the flames:

> According to Boston police scanner (via twitter)—the answer may be yes. . . . I would, however, like to caution against people now concluding that we should all be internet detectives / vigilantes, etc. Yes—it seems speculators here got it right this time. There have been plenty of cases in the past (even the recent past) where online communities (reddit included) have gotten it wrong and caused someone innocent a lot of grief. . . . So I hope people aren't patting themselves on the back too hard over this.[45]

Yet such cautions were thrown to the wind as numerous reporters, media personalities, and social media users began to repeat the accusation. Tragically, Tripathi had actually committed suicide nearly a month before the bombings, and his body was found floating in a river shortly after the FBI named Dzhokhar and Tamerlan Tsarnaev as the actual bombing suspects. Tripathi had been wrongfully accused by legions of amateur detectives armed with search engines. Afterward, Reddit admins issued a public apology to the Tripathi family, who suffered weeks of harassment due to the false claims. A few reporters also reflected on the faults of the news media in spreading the crowdsourced theory, turning online rumor into authoritative discourse. For example, Jay Caspian Kang suggested that the mechanisms of social media have now made journalism into a kind of video game for professionals and amateurs alike, establishing rules and scoring systems for leveling up, winning accolades, creating instant internet superstars:

> It helps to envision modern journalism as a kind of video game. If you're part of the Internet media, everything you put out into the world

comes with its own scoring system. Tweets are counted by retweets and favorites, stories are scored by page views and Facebook likes. A writer's reach and influence is visible right there, in the number of his followers and the number of "influencers" who subscribe to his or her feed. If you're wondering why so many writers and journalists from such divergent backgrounds would feel the need to instantly tweet out unconfirmed information to their followers, all you have to do is think of the modern Internet reporter as some form of super Redditor—to be silent is to lose points. To be retweeted is to gain them.[46]

In this manner, the ludic systems of the internet facilitate casual fantasies of the "super." Internet reporters strive to become "some form of super Redditor," while Redditors themselves jump to play online vigilante at a moment's notice. Switching into Batman mode—an orientation to high-tech methods of investigation and intervention, a media complex informed by superhero narratives and video games—becomes a commonplace, unrestricted practice. And like Batman's own methods, it affords both positive and negative outcomes at exactly the same time:

> Consider the Boston Bombing and Reddit's role in the aftermath. The Internet embraces superheroes like Batman: self-appointed justice-seekers at best, raging avengers at worst. After the tragic events at the Boston Marathon, the Internet, largely well-meaning, sprang into action, crowdsourcing hours of security footage, social media feeds, and other data to try to identify the twisted souls behind those events. After accusing several people wrongly, most users backed off the witch hunt. But the Internet also produced a wave of volunteer emergency responders. . . . Thanks to the Internet, that wave rippled around the world as Internet users paid medical bills, sent money and pizzas, created maps to shelter, or offered places to stay to stranded runners.
>
> People were as creative in finding ways to help as they are in creating parody videos. That day, we were truly a community.[47]

A double-edged sword, it seems—two sides of the same coin. This is a key point of *Batman: Arkham Knight*, as well, reflecting a persistent theme in the post–Frank Miller history of Batman stories. In the game, even as Batman uses his powerful gadgets and crimefighting techniques to restore order to Gotham, he ends up destroying major parts of the city and repeatedly gets his friends kidnapped, tortured, or killed. The neural-ghost of the Joker reminds Batman that his vigilante detective work, driven by an overwrought sense of moral superiority and an unwavering faith in high-tech solutions, can have disastrous consequences: "After all, you've seen what happens when you drag your friends into this crazy little game of ours."[48] As Batman makes a series of difficult decisions that further endanger the city and his allies—tearing through the streets in his tanklike Batmobile, routinely stopping to brutalize every petty thief and tough guy in his way—the "crazy little game" presents important considerations for real-life superheroes.

Significantly, by the end of the main game narrative, Batman has literally become his own worst enemy. Before the Joker died in *Batman: Arkham City*, he had infected Batman with a virus containing the Joker's genome. During the course of *Batman: Arkham Knight*, the Joker's biochemical signature and psychotic personality gradually take over. At the climax of the game, the final battle happens inside Batman's own mind: the game discloses a possible future where Batman, possessed by the sadistic drives of the Joker, rampages through Gotham and destroys everything he had once cherished. The player must suddenly take on the role of Joker-as-Batman, killing everyone, burning the city, while Alfred pleads with Batman to stop: "Please listen to me. After all the good you've done for the city, think about what you're doing. Sir, I'm begging you. Master Bruce. Batman! You have to listen. . . . Please, please stop this rampage." Here the game requires the player to inhabit multiple levels of identification simultaneously, temporarily aligning with the Joker—recognizing that, at this juncture, to keep playing means using Batman's own expert abilities to wreak havoc—while actively fighting against the remaining traces of Batman-as-hero inside the crumbling ruins of Bruce Wayne's psyche. Ultimately, the hero version of Batman emerges victorious, subduing the Joker personality by the force of will alone. Nevertheless, the virus remains in his system: the Joker infection could flare up again at any time. It serves as a commentary on the dangers of high-tech vigilantism while affirming the importance of heroic ideals and introspective deliberation. After all, however well intentioned they may be, in rushing to put on the mask of the online superhero—taking up the digital utility belt for some cause, rallying around a hashtag Bat-Signal—aspiring crusaders may misrecognize their own alignments, self-righteously obsessing over their own personal opinions and predilections, all the while overlooking their own latent Joker infections.

In recent years, for instance, online mobs of trolls have often descended on media critics who dare to offer negative reviews of geek movies, comics, or video games. On August 2, 2008, the entrepreneur Alyssa Royse posted a short essay on her blog called "Business Lessons from Batman and *The Dark*

Knight." Poking fun at the cinematic bloat of Christopher Nolan's 2008 film, *The Dark Knight*, Royse's blog post was about the branding challenges of startup companies, taking the film as "a cautionary parable for the mistakes entrepreneurs make." According to Royse, "*The Dark Knight* is a study in what happens when a director tries to do more than they can, loses focus, is fake, gets too big a team and misses opportunities. The death knell of both a film and a startup." She expressed her distaste for the film while reading it as an object lesson: "*The Dark Knight* was an orgiastic cocktail of chaos and delusion steeped in self-indulgent whining. It tried to do too much: psycho-analyze 4 characters, throw in some international intrigue, and oh, oh, oh, can we blow up a lot of stuff, and oh oh oh, how about that cool tech thing and that cool gadget and . . . You can't do that much in a single film. Just can't." Her thoughts about the movie seemed to hit a sensitive nerve in the interwebs. The post was viewed more than ten thousand times. Hundreds of people left vicious threats and sexist jokes in the comments section of the blog, excoriating Royse for her remarks about Batman: "Get a life you two dollar whore blogger, The Dark Knight doesn't suck, you suck! Don't ever post another blog or unless you want to get ganged up"; "you are clearly re-tarded, i hope someone shoots then rapes you"; "if you were my wife i would beat you"; "This is why women are TOO STUPID to think critically and intel-ligently about film; AND business for that matter."[49] As the trolls swept in to defend Batman, using the simple web tools at their disposal to punish the blogger for a misperceived slight, they proved to be less on the side of justice than the side of terror and mayhem—the dark side of the lulz.

They did not resemble Batman, after all, but rather Batzarro—the twisted Bizarro World clone of Batman, who seems to think he is a hero but is ac-tually the "world's worst detective," committing the very crimes he hopes to solve. If only these avid defenders of the Dark Knight had actually paid more attention to the comic books, in this regard! Or even had they played the "Bizarro" expansion pack for the 2014 LEGO *Batman 3: Beyond Gotham* video game, where the delusions of Batzarro and the other Bizarro World characters are rendered awkwardly playable: an ironic tale about the difficul-ties of saving the world while getting everything completely backassward. At inopportune moments, for example, Batzarro's high-tech cowl spins around so that he cannot see where he is going—and when he throws his exploding batarangs, they often come right back to smack his own head.

Or consider GamerGate. The trigger for this bleak moment in gaming history happened in August 2014, when Eron Gjoni, an ex-boyfriend of the indie game developer Zoe Quinn, published a bitter screed on the *Penny*

Arcade and *Something Awful* forums, as well as a WordPress blog called *The Zoe Post*. Gjoni accused Quinn of infidelity, claiming that she had slept with several men in the games industry as well as a *Kotaku* reporter during the period of their relationship. On 4chan, some readers saw *The Zoe Post* as evidence of foul play in the gaming world, alleging that Quinn had exchanged sex for career advancement and favorable media coverage of her 2013 game *Depression Quest*. These salacious allegations were false, bristling with misogyny, but they propagated among certain online communities, some ostensibly concerned with ethics in games journalism, others more concerned with the growing prominence of women in software development. Discussions raged on 4chan, *The Escapist* forums, YouTube, Twitter, and Reddit, fomenting a conspiracy theory that feminists and other left-leaning elements were actively trying to destroy gamer culture. The idea was that, evidently, progressive game developers, journalists, and academics were collaborating through backdoor channels to promote "fringe" titles such as *Depression Quest* while also trying to undermine the legitimacy of mainstream games, critiquing the gender and racial politics of popular franchises, apparently with the goal of changing the entire games industry and spoiling everything. From this perspective, the Quinn situation (the "Quinnspiracy") started to look like the tip of a vast iceberg. The actor Adam Baldwin, attending to these increasingly unhinged gamer discussions, coined the hashtag #GamerGate.

Now given a name, the sense of a movement, supporters began strategizing to confront the alleged conspiracy, specifically targeting Quinn, the game developer Brianna Wu, the media critic Anita Sarkeesian, the programmer Randi Harper, the journalist Leigh Alexander, and a number of other figures in the software industry, tech media, and academic game studies.[50] The GamerGate attacks included doxing, SWATting, hijacking social media accounts, and sending endless threats of rape, murder, and grotesque brutality. Over a period of months, Quinn, Wu, and Sarkeesian each had to flee their homes and cancel public appearances due to the escalation of violent threats. Anyone who publicly critiqued GamerGate or challenged sexism, racism, and homophobia in games risked becoming a new target.

On 4chan, the GamerGate debates became so explosive that Christopher Poole, the founder of the site, decided to ban discussion of these issues in September 2014. Despite 4chan's reputation as a space for relatively unrestricted speech, GamerGate was tearing the community apart. (For Poole, already fatigued from other recent scandals, it was the last straw: not long after he became a target of GamerGate's ire, Poole announced that he was selling 4chan and retiring as its administrator.) Undaunted, GamerGate simply relocated to 8chan and other sites that were more welcoming of its rancor. Nevertheless, it represented a pivotal moment in the history of 4chan, marking an ongoing transition from the more anarchic, collectivist shock discourse that had produced Anonymous toward the identitarian obsessions of the alt-right, which had been hiding in plain sight on 4chan for many years, especially on the /pol/ "Politically Incorrect" board. As one longtime 4channer later observed,

> Despite most of the rightist discussion being limited on /pol/, there was a website-wide rightening of 4chan culture. . . . While GamerGate started off as a very diverse, vocal opponent to what they saw was unethical journalism (before it was debunked), many of the anonymous /pol/ rightists would take advantage of its anti-left character by creating sock-puppets [i.e., alternate personas to amplify reactionary positions]. . . . Today it is hard to find a 4chan user that doesn't have an attachment to far right politics. By being anonymous, rightists took advantage of their lack of identity to spread a hateful world-view.[51]

The hacktivist vanguard of Anonymous had largely migrated to other online spaces by this time—and, of course, many other Anons had been arrested for their participation in Operation Sony and other protest activities, significantly chilling any lingering social-justice aspirations on 4chan. Yet some Anonymous hackers rallied to strike back against the troll armies of GamerGate, even launching a counteroffensive dubbed Operation GamerGate on October 24, 2014. Commander X, one of the operation's organizers, noted that both Anonymous and GamerGate had germinated on 4chan, seeing them as twin offspring of the same technogenic forces: "4chan and specifically /b/ is a breeding ground for Internet culture. Probably the most fertile breeding ground. That means it is going to give birth to both the good and evil, the full spectrum of moral memes."[52] It was therefore the duty of Anonymous to fight its 4chan doppelgänger, its Bizarro World duplicate. Planning to identify the IP addresses of those participating in the harassment campaigns and to expose their true names, Anonymous promised to end GamerGate with maximum carnage: "This is going to be a troll genocide, fucking beautiful."[53]

But before this operation even got off the ground, a different faction speaking in the name of Anonymous called on Operation GamerGate to stand down: "Many of Anonymous are gamers. We understand that gamers are diverse, and labels such as 'misogynist' and 'terrorist' make no sense to use for the entire group. The label 'gamer' is currently under attack by fringe feminists and corporate bullies. This is a message to any Anonymous involved in Operation GamerGate. Do not blindly follow others. . . . We condemn Operation GamerGate. . . . We do not endorse any of their actions. . . . WE ARE GAMERS. WE ARE ANONYMOUS. . . . WE ARE LEGION. EXPECT US."[54] The meaning was clear: if Anonymous tried to destroy GamerGate, it would also be at war with itself—hivemind versus hivemind, gamer versus gamer.

Meanwhile, GamerGate turned its wrath on particular websites that were disparaging of the movement or openly supportive of diversity in gaming culture, especially *Gamasutra*, *Kotaku*, *Ars Technica*, *Polygon*, and *Gawker*, even coordinating a massive letter-writing campaign to pressure advertisers to withdraw from these sites. The editor-in-chief of *Gawker*, Max Read, later reflected on the tenacity of the GamerGaters, their dogged, win-at-all-costs attitude honed by years of playing video games: "As Gawker was imploding in the summer of 2015, a group of teenage-video-game enthusiasts was throwing gasoline on the already-raging fire. These were the Gamergaters. Of all the enemies Gawker had made over the years—in New York media, in Silicon Valley, in Hollywood—none were more effective than the Gamergaters. . . . What I'd missed about Gamergate was that they were gamers—they had spent years developing a tolerance for highly repetitive tasks. Like, say, contacting major advertisers."[55] *Gawker* lost advertising revenue during the GamerGate debacle while gamers turned the site's survival into a playable challenge, a major boss battle. In 2016, Gawker Media—the parent company of *Gawker* and *Kotaku*—went bankrupt after losing a sex-tape lawsuit filed by Hulk Hogan. The *Gawker* website shut down. The GamerGaters rejoiced, claiming Hulk Hogan as one of their own.

Many were keen to emphasize that their experiences as gamers had prepared them for such media skirmishes. As one infamous bit of GamerGate copypasta explained,

> They targeted gamers.
> Gamers.
> We're a group of people who will sit for hours, days, even weeks on end performing some of the hardest, most mentally demanding tasks. Over, and over, and over all for nothing more than a little digital token saying we did.
> We'll punish our selfs doing things others would consider torture, because we think it's fun.
> We'll spend most if not all of our free time min maxing the stats of a fictional character all to draw out a single extra point of damage per

second. . . . These people honestly think this is a battle they can win? They take our media? We're already building a new one without them. They take our devs? Gamers aren't shy about throwing their money else where, or even making the games our selves. They think calling us racist, mysoginistic, rape apologists is going to change us? We've been called worse things by prepubescent 10 year olds with a shitty head set. They picked a fight against a group that's already grown desensitized to their strategies and methods. Who *enjoy* the battle of attrition they've threatened us with. Who take it as a *challange* when they tell us we no longer matter. Our obsession with proving we can after being told we can't is so deeply ingrained from years of dealing with big brothers/sisters and friends laughing at how pathetic we used to be that proving you people wrong has become a very real need; a honed reflex.

Gamers are competative, hard core, by nature. We love a challange. The worst thing you did in all of this was to challange us. You're not special, you're not original, you're not the first; this is just another boss fight.[56]

Rhetorically, the GamerGaters cast themselves as upstart insurgents confronting an entrenched army of "Social Justice Warriors" (or sjws) and "White Knights," imagining cartoonish, larger-than-life enemies committed to the eradication of fun and masculine privilege. Standing against such intolerable forces of change, GamerGaters fashioned their own side as the domain of true superheroes. On December 6, 2014, Brianna Wu inadvertently accelerated this figuration with a series of tweets comparing Batman's shadow war on crime to her own struggle against the trolls: "I watched Dark Knight again recently, and my God did it feel similar to my own life. . . . You have a city that ignored a problem to the point the criminals took over. Bruce Wayne, because of his painful past, stands up to them. . . . Meanwhile, you have Joker and his gang, who are simply having fun burning the city to the ground. They have no conscience. . . . And even though standing up to them comes at a deep, painful, personal cost to Batman, many people in the city have no gratitude. . . . It's not just me, it's all the women that have been targeted. The whole week has been hell for me, Zoe and Randi. And I'm exhausted."[57]

GamerGaters responded with disdain to Wu's tweets and other superhero references made by their victims, insisting that sjws were merely pretending to be heroes, posing in fake costumes, while GamerGaters were the real champions of truth and freedom. One issue of the *GamerGate Life* webcomic illustrates this common refrain (fig. 5.13). Kukuruyo, a Spanish cartoonist,

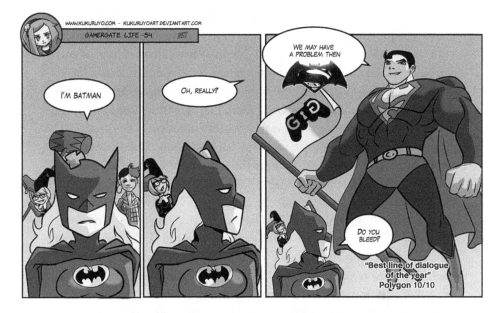

FIGURE 5.13. Kukuruyo, *GamerGate Life* #54, August 1, 2015. Available at *Kukuruyo Comics and Illustration*, http://kukuruyo.com/comic/gamergate-life-54-english/.

created *GamerGate Life* to bolster the movement: "Gamergate, a movement that started on august 2014 due to some related events in a shot period of time, all related to unethical behavior on games journalism and the invasion of the so called Social justice warriors, people who want to apply censorship and force changes into the industry while not playing games themselves. Those related events made people unite with a single goal, defend gaming and freedom of expresion."[58] The webcomic series features the cousins Vivian James (a character developed on 4chan to represent GamerGate) and Lillian Woods (a character developed by Nightwulfe1 to represent anti-GamerGate, later adopted by GamerGaters as a caricature of the Social Justice Warrior). In this particular episode, Lillian Woods wears a Batman costume and claims Batman's identity. However, the two figures behind her shoulders are wearing Harley Quinn and Two-Face costumes, suggesting that the sjw league is secretly aligned with criminals. Superman, bearing a GamerGate flag, swoops down and initiates a *Batman v Superman: Dawn of Justice* faceoff (dir. Zack Snyder, 2016). Superman's pro-GamerGate intervention here alludes to a comment made on July 31, 2015 by the actor Dean Cain, who played Superman in the 1990s TV show *Lois and Clarke*. As Kukuruyo

We Are Heroes   167

explains on his website, "Dean expressed his full support to gamers and the Gamergate movement, commenting how he has been a gamer all his life. So, yeah, we have Superman on our side."[59] In this regard, the cartoon allegory implies that Dean Cain playacting as Superman is more authentic than Lillian Woods playacting as Batman. The comic suggests that Superman—the true hero, bulging with muscles, towering above Lillian with clenched fists and a smile—will pound the gang of female sJws into submission.

It was a prevalent trope, a mode of self-fashioning. One GamerGater wrote, "They're not Batman. They are the side with the White Knights and the Jokers. We're the ones who Dark Knight the whole time trying to save our hobby from the corrupt while the general population think we're criminals. We're the ones banished to the Darknet but still fight for justice. We are all Batman."[60] Others instead found parallels with the Hulk: "I thought of GamerGate (as a whole) more like The Hulk. When at rest, it's brilliant and analytical, most often rational and up for debate. When angered it's a force of nature, unstoppable."[61] Yet others suggested comparisons to Spider-Man, pointing to the idea of an ordinary guy suddenly made extraordinary thanks to high-tech interventions (the radioactive spider and the homemade web-slingers), noting as well the similarly facetious attitude, the fraught relationship with the press ("The media is JJ Jameson and Gamergate is Spiderman"), and the tactical use of information technologies for archiving and distributing evidence. After all, both Spider-Man and GamerGate "work on the web."[62] As another GamerGater explained,

> If anything, I feel that GamerGate is Spiderman. . . .
> - Spiderman is a superhero who doesn't need any money to do good.
> - The press slanders him but he continues to do good anyway.
> - For some reason, we attract a lot of bad guys but we just want to do good.
> - He want proper press about himself.
> - He is an ordinary everyday sort of guy that no one sees that he can potentially be someone special.
> - He cracks jokes in the middle of a fight the same way we laugh at the foolish efforts of the other side.
> - He takes a lot of pictures of himself while fighting crime to send to get positive press about him the same way GamerGate screenshots and archives anything positive GG has done to show that we're good.[63]

Desperately wanting "to show that we're good," numerous supporters of GamerGate tried to forge a narrative of the virtuous crusade. Other Gamer-Gaters, however, came to embrace the tropes of villainy, conceding their antagonistic relationship to social values. The media personality Milo Yiannopoulos, for example, opportunistically jumped on the GamerGate bandwagon in September 2014 to promote the racist and misogynistic discourse of the alt-right, celebrating GamerGate as an antifeminist, antiliberal uprising. Although he had formerly dismissed gamers as "pungent beta male bollock scratchers" and social outcasts ("Few things are more embarrassing than grown men getting over-excited about video games"), at the time of GamerGate he made an abrupt about-face, professing a newfound admiration for geek culture. He also began to describe himself as the "most fabulous supervillain on the internet."[64]

Following suit, some GamerGate factions joined Milo in advertising a supervillain image. For example, a few suggested that Bane—the pharmaceutically enhanced criminal mastermind, one of Batman's recurring foes who sometimes, perplexingly, endorses ideas of social justice and economic equality through a murderous fundamentalism—could serve as the movement's moral compass. As one GamerGater tweeted, "Don't forget the words of Bane, #GamerGate 'It doesn't matter who we are. What matters is our plan.'"[65] Others said that Brianna Wu could keep her Batman quip, since GamerGaters were happy enough to cast their lot with the Clown Prince of Crime: "Brianna Wu is Batman and we're the Joker gang."[66] Such labile position-switching and adventitious principles characterized GamerGate as a whole, which actually comprised several distinct, even incompatible agendas and perspectives, united only by a shared sense of disenfranchisement, a commitment to a medium allegedly under attack by dominant cultural forces, and an emboldened, militarized rhetoric of geek warfare.[67]

The ambiguities, the incoherencies of GamerGate eventually folded back into video games themselves. For instance, one of the Batcomputer "City Stories" in the *Batman: Arkham Knight* game—unlocked by solving the Riddler's challenges—tells about the Riddler's "CrusaderGate" campaign, an attempt to turn the "internet's idiotic and easily roused rabble" against the Dark Knight (fig. 5.14). But the campaign failed. The rabble instead turned on the Riddler, harassing him with homophobic slurs:

"Y do u attack B@man? He is BASED! U r a fa—"
Riddler deleted the email, and all the others like it, as prickly hot anger and shame squirmed through his insides. No point in denying it: #CrusaderGate had been a disastrous social media campaign.

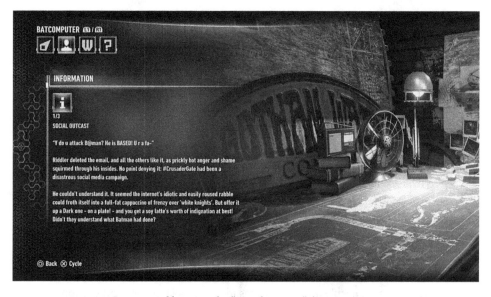

FIGURE 5.14. *Batman: Arkham Knight*: "Social Outcast" (Batcomputer—City Stories). Rocksteady Studios, 2015.

He couldn't understand it. Seemed the internet's idiotic and easily roused rabble could froth itself into a full-fat cappuccino of frenzy over "white knights." But offer it up a Dark one—on a plate!—and you get a soy latte's worth of indignation at best! Didn't they understand what Batman had done?

This tiny incident in *Batman: Arkham Knight* provided an ironic capstone to the GamerGate mess, showcasing the Riddler's befuddlement at the whole movement. Riddle me this: how could they rile themselves into a frenzy over White Knights and Social Justice Warriors but align themselves with Batman at the same time? "Didn't they understand what Batman had done?" ponders the Riddler—recalling not only his own humiliation at the hands of the Dark Knight, but also everything in Batman's career that would suggest an overriding commitment to social ideals of justice. No wonder that the Riddler seems confused here. It remains a puzzle that even the GamerGaters have been hard-pressed to resolve.

As these various examples indicate, the mapping of superhero mythologies onto video games and other computational tools—sometimes sincere, sometimes tongue-in-cheek—affords a potent set of resources for intervention in the networked world, frameworks or scripts for the practice of technogenic life. Playing superhero—whether on a gaming console, a search engine, or the interwebs of social media—rehearses a desire for resistance, a struggle against obstinate systems. Even if resistance fails, the superhero framework renders the stakes all the more sublime, narrated in continuity with a multitude of other endeavors, other fights to secure the future or disrupt it entirely.

Yet many different ideological positions and competing forces now situate themselves in relation to the discourse of high-tech superpowers—and they draw promiscuously from the same toolkits, employing all the same tactics and strategies. The distinction between the good guys and the bad guys, the superheroes and the supervillains, tends to get rather blurry. But this situation only further affirms the value of superhero stories for making sense of the transformative energies afoot in the world today, the ways in which games and computational media allow us to reach out from our own bedrooms and immediately intervene in the lives of others far away. As instruments of applied science fiction, superhero stories sometimes reinforce fascistic tendencies, aspirations to defend the status quo with overwhelming might—but they can also help us imagine a better tomorrow and unlock surprising achievements. As fables of high-tech enhancement, parables of the respawn function, they offer critical insights and ethical deliberations for a moment in history when fabulous secret powers can be activated at will, unleashed by the click of a button. Our world needs heroes, certainly— as well as the wisdom to survive our own superhuman condition.

As Spider-Man himself learned long ago, with great power there must also come great responsibility.

GREEN MACHINE

CH 6

At this point, it may seem perverse to venture a theory of green gaming—to utter the word "green" in the context of video games. After all, the video-game industry right now would seem to be a significant factor, a prime suspect, in the intensification of certain environmental problems, especially those associated with the worldwide production and disposal of consumer electronics. If we understand the video game, broadly speaking, as a particular assemblage of hardware and software, a medium that depends not only on the production of powerful computational devices but also on the expansion of the energy economy that enables these devices to operate, we therefore cannot speak of the video game without also conjuring a vocabulary of pollution, carbon footprints, greenhouse effects, habitat depletion, extinction: in short, the volatile language of environmental risk.

Let us briefly consider the scope of these problems, the penumbra of environmental hazard that surrounds the video game, from cradle to grave and beyond.[1] The engineering of game hardware relies on scarce resources, including critical metals caught up in far-reaching geopolitical conflicts. For instance, the metallic ore columbite-tantalite, or coltan, is required for making the capacitors of many common electronic devices, such as mobile phones, DVD players, computers, and video-game consoles. Mined in several different countries—Australia, Brazil, Canada, China, Ethiopia, and the Democratic Republic of Congo, among others—coltan ore is processed into tantalum powder and then sold to high-tech developers all over the world. As consumer appetites for all manner of electronic gadgets have been steadily growing in recent decades, the industrial market for tantalum has likewise kept apace. It is a matter of concern, to say the least.

The Second Congo War, for example, fueled in part by the mineral resources of central Africa, highlighted some of the unforeseen dangers related to digital technologies. A few commentators, not mincing any words, have even described the sprawling violence in Congo between 1998 and 2003 as the "PlayStation War."[2] The worldwide launch of the Sony PlayStation 2 in 2000 required the rapid production of a vast number of capacitors. But Sony could not meet the astonishing demand for its machine, due to an apparent shortage of tantalum on the open market. Thanks to the dot-com boom and the explosive growth of the mobile phone industry in the 1990s, much of the available coltan supply was already locked up in long-term contracts with other companies by the time Sony began to manufacture the new gaming console. The price of tantalum powder skyrocketed. In response, coltan mining in the rebel-occupied eastern region of Congo escalated for several years, helping to finance the invading forces from Rwanda and Uganda. Since then, coltan mining has continued to support armed conflicts in the region, even as some Congolese have come to see the ore as symbolic of their country's crucial function in the digital age.[3] Among the various human costs of the coltan operations, prisoners-of-war and children have been forced to work in the mines. As the former British Member of Parliament Oona King put it, "Kids in Congo were being sent down mines to die so that kids in Europe and America could kill imaginary aliens in their living rooms."[4]

To address the mounting public unease about "blood coltan," Sony announced that it long ago stopped acquiring any tantalum from illegal Congolese sources. However, it seems unlikely that the quantity of PlayStation 2 and later PlayStation 3 units distributed around the world could have been produced without some percentage of tantalum derived from black-market coltan, despite Sony's best efforts to document the supply chain.[5] Considering the complex international networks of transportation, processing, and brokerage that constitute the coltan trade, the number of intermediaries involved from the time ore comes out of the ground to the time tantalum powder and wires arrive at a manufacturing facility, global tech corporations are not always able to verify the specific source of these components, the origin of each atom of tantalum—and meanwhile, everyone else remains completely mystified.[6]

Whether in conflict zones or in more peaceful regions, the ecological impacts of coltan mining and other practices of resource extraction are extensive, including the devastation of wildlife habitats due to deforestation, surface stripping, and erosion, as well as the pollution of water sources with runoff from the mines. Polluted water sources can cause negative effects all along the food chain. In some mining regions, there are further threats to wildlife. For example, in the Democratic Republic of the Congo, coltan miners have moved into protected nature reserves and national parks, not only disrupting habitats but also hunting animals in the area. The miners and the militia groups, far removed from their normal food supplies, often eat the local bushmeat—including endangered elephants and gorillas. Coltan regions have suffered a ruinous depopulation of several species, such as the Grauer's gorilla. According to a report on the coltan boom published by the Dian Fossey Gorilla Fund and the Born Free Foundation, "The magnificent Grauer's gorilla will become the first great ape to be driven to extinction—a victim of war, human greed and high technology."[7]

The problems don't stop there. At the opposite end of the product life cycle, things look just as bleak. More and more gaming consoles, mobile devices, and computers are discarded as e-waste each year. Dumped into landfills or shipped on container barges to countries with less-than-stringent disposal regulations, they are often piled up in colossal heaps—sometimes set on fire, becoming infernos of plastic and metal—releasing toxic chemicals into the soil, the oceans, and the atmosphere.[8]

So throwing them away entails some dire risks, it seems. Yet video games present environmental challenges even while they are being used, even while they are still loved and wanted by their players. For instance, the proliferation of powerful console systems and high-performance PCs around the world puts additional demands on existing electrical infrastructures. The energy consumed by these legions of gaming machines is enormous—and getting worse. By all measures, video games leave a sizable carbon footprint.[9]

A 2007 Greenpeace machinima video called *Clash of the Consoles* emphasizes the scale of these issues. In the video, three iconic game characters—Mario (Nintendo), Master Chief (Microsoft), and Kratos (Sony)—confront the hazards posed by the manufacture and disposal of game consoles: "Three great heroes of the video game universe come together to battle the worst threat their world has ever known. Themselves." Kratos, star of the *God of War* series, scoffs at a PS3 unit in his hands: "How's one little box so dangerous? I'm here to battle, I'm the friggin' God of War!" The narrator responds: "One console may not sound like a threat, but try sixty million." The heroes now tremble as they face an enormous crumbling mountain of consoles (fig. 6.1). It begins to topple as the heroes dash off, in search of a better solu-

FIGURE 6.1. *Clash of the Consoles*: Kratos, Master Chief, and Mario face the tower of discarded gaming machines. Greenpeace, 2007.

tion: "With no safe way to dispose of or recycle these toxic video game systems, the only way these heroes can survive is to race for the greenest video game console ever." Yet even as Mario, Master Chief, and Kratos catch a glimpse of a glowing green console off in the distance, racing through a wasted landscape in pursuit of this chimera, the towering heap of discarded machines comes crashing down, rocking the earth while their backs are turned.

In this light, the term *green gaming* would appear oxymoronic, a mystification of its own material context. But even in this light, we might still consider how gaming might cultivate, provoke, or engender a cultural politics of green.[10] This is not simply a question of whether game manufacturers might continue to improve the environmental profiles of their products—which they no doubt can and perhaps will, even as more and more devices are produced. Rather, it is a question of whether gaming can create the conditions of ecological awareness necessary to address environmental risk, as well as the risk that gaming itself represents—the perils of technogenic life.

A number of video-game developers have experimented with green gaming: the possibility that games (a game, any game) might contribute to green politics, engaging players to recognize the precarious situation of our planet, and perhaps even providing the cognitive resources for actually doing something about it. Games with ecological themes have existed since the early days of the medium, to be sure. But green gaming would designate a specific form of gameplay and a narrative genre that posits the environment under threat, a conjectural state of imminent crisis, and tenders gaming itself as a meaningful response. Greening, in other words, as an affordance of gaming. By animating what the sociologist Ulrich Beck has described as "the anticipation of catastrophe," vivifying the potential consequences of everyday pollution, wilderness depletion, and high-tech consumerism, these games would become sites of green action in themselves, digital laboratories for remediating ecological and geopolitical risks in advance.[11]

From a cynical perspective, the existence of such games might seem to be a simple case of greenwashing, something like a public relations effort to absolve the video-game industry and video-game players from whatever degree of responsibility they might have for the problems of e-waste, strip mining, carbon emissions, and so forth. But more optimistically, these games may contain in themselves the potential for change, or at least for hope. In this regard, we might consider three distinct modes of green gaming, each featuring different capacities for promoting ecological thought: the games of environmental discipline, the games of environmental control, and the games of environmental responsibility.

Discipline

Although the historian and philosopher Michel Foucault situated the societies of discipline in the eighteenth and nineteenth centuries, formal elements of disciplinary society still persist, especially in the politics of securitization that have become ever more pronounced in recent years. Foucault described the societies of discipline as characterized by a conceptual infrastructure—an episteme—configured as a grid: a series of enclosures, both material and discursive, for shaping social organization, knowledge making, and the production of individual subjectivity. A logic of containment, manifested in specific institutions and architectural spaces, began to emerge or take on new determinate forms in the modern era: the clinic, the public school, the army barracks, the factory, and the prison. Disciplinary society formulates specific types of subjects, that is, subject positions created and reinforced by the bureaucratic organization of social order. Among these, of course, is the criminal as a type of person: abnormal, deviant, outside the social order, and yet also a category into which any normal person could risk sliding. Hence, the necessity of constant self-policing and self-surveillance. Foucault describes this condition of self-policing as the carceral function of modern society, the internalization of panoptic power: "He who is subjected to a field of visibility, and who knows it, assumes responsibility for the constraints of power; he makes them play spontaneously upon himself; he inscribes in himself the power relation in which he simultaneously plays both roles; he becomes the principle of his own subjection."[12]

A majority of the video games that address issues of environmental risk and crisis operate through the carceral function, for they typically situate environmental hazards under the category of criminal behavior. *Crimes against nature.* These games ask the player to occupy two roles simultaneously, acting as the policing agent who discovers and confronts some illicit activity, which appears therefore as the source of all environmental risk, and simultaneously self-policing against the risk of falling into the category of eco-criminal. For example, in *Sonic the Hedgehog*, developed for the Sega Genesis/Mega Drive in 1991, the valiant hedgehog is pitted against the evil technologist, Dr. Robotnik, who is depicted as a gross polluter. Similarly, the 1993 Sega Genesis game *Awesome Possum . . . Kicks Dr. Machino's Butt* features an intrepid possum who tidies up the wilderness by recycling discarded bottles ("I'm gonna clean up this world yet!") while thwarting the industrial aspirations of the wicked Dr. Machino and his army of contaminating robots. In the 1992 Sega Genesis game *Ecco the Dolphin*, the courageous cetacean faces off against aliens from outer space. These aliens plunder the oceans, sucking up all the sea life in a totally unsustainable way, and only Ecco can stop them. Likewise, the teenage heroes of the episodic 2008 PC game *Eco Warriors* must battle an invading force of necrobots. Controlled by the sinister Ecomafia, the necrobots dump illegal nuclear waste and other hazardous materials all over Italy. After defeating the toxic bots, the team of eco warriors dutifully recycles their metallic remains.

While the Manichean structure of these games perhaps speaks for itself, pitting ecological crusaders and virtuous animals against evil others—overfishing aliens, dastardly polluters, poisonous machines—it is worth noting how frequently the games of environmental discipline portray the eco-criminal as somehow beyond nature: inhuman, inorganic, not of this earth. By repudiating the eco-criminal, these games would tacitly immunize the game-playing subject against the risk of falling into the space of abjection.[13]

The operations of environmental discipline even become the plotline of the 2002 game *Super Mario Sunshine*, developed for the Nintendo Game

FIGURE 6.2. *Super Mario Sunshine*: Mario and friends observe the spreading pollution on the Isle Delfino. Nintendo, 2002.

Cube. Mario, Princess Peach, and a few other friends from the Mushroom Kingdom go for a holiday on the Isle Delfino. This island country has the shape of a dolphin—a familiar icon of environmentalist thought—and its energy infrastructure is driven by "Shine Sprites," creatures of solar power. When Mario and the gang arrive, they immediately discover that the island has been contaminated with glowing toxic waste. Slicks of "icky, paint-like goop," pools of acidic sludge, and splashes of graffiti are everywhere (fig. 6.2). The horrible pollution has driven away the Shine Sprites, and the island is now falling into darkness. The islanders have seen a shadowy figure resembling Mario at the scene of each crime.

The police arrest Mario, accusing him of befouling the island. He is abruptly put on trial: "The accused is charged with polluting our beautiful home, and yes, threatening our very way of life." To the islanders, Mario represents a danger to the environment ("our beautiful home") and the social order ("our very way of life"), and he is not even allowed to defend his innocence (fig. 6.3). At this moment, the game represents the democratic system in a *state of exception*: the extralegal suspension of the law in the name of public good, the failure of rules and procedures when the law faces an enemy of the nation, an enemy of natural order.[14] On the evidence of his appearance alone, Mario is sentenced to clean up the island. The rest of the game involves Mario washing up the mess and trying to redeem his reputation. He eventually discovers that the son of his archnemesis Bowser is

FIGURE 6.3. *Super Mario Sunshine*: The incarceration of Mario. Nintendo, 2002.

the real culprit, having disguised himself as Mario in order to frame him. Eventually, Mario trounces the monstrous Bowser and Bowser Jr., restores ecological purity to Isle Delfino, and returns to the status of hero, no longer tainted by association with the sinister shadow-Mario, the eco-criminal.

Super Mario Sunshine casts the eco-criminal as outside the natural and social orders: a figure who undermines society precisely by contaminating the environment. At the same time, in representing the act of environmental defacement through a parodic narrative of executive power and the legal system, it underscores the worry that anyone might blunder into eco-crime, that anyone might inadvertently find themselves on the dark side. Hero and villain are thus represented as mirror images of each other. In this game, the legal system is incapable of securing true justice without the intervention of a virtuous plumber who actively polices against his shadow self. It presents a startling literalization of Foucault's carceral logic. Like other games of environmental discipline, it depicts environmental risk as the result of illicit behavior—a deviancy that likewise threatens the interiority of the good citizen-subject, the good gamer, who therefore must be self-disciplined. Such games body forth an obligatory vigilantism, a form of policing in excess of the law: constant vigilance against pollution and the perils of self-pollution.

And yet, insofar as games like *Super Mario Sunshine* pivot on Manichean narratives, where mistaken identity might blur the distinction between hero and villain for a short while but never ultimately disrupt the sense in which the hero-avatar must stand for the forces of nature against the unnatural forces of desecration—where truth and justice are all sorted out correctly in the end—they ultimately affirm the game-playing subject as virtuous, clean, and nonpolluting. Though there may be danger of becoming a polluter, or at least charged as one, the ecological condition of the game player remains pure and disciplined.

In this respect, we might question the extent to which the games of environmental discipline could ever achieve an effective green politics. They prescribe normative behavior, a proper relation to the environment. They lay down the law. Yet any eco-crime they might commit themselves—as accessories to e-waste or toxic pollution, for example—is excused by their own narrative apparatus. This narrative organization positions the origin of environmental risk beyond the *zone of playability*, that is to say, outside the player's *zone of responsibility*. By conjuring eco-crime as irredeemably other and beyond legality, these games, in order to remain playable, must suspend the very laws that they have themselves posited. They must insist on a state of exception to their own green logic: eco-crime is not a crime if it is, as they say, just a game.

Control

In his short essay "Postscript on the Societies of Control," the philosopher Gilles Deleuze argued that the disciplinary formations of the modern era have been eroding away since the middle of the twentieth century, replaced by mechanisms of control:

> We are in a generalized crisis in relation to all the environments of enclosure—prison, hospital, factory, school, family. . . . It's only a matter of administering their last rites and of keeping people employed until the installation of the new forces knocking at the door. These are the *societies of control*, which are in the process of replacing disciplinary societies. . . . [T]he different control mechanisms are inseparable variations, forming a system of variable geometry the language of which is numerical (which doesn't necessarily mean binary). Enclosures are *molds*, distinct castings, but controls are a *modulation*, like a self-deforming cast that will continuously change from one moment to the other, or like a sieve whose mesh will transmute from point to point.[15]

As we note in Deleuze's language of numerical systems and modulations, he saw the societies of control constituted under a general compliance to feedback regulation, that is, the logic of cybernetics, classically described as the science of control and communication.[16] Deleuze understood postmodern societies to operate through feedback control rather than disciplinary power. The individual is no longer contained in a specific subject position or architectural space, normal only to the degree of avoiding abnormality, but rather distributed among other elements of the social system, transformed as statistical data, algorithmic models, risk calculations, and online passwords. The individual, according to Deleuze, becomes "dividual": an assemblage of components each subject to the regulatory mechanisms of control, whose prototype is the thermostat.

The thermostat keeps environmental conditions in dynamic equilibrium, oscillating around a fixed temperature. If the temperature in a house gets too cold, this information becomes input for the thermostat, which triggers the heater to warm things up; if this output now overshoots the set point, the information is once again input for the thermostat to turn the heater off or trigger the air conditioner, and so forth. A feedback cycle with no surveillance necessary, no sovereign or disciplinary power: it is autonomous, coordinated by the dumb mechanism.

Cybernetic logic informs popular discourse, everyday thought, as much as the fields of science and engineering. Even the sciences of environmental systems—from evolutionary ecology to geoengineering—draw on a cybernetic vocabulary to comprehend the circulations and transformations of matter, energy, and information across different scales.[17] And this is why so many video games, in addressing environmental risk, explicitly thematize processes and practices of feedback control. By locating environmental risk in the feedback loops between ecosystems, technological infrastructures, and the routines of everyday life, such games often present themselves as models of regulatory governance. They simulate the operations of sociotechnical networks so as to train players to better inhabit such systems and administer them from the inside. Procedures of cybernetic management and informatic coordination inflect the narratives as well as the ludic mechanisms of these games, manifested in the playing. As Alexander Galloway has written: "Video games are allegories for our contemporary life under the protocological network of continuous informatic control. In fact, the more emancipating games seem to be as a medium, substituting activity for passivity or a branching narrative for a linear one, the more they are in fact hiding the fundamental social transformation into informatics that has affected the globe during recent decades."[18]

The imagination of control has certainly inspired a surge of energy-awareness games, including *The Energy Balance, Energy Hog, Energyville,*

FIGURE 6.4. *PowerHouse*: The player becomes the thermostat. Nickelodeon, 2010. To optimize the energy efficiency of this particular room, the gaming console and other devices must be turned off, the boy must be dissuaded from watching TV, and the mom must be prevented from turning up the heater.

Stop the Guzzler!, *Power Planets*, and *CityOne*. These games feature interactive simulations of petroculture, focusing on the electrical infrastructures of industrialized nations, the habits and demands of high-tech consumers, and the vampiric nature of domestic appliances. For example, in the 2010 Nickelodeon game *PowerHouse*, players are tasked with reducing the energy consumption of various rooms in a private home to more environmentally friendly levels: "This house has some major energy usage issues. But you can solve them, if you figure out where energy is being wasted. . . . Be creative! Stay strong! You have the power to save power!" The game's instructions make it clear that behavioral modification is the goal. In playing the game, we learn how to live more efficiently and save the world in the process: "Get every room's POWER METER in the green, and you and the planet are both winners!" It is, essentially, a game that turns the player into a thermostat (fig. 6.4).

In 2006, Magnus Bang and his colleagues at the Interactive Institute in Sweden designed a similar game, also called *The PowerHouse*. It involves managing a household of seven people, trying to keep all of them happy while also balancing resource usage to achieve a more sustainable lifestyle.

It deliberately implements aspects of games like *The Sims* to motivate the player to keep playing, to learn the rules (the only viable solutions to energy reduction are those already programmed into the software) by spending more and more time at the computer: "Operant conditioning is a crucial component in almost every computer game. In the *PowerHouse*, we have applied different kinds of conditioning. Sound and visual effects attuned to the target group [teenage gamers] have been implemented to motivate users to stay at the computer. . . . The player also gets direct feedback in terms of bonus points immediately after executing a correct behavior in the game, for example when the microwave is used instead of the ordinary electrical oven. Naturally, the goal is to encourage players and direct them to perform the right actions."[19]

In asking players to optimize the domestic environment, discovering the rules of "correct behavior" and "right actions," *The PowerHouse* also narrates their subordination to the algorithm, oscillating within the parameters of better and worse choices. Programmed feedback and operant conditioning are part of the story, crucial to the winning experience. The game features a Big Brother figure, modeled after a TV game-show host, who watches over things and gives advice about how to proceed. Following the host's advice leads to rewards; ignoring it leads to less desirable outcomes. The player is in charge of the characters in the household, but success in the game means learning how to align the actions of characters with the advice of the host, who represents the rules of the energy economy, that is, the rules of the algorithm itself. Like other games in this genre, *The PowerHouse* persuades players to recognize, on the one hand, the cybernetic conditions of their own domestic spaces, and on the other hand, the possibility of a set of green practices that might modulate homeostatic conditions. It assiduously foregrounds our functionality as consumers in existing systems of energy production and distribution, vast networks that we engage only as end users, adapting ourselves to the infrastructure in order to make it work more efficiently.

The decentralized regulatory mechanisms of these energy networks are made yet further evident in a prototype game created by Bang and colleagues called *PowerAgent*:

> The person playing *PowerAgent* has the role of a secret agent, and the mobile phone is the main agent tool. Via the phone, the boss, the mysterious Mr. Q, gives the player special missions to save the planet from the energy crisis. . . . [Each mission] contains a suggestion on how to act in order to be energy efficient in the upcoming real-world task,

and it also holds information on how to influence family members. . . . Typical missions include (1) adjusting the heating in the house, (2) washing clothes, (3) cooking food, (4) switching off all stand-by appliances, and (5) minimizing the total household energy use for a day. . . . The mobile phone is connected to special equipment in the home that measures the use of electricity and heat water during the missions. In this way, it is possible for us to provide feedback on the success of the missions and reinforce behaviors that are appropriate from the standpoint of energy conservation.[20]

PowerAgent draws attention to the ways in which power—in all its forms— now operates through self-regulating modalities. They are self-contained: the outside is already inside, an object defined by the program. Even the boss is nowhere but inside the mobile phone—indeed, the boss *is* the mobile phone (fig. 6.5). The figure of social authority (boss, governor) appears as a terminal of the information network, a node in the computational architecture. What *PowerAgent* makes perfectly clear is the degree to which we are embedded in systems of control; we are mere accessories, invisible facilitators, *secret agents* of the power grid. We may be given specific tasks to improve functionality, or to keep things calibrated, but we are not ever outside—no more and no less than the boss. Our actions—the success of our missions, the reinforcement of our behaviors—may perturb the system, which eventually adjusts itself around the perturbation, resetting to new parameters, but they do not affect the formal dimensions of the system itself.

There is no outside imaginable in the games of environmental control. Unlike the games of environmental discipline, which establish a space of criminality beyond their own playable standards of virtue, the games of environmental control body forth the conditions described by Deleuze, which culminate in the "conception of a control mechanism, giving the position of any element within an open environment at any given instant (whether animal in a reserve or human in a corporation, as with an electronic collar)."[21]

Players of such games concede to the rules of the algorithm and, in some cases, automated systems of surveillance. To play *PowerAgent*, for example, you must install "special equipment in the home." Likewise, the 2011 *Power House* game developed by Stanford University, Kuma Games, and Seriosity required players to register their home utility SmartMeter and sign an informed-consent agreement, allowing the game to access information from their monthly utility bills. The energy-usage data became the basis for the self-deforming and reforming gameplay experience.[22]

FIGURE 6.5. *PowerAgent*: The boss is the mobile phone. Energy Design, Interactive Institute, and Mobile Interaction, 2008. Image from the *PowerAgent* promotional video.

Such games function according to logistics of infrastructure that cannot—or at least, this is how the societies of control perceive themselves—be radically changed, hacked, or reconfigured. They can only be modulated. This becomes especially clear in games such as *SimCity*, *Tropico*, and *Alpha Centauri*, which offer simulations of city planning or planetary engineering. These so-called god games, which empower players to decide specific elements of socio-ecological existence—for instance, whether to use coal, nuclear, or solar energy—actually lay bare the structural limits on meaningful change under existing regimes of technoculture, even as we are given more and more choices for clean energy and efficient technologies. Each of these games allows modification of certain features or parameters as the simulation progresses, but the system (the simcity or simplanet) presents itself as self-adjusting to these choices, running out the effects of any given alteration without impacting the nature of the algorithm as such, the programmed rules of possibility. Even the 2013 version of *SimCity*, for example, which emphasizes the ecological consequences of industrial development and the benefits of alternate energy sources, nevertheless concedes to prevailing logistics of infrastructure, the path dependencies of inherited sociotechnical systems. As one player complains, "The new *SimCity* [only] allows people to create car-dependent 1950s-style developments: 1) No subways; 2) No bicycle infrastructure; 3) No mixed-use development to encourage walkability; 4) The allowed density of development is tied to the size of the road, which makes no sense. It's great that *SimCity* allows people to see the impact of pollution on their sims, but in terms of urban planning ideas, the new *SimCity* is stuck in 1950 suburban sprawl mode."[23] Tweak the parameters, yes, but not the system itself. Greener, yes, but not quite green.

Responsibility

In contrast to the games of discipline and control, there are the games of environmental responsibility. These games do not correspond to an established form of social or epistemic organization. After all, societies of responsibility do not actually exist. Not yet, anyway. They remain conjectural. But this mode of green gaming would render responsibility as a technopolitical disposition, an emergent capacity. In her book *When Species Meet*, the historian of science Donna Haraway writes, "Response, of course, grows with the capacity to respond, that is, responsibility. Such a capacity can be shaped only in and for multidirectional relationships, in which always more than one responsive entity is in the process of becoming. . . . Responders are themselves co-constituted in the responding."[24]

The games of environmental responsibility animate our capacity to respond, to affect and be affected, to engage with others: other species, other people, and the otherness of our own planet. These games attend to their own involvement in the networks of the energy economy, while also drawing attention to players' culpability in enjoying media technologies that pose so many risks to the environment. So they represent a kind of counter-gaming, gaming turned against itself.[25] They rely on a certain subtlety, a certain faith in the power of irony. But their self-critical interventions are intensified by the interactive qualities of video games as a medium. Immersive engagement, which is to say, playing, heightens these ironies in ways that render responsibility *palpable*—shaped by systems of control, to be sure, and yet immanently transformable, open to the possibility that things could be otherwise.

A notable example is the game *Tasty Planet*, developed in 2006 for Mac, Windows, and Linux by the Canadian company Dingo Games and then later ported over to smartphones and touchscreen tablets. In this game, the player takes the role of an out-of-control nanotechnology blob—a gray goo.[26] Originally invented as a bathroom cleaner, the goo proves to have unintended consequences (fig. 6.6). Indeed, it begins to devour the world. *Tasty Planet*

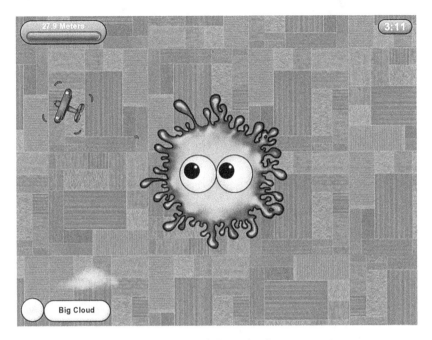

Big Cloud

FIGURE 6.6. *Tasty Planet*: The gray goo devours the planet. Dingo Games, 2006.

is a game about consumption. The point is to consume everything onscreen, absorb it, grow larger. The more the goo consumes, the more it can consume. The larger the goo, the larger the objects of its delectation. In the first levels, it can only eat molecules and microbes, but it soon progresses to higher organisms, cities, entire ecosystems, eventually growing so large that it can eat Earth itself, all the planets in the solar system, and ultimately, the fabric of spacetime as such.

The game presents an allegory of technological consumerism and the environmental impacts of our cultural appetites, the desire to guzzle more and more resources in order to grow, develop, expand: a neoliberal fantasy turned nightmare. The opening comic strip of the game presents the gray goo, our avatar protagonist, as the product of technoscience gone wrong. A laboratory experiment to develop a more efficient way of cleaning our private, domestic environment ends up destroying the common, planetary environment. It is unleashed upon the world though an act of industrial misconduct: the scientists, realizing that their invention has gone out of control, simply flush it down the drain. The allegorical elements are further sharpened in the sequel, *Tasty Planet 2: Back for Seconds*, in which the gray goo, prior to eating the whole planet, travels back in time. The bulk of the sequel

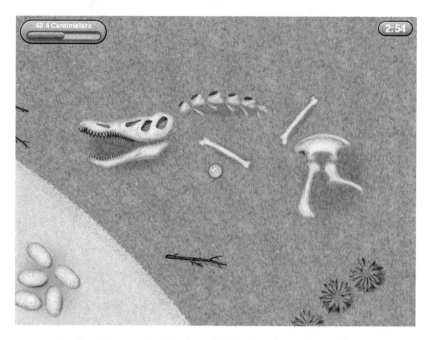

FIGURE 6.7. *Tasty Planet 2: Back for Seconds*: Traveling through time, the gray goo consumes prehistoric creatures. Dingo Games, 2010.

is spent consuming dinosaurs and other prehistoric flora and fauna, fossilized remains of ancient biology now turned into energy supply for the ravenous goo (fig. 6.7). So it is a fairly straightforward commentary on petroculture, our fossil-fuel dependencies that mobilize greater and greater levels of planetary exploitation.

The fun of the game is in the exuberance of consumption, the glee of eating everything in sight. The goo makes expressions of delight ("Yummy!"), and happy music plays in the background. We guide the goo along its path of destruction—and in this regard, in playing as the ravenous consumer, the game forces us to recognize our own responsibility. The goo can do nothing unless the player maneuvers it. So every act of consumption is caused directly by the player, even though there is no other choice if one wants to play. It also addresses our accountability as gamers—consumers of this video game, any video game—insofar as the goo is a figuration of the game itself: a high-tech medium of consumption, a *playable technology* taking over more and more of the world.

Online discussions of the *Tasty Planet* games among enthusiastic players frequently register an inherent ambivalence, namely, the fact that having fun with these games means taking responsibility for the destruction of the planet. The discourse of the players, self-conflicted and vacillating, indicates how interacting with the goo, responding to its insatiable behavior as it responds to commands, shapes a capacity for responsiveness and critical reflection. In these conversations, expressions of pleasure appear alongside discomfort, even grief. For example, one player writes, "The cat-eating levels are among my favorites, because the sad meowing cracks me up." But another writes, "I feel so guilty for eating the cats!" Indeed, consuming companion animals seems to upset a number of players: "i hate eating cats =("; "i have this empty feeling inside me after absorbing the cat D:"; and so on. Such mixed feelings of pleasure and remorse extend to other species featured in the games, as well, including dinosaurs: "I made Rex chase his tail how adorable but after 20 seconds i ate him sad."[27]

Players often express more concern for the nonhuman animals in *Tasty Planet* than the humans. According to one, "i felt worse eating the cats then i did people." And another: "I felt a little bad when eating those dogs and cats. But the several dozen police cars? meh." Yet others find the task of eating the policemen and their vehicles the most disturbing aspect: "At first it was fun eating all the little insects and animals, then it got kinda disturbing eating the police and cars, and finally it got epic when you were able to eat up all the planets in our solar system. Great game!" Reacting to the "disturbing" manner in which the game puts us outside the rule of law, this particular player nevertheless finds delight in the epic scale of the goo's crimes against nature. It is, of course, the nature of the game: "This game rocks. Where else do you eat the world?" Or: "It's easy, addictive, but also has an end. So it's not completely life-consuming (just world-consuming). Fun!"[28]

Many players seem especially keen to discuss the meanings of the final levels, where the goo must consume the planets in our solar system and then the whole universe. Some pretend to be awkwardly apologetic: "Sorry guys, but I . . . Eh ate the Earth." Or: "I felt bad for Pluto, as humans claimed it was not a planet anymore, so I tried to keep from eating it. One slip in my concentration, and I accidentally ate Pluto. I then imploded. I still feel bad for eating Pluto." The performance of emotional response is often a way of addressing and acknowledging the metaphorical aspects of these games: "And that kids is why we don't let untrained individuals experiment with the balance of nature . . . oh, never mind, we still do that." Or: "cat eat mice, dog eat cat, blob eat everything and that's the food chain any questions yeah is it true yes because as we are speaking a blob is eating our planet." Some see the *Tasty Planet* games as commenting directly on scientific responsibility: "unforturtanately the young scientists do not acknowledge that their series of actions can turn into such a catoshophy [catastrophe]." Or: "Well, Mr Scientist, it seems that your experiment went horribly right. It DID clean the Earth . . . From everything, but it cleaned the Earth. Just as planned?" Others see it as addressing even larger issues: "A good metaphor about capitalism. The more you grow, the more you want, no matter how many people under you you have to destroy, easily forgetting that you came from the streets in the beginning, and you had to eat shit and rats. At the end, Capitalism destroys the Earth."[29]

To avoid this outcome, the only solution is to refuse to play by the rules, or to opt out entirely: "i quit before he ate the earth. So the goo did not eat the earth! i made history there!" Another gamer, identifying with the goo, tries to behave responsibly—and loses the game: "I spared Earth just so they [the earthlings] would see me as their defender. They made me and thus it was my responsibility to show my gratitude. . . . [F]inally, after minutes of temptation to eat Earth, [I] devour Jupiter. Then I imploded. Nice, feel-good game!"[30] The sarcasm here foregrounds the double bind of the game (to win is to lose, to lose is to win) and its affective force.

In elevating environmental responsibility to the level of both theme and practice, *Tasty Planet* produces a communal field of affect—a complex of pleasure, humor, and discomfort. It brings players together, even in anonymity, to contemplate and work through what they have done: a common response, a responsiveness to the common and its precarity. The game cultivates an ironic sense of accountability for the fate of Earth and its creatures by ludicrously amplifying the pleasures of destruction. Responsibility emerges in responding to the game, recognizing the lethal dimensions of having a good time. And so, for some players, the real game becomes how to play otherwise.

Turning to *Ratchet & Clank*, developed for the PlayStation 2 by the American company Insomniac Games in 2002, we see a similar enactment of environmental responsibility. The setup for this game involves an ecological criminal, Chairman Drek, leader of the Blarg. After orchestrating the pollution and overpopulation of his own planet for the sake of corporate profit, Drek now intends to consume other planets:

My race, the Blarg, have a small problem. Our planet has become so polluted, overpopulated, and poisonous that we are no longer able to dwell here. But I, Chairman Drek, have a solution. We are constructing a pristine new world using the choicest planetary components available. So, what does this mean to you, you might ask? Using highly sophisticated technology, which you couldn't possibly understand, we will be extracting a large portion of your planet and adding it to our new one. Unfortunately, this change in mass will cause your planet to spin out of control and drift into the sun where it will explode into a flaming ball of gas, but, of course, sacrifices must be made. Thank you for your co-operation.

While the narrative is presented in terms of heroes and villains, *Ratchet & Clank*'s apparatus of gameplay resists the immunizing structure of the games of environmental discipline. For in order to combat Drek, the Blarg, and their corporate robots, our hero-avatar Ratchet (a lombax) and his companion Clank (a robot) must acquire weapons. To do so, they must acquire money. After acquiring the money—and much of the game is about collecting money—Ratchet and Clank can only spend the money at shops owned and maintained by the company Gadgetron. Gadgetron holds a monopoly on all technologies in the galaxy, including pharmaceuticals, domestic appliances, urban transport services, and computational systems. Gadgetron is also, perhaps even primarily, a munitions manufacturer. Part of the fun involves purchasing bigger and crazier weapons from Gadgetron, each with its own hyperbolic function: holocannons, glove bombs, chickenators, et cetera.

At one stage of the game, Ratchet and Clank get to visit the factory planet of Gadgetron—a completely technological world. By this point, however, we have already witnessed the vastness of Gadgetron's empire, distributed across inhabited and undeveloped planets alike. We have visited the planet where the Blarg are refining minerals needed to produce their technologies, filling the atmosphere with poison gas. We have been to other planets where they are dumping toxic waste. We have seen them eradicating indigenous populations. We have even explored the Blarg warships themselves. In every single location, financially benefiting from all the environmental destruction and the war economy, there is Gadgetron (fig. 6.8).

This PlayStation game therefore foregrounds the tangle of financial markets, military forces, and natural resources like coltan and other materials (figured in the game as the mineral ore "Raritanium") involved in systems of high-tech innovation. At the center of it all, the intrepid consumer-warrior—namely, the player guiding Ratchet in transaction after transaction, purchasing new weapon after new weapon—engages in a continuous process of *technological upgrade* that sustains the mystifications of the military-industrial complex, along with its environmental hazards.

FIGURE 6.8. *Ratchet & Clank*: Ratchet approaches a Gadgetron vendor on the war-torn planet Novalis. Insomniac Games, 2002. Remastered in HD for *The Ratchet & Clank Collection*, Insomniac Games and Idol Minds, 2012.

To play the game, to win, requires participating in the fictive economy. Like the games of control, *Ratchet & Clank* shows how the dividual subject is enmeshed in techno-economic networks, systems of global capital and transnational militarism. But this game also insists on our responsibility in playing in these systems, enabling them to prosper by devoting our labor—our playbor—to the economic infrastructure.[31]

Ratchet & Clank makes us work inside the systems of control and also on the fringes, playing in the junk, the detritus, and the spoiled remains of once-thriving planets. But these wasted worlds also serve to mark the edges of the techno-economic network, the threshold of other zones still beyond reach. By attending to our player agency, our role in enabling such systems to exist and endure—even though, or rather because it is the condition of playing the game—*Ratchet & Clank* makes responsibility manifest. In doing so, it denaturalizes the path dependencies of existing technologies and economies. It exposes the material foundations of the present and suggests that, as much as our playbor practices and consumer desires may support the status quo, they could instead be turned to other efforts. Indeed, the variety of planets that we visit in the course of the game, the developed and the undeveloped,

FIGURE 6.9. *Shadow of the Colossus*: The wanderer slays the second colossus. Team Ico, 2005. Remastered in HD for the PS3, Bluepoint Games and Team Ico, 2011.

the wild and the tamed, the sustainable and the unsustainable, serve as vivid reminders that another world is always possible, even in the here and now.

Shadow of the Colossus, a PlayStation 2 game developed in 2005 by the Japanese company Team Ico, further illustrates this point. In *Shadow of the Colossus*, we play as the wanderer, a young man venturing into a strange land. His desire: to resurrect a dead maiden, Mono, sacrificed for some unknown purpose back in his own country ("She was sacrificed for she has a cursed fate"). He steals a magical sword—so he is marked from the outset as a criminal—and he travels to this land where he knows he might bargain with the god Dormin to bring the young woman, his love, back to life. The price of this bargain: to kill the sixteen colossi, gigantic beasts that seem to be manifestations of the environments in which they live—and indeed, when we slay them, they deteriorate into earth, stone, and mulch. As we wander the land searching for each colossus, it becomes clear that this is a world that has moved on. There are few animals at all—the occasional bird and lizard are the only vertebrates visible in this world—and while there are trees and grasses, most are dead, barren, or wasting. There are ruins of an old human civilization here, traces of another age. But now remain only the colossi, and the whole purpose of the game is to slaughter them (fig. 6.9).

With each death, Dormin—a god of inky darkness, oil, and shadow—grows more powerful. The colossi each contain a portion of this god's essence. When they die, geysers of black fluid and smoke erupt from their vast corpses, and the wanderer's body absorbs these organic energies. After the final colossus is killed, Dormin at last becomes capable of possessing the wanderer's body, indicating how the wanderer has all along operated as an agent of this god whose dominion relies on extermination and extinction. Dormin is a figure of pure consuming power, taking far more energy and living essence than it returns to the world.

It is profoundly sad game, but a beautiful one. Many players comment on their discomfort with it, the evident narrative of environmental despoliation, and the difficulty of playing a character who ruthlessly destroys rare and wondrous creatures, not because he is malicious, but because he wants to save Mono, his love—which is to say, in order to play this game at all. To play the game means we must kill, and these deaths are our responsibility. As players of the wanderer, we are directly answerable for the extinction of the colossi. For example, one player has written,

> When I traversed these long stretches of scenery and the world, uninterrupted, I felt a greater sense of wonder and amazement; at the same time, I started questioning myself and the protagonist's journey. I was in doubt of myself. . . . . Every Colossus battle is unique in itself. Each holds its own personality, and some are completely harmless and docile. Which only comes back to reinforce the question of the morality of killing them. . . . My character, the very person I was playing, was the insinuator. I felt like a hunter of sorts, killing not out of necessity for my survival, but for the sake of my selfish goals and means.[32]

This is a common sentiment among players: intense remorse and, consequently, an active questioning of the meaning of the game. As one player posted, "I feel so bad killing the Colossi :(They are so innocent looking. (Some of them)."[33] Another responded, "Yeah some of them are just there just chilling and you stabbing them to death. Some of them are bit more hostile but if you look at the whole picture its no more than an animal being invaded would do, you're trying to bother them they defend. I wonder if the development team had this in mind and focused on making it feel wrong to kill them, or just happened. Probably it was intentional."[34]

As we see here, affective response to *Shadow of the Colossus* provokes deeper interrogations into the game's meanings, the intentions of the gamemakers, and whether it matters or not if meaning is intentional. In the elaborate fan discussions of this game, we see a kind of devotion emerge: a devotion to the game and its artistry, to the emotional experience that it provokes, and to the colossi themselves, their meanings, and the need for other players to be aware of these meanings even as the colossi pass from this world.

The sense of devotion is intensified for many players by a particular gameplay feature: the wanderer's horse, Agro. The wanderer relies on Agro to carry him over great distances, to take him into battle with the colossi—and, at a pivotal moment in the game, to sacrifice himself. Players likewise develop a haptic and emotional relationship with Agro, in that maneuvering the horse with the PlayStation controller is a process of coaxing and constant care. It becomes the condition for love: a commitment to the nonhuman other, the algorithm that comes to stand for the nonhuman as such. As one player writes,

> It's no secret that I love *Shadow of the Colossus*. That game was an incredible experience for me, and I will never forget it. When I think about love being conveyed in a video game, I think about *Shadow of the Colossus*. . . . Agro is your trusty steed throughout the journey. He carries you wherever you need to go, as far as he can. . . . As I played the game, I came to care deeply about Agro.
>
> This connection that you have to Agro is facilitated by the game's controls. . . . When you are riding Agro you use the X button to kick your heels and go forward and use the left analog stick to steer left or right. . . . What this scheme does is it make[s] you connect with Agro the way you would a real horse.
>
> You, the player, have to form a physical connection to Agro. . . . *Shadow of the Colossus* forces you to communicate with the controller in much the same way that Wander must communicate with Agro. . . . He's your only companion in this strange, harsh land, and you need him. You need him to survive. . . . I grew to love Agro. I could feel Wander's love for Agro, and I could feel Agro's love for Wander. . . . I hope to never forget.[35]

The durable relationship with the horse that grows through playing *Shadow of the Colossus* concretizes various thematic dimensions of the game. The transspecies connection between the wanderer and Agro reproduces at a narrative level the technogenic connection between the human player and the gaming system. In this way, it highlights the profound sacrifices made in service to

Dormin, in the name of love—a love not only for Mono or Agro but also for the game itself ("I love *Shadow of the Colossus*")—and our responsibility as players to the worlds in which we play:

It is as the hero rides his horse to the final colossus' lair that the game begins to reveal its true genius. The hero is riding Agro across a bridge across a ravine when, suddenly, the ancient stone structure begins the crumble. In a desperate attempt to save her rider, the horse throws Wander to the other side before falling into the depths of the chasm. Years ago, when I had first watched Wander lean over the cliff edge and scream in despair, I honestly set my controller onto the floor and cried. Although my reaction to it is no longer as strong, the scene still touches me in some way whenever I replay it, even today.

I don't think that Agro's act of sacrifice would have been as meaningful if *Shadow* were retold in any other medium. Games offer the player a different perspective, as a participant, in the world in which a story is told compared to films or novels, which can only offer the perspective of an observer. By the end of the game, I, as the player, had developed a relationship with Agro similar to Wander's. I had spent as much time riding her across the Forbidden Land as he had, and when she sacrificed herself, his cry of anguish was very much my own.

Wander, after suffering the loss of his horse, goes on to slay the final colossus. Upon doing so he returns to the temple, his body possessed by Dormin and sporting two small horns protruding from his head. . . . Despite having used Wander for its own purposes, Dormin keeps his word and restores Mono back to life. At the same moment, Agro limps into the shrine with a broken leg, alive but unable to ever run again. The game ends with them finding the infant in the temple, an ending that had left me with an incredible feeling of remorse. After all, I did not merely observe the story's events unfold, I was responsible for them. I was the one who killed the colossi, revived Dormin, crippled my horse, destroyed my body, reduced myself to a child, and left my love stranded in an uninhabited land for the rest of her life. . . . It is a game about desperate love, self-sacrifice, tragic mistakes, and the friendship between a young man and his horse. For me, *Shadow of the Colossus* represents everything that games could be.[36]

With the sense of what games could be—what they could be but are not quite yet, namely, instruments to improve the world rather than injure it—

some players of *Shadow of the Colossus* come to realize that they simply cannot keep playing as if nothing had changed. For these players, to take the game seriously means acknowledging their own complicity—and refusing any longer to play by the rules, before it is too late: "I want the colossi to live, as the beautiful giants they are. The game sits on my shelf because I have no desire to stab these animal gods to death anymore, as they seem so harmless when left to themselves. I let them live by not playing, as little bits of code, unchanged."[37] No longer content to simply play along, these players feel compelled to take a stand:

> I continued killing colossi but as my blade pierced through their flesh I began to feel a morsel of guilt and pain. These magnificent beasts intended me no harm, yet I murdered each in cold blood. I quickly brushed the thought aside. I mustn't lose focus. I'm doing this for Mono, the one I love. . . . Agro and I headed toward the sixteenth and final colossus. A bridge was all that stood between us and the colossus. Agro sauntered across the bridge, but halfway across the rope snapped. The bridge began to give way, I snapped the reigns but Agro was already in full sprint. I knew we weren't quick enough to make it to the end. I prepared myself for the fall. The memories of the colossi flashed before my eyes. I felt sorry that I had killed them. Were they not creatures too? Do they not have a right to live as much as I or even Mono did? Agro reached the edge of the bridge, but it was too late. There wasn't enough momentum to keep us from falling.
>
> I felt a thrust my back. Agro used the last of his energy to fling me onto land. Agro fell into the canyon sacrificing his life so that I may live. I tumbled onto gravel and rocks, which scraped against my skin. I lay there for two or three minutes before I had the muscle to get up. I stood and looked over the edge of the canyon. Agro was nowhere to be found, the river had swept him away. Sadness filled me inside and I wept.
>
> The final colossus stood a few hundred meters before me but I had no will to go on. Death and destruction was all that surrounded me. Everything I loved was taken from me and in return I sought justice by killing innocent beings. My selfishness and pride caused so much pain. It did not feel right to continue my journey any further. Dormin had told me from the beginning that the price for Mono's life would be great. I did not know that the price would be my own soul and my human-

ity. *What does it profit a man to gain the whole world and lose his soul?* I could go no further; this was the end. I turned off my PS2 and TV.[38]

In the various experiences recorded by players of *Shadow of the Colossus*, as with other games of responsibility, we see emerging, in fits and starts, as a desire for a different game, a gaming of the game. It is an opening of ecological awareness and a responsibility to act responsibly, not merely though techniques of discipline or control, not merely through heroic feats or virtuous activism, but rather through the capacity of games to touch us, to move us, and to awaken our empathy.

PWN

There is a common refrain among fans of the 1997 Japanese video game *Final Fantasy VII*: "This game pwns."[1] Developed by Square (now Square Enix) for the Sony PlayStation and Windows, the game has attained legendary status: "This game PWNS ALL."[2] It beggars description, virtually sublime: "FFVII pwns. . . . I don't even think pwns describes it."[3] For many gamers, it represents not only the pinnacle of the long-running *Final Fantasy* series, but also the climax of video-game culture at large: "Final Fantasy VII frigin pwns anyone and anything!!!"[4] By now, the widespread adoration of this game has even become a cliché, a stereotype of geek zealotry: "I dont care what you say, ff7 pwns all."[5]

The gamer vocabulary of "pwning" signifies the domination of an opponent—owning, conquering. But it also represents a quality of excellence, brilliance, and delight. According to gamer lore, the verb "to pwn" originated in the gaming community itself, born from a typographic error. One popular theory points to a multiplayer map in the 1994 game *Warcraft: Orcs & Humans*, allegedly the result of a developer's hasty misspelling. Another common theory holds that the term arose during a deathmatch session of the 1996 game *Quake*, beginning with a player's slip of the keyboard when proudly announcing that an adversary had been "owned." Instead of being ignored or overlooked in the reckless pace of the game, the mistake was called out and then wildly embraced. Yet others have suggested that the term goes back deeper in gaming history, born from chess: a corruption of the word *pawn* and the tactics of taking down an opponent by using the lowliest pieces on the board.[6]

Despite such origin stories, the notion of pwning as coeval with gaming remains dubious, unproven, an enigma of leetspeek. But in their desire to establish the mythic roots of pwning among games and gamers, these folk etymologies suggest the strong communal value of a term that can mean both a smackdown and a reckoning, a mark of virtuosity as well as virtue. For as much as it might indicate a glorious owning, it also suggests a condition of accountability: an owning that owns up to its mistakes, its failures.

In a ridiculously ironic way, after all, the recycling of the mistaken *p* signals a reclaiming of error, even if nothing more than a typographical error, yet expanded into a hallmark of gamer identity. It takes seriously the error as belonging to *us*—our group, our community—owning it and then finding ways to transform it, rendering it surprisingly productive of other ways of thinking, with pleasure, in common.

It is a term that recognizes, in its playfulness, that one cannot simply undo past wrongs, but instead discovers renovated potential precisely by playing through, learning from the blunder, and responding to such unexpected risks of goofing around with technology: a *mistaken owning* now troped into a way of taking charge of the game, taking responsibility.

In this regard, then, pwning might be understood as an ironic ethical concept, a ludic if not ludicrous ethics. Especially in the context of a game such as *Final Fantasy VII*, widely recognized as a richly layered allegory of environmental crisis and the planetary impacts of technological development, the ironies and paradoxes of pwning are front and center.

Like other games of environmental responsibility, *Final Fantasy VII* recursively implicates game technologies in environmental risk and ecological despoliation. It is a relentlessly self-reflexive game that provides players with conceptual and affective resources to address the consequences of their own recreational pleasures. While encouraging them to love their hardware, it simultaneously galvanizes some players to love responsibly and to take a stand for sustainable media—developing alternative practices of technogenic life.

A Bird in the Hand

There is a scene in *Final Fantasy VII* where our intrepid band of heroes, led by the ex-corporate soldier Cloud Strife, encounters a nest of monstrous baby birds. The game prompts the player: "What should we do?" If the player chooses that Cloud and his companions should leave the nest in

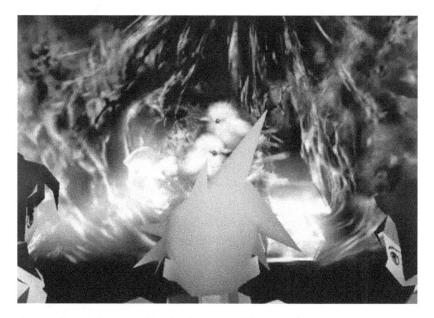

FIGURE 7.1. *Final Fantasy VII*: Cloud and friends look at the cokatolis's nest and contemplate what they have done. Square, 1997.

peace, Cloud's childhood friend Tifa responds, "Right! That was admirable of you." If, however, the player chooses to pilfer the nest, the mama bird immediately descends to defend her young. The player is then locked in mortal combat with the mama bird, with no other choice remaining but to destroy her or lose the game. As soon as the mama bird dies, the heroes receive the treasure in the nest: a bundle of magical Phoenix Downs for restoring life to fallen characters. The scene concludes with Cloud silently staring at the nest of newly orphaned birds, scratching his spiky head, as if recognizing that he and his friends have now doomed these young creatures as surely as they have destroyed the mother, all for the sake of gaming advantage (fig. 7.1).

The scene has provoked considerable debate. Some players see it purely as a tactical moment, another opportunity to maximize utility: "I always took [the Phoenix Downs]. . . . I say if it only helps to take them then take them. Don't give in to cute little 10001001, come on its just a computer animated bird." For these players, the game is simply a game, an algorithmic system. To think otherwise is to be duped by fiction: "always take them [the Phoenix Downs]. There's no reason not to except for role-playing purposes." Others take the representation more seriously while still advocating a hard-nosed financial calculus: "I always take the phoenix downs because they are useful and the items are expensive. So it is money saved. Yeah it is sad that momma bird dies, but hey in real life it happens also." Yet even for these pragmatic players, the scene often induces a role-playing effect, an affective response, precisely because it shows the collateral impacts of the most profitable course of action: "i always take them. it saves money and all that, exp [experience points] and such. do i feel guilty? sort of."[7]

While many are perfectly content to live with this choice and its instrumental rewards, others find it intolerable: "I only ever took them the first time I ever played it, then promoptly felt guilty for ages after when I killed the parents :gasp: So Ive never taken them since xD I just can't bring myself to do it, even though I know they would come in handy. . . . I look at the little chicks and Im like awwwwww. I think about it for afew minutes then come to the conclusion that I just can't do it." It is a common experience: "I took it once, then guilt ate away at me and I ended up restarting the game. Guess I just felt bad for the little birdies." Some even translate the moment into a moral imperative: "I have never taken the phoenix downs from the nest. If I did i could not live with my self literaly the birds are so cute . . . Please dont take them."[8]

It is a strangely poignant moment in a game that, up to this point, has consistently rewarded the player for ransacking every hidden treasure and slaying all manner of other creatures. Following the model of earlier games in the *Final Fantasy* series—and like most role-playing games (RPGS) in general—*Final Fantasy VII* structures its gameplay around "level grinding," the process of gaining power, money, and equipment by fighting monsters and wildlife, becoming stronger and more experienced with each victory. The baby bird scene merely highlights the fact that the entire game, characteristic of RPGS as a genre, encourages us to carve a path of carnage across the planet in order to level up. More than one player has noted the irony: "RPG characters are always trying to fix the world (while killing as much flora and fauna as it takes to reach level 99)."[9]

It is a particular irony in the context of *Final Fantasy VII*, which focuses on the efforts of Cloud and his scrappy companions to save the planet from the exploitations of Shinra, Inc. Shinra is a ruthless technology corporation that controls the global energy infrastructure. Running its own private army called SOLDIER, Shinra dominates the political economy of the world. The Shinra business plan is based on constructing powerful reactors to extract Mako energy from the geological depths of the planet. Mako is a natural resource, converted into fuel by the reactors. In concentrated form, it is also the source of numerous strange phenomena that are commonly considered "magic" (though some characters point out that any mysterious power is just unexplained science: "It shouldn't even be called 'magic'").

Eager for profit, Shinra supplies more and more Mako to feed the energy demands of the human population, especially in the high-tech city of Midgar. At the outset of the game, Shinra's extraction of Mako has reached a crisis point, threatening the integrity of the planet, the vitality of its ecosystems past and present (the "Lifestream"). The Mako economy has also created enormous social disparities. In Midgar, the poor live in the bottom tier of the city, below the surface, no other choice but to inhabit an urban stratum filled with pollution from the Mako reactors: "The upper world . . . a city on a plate . . . people underneath are sufferin'! And the city below is full of polluted air. On topa that, the Reactor keeps drainin' up all the energy."

Riding the train that connects the different sectors of the city, Cloud suddenly observes the path dependencies of existing technological infrastructures and socioeconomic orders, the extent to which choices made in the past lock in certain futures that often seem impossible to change: "I know . . . no one lives in the slums because they want to. It's like this train. It can't run anywhere except where its rails take it." A train on a track: a metaphor for what the philosopher Martin Heidegger called the technical ordering of destining, that is to say, technological enframing.[10] It indicates a dominant mode of existence in the modern world, the manner in which all things are challenged forth as standing-reserve, component resources in the relentless drive of technologization. This theme is reinforced throughout *Final Fantasy VII*. Indeed, the head of the Shinra Public Safety division—that is, the Shinra military—is even named Heidegger.

The game puts the player in charge of a group of characters actively resisting Shinra and the environmental crisis it has created. Cloud and the other protagonists are members of the militant ecological group AVALANCHE, whose tactical ops focus on blowing up the Mako reactors. AVALANCHE's activities—lauded by some, vilified by others—foment an eschatological discourse on environmental justice, as suggested by scattered graffiti in Midgar:

Don't be taken in by the Shinra.

Mako energy will not last forever.

Mako is the life of the Planet and that life is finite.

The end is coming.

Saviors of the Planet: AVALANCHE

To the extent that the game presents its core conflict as an epic struggle for the fate of the planet, with Cloud and AVALANCHE fighting a guerrilla war against the militarized corporate power of Shinra, the fact that the heroes must procedurally depopulate the wildlife of every region they visit would perhaps seem an instance of ludonarrative dissonance—a radical disjunction between gameplay mechanics and narrative content.[11] Yet this is exactly the point. The game draws attention to the ways in which its own conventional gameplay design, its random encounters and accumulative leveling structure, allegorize a general predicament: to play a video game, any video game, is to contribute however indirectly to the environmental hazards represented by electronic media.

Final Fantasy VII encourages us to remember, precisely in the conflict between its narrative of environmental heroism and its ludic insistence on random acts of animal slaughter, how video games and other technologies of entertainment exacerbate global ecological problems. Pointedly, repeatedly, it emphasizes the links between digital media and the world's unsustainable energy economy. For example, a citizen of Midgar advises Cloud about their media dependency on Mako: "If you knock out Midgar's power, then all of its computers and signals are going to be knocked out too." When playing the game, whether on a personal computer or a PlayStation console, we are reminded that, as gamers, we are contributing to the environmental crisis—even as the narrative of the game charges us, at least fictively, to do something about it.

Runaway Train

Barret, the leader of AVALANCHE, addresses the technological condition of the world with a recurring metaphor—his personal motto: "There ain't no gettin' offa this train we on! The train we on don't make no stops!" The figure of the runaway train suggests the deterministic force of industrialization and the path dependency of the energy economy, the acceleration of petroculture. The game depicts energy consumption speeding up as the result of new technologies, especially in the transition from coal-powered systems to the Shinra-controlled Mako reactors. However gradually at first, the fate of the planet was set once humans began to extract machine fuel from the remains of living things (symbolized as a fluid "Spirit energy" that flows into the underground Lifestream). As the scientist-mystic Bugenhagen says, "Every day Mako reactors suck up Spirit energy, diminishing it. Spirit energy gets compressed in the reactors and processed into Mako energy. All living things are being used up and thrown away. In other words, Mako energy will only destroy the planet."

Recognizing that technological decisions of the past have become self-reinforcing, Barret repeatedly admonishes his companions that they must fight to change the system in its entirety: "But you gotta understand that there ain't no gettin' offa this train we on, till we get to the end of the line." His metaphor points to the material infrastructures underpinning the social order, while also emphasizing that we are all in it together, for better or worse. Barret's insistence that we are all passengers on the same train distributes responsibility to everyone, in pointed contrast to the polarized structure of the game's playable narrative, which identifies the corporate greed and unethical scientific experiments of Shinra as the primary threats to environmental sustainability.

Certainly, Shinra represents the worst excesses of high-tech global capitalism. Even as the existing Mako sources threaten to run dry, destabilizing the integrity of the entire world, Shinra strives to locate the so-called Promised Land, a hidden region of vast Mako reserves, and drain it completely. Irritated by the AVALANCHE insurgents and their strikes against the Mako reactors in Midgar, Shira responds by detonating the supporting structures of the Sector 7 plate, which divides the gentrified upper level of the city from the slums below. The slum area is crushed by the collapse of the massive plate: a shocking display of corporate force that callously destroys the lives of thousands of people simply to stifle a handful of rebels.

Moreover, it is Shinra's work on the military applications of Mako and the company's unethical biotechnology research that shifts the "slow violence" of the energy economy into a climax crisis: the existential threat represented by Sephiroth and his summoning of the Meteor, a potential extinction event.[12] Sephiroth, the most powerful member of SOLDIER, is the product of Shinra's experimental research, engineered from human and alien materials, as well as heavy doses of Mako. He is both the pinnacle of Shinra's military science program and its foreclosure, for upon discovering his synthetic origins, Sephiroth turns against Shinra and the entire biosphere. Another figure of the runaway train, Sephiroth is an uncontainable force produced by techno-scientific choices of the past—and now driving the entire planet headlong toward catastrophe.

Despite that Shinra is a war-mongering, criminal corporation, most people of the world are willingly duped by its propaganda ("Shinra's Future Is The World's Future!! Mako Energy For A Brighter World!!"). In the complacent town of Kalm, for example, an old man says, "Thanks to Shinra, Inc. developing Mako energy for us, everything's more convenient now." A woman says, "I'd hate to think of what life'd be like without Mako energy. . . . Yeah, Mako energy's made our lives much easier. And it's all thanks to Shinra, Inc." Even awareness of the looming crisis cannot shake this attitude. "I hear that the natural resources near the reactors are being sucked dry," says one villager. But he nevertheless concludes, "We're better off with them bringing in the Mako energy." This widespread feeling, according to the president of Shinra, cannot even be threatened by the rising prices of Mako: "It'll be all right. The ignorant citizens won't lose confidence, they'll trust Shinra, Inc. even more." The citizens of the world are happy to accept exploitation as long as they can avoid changing their way of life.

But no one is innocent. Even Cloud bears the evidence of complicity in his own flesh. His glowing blue eyes indicate that he was literally showered in Mako to enhance his capabilities as a corporate warfighter: "That's the sign of those who have been infused with Mako. . . . A mark of SOLDIER." Barret, likewise, sports a prosthetic gun-arm, a constant remembrance of the catastrophic destruction of his hometown of Corel. Barret had urged the people of Corel to give up coal and allow Shinra to build a Mako reactor near the town ("No one uses coal nowadays. It's the sign of the times.") But disaster falls: "There was an explosion at [the] reactor. Shinra blamed the accident on the people. Said it was done by a rebel faction." The Shinra army burned the town, killing Barret's wife and shooting off his arm while he tried to save a friend. Replacing his ruined arm with a gun, Barret became the leader of AVALANCHE to alleviate his own culpability: "But more than Shinra, I couldn't forgive myself. Never should've gone along with the building of the reactor." But as Tifa says, "We were all fooled by the promises Shinra made back then." The mistakes are ours, we must own them. We are all passengers. We are all playing the game.

Whenever his companions start to lose track of the technopolitical objective—that is, the goal of this game—Barret rallies them with the familiar refrain: "C'mon, let's think about this! No way we can get offa this train we're on." The insistence on the technically determined pathway also self-reflexively points to the narrative of *Final Fantasy VII* itself, to the software of the game and its predetermined range of possible choices. For the player of *Final Fantasy VII*, just as for the characters in the story, the only apparent option is to play through to the end or to quit entirely. It is a reminder that our own participation in the game is coterminous with the journey of Cloud and friends to defeat Shinra, a journey that shows how they have always been as responsible as everyone else in maintaining the status quo, the Mako economy and the corporate systems accelerating its expansion.

The central drama of *Final Fantasy VII*, after all, is about discovering the extent to which even those who resist the prevailing systems of control are likewise products of those same systems, mystified by the conditions of high-tech living to overlook everyday failures of responsibility, including their own failures. It is drama about accepting the fact that we are all puppets of the technopolitical regimes we inhabit, for only by owning up to this can we begin to find ways of turning our puppet condition to advantage, to game the game.

No Strings Attached

The big twist in *Final Fantasy VII* is that Cloud is not who he thinks he is—and in more ways than one. He has played out an elaborate fantasy in his own mind, creating a fictive backstory to avoid grappling with his inability to achieve his ambitions. It blinds him to the fact that he is also being controlled by an external agency: "There's something inside of me. A person who is not really me." He discovers that he is a pawn, a doll, a marionette: "I'm . . . a puppet?"

This puppet condition is the result of a series of failures: "I never was in SOLDIER. I made up the stories about what happened to me five years ago, about being in SOLDIER. I left my village looking for glory, but never made it in to SOLDIER. . . . I was so ashamed of being so weak; then I heard this story from my friend Zack. . . . And I created an illusion of myself made up of what I had seen in my life. . . . And I continued to play the charade as if it were true." Haunted by anxieties of weakness, Cloud's personality is further destabilized when Professor Hojo of the Shinra science division tries to turn him into a copy of Sephiroth: "You are just a puppet. . . . An incomplete Sephiroth-clone. Not even given a number. That is your reality." Cloud is rescued by his friend Zack, an accomplished member of SOLDIER, but the nefarious experiment nearly destroys him: "I was a failed experiment." Cloud's mental stability crumbles completely when Zack dies in combat. Cloud then constructs a fake history for himself. His persona as an ex-SOLDIER resistance fighter is merely an avatar, a puppet identity without substance. He is a shell, a fictive version of himself secretly manipulated by Sephiroth ("I wasn't pursuing Sephiroth. I was being summoned by Sephiroth.").

By owning up to being a failed hero and a failed experiment, conceding his puppet condition and working to move beyond it, Cloud gains the upper hand: "I never lived up to being 'Cloud,'" he tells Tifa. "Maybe one day you'll meet the real 'Cloud.'" He does not accomplish this alone, of course, but with the help of friends. Tifa guides him to reconstruct an identity from the stream of his memories tinged with fantasies of Zack's exploits: a composite fiction that ultimately becomes real life. "I'm . . . Cloud . . . the master of my own illusionary world. But I can't remain trapped in an illusion any more. . . . I'm going to live my life without pretending."

This process represents the pwning of error, taking responsibility for the failed experiment. Cloud was a victim of Shinra's military research program, certainly—but only because he had already volunteered for the Shinra ranks in a misguided effort to join SOLDIER. He was a puppet of the military-petroleum complex, from the beginning. Only by recognizing his personal contribution to the onrushing environmental calamity (under Sephiroth's influence, he even hands over the Black Materia for summoning Meteor) can he change the course: "I'm the reason why Meteor is falling towards us. That's why I have to do everything in my power to fight this thing. . . . There ain't no gettin' offa this train we on!" Taking charge of his own mystification, he actually becomes the virtuous warrior he was not supposed to be. Cloud's pwning of the environmental crisis, even in going forward "without pretending," thus depends on an elaborate role-playing game, adopting the role of the "real Cloud" who emerges from the other side of his own puppet condition, the "real Cloud" who turns out to have been a hero in sufferance, all along.

These narrative twists allegorize the gameplay situation itself. The player, having puppeted Cloud throughout the game, occupies two roles simultaneously: both the puppet, identifying with Cloud, controlled by Sephiroth's will—which is to say, controlled by the game software and its narrative that inexorably drives us through the action—and the puppeteer, the controlling agency behind the console in whose hands the action lies. It is a recursive allegory that valorizes the capacity of RPGs to create an ecologically responsive subject, an eco-warrior fighting for the planet by taking responsibility for past mistakes. Playing the role of "Cloud" is literally the means by which Cloud works though failure to become better than himself. We, as players of Cloud, are invited to take the same initiative.[13]

In this way, *Final Fantasy VII* fashions itself as an instrument of ecologically responsible technopolitics, an instrument of change. Over and again, its narrative recursively emphasizes the transformative power of games, the subversive potential of role-playing and other forms of ludic recreation. The secret AVALANCHE hideout in Midgar, for example, is actually hidden beneath a pinball machine (fig. 7.2). Or consider the Gold Saucer: a vast

FIGURE 7.2. *Final Fantasy VII*: Cloud, Barret, and other AVALANCHE members arrive at Tifa's bar in the Sector 7 slums of Midgar. Square, 1997. The AVALANCHE hideout and the activists' networked computers are located below the pinball machine: a secret zone of technopolitics disguised as a game.

pleasure dome, an amusement park offering a wealth of playable minigames, including video arcades, chocobo races, basketball, VR battles, and more. The Gold Saucer bodies forth the culture of fun and games as such. On the one hand, it represents gaming as a distraction from real environmental crisis, a temporary escape from the problems of modern life. When the AVALANCHE crew enters the Gold Saucer, hot on the trail of Sephiroth, Aeris says, "Wow! Let's have fun! I know this isn't the right time to do this. I wish we could just forget everything and have fun!" The Gold Saucer is an alluring diversion, beguiling the AVALANCHE team to waste time while the fate of the world remains at stake. But on the other hand, the Gold Saucer episode shows how games also provide clues, tools, and skills for addressing the material conditions of the present.

After all, when exploring the entry hub to the Gold Saucer, Cloud finds the following poster: "Many attractions await you here at Gold Saucer. You will be moved and excited, thrilled and terrified! Led from one zone to another . . . unlike anything you've ever experienced!" And at the bottom of the poster: "Shinra." In other words, the Gold Saucer and its ludic pleasures have

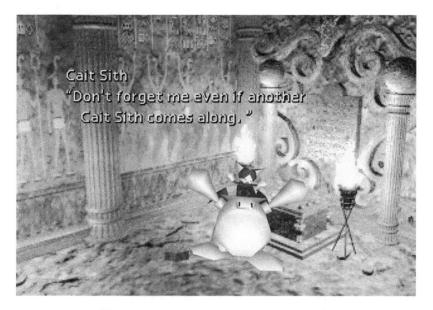

FIGURE 7.3. *Final Fantasy VII*: Avatars upon avatars—respawned. Square, 1997. Cait Sith (a robotic cat piloting a synthetic moogle, puppeted by Reeve, playable as a game character) sacrifices himself in the Temple of the Ancients to help AVALANCHE secure the Black Materia. He asks to be remembered after death, even while anticipating his return, already looking ahead to respawning in another toy body. Cait Sith renders visible the conditions of technogenic life, the transfiguration of what it means to live through computational machines.

been developed by the very same company controlling the energy economy and driving the planet to disaster.

It also becomes clear that the entire Gold Saucer structure has been built upon the ruins of Old Corel, Barret's hometown, which had been decimated by the Mako reactor explosion, razed by Shinra's army, and then repurposed as a prison. The pleasure dome has risen from the ashes of this calamity. The lucrative chocobo races inside the Gold Saucer even rely on convicts from the Corel prison below, who are lured into the races in hopes of winning their freedom. If Cloud therefore learns that games contribute to petroculture and environmental despoilation, corporate power and securitization, we as players must also reckon with the idea that the gaming console in our hands is a node in a much larger system of technopolitical forces and material flows. Certainly, some *Final Fantasy VII* players become acutely attentive to such connections: "You are aware how god-awful video games are for the environment right?"[14] Or as another player explains, "*Why are we still so dependent on oil?* Because we need the electricity to play Final Fantasy VII, of course. Speaking of which, am I the only one who thinks that it's a bit hypocritical . . . it's kind of annoying to get an environmental message from a video game that essentially wastes electricity for the sake of entertainment."[15]

But this shocking revelation of the impurity of gaming is, of course, afforded by gaming itself—a type of double agency. It is for this reason that our first exploration of the Gold Saucer also introduces the playable character of Cait Sith. Like Cloud, Cait Sith is a self-reflexive figure of the puppet. Cait Sith has a robot moogle body, apparently piloted by the intelligent cat riding on the robot's head (fig. 7.3). Cait Sith joins the AVALANCHE team to fight Shinra and Sephiroth. But it turns out that Cait Sith is a double agent. The intelligent cat is actually a cybernetic avatar teleoperated by Reeve, a Shinra employee who runs the urban development department back in Midgar: "This [Cait Sith] body's just a toy anyway. My real body's at Shinra Headquarters in Midgar. I'm controllin' this toy cat from there." A remote-controlled toy, Cait Sith was set up in the Gold Saucer to infiltrate Cloud's group and undermine the resistance from inside.

Yet as an effect of role-playing as an eco-warrior, Reeve starts to identify with the insurgency. Speaking through the Cait Sith puppet body, he confesses to the AVALANCHE group: "Alright, yes, I am a Shinra employee. But we're not entirely enemies. . . . Something bothers me. I think it's your way of life. You don't get paid. You don't get praised. Yet, you still risk your lives and continue on your journey. Seeing that makes me . . . It just makes me think about my life. I don't think I'd feel too good if things ended the way they are now." Reeve switches sides, turning against his employer and embracing the Cait Sith role. He emerges as the virtuous defender of the planet he had not planned to be. In playing along, even from the compromised position of Shinra middle management, Reeve discovers hope—and becomes otherwise.

If at First You Don't Succeed . . .

Hope—even faced with the scope of the problem, recognizing the difficulty of solving a crisis while contributing to it, the double agency of pwning says to play through, try again. Bugenhagen reflects on this conundrum: "Cloud says they are trying to save the planet. Honestly, I don't think it can be done. For even if they stop every reactor on the planet, it's only going to postpone the inevitable. Even if they stop Sephiroth, everything will perish. But . . . I've been thinking lately. I've been thinking if there was anything WE could do, as a part of the planet, something to help a planet already in misery. . . .

No matter what happens, isn't it important to try?" For Bugenhagen, this entails responsible innovation: not a relinquishment of modern science and technology, but an obligation to find other ways, different technopolitics.

For example, during the companions' adventure in the wild northern snowfields, Barret observes that some human modification of the environment might be desirable: "Seein' a place like this, makes you realize how awesome nature is. But, if anyone ever told me to live here, I'd tell them to . . . you know . . . I'll tell you one thing though, If I did have to live here I'd change things around 'n' make it better. I guess the total opposite of this would be . . . Midgar. When you think of it that way, Shinra don't seem so bad. . . . Uuuuuurrrrrgh!! What the hell am I sayin'!? The Shinra, not bad!?" Barret begins to consider Shinra's industrial expansion less as a symbol of evil than as a failure of responsible innovation, a symptom of capitalist profiteering. Indeed, the game implies that other options for the flourishing of high-tech human civilization and the planetary ecosystem are possible. Bugenhagen, for instance, imagines an alignment of natural processes and human ingenuity: "Smells like machinery. I love this smell. Of course, I also love the smell of nature, too. . . . I can feel the workings of the planet in the smell of the wind. I also feel the greatness of man's wisdom and the knowledge in the smell of machinery." It turns out that Bugenhagen had also formerly been a Shinra employee, and his deep understanding of the planet, his holistic notions, and his ethics were not shaped in isolation from Shinra technologies but in relation to them. Living in the ecotopian village of Cosmo Canyon, Bugenhagen has put Shinra's machines to more sustainable purposes: "Wrapped up in the planet's strange notions surrounded by Shinra-made machines . . . Science and the planet lived side by side in that old man's heart."

It is a vision of sustainable media, conjured forth through the mechanisms of unsustainable media. The provocation that a source of danger could itself become a saving power, that the conditions of modern technologization might be the means of their own transformation—a Heideggerian paradox, to be sure—is everywhere affirmed in the game.[16] Debating the merits of high-tech solutions versus the power of nature (e.g., magic) for averting global catastrophe, Cid Highwind, the ace pilot who joins Cloud and his companions, says, "I don't give a rat's ass whether it's science or magical power. No, I guess if I had to choose, I'd rather put my money on the power of science. . . . Science is a 'Power' created and developed by humans. And science just might be what saves this planet." Certainly, the future is filled with risk. Every choice is a gamble ("put my money"), a maneuver in a game. But winning this game—that is, arriving at the conclusion of *Final*

Fantasy VII—means using a high-tech system (the console, for example) to work through the crises of high-tech globalization and achieve a different outcome. This is the point of the game's coda. Several centuries after the collision of Meteor and the Lifestream, Nanaki—once known as the experimental test subject Red XIII—and his cubs gaze on the ruins of Midgar that have grown verdant with new life. The coda suggests that human civilization successfully let go its reliance on Mako, allowing the planet to restore itself.[17] It is the result of the playable events in the game—a consequence of playing through, committing to the challenges. In this manner, *Final Fantasy VII* discloses its own final fantasy of recuperation and rehabilitation. The failed experiment of the digital media industry, with all its contributions to environmental problems, here represents itself as affording something better in the long run . . . by putting the future in the hands of players.

Responding to these recursive thematizations of responsibility, fans of the game endlessly discuss its potential to elicit critical thought about the conditions of our technological society. Of course, some prefer to overlook the environmentalist motifs and simply enjoy the fun of slaying monsters. Others are overtly skeptical about the green politics of the game, much to the dismay of those more committed to its ethical twists.[18] But for many players around the world, *Final Fantasy VII* has encouraged them to consider, for example, "how deeply the fights for economic democracy and environmental sustainability are intertwined."[19] It has helped them to conceptualize the stakes: "We're all aware of the idea that Mako energy and all that is a metaphor for the way we mistreat our planet but parts of Final Fantasy VII seem to hint in an even stronger way towards the effects of climate change/global warming."[20] The parallels between fiction and real life become abundantly clear: "Shinra, like so many real corporations, are ruthlessly upsetting that balance with no thought of the future. . . . This is exactly the same problem that we face today. We have wreaked havoc on the environment and are causing many species to become extinct. How are Mako reactors any different than nuclear or other real-life power plants?"[21] For some, engaging with the game on this level can lead to exasperation: "The ideological strife here [in the game] mirrors an obvious—and also often ignored—issue in the real world. Fossil fuel consumption, global warming, and ongoing pollution are problems that have gone on relatively unchecked since the Industrial Revolution and have continued to increase in severity as technology and a growing population demand more use of coal and gasoline. . . . Gaia is dying, the people are loosely aware of it, and pretty much no one is doing anything about it. In many ways, the same thing is happening on Earth."[22] Yet for others, the figural aspects of the game entice them to imagine differently, turning erstwhile fantasy into proactivity.

In online discussions about the lessons of *Final Fantasy VII*, ranging from the tongue-in-cheek to the sincere, numerous players have attested to the impact of gaming on their own ecological sensitivities. As one player has put it, "I'd also like to thank Final Fantasy VII, EcoQuest I and II, and Chrono Cross for turning me into a raging environmentalist." According to another player, "*FFVII* changed the way I think about the planet, I can tell you that much lol. Hurry! Let's all rebel against giant companies and industries because they're polluting the planet!" Another has said, "It made me newly aware about matters like ecology, the need to fight for your rights without hurting anyone else, and most of all it made me think a lot about bioethics." And another: "it made me question a lot of things, including the way we live." And another: "It made me realize that the whole world needs improving . . . and I've gotta help."[23]

It is certainly the case that these insights, these ethical urges and emergent dispositions, are shaped by experiences with a game, or rather, an entire media ecology that is not remotely sustainable in its current form. Ironic, yes. But such irony often cultivates perspicacity. Consider the Spanish console modder MakoMod, who made headlines in 2015 by transforming an old PlayStation console into a physical replica of Midgar (fig. 7.4). This Midgar PS1 mod is a fully functional gaming machine that also features small details of narrative significance: the Mako reactors, the poisoned terrain beneath the city, the train system, and Aeris's reclaimed church where she grows flowers in the midst of industrial ruin. It reaffirms the game's allegory of environmental crisis and responsibility, identifying the unsustainable city of Midgar with the PlayStation itself: the city is the console, the Mako reactors draw power from a real electrical outlet. The mod does not obscure the material and geopolitical histories that converge at the site of the console, but instead brings them to light and recycles them. In this regard, it also represents a small gesture of resistance, pushing back against the game industry's calculus of planned obsolescence by refurbishing the vintage hardware, giving it new life.[24]

This modding experiment and others like it, modest though they are, can be considered affirmative exercises of remediation, homebrew efforts to reclaim the toxic infrastructures of the present. Some players have likewise suggested that the massive fan re-creations of Midgar in *Minecraft* are comparable to Aeris's flower garden in *Final Fantasy VII*, insofar as they represent DIY attempts to revamp the contaminated city of Midgar and all

FIGURE 7.4. PlayStation as Midgar: A console mod created by MakoMod. Video demonstration uploaded to YouTube by MakoMod, "Midgar PS1—Working," February 7, 2015, https://www.youtube.com/watch?v=VPrpFdgjEvE.

FIGURE 7.5. "Midgar Restoration Project": Steve from *Minecraft* visits Aeris's flower garden in the ruined church of Midgar's Sector 5 slums. Created by Killerx20, Volagarenthor, Ksun, Anniixo, Flock, and collaborators, *Minecraft*, 2012–17. Midgar Explorer v. 2.2 modpack, created on *Minecraft* v. 1.7.10, played with Technic Launcher. Modpack uploaded to Technic Platform by Killerx20, August 18, 2016, https://www.technicpack.net/modpack/midgar-explorer.504534.

it signifies from the bottom up (fig. 7.5). As one player puts it, "If everyone grew flowers in Midgar, it'd be a better place. She [Aeris] tried to change that place for the better."[25] Expressing a shared desire for change, such practices of media appropriation confront the givenness and intractability of our high-tech modes of existence, indicating in minuscule ways that other futures are yet possible: alternate tracks for this train we are on.

Problem and solution, poison and remedy, video games propagate pharmacologically in the ecosystems of our world. They represent the danger and the saving power of technology, the threat and the promise. As the philosopher Bernard Stiegler writes, "This is the case because technological knowledge is pharmacological, that is, it has the ambivalent structure of a *pharmakon*: it is always at once potentially beneficial and potentially harmful. The following question therefore arises: under what conditions can therapeutic knowledge be elaborated and transmitted, that is, knowledge that cultivates curative capacities and that fights against the toxicity of technical knowledge insofar as it is essentially pharmacological."[26] This is the core question pertaining to video games today, after all, the question at the heart of the technopolitics surrounding video games, the sociogenesis of gamer culture. For even while contributing to high-tech problems and environmental hazards, games tend to animate a playful and experimental attitude toward technology as such, a sense that innovation pathways and technopolitical trajectories can always be hacked, transmogrified. As mechanisms for working through error, overcoming failure, they afford visions of a future reloaded, played with renewed virtuosity, thanks to skills learned from past experience. In a word, pwned.

It is the task at hand, the game in hand. It is not at all impossible, this final fantasy. So can we get from here to there, from this world of corporate control, securitization, and environmental devastation to a world of free play, openness, and responsibility—from a world full of own, to a world full of pwn?

"Get ready to start a new life!"[1] In the 2005 Nintendo DS game *Animal Cross-ing: Wild World*, our player-character takes up residence in a village of diverse humanoid animals. If our adventure goes awry, if we make some unhappy decisions, we might be tempted to shut off the DS without saving and then reload the game from an earlier point in the narrative. Yet doing so triggers a reprimand. Upon relaunching the software, a mole character called Resetti appears onscreen and chides us, sputtering in consternation, as if the familiar gamer tactic of resetting were somehow an affront to life itself. "Well," he says, "I'll TELL you what this mole knows: you gotta treasure life. Every second!" (fig. c.1). Like an evangelist for Iron Man mode, Resetti insists that restarting the game amounts to a disavowal of finitude, taking life for granted. If the player does it again, Resetti comes back: "OK, listen. Everybody, and I mean everybody, makes mistakes. That's just life. . . . It's takin' whatever comes your way, the good AND the bad, that gives life fla-vor. It's all that stuff rolled together that makes life worth livin'. Turnin' the power off 'cause you didn't get an item you really, really wanted? Or tryin' to backtrack and avoid some kinda sticky situation? . . . Stop playin' like that. Stop LIVIN' like that! . . . Deal with the consequences of your actions, 'cause life ain't no video game. You feel that irony, punk? Aw, for the luvva dirt!"

Resetti knows irony, it seems, and he asks us to feel it, to internalize the impurities and paradoxes of the game in our own flesh. Life is not a game, says Resetti, but he suggests that playing games can teach us how to live. He

FIGURE C.1. *Animal Crossing: Wild World*: Resetti tunnels out from the depths of the Nintendo DS to lecture about the ethics of saving. Nintendo, 2005.

implores us to play responsibly—to save ourselves, to save our progress—even while implicitly encouraging us to reset yet again, precisely to see what further morsels of wisdom he might offer about life in the age of computer games: "You doin' this on purpose? Are you maybe turnin' the power off without savin' for laughs? You wanna get the crazy mole out here and see what he says next, that it? This entertains you, punk?" Lol!

Resetti is an animated metaphor of the reload, the reboot—a figure for the respawn function as such. He suggests the affordances of resetting even while telling us not to do it, advertising the values of starting over despite his own assurances that we cannot turn back the clock, that we must take responsibility for our choices. After all, Resetti's recurring performance indicates that the reset is not a reset, at least, not in any absolute sense. As players, we remember each previous encounter. And, indeed, so does Resetti. As a software function, he keeps track of the number of times he has been called out, and his speeches note the persistence of the past, the recalcitrant traces of history stored in computer memory and player memory alike: "Read my lips: save first, and then, and ONLY then, turn the power off. . . . How many times I gotta tell you that?"

Like the narrator of Crowther and Wood's *Adventure*, like SHODAN and GLADOS, Resetti personifies the obstinate algorithms of digital culture, mediating the relationship between the player and the computational hardware: "Just shuttin' down is the same as resettin', and you know what that means! Yeah! I gotta tunnel out here and lecture you!" Traveling through the twisty little passages of the gaming system, emerging onscreen, Resetti insists that we must save before we restart. And yet, insofar as his own appearances actually incentivize players to not save the software state—even if for no other reason than to experiment with Resetti himself—his pleas take on extra nuances: "If you're gonna quit, you gotta SAVE first!" By repeatedly disobeying his commands, we learn that quitting is less an issue of erasing the past than figuring out what we ought to save, how we ought to save, before we delete unexplored futures.

And what is there to save, in this game? It's more than our gameplay progress, after all. The game focuses on the relations of humans to other organisms, emphasizing an ethos of care and cultivation, encouraging us to assess the conditions of the village and do whatever we can to improve things. Pelly, an anthropoid pelican who offers advice for renovating the village, remarks from time to time, "You know, I think if we added some green, it would really help." Keeping the village hospitable requires good stewardship, attentiveness to diversity. While the protagonist is human, the other characters are biological chimeras or animal robots (the adorable Ribbot, for example). These creatures mingle in the bucolic setting where common pastimes include observing the stars and constellations, classifying fossils and insect specimens, or breeding hybrid flowers. The experimental activities, the various tasks of collecting and taxonomizing, reflect the deeper technoscientific systems running beneath the rustic landscape. In the course of our explorations, after all, we discover that our village is just one node in a high-tech network. To visit other players' villages, for example, the player-character can talk to a gatekeeper named Copper. Copper asks if we want to transfer between DS devices using the local multiplayer function or instead using the Nintendo Wi-Fi Connection (WFC) for remote linkups, prompting us to configure our device settings. Traveling between villages thus highlights the technical infrastructures of the world, the extent to which even the aesthetics of the pastoral and the georgic now express the logics of networked computing.[2]

So *Animal Crossing: Wild World* is about the practice of technogenic life. It thematizes continuity in relation to change, the past in relation to the uncertain future—ways of opening up or remembering alternate possibilities that may have been neglected, foreclosed, or yet to emerge. It is a game that provokes us, teases us with the prospect of making the world better by playing better, playing responsibly—and learning how to save. All this, not despite our experiments with Resetti, but precisely because of them.

Wendy Chun has argued that, in our era of constant technoscientific change, the urgency to secure the familiar and the known regularly translates into archival projects of mass digitization, the analytic promises of big data, and the mandate to keep things the same by constantly upgrading our consumer technologies. Yet rather than resolving crisis, the pressure to save our comfortable habits and cultural patterns results in never-ending crisis: a present that never actually progresses despite the ongoing sense of acceleration, a metastasis of the present that compels us to save all the time without questioning what exactly we are saving, without asking whether the drive to save may actually make things less safe, less sustainable. Instead, Chun suggests that there are other ways to save—not just the present, but the future. Sometimes, in order to save, we must also delete: "we need to forego the desire to reduce memory to storage, and we must develop a politics of fore-giving that realizes that to delete is not to forget, but to make possible other (less consensually hallucinatory) ways to remember."[3] Saving means more than locking down the past and narrowing the horizon of things to come. It also means recognizing that the present is made by continually performing the past, recollecting other pathways that might be yet worth exploring, revisiting alternatives obscured by our obsessive struggle to preserve the way things are:

> Saving is something that technologies or bodies cannot do alone; the battle to save is a crisis in the strongest sense of the word. This necessary repetition makes us realize that our desire for safety as simple securing, as ensured by code, actually puts us at risk of losing what we value, whether it is data stored on old floppy drives or habituations. It also forces us to engage with the fact that if some things stay in place, it is not because they are unchanging and unchangeable, but rather because they are constantly implemented and enforced. . . . Further, acknowledging this necessary repetition moves us away from wanting an end (because what ends will end) and toward actively engaging and taking responsibility for everything we want to endure.[4]

From this perspective, then, the character of Resetti proves to be not merely a comic distraction but a potent figure of philosophical depth, asking us to think about how our own apparently minor actions—shutdown, save, reboot, replay—entail much more profound implications and consequences. The procedures of gameplay both mirror and recode the technopolitical processes at stake in our world. It is no wonder, then, that the blustery character of Resetti has been known to make children cry! Nintendo even had to tame him down in later installments of the *Animal Crossing* series, including the 2012 entry *Animal Crossing: New Leaf*, because so many young players had been distressed by the diatribes of the angry mole.[5] No doubt, Resetti's vehement claim that our choices as gamers reflect how we live, how we want to live, is a hard lesson to swallow. For it implies that the casual, quotidian act of saving or resetting gameplay data itself models an orientation to social change, affirming that duration and persistence are not givens but are always active processes of construction. Moreover, it suggests how we can affect what gets carried forward, what structural conditions and institutions are made to endure—not by erasing or overwriting the past, but rather by remembering it, learning from it, and choosing how to go on from here.

The mechanisms, the practices, the technologies of video games now bring the weightiest dilemmas of contemporary society into focus—to save or not to save, to pwn or not to pwn, to spawn or to respawn. A variety of creative works that recapitulate the forms and conventions of video games have now addressed this situation directly, reflecting on a moment in history when games have become a cultural dominant, responding to the forms of life afforded by ludic modes of experimentation. For example, in the 1998 German film *Run, Lola, Run*, the protagonist Lola navigates a hazardous series of events at high speed, discovering the most effective pathways, the most responsible choices, by respawning and starting over again when the story goes disastrously wrong. She learns from playing through the different branching pathways of her adventure not only how to save her own life, her boyfriend's life, and the lives of a few other people she encounters, but also how to influence the whims of chance by bending the rules of the game to her own will.

Similarly, the 2014 American film *Edge of Tomorrow*, loosely based on Hiroshi Sakurazaka's 2004 light novel *All You Need Is Kill*, depicts an extraterrestrial invasion of Earth. Although the nations of Earth put up a massive military resistance, the aliens win nearly every battle because they have the power to turn back time whenever one of their Alpha members gets killed. Serendipitously, the inexperienced soldier William Cage (played by Tom Cruise) acquires the aliens' ability to replay the previous day each time he dies in combat. By respawning over and again, Cage learns how to survive a seemingly unsurvivable future. He eventually manages to reset the future entirely, restoring history to a trajectory in which the catastrophic alien war ended before he even arrived on the front line.

If these narratives literally represent the resetting of reality, they figuratively rehearse the extent to which video games provide a model for the conscientious shaping of the future: the forward-looking evaluation of innumerable choices that we make in the here and now, refined by testing and retesting those choices over and again in the speculative mode, learning from repeated errors to preserve, the remember, to carry forward felicitous decisions and to relegate infelicitous pathways to the status of alternate history.

This is why, according to the fictions of digital culture, the practices, the dispositions of gaming can inform political choices, responsible policy decisions, and collective actions. For example, in Cory Doctorow's 2010 novel *For the Win*, several of the world's largest economies are represented by online games, owned and operated by powerful transnational corporations. Teenage gamers, gold farmers, and Mechanical Turk workers from all around the world coordinate an uprising against these companies that control the infrastructures of technogenic life, unionizing against the corporate exploitation of play and immaterial labor. Applying their gamer skills to the challenge of labor organization, discovering their collective agency, the unionized gamers and webworkers, now dubbed the "Webblies," suddenly find themselves in a position to impact the global economy, to decide the fate of the game companies. The gamers evaluate possible futures, and rather than choosing a radical reboot, they instead propose a decisive reform. The gamer Wei-Dong, representing the Webblies' interests to one of the game companies, puts it this way: "I'd prefer *not* to destroy the game. I love it. I love playing all these games. You have my record there, you know it. We all feel that way, all the Webblies. It's where we go to work every day. We *want* it to succeed. But we want that to happen on terms that are fair to us. So believe me when I tell you that I am calling to strike a bargain that you can afford, that we can live with and that will save the game."[6] Having learned to play with the digital economy, discovering the great power of the online swarm and the hive-mind, the gamers maneuver to negotiate with the corporate opposition and develop common ground, mutual flourishing. They aspire to make a future that is neither a propagation of the status quo nor a discontinuous future in which the lessons of the past are deleted or forgotten, but rather a respawned future that takes responsibility for the things that are made to endure.

The imagination of technopolitical change as respawning, venturing forth through a deliberate recollection of other paths not yet traveled, likewise affords reflexive questioning of the current moment, the era in which video games and their extended media networks present ever more significant impacts on the social order. This is the point, for example, of Ernest Cline's 2011 novel *Ready Player One*. In the near future, the worldwide degradation of environmental and economic conditions has become so severe that the majority of people have reoriented their lives around the OASIS, a massive gaming environment that has become the default interface to the internet itself: "It was the dawn of a new era, one where most of the human race now spent all of their free time inside a videogame."[7] The open-access OASIS improves society in some ways, by providing access to top-notch education and offering employment opportunities to billions of people; fostering communities, friendships, and relationships; and promoting new forms of technogenic life. But the pleasures of the OASIS have also distracted everyone from the formidable problems of ecological destruction and worsening economic disparities. When the creator of the OASIS, James Halliday, passes away, he sets up a contest inside the OASIS: a difficult "Easter egg hunt," inspired by Warren Robinett's *Adventure*, involving a series of puzzles and challenges that only the most talented gamers might navigate. Halliday's will declares that the winner of the contest will inherit his vast fortune and control over the fate of the OASIS.

The story follows young Wade Watts and his friends as they try to solve the mysteries of Halliday's contest. Meanwhile, the world's biggest internet service provider, Innovative Online Industries (IOI), mobilizes its vast resources to secure control of the OASIS. Not merely content to own the hardware infrastructure of global telecommunications, IOI also wants to own the OASIS system so as to dictate the contents of the internet, to lock down its accessibility and monetize every aspect of the OASIS experience. Transparently, then, the OASIS is a figure for digital culture in its entirety, the mediascapes and technoscientific institutions of our own world, caught between competing values of open-culture gamers and closed-culture corporate goons. Fortunately, Wade and his friends manage to win the contest, thanks to their ingenuity, their determination to fight for the open OASIS, and, most importantly, their mastery of geek lore. As it turns out, winning Halliday's game requires an encyclopedic knowledge of science fiction, video games, and 1980s pop culture. The novel proposes that living, navigating, and surviving in the network society requires a deep familiarity with geek media and the practices of applied science fiction—and, of course, exquisite gamer skills.

At the end of the book, when Wade inherits the Halliday estate and the operations of the OASIS, Wade learns that he has also inherited a sobering responsibility. Halliday's avatar (a computer persona that persists long after Halliday's own death) draws Wade's attention to a large red button hidden inside an inaccessible castle in the OASIS:

> "I call this the Big Red Button," Halliday said. "If you press it, it will shut off the entire OASIS and launch a worm that will delete everything stored on the GSS [Halliday's Gregarious Simulation Systems] servers, including all of the OASIS source code. It will shut down the OASIS forever." He smirked. "So don't press it unless you're absolutely positive it's the right thing to do, OK?" He gave me an odd smile. "I trust your judgment."[8]

Whatever degree of wisdom and good judgment that the eighteen-year-old Wade might possess, it derives from his complete immersion in media archaeology. As a character living in the future but intensively researching the media of the past—specifically, the pivotal decade of the 1980s—he has a refined appreciation for the ways that video games and popular fiction have shaped high-tech society.[9] By playing every game, reading every novel, memorizing every film that informed Halliday's development of the OASIS, Wade finds himself awash in stories, attentive to the experiences and memories of more lives than his own.

Recall the old gamer adage: "I am a gamer, not because I don't have a life, but because I choose to have many." The idea that Wade has gained extra life, extra knowledge, and extra wisdom, thanks to his meticulous engagement with games and geek media, is made clear during the climactic OASIS battle between the IOI clone army and the gamer legions vying for access to Halliday's puzzle. The corporation detonates a weapon of mass destruction that kills every avatar in the vicinity. But just when all hope seems lost, Wade saves the day, thanks to a surprise respawn—a bonus life he gained earlier in his quest by completing a perfect game of *Pac-Man*. Springing back to life amid the devastation, Wade presses forward. As the last avatar standing, he now represents all the gamers, the entire community united against corporate predation. By virtue of all the lives he has played as a gamer, getting by with a little help from his friends, Wade reaches the end, the final victory, and the choice represented by the Big Red Button: whether the OASIS and everything it stands for ought to be allowed to persist unchanged or totally shut down, opening the way for something else. By the time he gets to this point, standing on the brink between two options—maintaining a system that, despite all its good qualities, is ultimately not sustainable, or instead hitting the kill switch, starting over—Wade already knows more than he knows. From inside the game, he has discovered a new appreciation for life outside the game, for living in the world and refusing to flee from its complications.

Importantly, the novel ends without precisely telling us what Wade decides. But even if he decides to delete the OASIS—and there is perhaps a hint that this is what Wade does choose, eventually—it would not be an erasure of what the OASIS had been but rather an affirmation, a remembrance as well as a fore-giving, of how it had empowered Wade and his friends to finally get to the point of wanting to change it.[10]

So it is not simply a choice of one or the other, this world or that world. Rather, it is about evaluating the desire to reproduce more of the same against the urge to reload, to save by playing otherwise. While the game may be rigged, obstinate, the important thing is not to give up.[11] For the people who are still inside, rage quitting is no solution—because there ain't no gettin' offa this train we're on. In a world of technogenic life, where we always live more lives than one, always responsible for more lives than our own and more worlds than we know, getting to the save point may take a few tries. The real question is what to save when we get there.

Game on.

This book emerged from conversations and collaborations with friends around the world. At UC Davis, my colleagues and students in the Department of English, the Program in Science and Technology Studies, and the Department of Cinema and Digital Media have been wonderfully supportive. Special thanks to everyone who has helped to make the UC Davis ModLab such an exciting space for working on games, media, and technoculture, particularly Treena Balds, Ashlee Bird, Gina Bloom, Larry Bogad, Stephanie Boluk, Katherine Buse, Evan Buswell, Alexis Caligiuri, Jordan Carroll, Gerardo Con Diaz, Ranjodh Singh Dhaliwal, Joe Dumit, Kris Fallon, Ksenia Fedorova, Colin Johnson, Sawyer Kemp, Evan Lauteria, Patrick LeMieux, Tim Lenoir, John Marx, Josh McCoy, Michael Neff, Josef Nguyen, Amanda Phillips, Kriss Ravetto-Biagioli, Justin Siegel, Alison Tam, Nick Toothman, Emma Leigh Waldron, Marty Weis, and Melissa Wills.

I worked on this project for almost ten years. Needless to say, a lot has changed in that time. The world looks different than it did when I first started thinking about technogenic life in a long-gone IRC channel. But through it all, I benefited from the advice and encouragement of many people. My sincere thanks to Aimee Bahng, Bernadette Bensaude-Vincent, Mario Biagioli, Sylvie Bissonnette, Marianne Boenink, Alisa Braithwaite, Luis Campos, Cesare Casarino, Seeta Chaganti, Alenda Chang, Wendy Chun, Bruce Clarke, Christopher Coenen, Gabriella Coleman, Karen Collins, Lucy Corin, Jeanne Cortiel, Kathleen Frederickson, Paweł Frelik, Yulia Frumer,

Christine Gerhardt, Bishnu Ghosh, Jeremy Greene, Jim Griesemer, Alexei Grinbaum, Orit Halpern, Kate Hayles, Ursula Heise, Veronica Hollinger, Nalo Hopkinson, Zach Horton, Eddy Hubert, Ben Hurlbut, Patrick Jagoda, Mark Jerng, Melody Jue, Chris Kelty, Susanne Lachenicht, Sacha Loeve, Sylvia Mayer, Jonah Mitropoulos, Dave Munns, Alfred Nordmann, Laura Oehme, Katy Park, Geeta Patel, Sharrona Pearl, Rita Raley, Neil Randall, Alisha Rankin, Arie Rip, Kim Stanley Robinson, Russell Samolsky, Bhaskar Sarkar, Daniel Schrimshire, Astrid Schwartz, Sudipta Sen, Hanna Shell, Rasmus Slaattelid, Nicole Starosielski, Tsjalling Swierstra, Elly Truitt, Tim Valdepena, Simone van der Burg, Harro van Lente, Sherryl Vint, Priscilla Wald, Janet Walker, Emily Wanderer, Alexa Weik von Mossner, and Fern Wickson.

Several ideas came out of discussions with Jonathan Alexander, Megan Arkenberg, Brian Attebery, Stina Attebery, Clara Barr, Michael Bennett, Etienne Benson, Vincent Bontems, Diana Bowman, Finn Brunton, Joseph Bustos, Laurel Carney, Siobhan Carroll, Michaela Castellanos, Ted Chiang, Tim Choy, Joshua Clover, Christina Cogdell, Bryan Coller, Seth Cooper, Victoria de Zwaan, Claudia Deetjen, Fran Dolan, Sydney Duncan, Brian Egan, Kevin Elliott, John Fekete, Margie Ferguson, Arianna Ferrari, Ed Finn, Beth Freeman, Jennifer Gabrys, John Garrison, Ken Goldberg, Axel Goodbody, Kathleen Ann Goonan, Jack Gosse-Fuchs, Jessica Gray, Dave Guston, Andy Hageman, Jenni Halpin, Mark Hancock, Bridget Heaney, Jeff Hicks, David Higgins, Robbie Hoile, Katherine Isbister, Alessa Johns, Mario Kaiser, Caren Kaplan, Sharon Kingsland, Zach Kissinger, Kornelia Konrad, Oliver Kreylos, Anthony LaBella, Ingrid Lagos, Rob Latham, Christina Lee, Katie Leveling, Eira Long, Victor Luo, Desirée Martín, Emilee Mathews, Juliet McMullin, Elizabeth Miller, Liam Mitchell, Donald Morse, Projit Mukharji, Rahul Mukherjee, Natasha Myers, Julia Neil, Brandon Norris, Amanda Ong, Josh Pearson, Constance Penley, David Rambo, Mark Ranstrom, Jerry Ravetz, John Rieder, Gabe Romaguera, Bonnie Ruberg, Nicholas Sanchez, Christian Schmidt, Birgit Schneider, Robin Schramm, Tyler Sciacqua, Cynthia Selin, Lorenzo Servitje, Steven Shaviro, Adrienne Shaw, Scott Shershow, Scott Simmon, Dana Simmons, David Simpson, Greg Siu, Eric Smoodin, Braxton Soderman, Erik Stayton, Matthew Stratton, Josh Tanenbaum, Cameron Taylor, Lindsay Thomas, Aaron Trammell, Victoria Trang, Chris Toumey, Chris Tung, Nora Vaage, Arjan Wardekker, Claire Waters, Emily West, Steve Wilcox, Gary Wolfe, Emily York, Meagen Youngdahl, and Mike Ziser. I also deeply appreciate the students who participated in my seminars "Video Games and Literature," "Cyberpunk and Cyberculture," and "Video Games and Digital Narratives."

For their assistance at numerous points throughout this project, I am grateful to Agata Antkiewicz, Aaron Barstow, Jenny Bickford, Kevin Bryant, Yoke Dellenback, Stefanne Haro-Maendly, Lynda Jones, Melissa Lovejoy, Molly McCarthy, Karen Nofziger, Ron Ottman, Darolyn Striley, Vicki Higby Sweeney, Darla Tafoya, and Mary White. It has been lovely to work with everyone at Duke University Press, and I'd like to acknowledge especially Courtney Berger, Sandra Korn, and Christine Choi Riggio. Two anonymous reviewers offered brilliant insights and suggestions that helped me tremendously during the revision process. Many thanks to Nils Knoblich and Jürgen Keil for providing images and inspirations.

Several parts of this book were first tested out in seminars and conferences. I am indebted to the audiences who attended my talks at MIT, the University of Bayreuth, Maastricht University, the University of Bergen, the University of Pennsylvania, the University of Rhode Island, Texas Tech University, Sonoma State University, the University of Waterloo, the European University of St. Petersburg, Arizona State University, New York University, the Cyprus Institute, UC Berkeley, UC Irvine, UC Riverside, UC Santa Barbara, the Library of Congress Blumberg Dialogues, several meetings of the Society for Studies of New and Emerging Technologies (S.NET), the Queerness and Games Conference (QGCon), and the International Conference on the Fantastic and the Arts (ICFA). Some sections of this book previously appeared in different form in the following publications: "Long Live Play: The PlayStation Network and Technogenic Life," in *Research Objects in Their Technological Setting*, ed. Bernadette Bensaude-Vincent, Sacha Loeve, Alfred Nordmann, and Astrid Schwartz (London: Routledge, 2017), 105–22; "Hacking the Scientific Imagination," *Journal of the Fantastic in the Arts* 27 (2016): 28–46; "'Ain't No Way Offa This Train': *Final Fantasy VII* and the Pwning of Environmental Crisis," in *Sustainable Media*, ed. Janet Walker and Nicole Starosielski (London: Routledge, 2016), 77–92; "Video Games—Science Fiction to the Core," *Science Fiction Studies* 43 (2016): 10–11; and "Green Gaming: Video Games and Environmental Risk," in *The Anticipation of Catastrophe: Environmental Risk in North American Literature and Culture*, ed. Sylvia Mayer and Alexa Weik von Mossner (Heidelberg: Universitätsverlag Winter, 2014), 201–19.

The book developed significantly through my involvement with the IMMERSe Research Network for Video Game Immersion, supported by the Social Sciences and Humanities Research Council of Canada, as well as the UC Davis Mellon Research Initiative in Digital Cultures, supported by the Mellon Foundation. My research was further supported by a New

Directions Fellowship from the Mellon Foundation, which allowed me to retrain in computer science.

My whole family has been there for me, through thick and thin. My partner, Peter Holman, has been an endless source of strength and joy. Our two cats, Carmen and Figaro, were at my side virtually every day while I was writing this book. Carmen passed away in the autumn of 2016. Leukemia. I am still heartbroken. But I always think of the things she taught me: love without hesitation, cuddle with abandon, and play whenever you can.

Comment on sources: To preserve the flavor of contemporary discourse, quoted sources are presented verbatim, including any grammatical peculiarities or typographical errors, and without editorial intervention unless needed for clarity. For the sake of accuracy, citations of online materials are historically specific whenever possible, referring to original hosting websites, full URLs, and dates of first publication or appearance unless otherwise indicated. Although some websites may have disappeared or changed over time, for the most part, the specific materials cited here can still be accessed through the Internet Archive's Wayback Machine or other web-archiving initiatives. However, other materials—such as those hosted on sites that block web crawlers—have not been publicly archived. Copies of all cited documents and media materials are on file with the author.

Introduction

1. Developed by Toaplan in 1989, *Zero Wing* was originally an arcade game before it was ported to the Mega Drive in Japan in 1991. For the console version, Toaplan added the introductory scene to expand the narrative context. Sega published the English-language version for the European market in 1992.

2. Many gamers have noted that CATS bears an uncanny resemblance to the Borg from *Star Trek*, not only visually but also rhetorically, insofar as the CATS leader echoes the Borg's characteristic threats of total assimilation. As one *Zero Wing* fan explains, "The introduction shows the bridge of a starship in chaos as a Borg-like figure named CATS materializes and says, 'How are you gentlemen!! All your base are belong to us.' . . . Has many of the connotations of 'Resistance is futile; you will be assimilated.'" See Biohertz, "All Your Base Are Belong to Us," *Urban Dictionary*, January 30,

2003, http://www.urbandictionary.com/define.php?term=all+your+base+are+belon g+to+us&defid=27690. The Borg first appeared in the 1989 "Q Who" episode of *Star Trek: The Next Generation*.

3. See Poster, *Information Please*; Jenkins, *Convergence Culture*; Krapp, *Noise Channels*; and Nunes, *Error*.

4. Around 1999, a GIF made from the English-language opening scene of *Zero Wing* began to replicate on the internet, hosted on the *Rage Games* forum, the *Zany Video Game Quotes* website (http://zanyvg.overclocked.org), and elsewhere. By 2000, remixes and dubs started to appear, such as the Zero Wing Dub Project on *OverClocked*, along with an explosion of image macros developed on *Something Awful* and the *TribalWar* forums. In 2001, Bad_CRC of the *TribalWar* forums created a music video for "Invasion of the Gabber Robots" by The Laziest Men on Mars—a hardcore techno song that samples liberally from the *Zero Wing* soundtrack—showcasing a variety of the joke macros and media pranks inspired by *Zero Wing*. As this video went viral, it triggered other remix experiments. Since then, the *Zero Wing* meme has continued to evolve and diversify—even if some of the ineffable humor of its early years has diminished over time. On the development of the meme, see Jeffrey Benner, "When Gamer Humor Attacks," *Wired*, February 23, 2001, http://www.wired.com/2001/02/when -gamer-humor-attacks/; Chris Taylor, "All Your Base Are Belong to Us," *Time*, February 25, 2001, http://content.time.com/time/magazine/article/0,9171,100525,00.html; and Triple Zed, Jamie Dubs et al., "All Your Base Are Belong to Us," *Know Your Meme*, May 1, 2016, http://knowyourmeme.com/memes/all-your-base-are-belong-to-us. On the propagation and cultural effects of such internet memes, see Shifman, *Memes in Digital Culture*; W. Phillips, *This Is Why We Can't Have Nice Things*; and Milner, *World Made Meme*.

5. For key accounts of technogenesis, the emergence of technical beings and collectivities in relation to the technical production of the human itself, see Simondon, *On the Mode of Existence of Technical Objects*; Stiegler, *Technics and Time, 1*; Waldby, *Visible Human Project*; Hansen, *Bodies in Code*; Loeve, "About a Definition of Nano"; Denson, *Postnaturalism*; and Hayles, *How We Think*.

6. S. Mitchell, *Technogenesis*, 28, 94.

7. McCarthy, *Bloom*, 6, 100.

8. The philosophers Jacques Derrida and Bernard Stiegler have theorized this condition as *originary technicity* or *originary prostheticity*. See Derrida, *Of Grammatology*; Derrida, *Archive Fever*; Derrida and Stiegler, *Echographies of Television*; and Stiegler, *Technics and Time, 2*. For context, see Beardsworth, *Derrida and the Political*; Bennington, *Interrupting Derrida*; and Mackenzie, *Transductions*.

9. See Genosko, *When Technocultures Collide*; Beyer, *Expect Us*; Burkart, *Pirate Politics*; Dunbar-Hester, *Low Power to the People*; Hurley, *Geek Feminist Revolution*; Postigo, *Digital Rights Movement*; Sarkar, "Media Piracy and the Terrorist Boogeyman"; W. Phillips, *This Is Why We Can't Have Nice Things*; and Coleman, *Hacker, Hoaxer, Whistleblower, Spy*. Riffing on James Scott's concept of "weapons of the weak" and forms of peasant resistance, Coleman describes such technopolitical practices as "weapons of the geek." She writes that "weapons of the geek is a modality of politics

exercised by a class of privileged and visible actors who often lie at the center of economic life. . . . What they all have in common is that their political tools, and to a lesser degree their political sensibilities, emerge from the concrete experiences of their craft, like administering a server or editing videos. Often these skills are channeled into activities in order to bolster civil liberties, such as privacy. Unlike peasants who seek to remain inconspicuous and anonymous even as a group, geeks and hackers—even the anonymous Anonymous—explicitly call attention to themselves via their volatile, usually controversial, political acts" (107). See also Coleman, "From Internet Farming to Weapons of the Geek." On technopolitics as the enactment of political processes through technological use and development, as well as the political qualities of technologies themselves, see Hecht, *Radiance of France*; T. Mitchell, *Rule of Experts*; Conway, *High-Speed Dreams*; and Edwards, *Vast Machine*.

    10. Galloway, *Protocol*, 244.

    11. On the history of cybernetics and its fashioning of self and other as mechanisms in extended feedback systems, blurring distinctions between human and technology, see Haraway, "Cyborg Manifesto"; Galison, "Ontology of the Enemy"; and Hayles, *How We Became Posthuman*.

    12. Will Wright, "Spore, Birth of a Game," TED, March 2007, http://www.ted.com /talks/will_wright_makes_toys_that_make_worlds. On video games as instruments that extend practices of experimentation and modes of scientific thinking, see Milburn, *Mondo Nano*.

    13. *Doom* instruction manual (Mesquite, Tex.: id Software, 1993), 7. The "-RESPAWN" parameter is described in the *Doom* "README.TXT" file as follows: "-RESPAWN tells DOOM that, yes, you are a badass, and yes, you want all the monsters to respawn around 8 seconds after you kill them." See "Welcome to v1.8 of DOOM!" README.TXT, *Doom* version 1.8 (id Software, 1995).

    14. See Doyle, *On Beyond Living*; Helmreich, *Silicon Second Nature*; Kay, *Who Wrote the Book of Life?*; Thacker, *Biomedia*; Parikka, *Digital Contagions*; Parikka, *Insect Media*; Chun, *Programmed Visions*; Kember and Zylinska, *Life after New Media*; and M. Y. Chen, *Animacies*.

    15. See Thacker, *Global Genome*; Sunder Rajan, *Biocapital*; Cooper, *Life as Surplus*; and Stevens, *Life out of Sequence*. As Stevens writes, "Biological databases are not like archives and museums—they are oriented toward the future more than the past" (138–39).

    16. Massingham and Goldman, "All Your Base." On the computerization of biology, see November, *Biomedical Computing*. On machinic vitalism and convergences with digital media, see Doyle, *Wetwares*; Johnston, *Allure of Machinic Life*; and Milburn, *Nanovision*.

    17. See Weis, "Bio-Gaming"; Weis; "*Assassin's Creed* and the Fantasy of Repetition"; and Parkin, *Death by Video Game*.

    18. See Markey and Ferguson, *Moral Combat*.

    19. On the ways in which games isolate themselves from normal life, crafting temporary spaces apart, see Huizinga, *Homo Ludens*; Caillois, *Man, Play and Games*; Suits, *Grasshopper*; and Salen and Zimmerman, *Rules of Play*. On modes of existence,

see Simondon, *On the Mode of Existence of Technical Objects*, and Latour, *Inquiry into Modes of Existence*.

20. See Jenkins, *Fans, Bloggers, and Gamers*; Taylor, *Play between Worlds*; Taylor; "Pushing the Borders"; Jones, *Meaning of Video Games*; and Consalvo, "There Is No Magic Circle." On wavedashing and other specialized practices that enable new emergent forms of play in and around existing game objects, see Boluk and LeMieux, *Metagaming*. As Boluk and LeMieux argue, the expansion of a game beyond itself into other games and gamelike practices (*metagaming*) always redefines the game, recursively producing and re-producing its conditions of playability, such that the game becomes less the origin than the effect of the metagame: "Before a videogame can ever be played—before software can be considered a game in the first place—there must be a metagame" (9).

21. See Bogost, *How to Do Things with Videogames*; McGonigal, *Reality Is Broken*; Walz and Deterding, *Gameful World*; Schrier, *Knowledge Games*; and Jagoda, "Gamification and Other Forms of Play."

22. Anonymous Network, "Message to NSA—Anonymous #OpNSA," YouTube, August 1, 2013, http://www.youtube.com/watch?v=T1nLuKuSnaU. This video was originally released in early June 2013. It was uploaded many times to YouTube and other websites over the following two years, along with several related Anonymous videos about OpNSA. For additional details about OpNSA activities, see the AnonOps website, *Operation NSA: Make Privacy Matter*, 2013, https://anonops.com/opnsa/. See also the @AnonymousOpNSA Twitter stream, https://twitter.com/AnonymousOpNSA, which helped to propagate the #OpNSA hashtag. Some members of Anonymous had previously tried to launch #OpNSA in January 2012, responding to emerging details about surveillance activities of the U.S. cyber-military-industrial complex that were already becoming known prior to the Snowden revelations. For example, NSA's secret Turbulence program (designed to monitor hackers around the world and launch preemptive cyberattacks) as well as some other electronic eavesdropping practices had been reported as early as 2007. See Bamford, *Shadow Factory*. Further indications of mass surveillance had come to light thanks to the Anonymous-affiliated Operation Metal Gear team coordinated by Barrett Brown, later rebooted as Project PM. (Notably, the focus of Operation Metal Gear on exposing mysterious cybersecurity projects took a cue from the *Metal Gear* and *Metal Gear Solid* video game series.) These efforts had found evidence of various spying programs by analyzing email data from the Anonymous hack of the HBGary security firm in February 2011, as well as additional data gathered from other security contractors in the same year. The first Anonymous video to declare OpNSA explained:

> Greetings Citizens of the World. We are Anonymous. For years, the NSA has been tasked with protecting the United States by gathering foreign intelligence of threats against its citizens and military. But this agency has unlawfully been monitoring civilian Internet and communications. The media and U.S. government has been frowning on our Operations when they themselves have done their fair share of what they call "hacking." The Nixon, George W. Bush, and Obama administration have been involved in wiretapping of the public.

Operation Turbulence is the current reincarnation of the NSA's programs that include data mining and malware injection into computers. Congress and politicians know of these programs and support them, even when they break our privacy. This is a formal message to the NSA, Congress, and the current administration . . . STOP! You have been warned. . . . We are Anonymous. We are Legion. We do not forgive. We do not forget. Expect us. (runmonkey75, #OpNSA.wmv, YouTube, January 26, 2012, https://www.youtube.com/watch?v =u7LOWGmGXiE)

Despite such early provocations, OpNSA was left simmering until the Snowden leaks happened. At that point, Anonymous turned it up to a full boil, organizing diverse protest actions.

23. See Raley, "Dataveillance and Countervailance."

24. Greenwald, *No Place to Hide*, 45–46.

25. Greenwald, *No Place to Hide*, 46. On the various ways that games can intervene in politics, including via content, narrative form, procedural rhetoric, and other means, see Bogost, *Persuasive Games*; Losh, *Virtualpolitik*; Dyer-Witheford and de Peuter, *Games of Empire*; Burak and Parker, *Power Play*; and Jagoda, "Videogame Criticism and Games in the Twenty-First Century."

26. *Eddy's Run: The Prism Prison*, Binji Games, May 8, 2013, http://www.eddysrun.com.

27. See James Ball, "Xbox Live among Game Services Targeted by US and UK Spy Agencies: NSA and GCHQ Collect Gamers' Chats and Deploy Real-Life Agents into *World of Warcraft* and *Second Life*," *Guardian*, December 9, 2013, https://www .theguardian.com/world/2013/dec/09/nsa-spies-online-games-world-warcraft-second -life. See also Justin Elliott and Mark Mazzetti, "World of Spycraft: NSA and CIA Spied in Online Games," *ProPublica*, December 9, 2013, https://www.propublica.org/article /world-of-spycraft-intelligence-agencies-spied-in-online-games (published simultaneously as Mark Mazzetti and Justin Elliott, "Spies Infiltrate a Fantasy Realm of Online Games," *New York Times*, December 9, 2013, http://www.nytimes.com/2013/12 /10/world/spies-dragnet-reaches-a-playing-field-of-elves-and-trolls.html). The leaked documents include an NSA briefing, "Exploiting Terrorist Use of Games and Virtual Environments" (2008); a memo reporting work by the NSA's Menwith Hill Station and the British GCHQ, "MHS and GCHQ 'Get in the Game' with Target Development for World of Warcraft Online Gaming" (2008); and a report developed by the defense contractor Science Applications International Corporation, *Games: A Look at Emerging Trends, Uses, Threats and Opportunities in Influence Activities* (2007). Released by the *Guardian* in coordination with the *New York Times* and *ProPublica*, the documents are available on DocumentCloud at https://assets.documentcloud.org /documents/889134/games.pdf. On the racialized history of surveillance in online game worlds, see Nakamura, "Socioalgorithmics of Race."

28. NSA, "Exploiting Terrorist Use of Games and Virtual Environments," 2.

29. See Lenoir and Caldwell, *Military-Entertainment Complex*; Der Derian, *Virtuous War*; Kline, Dyer-Witheford, and de Peuter, *Digital Play*; Crogan, *Gameplay Mode*; Halter, *From Sun Tzu to Xbox*; Huntemann and Payne, *Joystick Soldiers*; Mead, *War Play*; Payne, *Playing War*; and Allen, *America's Digital Army*.

30. Michael Hsieh, "Crowd Sourced Formal Verification (CSFV)," Defense Advanced Research Projects Agency, 2015, http://www.darpa.mil/program/crowd-sourced -formal-verification. As the DARPA Information Innovation Office has elaborated, "This is particularly an issue for the Department of Defense because formal verification, while a proven method for reducing defects in software, currently requires highly specialized talent and cannot be scaled to the size of software found in modern weapon systems." See DARPA Information Innovation Office, "DARPA-SN-12-17: Crowd Sourced Formal Verification Proposers' Day—December 8, 2011," Federal Business Opportunities, November 22, 2011, https://www.fbo.gov/index?s=opportunity&mode =form&id=7568977f9618c969b17a6deddd73aa84&tab=core&_cview=0, p. 1.

31. "About Us," *Verigames*, September 16, 2013, http://www.verigames.com/about -us.html. As indicated of the FAQ page of the website, "If gameplay reveals potentially harmful code, DARPA will implement approved notification and mitigation procedures. . . . Prompt notification is essential to correct the software rapidly and mitigate risk of functional or security breakdowns." See "FAQ," *Verigames*, October 4, 2013, http://www.verigames.com/faq.html.

32. TheTrueHOOHA, response to Chickenlegs, "Clicking Power Supply on My Xbox 360," *Ars Technica*, May 19, 2006, http://arstechnica.com/civis/viewtopic.php ?p=6726096#p6726096. On Snowden's history as TheTrueHOOHA, see Joe Mullin, "NSA Leaker Ed Snowden's Life on *Ars Technica*," *Ars Technica*, June 12, 2013, http:// arstechnica.com/tech-policy/2013/06/nsa-leaker-ed-snowdens-life-on-ars-technica/.

33. On the ways in which new forms of life arise in technoculture as contests over structures of meaning and the rules of play, see Fischer, *Emergent Forms of Life and the Anthropological Voice*; Fischer, *Anthropological Futures*; Epstein, *Impure Science*; Juris, *Networking Futures*; and Choy, *Ecologies of Comparison*. On gaming as a zone of sociopolitical conflict, see Dyer-Witheford and de Peuter, *Games of Empire*, and J. Wright, Embrick, and Lukács, *Utopic Dreams and Apocalyptic Fantasies*.

34. W. A. Higinbotham, "The Brookhaven TV-Tennis Game," circa 1983, Brookhaven National Laboratory, 2013, https://www.bnl.gov/about/docs/Higinbotham_Notes.pdf. See also Higinbotham, "BNL Tennis Game," April 29, 1976, Brookhaven National Laboratory, 2013, https://www.bnl.gov/about/docs/Higinbotham_Deposition.pdf. On the development of *Tennis for Two* and its role in the history of gaming, see Guins, *Game After*.

35. Andy McNamara, "Games Are Science Fiction Come to Life," *Game Informer* 261 (2015): 4.

36. On the rhetoric of futurity that often adheres to gaming hardware, see Maher, *Future Was Here*; Milburn, *Mondo Nano*; and Altice, *I Am Error*. As Michael Newman shows, the early personal computer industry also pushed the idea of computers as toys while emphasizing their futuristic orientation, advertising them as serious high-tech devices that would transform both labor and leisure in the society of tomorrow. Ads for personal computers such as the Radio Shack TRS-80 and the Commodore VIC-20 featured Isaac Asimov, William Shatner, and other figures from the world of science fiction playing video games on home computers while indicating that these devices were capable of far more than mere entertainment. See M. Newman, *Atari Age*, 115–52.

By the time Apple launched the Macintosh in 1984 with its famous Orwellian Super Bowl ad, presenting the Macintosh as a sporty hacker weapon against technological authoritarianism, the science-fictional sheen of personal computing and video games had been well established. See Friedman, *Electric Dreams*, and Bukatman, *Terminal Identity*.

37. De Certeau, *Practice of Everyday Life*, 18.

38. On GamerGate, see Cross, "'We Will Force Gaming to Be Free'"; Chess and Shaw, "Conspiracy of Fishes"; and Braithwaite, "It's about Ethics in Games Journalism?" On the politics of diversity and representation in video-game culture, see Shaw, *Gaming at the Edge*; Anthropy, *Rise of the Videogame Zinesters*; Wysocki and Lauteria, *Rated M for Mature*; Russworm and Malkowski, *Gaming Representation*; A. Phillips, "Shooting to Kill"; and Ruberg and Shaw, *Queer Game Studies*.

39. See Jenkins, Ito, and boyd, *Participatory Culture in a Networked Era*; Jenkins et al., *By Any Media Necessary*; Raley, *Tactical Media*; Stokes and Williams, "Gamers Who Protest"; Schrank, *Avant-Garde Videogames*; Schleiner, *Player's Power to Change the Game*; and Boluk and LeMieux, *Metagaming*.

ONE. **May the Lulz Be with You**

1. On *Spacewar!* and its role in the evolution of hacking, see Brand, "Spacewar"; Levy, *Hackers*; Barton and Loguidice, "History of *Spacewar!*"; and Turkle, *The Second Self*. The *Spacewar!* project and other hacker experiments indicate how computer programming is itself a form of play; see Wells, "Programmer as Player." On ways that *Spacewar!* and university labs influenced the development of the games industry, see Lowood, "Videogames in Computer Space." While *Spacewar!* has often functioned as an origin myth for hackers, the history of hacking actually reveals multiple genealogies and microcultures, especially in global context; see Coleman and Golub, "Hacker Practice," and Kelty, *Two Bits*.

2. Russell, quoted in Brand, "Spacewar."

3. Graetz, "Origin of *Spacewar!*," 42.

4. Graetz, "Origin of *Spacewar!*," 48.

5. See Frelik, "Video Games"; Jagoda, "Digital Games and Science Fiction"; and Tringham, *Science Fiction Video Games*. On the contrivances of video games that evert the irrealisms of virtual environments into ordinary human environments, reframing the gaming apparatus and other material contexts through fiction, see Welsh, *Mixed Realism*. On video games as mixtures of technical rules and fictional worlds, see Juul, *Half-Real*.

6. Milhon (St. Jude), quoted in Jon Lebkowsky, "St. Jude Memorial and Virtual Wake," *The WELL* (*Whole Earth 'Lectronic Link*), August 1, 2003, https://www.well.com /conf/inkwell.vue/topics/190/St-Jude-Memorial-and-Virtual-Wak-page01.html. Partially quoted in Coleman, *Hacker, Hoaxer, Whistleblower, Spy*, 167. A similar definition of hacking appears in St. Jude, Sirius, and Nagel, *Cyberpunk Handbook*: "A hijack of The Way Things Are. A brilliant *détournement*. An elegant solution to a technical problem. A fiendishly clever circumvention of regulation reality" (52).

7. See Suvin, *Metamorphoses of Science Fiction*; Scholes, *Structural Fabulation*; Toumey, *Conjuring Science*; Csicsery-Ronay, *Seven Beauties of Science Fiction*; Barry, *Technobabble*; and Vint, *Science Fiction*.

8. On science fiction as a resource for hackers, see Sterling, *Hacker Crackdown*; Ross, *Strange Weather*; Thomas, *Hacker Culture*; Latham, *Consuming Youth*; Kline, Dyer-Witheford, and de Peuter, *Digital Play*; Burrill, *Die Tryin'*; and Ferro and Swedin, *Science Fiction and Computing*.

9. Raymond, *Cathedral and the Bazaar*, 207.

10. Pesce, "Magic Mirror." Notably, in 1991 Pesce founded Ono-Sendai, one of the earliest VR startups, taking its name from a fictional corportation in *Neuromancer*.

11. On the influences of fantasy and speculative fiction—especially the works of J. R. R. Tolkien and the role-playing game *Dungeons & Dragons*—in the history of computing and video games, see King and Borland, *Dungeons and Dreamers*. On the fetishistic rhetoric of magic and demonic processes in computer programming, see Chun, *Programmed Visions*. On ways in which science fiction concepts are put into practice by hackers, see D'Andrea, De Paoli, and Teli, "Open to Grok." The concept of grokking comes from Heinlein's 1961 novel, *Stranger in a Strange Land*.

12. The hacker and security researcher Raphael Mudge originally released Armitage in November 2010. Armitage is a graphical interface for the Metasploit framework, named after the character Armitage in *Neuromancer*, a former military cyberopera-tive who is controlled by the AI Wintermute. Mudge developed Cortana in 2013 as a scripting engine to extend the capacities of Armitage and to create automated bots for penetration testing. The Cortana scripting engine is named after the friendly AI in the *Halo* games, a companion to the Master Chief and an efficient instrument of netwar. (As a hacker tool, Mudge's Cortana seems well aligned with the character of Cortana in the *Halo* series, unlike Microsoft's own virtual personal assistant for Windows 10 and Xbox One, which is also named Cortana but proves to be rather less hack-friendly.) Mudge has often pointed to a range of speculative ideas and concerns raised by hacking tools such as Armitage and Cortana, even beyond their allusive names. For instance, in a tutorial document for Cortana, he quips, "To prevent self-aware bots from taking over the world, Cortana has blanket safety features to provide positive control when enabled." See Raphael Mudge, *Cortana Tutorial*, May 21, 2013, avail-able at http://www.fastandeasyhacking.com/download/cortana/cortana_tutorial.pdf. On Berlin's c-base and its wonderful mythology, see the website *c-base >>> Raum-station unter Berlin*, www.c-base.org. See also the book *c-book: 20 Years of the c-base* (Berlin: c-base e.v., 2015).

13. On Emmanuel Goldstein, hagbard, the Legion of Doom, and their relations to science fiction, see Goldstein, *Best of 2600*; Sterling, *Hacker Crackdown*; Hafner and Markoff, *Cyberpunk*, 160–61, 234–35; and Slatalla and Quittner, *Masters of Deception*. Count Zero of the Cult of the Dead Cow (cDc) is one of several hackers who have sported the same handle. He has often narrated his own backstory using elaborate science fiction tropes: "Count Zero is a man of science. Abandoning a promising career as a neurologist and cabaret dancer, he joined the cDc as their official Surgeon General where he performs surgical bio-enhancements on all members to keep them

operating at peak performance during space battles and onstage performances. He is a hacker of the human brain and a connoisseur of fine Bordeaux and crunchy breakfast cereals. Ultimately scorned by the medical establishment for his radical ideas and flashy jewelry, he operates out of a hidden medical laboratory beneath the ice cap in Antarctica. When fighting crime, he outfits himself in a black jumpsuit augmented with bio-mechanical weapons and surgically attached robotic homunculi. Turn-ons include long walks in the park and sunsets. Zero fights the good fight, preparing for the future showdown against the evil robots for the fate of mankind." See Count Zero, "About—Team Bio," *Cult of the Dead Cow*, 2008, http://w3.cultdeadcow.com/cms /team_bio.html.

On Team GhostShell's global hacking activities and its manifestos about Dark Hacktivism ("Information Is Everything"), see Team GhostShell's Pastebin, https:// pastebin.com/u/TeamGhostShell. On Sandworm Team, see Ward, "isIGHT Discovers Zero-Day Vulnerability," isIGHT Partners, October 14, 2014, http://www.isightpartners .com/2014/10/cve-2014-4114; and Zetter, "Russian 'Sandworm' Hack Has Been Spy- ing on Foreign Governments for Years," *Wired*, October 14, 2014, https://www.wired .com/2014/10/russian-sandworm-hack-isight/. While studying the hackers' attacks on foreign governments and infrastructures, researchers at the isIGHT security firm came up with the name after noticing a surprising number of *Dune* connections, for example, in the hackers' use of base64-encoded URLs for command-and-control serv- ers that would translate as "arrakis02," "houseatreides94," and so forth. On the Shadow Brokers and the geopolitical implications of the NSA exploit leak, the ways in which citizens and businesses become collateral damage in the games of cyberwarfare played by government actors, see van Der Walt, "Impact of Nation-State Hacking on Com- mercial Cyber-Security." On the Decepticons, the Shadow Brokers, and the concept of a "public interest hack" where private information is dumped on the internet for the sake of public, sometimes even civic interest, see Coleman, "Public Interest Hack."

14. Heinlein, *Rocket Ship Galileo*, 21.

15. Asimov, "Nightfall," 137.

16. See Canaday, *Nuclear Muse*; Brake and Hook, *Different Engines*; Milburn, "Mod- ifiable Futures"; Milburn, "Ahead of Time"; Shoch and Hupp, "'Worm' Programs."

17. "Parallel Worlds Galore," *Nature* 448 (2007): 1.

18. Fleischmann and Templeton, "Past Futures and Technoscientific Innovation," 1. Other sociological studies have offered similar assessments. In 1954, for example, the sociologist Arthur S. Barron noted that the most avid consumers of science fiction at the time tended to be scientists, engineers, and others working in technical fields, sug- gesting the genre's capacity to affirm and cultivate a scientific disposition. See Barron, "Why Do Scientists Read Science Fiction?"

19. Dick, *Do Androids Dream of Electric Sheep?*, 150–51.

20. See Jameson, *Archaeologies of the Future*, and Wegner, *Shockwaves of Possibility*. On the ways in which different communities of practice shape the cogntive and social affordances of speculative fiction, including its political horizons, see Hassler-Forest, *Science Fiction, Fantasy and Politics*, and Rieder, *Science Fiction and the Mass Cultural Genre System*.

21. See the documentaries *Trekkies* (1997, dir. Roger Nygard) and *Trekkies 2* (2004, dir. Roger Nygard). See also Jenkins, *Textual Poachers*.

22. See Cusack, "Science Fiction as Scripture."

23. See Krulos, *Heroes in the Night*, as well as the documentaries *Superheroes* (2011, dir. Mike Barnett) and *Legends of the Knight* (2013, dir. Brett Culp). See also Peter Tangen's online photographic exhibit, *The Real Life Superhero Project*, 2011, http://reallifesuperheroes.com.

24. On the history of hacktivism, see Jordan and Taylor, *Hacktivism and Cyberwars*. On Anonymous, the evolution of its activist orientation through online pranks, and its often conflicted commitments to technopolitical justice, see Coleman, *Hacker, Hoaxer, Whistleblower, Spy*; Stryker, *Epic Win for Anonymous*; Olson, *We Are Anonymous*; Wesch et al., "Anonymous, Anonymity"; Greenberg, *This Machine Kills Secrets*; Mitchell, "'Because None of Us Are as Cruel as All of Us'"; Beyer, *Expect Us*; Ravetto-Biagioli, "Anonymous"; Deseriis, *Improper Names*; and W. Phillips, *This Is Why We Can't Have Nice Things*. On the extent to which hackers imagine technical acumen as a means of transforming society, see Kelty, *Two Bits*, and Coleman, *Coding Freedom*. On global icons as symbolic nodes of the collective imagination, see Ghosh, *Global Icons*.

25. ChurchOfScientology [Greg Housch], "Message to Scientology," YouTube, January 21, 2008, https://www.youtube.com/watch?v=JCbKv9yiLiQ.

26. Coleman interviewed in *We Are Legion* (2012, dir. Brian Knappenberger). There is actually a long history of conflict between hacker geeks and the Church of Scientology. In 1995, for example, one of the church's lawyers tried to shut down the alt.religion.scientology Usenet group for distributing proprietary Scientology documents and facilitating abusive discussions of the church. In response, the Cult of the Dead Cow declared war on the church, leading to sustained hacker interest and scrutiny of Scientology as a symbol of information suppression.

27. On the development of LOIC and the practices of DDOS, see Sauter, *Coming Swarm*.

28. "The Chanology Experiments," *Encyclopedia Dramatica*, 2009, https://encyclopediadramatica.se/The_Chanology_Experiments.

29. "Anonymous," Fox 11 News, KTTV Los Angeles, July 26, 2007, archived by LOL Money, "Anonymous on Fox 11," YouTube, July 27, 2007, https://www.youtube.com/watch?v=DNO6G4ApJQY.

30. "Denial of Service," *Encyclopedia Dramatica*, 2011, https://encyclopediadramatica.se/Denial_of_Service.

31. "Chanology Experiments." See also "The Comprehensive Theory of Lulz," *Encyclopedia Dramatica*, 2011, https://encyclopediadramatica.se/The_Comprehensive_Theory_of_Lulz.

32. LulzSec member [Topiary], quoted in Olson, "Interview with PBS Hackers: We Did It for 'Lulz and Justice,'" *Forbes*, May 31, 2011, https://www.forbes.com/sites/parmyolson/2011/05/31/interview-with-pbs-hackers-we-did-it-for-lulz-and-justice/. For a fuller accounting of LulzSec's sometimes principled but generally chaotic motives, see Olson, *We Are Anonymous*; Coleman, *Hacker, Hoaxer, Whistleblower, Spy*.

33. See LulzSec, "LulzSec versus FBI (We Challenge You, NATO!)," Pastebin, June 3, 2011, https://pastebin.com/MQG0a130.

34. Topiary, "You Cannot Arrest an Idea," Twitter, July 21, 2011, 7:02 p.m. (PT), https://twitter.com/atopiary/status/94225773896015872. Topiary was responding to a wave of Anonymous arrests in North America and Europe. His pointed allusion to *V for Vendetta* has become legendary, inspiring further adaptations. The Lizard Squad, for example, has reinvented Topiary's aphorism with a reptilian wink. Following their attacks against various online game servers on November 23, 2014, and promising bigger stunts to come ("Cooking up something nice for later")—perhaps looking ahead to their big Christmas 2014 takedown of the PlayStation Network and Xbox Live—the Lizard Squad tweeted, "You cannot arrest a lizard." See Lizard Squad @LizardPatrol, "You Cannot Arrest a Lizard," Twitter, November 24, 2014, https://twitter.com/LizardPatrol/status/536633313361141760. It has since become one of Lizard Squad's mottos.

35. Video uploaded by CockSec, "LulzSec: ALL YOUR BASE ARE BELONG TO US," YouTube, June 3, 2012, http://www.youtube.com/watch?v=cRZ5fDS_A4Q. *Star Wars* pastiches have been prevalent in the self-narration of hacker culture since the late 1970s; see Mark Crispin, "Software Wars," 1978, archived at *Temple of the Moby Hack*, http://hack.org/mc/writings/hackerdom/softwars.text; Eric S. Raymond, "Unix Wars," *Eric S. Raymond's Home Page*, 1998, http://www.catb.org/esr/writings/unixwars.html; and David Madore, "The Net Wars Trilogy," *David Alexander Madore's Web Site*, 1999, http://www.madore.org/~david/computers/netwars.html.

36. On the logics of conspiracy theory that inform the practices of hacktivism, see Krapp, *Noise Channels*.

37. OpLastResort, "United States Sentencing Commission Owned by #Anonymous," Twitter, January 25, 2013, 8:41 p.m. (PT), https://twitter.com/OpLastResort/status/295028645993517056. The website defacement took place over the span of several hours that night. Although some of the initial changes to the site seemed haphazard, the attack plan had been set up long beforehand.

38. Anonymous, "Operation Last Resort," U.S. Sentencing Commission website, January 25, 2013, http://www.ussc.gov. Approximately twenty minutes before the Sentencing Commission site shut down, the final version of its defacement was archived at Freze, January 26, 2015, 12:43 a.m. (PT), http://freze.it/1mT. The embedded video was uploaded by Aarons ArkAngel, "Anonymous Operation Last Resort," YouTube, January 25, 2013, republished with new captions, January 26, 2013, https://www.youtube.com/watch?v=WaPni5O2YyI.

39. Anonymous, "Operation Last Resort."

40. Anonymous, "Operation Last Resort." OpLastResort was only one—albeit the most spectacular—of several attacks by Anonymous factions around the world against U.S. agencies in retaliation for the death of Aaron Swartz. For an overview of Swartz's life and death, see the documentary *The Internet's Own Boy* (2014, dir. Brian Knappenberger).

41. OpLastResort, "USSC.GOV --> Enter Konami Code," Twitter, January 27, 2013, 2:22 p.m. (PT), https://twitter.com/OpLastResort/status/295657943230210048.

42. On the development of *Asteroids* and its genealogical debts to *Spacewar!*, Atari's 1971 *Computer Space* (itself a commercialized reinvention of *Spacewar!*), Larry Rosenthal and Cinematronics's 1977 *Space Wars* (the pioneering vector-graphics arcade

game, likewise an adaptation of *Spacewar!*), and other ancestors, see Drury, "Making of *Asteroids*," and Burnham, *Supercade*, 62, 184, 194–97. Ed Logg, the developer of *Asteroids*, has often emphasized the *Spacewar!* connection: "For example, when *Asteroids* was in development I used the ideas from *Spacewar!* to provide the game with hyperspace as well as the shape of the player's ship"; Logg, quoted in Lorge and Antonucci, "Game Changers," 49 (foldout sidebar). On the history and design constraints of *Asteroids* and other Atari games of that era, see Montfort and Bogost, *Racing the Beam*.

43. OpLastResort, "USSC.gov Can't Seem to Handle the Traffic," Twitter, January 27, 2013, 8:17 p.m. (PT), https://twitter.com/oplastresort/status/295747510163632128.

44. "Operation Last Resort" game, hosted by the United States Probation Office of the Eastern District of Michigan website, January 27, 2013, http://www.miep.uscourts.gov.

45. John Leyden, "FBI Sends Memo to US.gov Sysadmins: You've Been Hacked . . . for the Past Year," *Register*, November 18, 2013, http://www.theregister.co.uk/2013/11/18/anon_us_gov_hack_warning/. Aside from bank-executive and witness-protection information, whatever data the hackers may have captured during Operation Last Resort has never been publicly released, allowing the criminal justice system to frame the legal and political stakes in an interpretive vacuum; see Follis and Fish, "Half-Lives of Hackers and the Shelf Life of Hacks."

TWO. **Obstinate Systems**

1. On the development of *Adventure*, see Jerz, "Somewhere Nearby Is Colossal Cave." On *Adventure* in the context of interactive fiction and electronic literature, see Montfort, *Twisty Little Passages*; Aarseth, *Cybertext*; and the documentary film *Get Lamp* (dir. Jason Scott, 2010). On the salience of *Adventure* in its particular historical moment—including its status as an ingenious hack—see Lessard, "*Adventure* before Adventure Games." On the ways in which *Adventure* produces a sense of spatial navigation, environmental interaction, and worlding, see M. Wolf, "Genre Profile: Adventure Games"; Chang, "Games as Environmental Texts"; and Seegert, "Doing There vs. Being There." On the flickering signifiers of computational media and the production of navigable space, see Hayles, *How We Became Posthuman*, and Hayles, *My Mother Was a Computer*. To consider *Adventure* in its original computational environment—namely, the TOPS-10 operating system for the DEC PDP-10—research for this chapter relied in part on "TOPS-10 in a Box," packaged and compiled by Jimmy Maher, *The Digital Antiquarian*, May 20, 2011, http://www.filfre.net/2011/05/tops-10-in-a-box/, as well as the SIMH PDP-10 emulator developed by the Computer History Simulation Project, http://simh.trailing-edge.com/. Crowther and Wood's 1977 PDP-10 FORTRAN source code for *Adventure* is available at the Interactive Fiction Archive, curated by Mark Musante, Doug Orleans, and David Kinder, with technical assistance from Goob and Zarf, http://www.ifarchive.org/. Crowther's circa 1976 code is available at Dennis Jerz, "Colossal Cave Adventure Source Code," *Jerz's Literacy Weblog*, http://jerz.setonhill.edu/intfic/colossal-cave-adventure-source-code/.

2. Anderson, "History of *Zork*," 7.

3. See McDonough et al., "Twisty Little Passages Almost All Alike."

4. See Murray, *Hamlet on the Holodeck*; Turkle, *Second Self*; and Golumbia, *Cultural Logic of Computation*.

5. Baudrillard, *Simulacra and Simulation*, 12–13.

6. Crowther, quoted in Peterson, *Genesis II*, 188.

7. Woods, quoted in Francesco Cordella, "Interactive Fiction? I Prefer Adventure [Interview with Don Woods]," *L'avventura è l'avventura*, June 2001, http://www.avventuretestuali.com/interviste/woods-eng/.

8. Woods, quoted in Cordella, "Interactive Fiction?"

9. Brand, "Spacewar," 50. For context, see Turner, *From Counterculture to Cyberculture*; B. Clarke, "Steps to an Ecology of Systems"; and B. Clarke, "From Information to Cognition."

10. "MAGIC adj.," Jargon File 1.2 (1981). Available at the *Jargon File Text Archive*, curated by Steven Ehrbar, http://jargon-file.org/.

11. A. Clarke, *Profiles of the Future*, 21. The third law appears in the 1973 revised edition of *Profiles of the Future*, and, with slightly different language, in A. Clarke, *Report on Planet Three and Other Speculations*, 139. The other two laws are (1) "When a distinguished but elderly scientist states that something is possible, he is almost certainly right. When he states that something is impossible, he is probably wrong"; and (2) "The only way of discovering the limits of the possible is to venture a little way past them into the impossible." Clarke revised the wording of these laws several times, even in later editions of *Profiles of the Future* (see especially his foreword to the Phoenix "Millennium Edition"). On the dispositions of wizard hackers and their relation to fictive archetypes, such as Gandalf and Jedi knights, see Brunton, *Spam*, 17–48.

12. Boluk and LeMieux, "Annotating *Adventure*."

13. Steele et al., *Hacker's Dictionary*, 66–67.

14. Chun, *Programmed Visions*.

15. Levy, *Hackers*, 141.

16. Crowther, quoted in Katie Hafner, "Will Crowther Interview," Internet Archive, 1994, https://archive.org/details/WillCrowtherInterview.

17. Jimmy Maher, "The Completed Adventure, Part 2," *The Digital Antiquarian: A History of Computer Entertainment*, June 3, 2011, http://www.filfre.net/2011/06/the-completed-adventure-part-2/. Woods added this puzzle to Crowther's original game, seemingly motivated by the idea that, since the game's text parser recognizes "BLAST" and other explosive synonyms, there should be some moment in the game when explosions are actually possible; see Jerz, "Somewhere Nearby Is Colossal Cave."

18. Woods, quoted in Hafner and Lyon, *Where Wizards Stay Up Late*, 208. On the extent to which the game informed the practices and dreams of other hackers, programmers, and technology professionals, see Levy, *Hackers*; Montfort, *Twisty Little Passages*; and Nooney, "Let's Begin Again."

19. See Tim Berners-Lee, "Information Management: A Proposal," archived at the World Wide Web Consortium (W3C), March 1989, http://www.w3.org/History/1989/proposal.html.

20. Robinett, "Adventure as a Video Game," 691.

21. Atari, *Adventure: Game Program™ Instructions* (Sunnyvale, Calif.: Atari, Inc., 1980), 1.

22. Robinett, quoted in Jaz Rignall, "'Could They Fire Me? No!' The Warren Robinett Interview," *usgamer*, January 2, 2016, http://www.usgamer.net/articles/warren-robinett-interview.

23. On Robinett's virtuosic approach to the platform limitations of the Atari 2600 as opportunities for innovation, likewise constrained by the uncongenial working conditions at Atari, see Montfort and Bogost, *Racing the Beam*.

24. Robinett, "Adventure as a Video Game," 713, 699.

25. Robinett, quoted in Hague, *Halcyon Days*.

26. Robinett, quoted in Rignall, "'Could They Fire Me? No!'" On Robinett's later impacts on VR and nanotechnology, see Rheingold, *Virtual Reality*; Lenoir, "All but War Is Simulation"; and Milburn, *Mondo Nano*.

27. Dyer-Witheford and de Peuter, *Games of Empire*.

28. Robinett, "Adventure as a Video Game," 713.

29. Adam Clayton, Letter to Atari, Inc., August 4, 1980. A scanned PDF of Warren Robinett's copy of Clayton's original letter was made available as early as 2011 through Scott Stilphen's "Easter Egg Compendium" on *Digital Press: The Video Game Database*, 2011, http://www.digitpress.com/eastereggs/adventure_letter.pdf, and, shortly thereafter, at *2600 Connection: The Complete Atari 2600 Video Computer System Resource*, 2012, http://2600connection.atari.org:80/eastereggs/adventure_letter.pdf, Stilphen has since archived the letter at *Atari Compendium*, March 29, 2017, http://www.ataricompendium.com/game_library/easter_eggs/vcs/adventure_letter.pdf.

30. On the history of the 1983 game market collapse in North America, see Stanton, *Brief History of Video Games*; Campbell-Kelly, *From Airline Reservations to Sonic the Hedgehog*; and Guins, *Game After*.

31. Galloway, *Gaming*; Nichols, "Work of Culture in the Age of Cybernetic Systems"; Dyer-Witheford and de Peuter, *Games of Empire*; Jagoda, "Gamification and Other Forms of Play"; and Milburn, *Mondo Nano*.

32. Wark, *Gamer Theory*, 020.

33. In this regard, *System Shock* echoes Michel de Certeau: "In the arena of scientific research (which defines the current order of knowledge), working with its machines and making use of its scraps, we can divert the time owed to the institution; we can make textual objects that signify an art and solidarities; we can play the game of free exchange, even if it is penalized by bosses and colleagues when they are not willing to 'turn a blind eye' on it; we can create networks of connivances and sleights of hand; we can exchange gifts; and in these ways we can subvert the law that, in the scientific factory, puts work at the service of the machine." See de Certeau, *Practice of Everyday Life*, 27–28. On the ways in which video games both replicate and sometimes resist the corporate logics of the neoliberal era, see Dyer-Witheford and de Peuter, *Games of Empire*.

34. Billy Idol, "Shock to the System," *Cyberpunk* (Chrysalis Records, 1993). On Idol's *Cyberpunk* album in the context of science fiction discourse, as well as the cultural and racial politics of the "shock to the system" motif, see Foster, *Souls of Cyberfolk*.

35. smiley, "SS1—Most Favourite In-Game 'Game'?," *Through the Looking Glass*, July 10, 2003, http://ttlg.com/forums/showthread.php?t=70901.

36. See Kilgore, *Astrofuturism*; Markley, *Dying Planet*; and Stuhlinger and Ordway, *Wernher von Braun*.

37. On games as educational and skill-building tools, see Gee, *What Video Games Have to Teach Us*; S. Johnson, *Everything Bad Is Good for You*; Ching and Foley, *Constructing the Self in a Digital World*; Davidson, *Now You See It*; Ito, *Engineering Play*; and Nguyen, "*Minecraft* and the Building Blocks of Creative Individuality."

38. Kay et al., *System Shock 2: Prima's Official Strategy Guide*, 128–33. On cheat codes, walkthroughs, strategy guides, and other forms of licit illicitness in gamer culture, see Consalvo, *Cheating*, and Consalvo, "*Zelda 64* and Video Game Fans." On paratextual materials as shaping the meaning of gameplay and game narratives, see Jones, *Meaning of Video Games*. On out-of-game practices as reconstituting and renewing the game as such, see Boluk and LeMieux, *Metagaming*.

THREE. **Still Inside**

1. See Burden and Gouglas, "Algorithmic Experience." These same themes extend through *Portal 2* and its pointed satire of corporate agricultural biotechnology; see Wills, "Corporate Agriculture and the Exploitation of Life in *Portal 2*." The GLaDOS-controlled Aperture facility, like the SHODAN-controlled Citadel and *Von Braun*, represents an archetypal space of the military-industrial imagination, what Paul Edwards has called *the closed world*: "enclosed and insulated, containing a world represented abstractly on a screen, rendered manageable, coherent, and rational through digital calculation and control." See Edwards, *Closed World*, 104.

2. Raley, *Tactical Media*, 6, 12. For further analysis of tactical media practices as modes of resistance and critique, see Lovink, *Dark Fiber*; Galloway, *Protocol*; Thacker, *Global Genome*; and da Costa and Philip, *Tactical Biopolitics*.

3. On ways that consumers transformatively appropriate media technologies and media narratives, see Jenkins, *Textual Poachers*; Penley, *NASA/Trek*; Eglash et al., *Appropriating Technology*; and Hilderbrand, *Inherent Vice*.

4. The 2011 graphic novel *Portal 2: Lab Rat*, published by Valve to create retroactive continuity between the first game and its sequel, establishes that the other survivor in the facility is Doug Rattman, a former lab technician at Aperture.

5. GLaDOS's mind games here resemble the infamous Milgram experiment on obedience to authority figures; see Burden and Gouglas, "Algorithmic Experience."

6. Kim Swift, quoted in Elliott, "Beyond the Box," 56 ("Afterthoughts: *Portal*").

7. For a demonstration, see 4perture5cience, "How to Save Your Faithful Weighted Companion Cube!," YouTube, November 27, 2008, https://www.youtube.com/watch?v=drdvWGEt7Vk.

8. On glitching as subversive play that nevertheless affirms the exploratory spirit of gaming, see Consalvo, *Cheating*; Boluk and LeMieux, *Metagaming*; and Schleiner, *Player's Power to Change the Game*. On glitches and glitch gaming as both intrinsic and resistant to the dominant logics of efficiency and control, see Krapp, *Noise Channels*.

9. Magnus Persson, "The Weighted Companion PC," *Bit-Tech*, January 21, 2008, https://www.bit-tech.net/modding/2008/01/21/the_weighted_companion_pc.

10. Paul Miller, "The Weighted Companion PC Isn't Bitter or Anything," *Engadget*, January 21, 2008, https://www.engadget.com/2008/01/21/the-weighted-companion-pc -isnt-bitter-or-anything/.

11. Latour, "Give Me a Laboratory and I Will Raise the World," 258.

12. wearelegionanon2, "GLaDOS Guide to February 10th," YouTube, January 29, 2008, https://www.youtube.com/watch?v=PkMIhR79ujw. The GLaDOS guide drew mainstream media attention to Anonymous, which was until then largely unknown outside of inter-net culture. As *Cinema Blend* reported the following day, "Not much is known about the group [Anonymous] as they have refused to identify themselves on all counts and were instructed to obscure their identities by a familiar voice, GLaDOS. . . . 'Anonymous' has been building support, as was evident yesterday when hundreds of protestors showed up outside of Scientology centers worldwide. Evidence of this, as GLaDOS instructed, has appeared on YouTube in the past twenty-four hours." See Tim Beringer, "GLaDOS Protests Scientology with Anonymous," *Cinema Blend*, February 11, 2008, http://www .cinemablend.com/games/GLaDOS-Protests-Scientology-With-Anonymous-8832.html.

13. anherosipod, "GLaDOS Anonymous Protest Training," YouTube, March 8, 2008, https://www.youtube.com/watch?v=LhW7lZfW57k.

14. NotAnonymousGreenie, "Anonymous Song," YouTube, March 10, 2008, http:// www.youtube.com/watch?v=WYKApdn1e7o.

15. Thetan Bait, "Anonymous: Still Alive II," YouTube, February 2, 2010, http://www .youtube.com/watch?v=ZLRhHCGcYQY.

16. SomeAnonymousPerson1, "A Message to Lt. Pike of UC Davis Police," YouTube, November 20, 2011, https://www.youtube.com/watch?v=XGHX9blEngM.

17. For example, see sexxespat, "Anonymous—Message to Occupy Police," YouTube, November 23, 2011, https://www.youtube.com/watch?v=CjcJWyu3LVU.

18. TWOLF1, "Portal Pepper Spray Cop," *Dorkly*, November 28, 2011, http://www .dorkly.com/post/27991/portal-pepper-spray-cop. On the media dynamics of the Pepper Spray Cop meme, see Milner, *World Made Meme*. On the extent to which the remixed images of the Pepper Spray Cop meme were acts of affirmative speculation akin to science fiction, parodying the present to potentialize a different future, see uncertain commons, *Speculate This!*

19. anonnyminstrel, "Still Alive—Anonymous," YouTube, February 18, 2008, http:// www.youtube.com/watch?v=XFs5ORsAN8s.

20. Miguel Concha, "GLaDOS and Anonymous," YouTube, April 1, 2011, https:// www.youtube.com/watch?v=UF-AEDt3clQ.

FOUR. **Long Live Play**

1. Jay Leno, opening monologue, *Tonight Show*, NBC, May 4, 2011.

2. Matt1246, response to Cybernetic56, in response to Joe Wilcox, "Happy Day! PlayStation Network Is Back Up—Well, Almost," *BetaNews*, May 14, 2011, http:// betanews.com/2011/05/14/happy-day-playstation-network-is-back-up-well-almost/.

3. ted2112, "Remembering the Great PSN Outage of 2011," *Homestation Magazine*, April 16, 2012, http://www.hsmagazine.net/2012/04/remembering-the-great-psn-outage -of-2011/. The date has become commemorative: "April 20 will live in infamy among the PlayStation Faithful as a result of The Great PlayStation Network Outage of 2011" (Colin Moriarty, "One Year Later: Reflecting on the Great PSN Outage," *IGN*, April 20, 2012, http://ps3.ign.com/articles/122/1223464p1.html). As another gamer writes, "We will never forget and here's hoping for a better tomorrow on PSN. ASCEND!!!" (Eric, response to Moriarty, "One Year Later"). And another: "I can never forget about what happened that day!" (xXcloWn23, March 2012, response to curiousjoi, "Enjoiable: PSN Shut Down! Sad Gamers Everywhere!" YouTube, April 27, 2011, https://www.youtube .com/watch?v=IoeOOXmgnkA). And another: "Oh my do I remember the GREAT OUTAGE! It was a, on one hand miserable situation, and on the other hand a real eye-opener. I also learned how much the [PSN] Home community meant to me! I missed Home and all my friends terribly . . . but, in the end we got . . . a greater appreciation for each other and Sony" (Boxer_Lady, response to ted2112, "Remembering the Great PSN Outage of 2011," April 19, 2012). Such performances of remembrance—as often ironic as they are sincere—are now commonplace in the PlayStation community.

4. Matt Parker, "Happy Birthday—A Year on from the PSN Hack," *RinseWashRepeat*, May 2, 2012, http://rinsewashrepeat.co.uk/2012/05/02/happy-birthday-a-year-on -from-the-psn-hack/.

5. ted2112, "Remembering the Great PSN Outage of 2011."

6. On the human and nonhuman aspects of networks, see Galloway and Thacker, *Exploit*. On networks as dominant social models whose pervasiveness becomes most evident in moments of network disruption, see Mejias, *Off the Network*. On the ways in which system-crashing bugs, hacks, spam, viruses, and other network pathologies expose technical functions while also highlighting the conditions for online community, see Parikka, *Digital Contagions*, and Brunton, *Spam*. In *Updating to Remain the Same*, Wendy Chun argues that networks become imaginable and inhabitable through familiarity and repetition. As habitual experiences, they enkindle anxieties of loss— "Habit is becoming addiction: to have is to lose" (8)—refined by crisis, resolved by updating (or, alternatively, respawning in a new direction). As Patrick Jagoda suggests, "Networks, a limit concept of the historical present, are accessible only at the edge of our sensibilities." See Jagoda, *Network Aesthetics*, 3. However, Jagoda shows how networks are rendered perceptible through aesthetic forms and cultural productions (including video games, films, and novels), as well as user discourses and experiences (including ordinary encounters with lag, broken links, crashes, fatal errors, dissapearances) that constitute the network imaginary and articulate its sociopolical affordances. Science fiction, in particular, often serves an important function in situating networked subjects relative to the network imaginary. See Shaviro, *Connected*. Certainly, many PlayStation gamers grappled with the network outage and its implications by resorting to the resources of science fiction.

7. Serres, *Parasite*, 225. Serres's privileged example of a quasi-object is the ball in a ballgame, the focal element in a system of play that binds the players together.

8. Latour, *We Have Never Been Modern*, 89.

9. On the stakes of access, see Mueller, *Ruling the Root*; DeNardis, *Protocol Politics*; Hilderbrand, *Inherent Vice*; MacKinnon, *Consent of the Networked*; and Postigo, *Digital Rights Movement*. On the cultural politics of free and open technoscience, see Kelty, *Two Bits*; Coleman, *Coding Freedom*; and Delfanti, *Biohackers*.

10. See Ken Weeks, "4D Kutaragi 'Live' and Unhinged," *Joystiq*, March 15, 2006, http://www.joystiq.com/2006/03/15/kutaragi-live-and-unhinged/; César A. Berardini, "Kutaragi Superhypes PlayStation Network," *TeamXbox*, March 15, 2006, http://news .teamxbox.com/xbox/10467/Kutaragi-Superhypes-PlayStation-Network/; and Chris Roper, "PS Biz Brief 06: PS3 Is 'Live'," *IGN*, March 14, 2006, http://www.ign.com/articles /2006/03/15/ps-biz-brief-06-ps3-is-live.

11. For example, see Standage, *Future of Technology*, 198–200 ("The Cell of a New Machine"). The Cell processor was developed through a collaboration among Sony, IBM, and Toshiba.

12. Masakazu Suzuoki, "Cell—The Dream Processor," Sony Global, "Interviews with Engineers," vol. 4, 2009, http://www.sony.net/SonyInfo/technology/interview /engineer04.html. For Suzuoki, the idea of an evolving network latent in the Cell's architecture provokes an embodied response, a vital frisson: "When I first heard about the Cell concept, I felt a pure chill of excitement."

13. The notion of "PlayStation DNA" had become part of Sony's marketing repertoire as early as May 9, 2006, when Kazuo Hirai introduced it during Sony's press conference at the 2006 Electronic Entertainment Expo (E3). Hirai had replaced Ken Kutaragi as the president of Sony Computer Entertainment shortly after the launch of the PS3. Celebrating the power of the Cell processor and announcing some new Sony initiatives, Hirai also claimed, notoriously, that the "essence of the PlayStation DNA is real change and the consumers are ready," even as he showcased some rather familiar game concepts. But the notion of "PlayStation DNA" stuck, with a range of associated meanings. In an interview at E3 2010, for example, Hirai suggested a different interpretation: "I think that PlayStation DNA has always been about stability and not making changes midcourse" (quoted in Nick Cowen, "E3 2010: Kazuo Hirai Interview," *Telegraph*, July 7, 2010, http://www.telegraph.co.uk/technology/video-games /7877149/E3-2010-Kazuo-Hirai-interview.html). The flexible notion of "PlayStation DNA" would therefore encompass both "real change" and "stability," revolutionary upgrades as well as "not making changes." In this regard, it might seem rather analogous to the actual hereditary material on which this metaphor is based, affording the transmission of stable genetic traits across generations even in the context of mutation, recombination, and long-term evolutionary forces. Featured in publicity announcements for several PlayStation products, the concept also appeared in a promotional video released for the fifteenth anniversary of the PlayStation brand, *The PlayStation DNA: 15 Years of PlayStation*, available at the Sony Computer Entertainment America "sceablog" channel, YouTube, October 26, 2010, https://www.youtube.com/watch?v =YKpwrC8kk-8.

14. Sony Computer Entertainment, "PlayStation°Vita, PlayStation°3, PSP° (PlayStation°Portable) and PlayStation°2 Retail Sales Exceed 6.5 Million Units Worldwide during the Holiday Sales Season," press release, January 10, 2012. Original document

archived at the Investor Relations News section of Sony's main website, https://www
.sony.net/SonyInfo/IR/news/20120110E.pdf. A similar assertion about PlayStation
DNA and technosocial connectivity had appeared in the first public announcement for
the PS Vita in January 2011, when the device was still codenamed "NGP" ("Next Generation Portable Entertainment System"): "Deep and immersive gaming is at the core
of PlayStation's DNA, and NGP is the latest embodiment of this vision. By having both
Wi-Fi and 3G network connectivity, together with various applications, NGP will enable infinite possibilities for users to 'encounter,' 'connect,' 'discover,' 'share' and 'play'
with friends wherever they are. Within the device are a range of features that provide
a genuinely cutting-edge, next generation ultimate portable entertainment experience"; Sony Computer Entertainment, "Sony Computer Entertainment Announces Its
Next Generation Portable Entertainment System," January 27, 2011, archived at Play-
Station.com, http://us.playstation.com/corporate/about/press-release/next-generation
-portable-entertainment-system.html.

15. Sony, "PlayStation Family: The Best Place to Play—Welcome to the Future of
Play," PlayStation.com, January 1, 2017, https://www.playstation.com/en-us/explore
/playstation-family/. Rob Gallagher offers an incisive analysis of Sony's rhetoric of the
"PlayStation family" and the game industry's obsession with hardware generations
("next-gen consoles") as indicative of heteronormative ways of thinking, a reproductive futurism that gets baked into gamer discourse at large—though the implicit
narrative of progress is sometimes queered by certain video games themselves. See
Gallagher, "Intergenerational Tensions."

16. ADAMPwns, message 31, July 21, 2009, response to gts1234567890, "Getting a Life
on Home," PlayStation Community, July 20, 2009, http://community.us.playstation
.com/t5/PlayStation-Home/Getting-a-life-on-Home/td-p/15568731. In the long-
running "Getting a Life on Home" forum thread and other online discussions, PSN
users took seriously the idea of Home as a place to "get a life," even while often making fun of themselves in the process.

17. Sony Computer Entertainment, "Sony Computer Entertainment Joins Stanford University Folding@Home Program to Further Medical Research," PlayStation
.com, March 15, 2007, http://us.playstation.com/corporate/about/press-release/386.html.

18. Lisa Baertlein, "Sony's PS3 Gives Gamers a Shot at at [sic] Saving Lives,"
MediaFile blog, Reuters, March 15, 2007, http://blogs.reuters.com/mediafile/2007/03
/15/sonys-ps3-gives-gamers-a-shot-at-at-saving-lives/. The claim that the PlayStation
would help save lives was widely repeated. For another example, see Jessica Aldred,
"Turn It On: How Your PlayStation 3 Can Save Lives," Mortarboard blog, Guardian,
March 28, 2007, http://www.guardian.co.uk/education/mortarboard/2007/mar/28
/turnitonhowyourplaystatio.

19. Rimon, quoted in Dave Tach, "After Contributing to the Fight against Alzheimer's, Sony's Folding@Home Lead Reflects on 'Overwhelming' User Support," Polygon,
November 16, 2012, http://www.polygon.com/2012/11/16/3580590/playstation-3-sony
-folding-at-home-alzheimers.

20. Pande, quoted in "Termination of Life with PlayStation," Life with PlayStation,
November 6, 2012, http://www.playstation.com/life/en/index.html.

21. Vijay Pande, "Life with PlayStation Ending, FAH Team Continuing to Look to Push the Envelope," *Folding@home: A Blog All about Folding@home, from Its Director, Prof. Vijay Pande*, October 22, 2012, http://folding.typepad.com/news/2012/10/life-with-playstation-ending.html.

22. For example, see Luttmann et al., "Accelerating Molecular Dynamic Simulation on the Cell Processor and PlayStation 3."

23. Pande, quoted in Ben Dutka, "Guiness Recognizes Power of Folding@home," *PSX Extreme*, October 31, 2007, http://www.psxextreme.com/ps3-news/2080.html.

24. "Michael," dir. Simon McQuoid (Deutsch LA/Sony Computer Entertainment America, 2011).

25. "Double Life," dir. Frank Budgen (TBWA/Sony Computer Entertainment Europe, 1999).

26. crashmash01, "A 'Regular' Story about Me and My Life with PlayStation," *PlayStation Community*, April 7, 2012, http://community.us.playstation.com/t5/PSN-Community-Meets-the-PS-Blog/A-Regular-Story-about-me-and-my-life-with-playstation/td-p/37259218. Interestingly, the *Crash Bandicoot* games featured in crashmash01's autobiography were developed by Naughty Dog, a game company that Vijay Pande (the director of Folding@home) helped to launch while he was still a high school student.

27. Lacan, *Seminar of Jacques Lacan, Book XI*, 198.

28. c_m_f_g, comment #89, April 26, 2011, response to Andrei Dobra, "PlayStation Network Still Down, Might Not Be Fixed for Another Two Days (Updated)," *Softpedia*, April 22, 2011, http://news.softpedia.com/news/PlayStation-Network-Still-Down-Might-Not-Be-Fixed-For-Another-Two-Days-196441.shtml.

29. Patrick Seybold, "Update on PSN Service Outages," *PlayStation.Blog*, April 20, 2011, http://blog.us.playstation.com/2011/04/20/update-on-psn-service-outages-2/#comments.

30. Patrick Seybold, "Updates on PlayStation Network/Qriocity Services," *PlayStation.Blog*, April 22, 2011, http://blog.us.playstation.com/2011/04/22/update-on-playstation-network-qriocity-services/.

31. sephron9, comment #55, April 24, 2011, response to Dobra, "PlayStation Network Still Down."

32. RyuuSkyez, response to Patrick Seybold, "Latest Update on PSN Outage," *PlayStation.Blog*, April 21, 2011, http://blog.us.playstation.com/2011/04/21/latest-update-on-psn-outage/.

33. Reaver, response to Khari Robinson, "Why Is the PSN Network Down?," *Yahoo! Answers*, April 2011, http://answers.yahoo.com/question/index?qid=20110421142611AARiRuF.

34. Sebastian Nygård, "PSN Network Is Down!," YouTube, April 23, 2011, http://www.youtube.com/watch?v=__yLhnwovSc.

35. erick_34, response to Seybold, "Latest Update on PSN Outage."

36. Ambroster, comment #464, April 24, 2011, response to Seybold, "Latest Update on PSN Outage."

37. Jay, response to Robinson, "Why Is the PSN Network Down?"

38. Gideon, "PSN Outage: An Opportunity," *Homestation Magazine*, April 24, 2011, http://www.hsmagazine.net/2011/04/psn-outage-an-opportunity/.

39. stevev363, response to Gideon, "PSN Outage."

40. Dan, "Fold Your Way through the PSN Outage," *One of Swords*, April 28, 2011, http://oneofswords.com/2011/04/fold-your-way-through-the-psn-outage/.

41. Sophronia, response to Patrick Seybold, "Latest Update for PSN/Qriocity Services," *PlayStation.Blog*, April 23, 2011, http://blog.us.playstation.com/2011/04/23/latest-update-for-psnqriocity-services/.

42. Patrick Seybold, "Update on PlayStation Network and Qriocity," *PlayStation.Blog*, April 26, 2011, http://blog.us.playstation.com/2011/04/26/update-on-playstation-network-and-qriocity/.

43. Harrison, quoted in Donald Melanson, "Sony's Phil Harrison Talks PS3 Homebrew Possibilities," *Engadget*, April 23, 2007, http://www.engadget.com/2007/04/23/sonys-phil-harrison-talks-ps3-homebrew-possibilities/.

44. geohot, "Geohot: Here Is Your PS3 Root Key!," *PSX-Scene*, January 2, 2011, http://psx-scene.com/forums/f6/geohot-here-your-ps3-root-key-now-hello-world-proof-74255/.

45. geohot, "Jailbroken PS3 3.55 with Homebrew," YouTube, January 7, 2011, http://www.youtube.com/watch?v=UkLSXsCKDkg. In addition to the "sup dawg" program featured in the video (geohot_1st.self), GeoHot also released a small PS3 application that would create a blank text file called "geohot.txt" (Lv2diag.self).

46. "A Statement of Purpose from Your Anonymous Friends," reposted by AnonymousIsBeast, "Anonymous: Sony Website Hacked (April 1st 2011)," YouTube, April 5, 2011, http://www.youtube.com/watch?v=zMSVTLMyEqI. The video statement was reposted again by several others, including Anon19861, "OpSony: Sony Press Release," YouTube, April 8, 2011, http://www.youtube.com/watch?v=mSiK35dCRgM.

47. Ask PlayStation, "PSN Currently Undergoing Sporadic Maintenance," Twitter, April 4, 2011, 9:35 a.m. (PT), https://twitter.com/AskPlayStation/status/54945167689515008.

48. Anonymous, "OpSony Update, to All," *AnonNews*, April 7, 2011, http://www.anonnews.org/?p=press&a=item&i=797.

49. Hotz, quoted in Patrick Seybold, "Settlement in George Hotz Case: Joint Statement," *PlayStation.Blog*, April 11, 2011, http://blog.us.playstation.com/2011/04/11/settlement-in-george-hotz-case/.

50. George Hotz, "Joining the Sony Boycott," *GeoHot Got Sued*, April 11, 2011, http://geohotgotsued.blogspot.com/2011/04/joining-sony-boycott.html.

51. Anon19861, "Anonymous_ Message to Sony WE RUN THIS . . . ," YouTube, April 12, 2011, http://www.youtube.com/watch?v=0GzPAa9YrTo. The video was widely reposted. For the full press release, see Anonymous, "#OpSony Update, Geohot Settlement, and April 16th IRL Protest," *AnonNews*, April 12, 2011, http://anonnews.org/?p=press&a=item&i=809.

52. AnonOps, "For Once We Didn't Do It," *AnonNews*, April 22, 2011, http://anonnews.org/?p=press&a=item&i=848.

53. Anonymous statement provided to *VGN365*, quoted in Jim, "Anonymous Responds to Halting Attacks on Sony; Releases Statement," *VGN365*, April 22, 2011, http://vgn365.com/2011/04/22/anonymous-responds-to-halting-attacks-on-sony-releases-statement/.

54. Kazuo Hirai, chairman of the board of directors, Sony Computer Entertainment America LLC, "Letter to Mary Bono Mack, Chairman, and G. K. Butterfield, Ranking Member, Subcommittee on Commerce, Manufacturing, and Trade, United States Congress," May 3, 2011, posted to the *PlayStation.Blog*'s Flickr photostream on May 4, 2011, http://www.flickr.com/photos/playstationblog/5686965323/in/set -72157626521862165/.

55. Hirai, "Letter to Mary Bono Mack."

56. George Hotz, "Recent News," *GeoHot Got Sued*, April 28, 2011, http:// geohotgotsued.blogspot.com/2011/04/recent-news.html.

57. The Lulz Boat, "#Sownage (Sony + Ownage)," Twitter, May 29, 2011, 1:16 p.m. (PT), http://twitter.com/LulzSec/status/74932233550569472.

58. The Lulz Boat, "Hey @Sony," Twitter, May 31, 2011, 2:09 a.m. (PT), https://twitter .com/LulzSec/status/75489095371079680.

59. The Lulz Boat, "You Sony Morons," Twitter, May 31, 2011, 10:12 a.m. (PT), https:// twitter.com/LulzSec/status/75610558178668544. Perhaps in response to the growing backlash from the gamer community, however, LulzSec then began to target other online games directly—hacking the servers of *EVE Online*, *Minecraft*, and others—which further enraged many gamers, even some who were otherwise sympathetic to the hacker perspective.

60. Donne, response to Robinson, "Why Is the PSN Network Down?"

61. For examples, see Adrianisen, "Osama bin Laden Sony PSN Account?! Anonymous Help U.S. Government Capture PS3 Terrorist?!," YouTube, May 1, 2011, http://www.youtube.com/watch?v=AX9F6EXcdM8; PSN Survivor, "Osama bin Laden Taken Down Thanks to the Playstation Network?!?!," YouTube, May 1, 2011, https:// www.youtube.com/watch?v=YjF4rjvojaw; and Dan Farrimond, "Source: Bin Laden Found via PlayStation Network," *The Simpleton*, May 6, 2011, http://thesimpleton .squarespace.com/humour/2011/5/6/source-bin-laden-found-via-playstation-network .html.

62. See Will Greenwald, "Bin Laden Might Have Trained Terrorists with a Video Game," *PC Magazine*, May 21, 2015, http://www.pcmag.com/article2/0,2817,2484504,00 .asp. On the digital and hard-copy documents recovered from bin Laden's compound, see "Bin Laden's Bookshelf," U.S. Office of the Director of National Intelligence, May 20, 2015, https://www.dni.gov/index.php/resources/bin-laden-bookshelf.

63. "Osama bin Laden Was Killed for Hacking the PlayStation Network," Facebook, May 2, 2011, https://www.facebook.com/Osama-Bin-Laden-was-killed-for-hacking -the-PlayStation-Network-146288458773719. For a more elaborate version of this joke, see Un-Jokerman, "Sony Breach by Al-Qaeda Helps Find Osama bin Laden; PlayStation Geeks Compensated," *Uncyclopedia: UnNews*, May 2, 2011, http://uncyclopedia .wikia.com/wiki/UnNews:Sony_breach_by_Al-Qaeda_helps_find_Osama_bin _Laden;_Playstation_geeks_compensated. On the tendency of neoliberal discourse to conjoin media piracy with terrorism and murder, see Sarkar, "Media Piracy and the Terrorist Boogeyman," and Hilderbrand, *Inherent Vice*. On the related tendency of digital rights management schemes and copy-protection software to pose as forces of geopolitical stabilization, see Postigo, *Digital Rights Movement*.

64. Marsh Ray, "Sony's Precarious PlayStation 3," *Extended Subset*, April 25, 2011, http://extendedsubset.com/?p=47. For further discussion of this scenario, see Dan Goodin, "Did PlayStation Network Hackers Plan Supercomputer Botnet? Sony 'Arrogance' Fuels Doomsday Scenario," *Register*, April 29, 2011, http://www.theregister .co.uk/2011/04/29/sony_playstation_breach_analysis/; and Michael R. Gideon, "Did PlayStation Network Hack Threaten to Create World's Largest Botnet Super Computer? #PSN," *100gf: Politics and Computers*, May 1, 2011, http://100gf.wordpress.com /2011/05/01/did-playstation-network-hack-threaten-to-create-worlds-largest-botnet -super-computer-psn/.

65. MuffintopX, response to Tor Thorsen, "'External Intrusion' Causing the PSN Outage," *GameSpot*, April 22, 2011, http://www.gamespot.com/news/external-intrusion -causing-psn-outage-6310113.

66. Steven Vargas, "Emergency: PSN Is Down," *The Lazy Geeks*, April 21, 2011, http://thelazygeeks.com/2011/04/21/emergency-psn-is-down/.

67. Joel, "Skynet Wins: Sony Can't Get It Up," *Save Point*, May 9, 2011, http://www .loadsavepoint.com/tag/skynet-wins/.

68. bible-man, message #67, reply to RabidWalker, "PSN Outage and FAQ—Updated Tuesday 18th May," *PlayStation Forum*, April 21, 2011, http://community.eu.playstation .com/t5/PlayStation-Network-General/PSN-Outage-and-FAQ-Updated-Tuesday-18th -May/td-p/12758774.

69. PacManPolarBear, "Folding@Home with Skynet," *Sarcastic Gamer*, February 15, 2008, http://forums.sarcasticgamer.com/showthread.php?t=3822. Other versions of this facetious scenario have often flared up in times of network trouble. For instance, on March 1, 2010, some PS3s were unable to connect to the network due to a clock bug. The YouTube video blogger sWooZie (Adande Thorne) responded to this incident with an animated cartoon called "How Skynet Caused the PS3 Apocalypse," You-Tube, March 5, 2010, http://www.youtube.com/watch?v=KRRpzZYFDRc. The cartoon focuses on a handful of Sony executives trying to manage the crisis. Apparently, a new virus is responsible: "It's like nothing we've seen before. It keeps growing and changing and evolving, like it has a mind of its own." Hoping to reverse the situation before it is too late, the chairman gives the order to uplink the new Skynet defense technology: "If we plug Skynet into all our systems, it'll squash this thing like a bug and give me back control of Sony." But the decision proves fatal. Seconds later, the executives hear sirens and gunfire as Skynet becomes self-aware and launches a war on humanity. When will they ever learn?

70. quaappybla, response to Blazerdt47, "Five Reasons Why the PlayStation Network Is Down," *GameSpot*, April 25, 2011, http://www.gamespot.com/forums/system -wars-314159282/five-reasons-why-the-playstation-network-is-down-28584028/. Similarly, for jho, who reposted the image in figure 4.12, the coincidence of Skynet Day 2011 served as both a convenient metaphor of technocratic control as well as actual evidence of a conspiracy: "Allow me to reiterate my suspicions . . . are we witnessing an internet false-flag designed to introduce the White House's proposed internetID [cybersecurity program]? A case of problem, reaction, solution? Could this be an attempt to piss off the gamers whom are suffering gaming withdraw and concerned

about this happening again? Will they ultimately sacrifice their anonymity online due to the fear of not being able participate in their preferred method of escapism?" Regardless, jho did find some surprising benefits to the recent turn of events: "I definitely had lots of time to meditate and enjoy my family . . . [because] I couldn't play DC Online due to the PSN outage." See jho, "4/21/11 The Day Skynet Becomes Self-Aware," *Synchromysticism*, April 22, 2011, http://www.synchromysticismforum.com /viewtopic.php?f=5&t=2244.

71. Domin666, April 6, 2011, response to Tom Ivan, "Sony Comments on PSN Service Outages: Platform Holder 'Working on a Solution' to Intermittent Service Problem," *Computer and Video Games*, April 5, 2011, http://www.computerandvideogames .com/296812/sony-comments-on-psn-service-outages/.

72. Philip Reitinger, "Enabling Distributed Security in Cyberspace: Building a Healthy and Resilient Cyber Ecosystem with Automated Collective Action," U.S. Department of Homeland Security website, March 23, 2011, https://www.dhs.gov/xlibrary /assets/nppd-cyber-ecosystem-white-paper-03-23-2011.pdf. Under Reitinger's direction, this white paper was originally drafted for a National Protection and Programs Directorate workshop in 2010. On later prospects of security research building from this proposal, see National Protection and Programs Directorate in conjunction with U.S. Department of Commerce, U.S. Department of Homeland Security, and National Institute of Standards and Technology, "RFI-OPO-12-0002: Developing a Capability Framework for a Healthy and Resilient Cyber Ecosystem Using Automated Collective Action," Federal Business Opportunities website (FedBizOpps.gov), September 10, 2012, https://www.fbo.gov/spg/DHS/OCPO/DHS-OCPO/RFI-OPO-12-0002/listing.html.

73. Reitinger, "Enabling Distributed Security in Cyberspace."

74. Stringer, quoted in Stephen Shankland, "CEO: PlayStation Network Growth Recovers after Hack," *CNET*, August 31, 2011, http://www.cnet.com/news/ceo-playstation -network-growth-recovers-after-hack/. Stringer made these comments at the IFA electronics show in Berlin on August 31. Less than a week later, Sony announced Reitinger's hire. See Chloe Albanesius, "After PlayStation Hack, Sony Hires Homeland Security Official," *PC Magazine*, September 6, 2011, http://www.pcmag.com/article2 /0,2817,2392468,00.asp; and Sony Corporation, "Philip R. Reitinger Is Named Senior Vice President and Chief Information Security Officer, Sony Corporation," Sony website, September 6, 2011, http://www.sony.net/SonyInfo/News/Press/201109/11-109E/. Reitinger kept his position at Sony for three years. He departed in September 2014 to start his own security consulting business, VisionSpear.

75. Wraith07, "Zombies of the ApocalyPSN," *PlayStation Forum*, April 30, 2011, http://www.community.eu.playstation.com/t5/General-Discussion/Zombies-of-the -ApocalyPSN/td-p/12795108. For some PlayStation users, however, things would never be quite the same. Years later, without admitting any wrongdoing, Sony settled a $15 million class action lawsuit on behalf of those users whose personal information may have been compromised during the network breach—though Sony representatives also pointed out that no cases of identity theft had ever been credibly linked to the incident, and, of course, the PSN user agreement and privacy policy does clearly state that "there is no such thing as perfect security." See Judge Antony J. Battaglia, "Order

Granting in Part and Denying in Part Defendant's Motion to Dismiss Plaintiffs' First Amended Consolidated Class Action Complaint" (Doc. No. 135), *In Re Sony Gaming Networks and Customer Data Security Breach Litigation*, U.S. District Court for the Southern District of California, MDL No. 11md2258 AJB (MDD), January 21, 2014. Sony distributed more free games and subscriptions to PlayStation Plus as part of the settlement. Afterward, Sony also settled a class action lawsuit on behalf of all the U.S. owners of the original "fat" PS3 who had "suffered injury" from the removal of OtherOS and the erasure of whatever DIY future it represented. See William N. Hebert, Rosemary M. Rivas, and James Pizzirusso, "Second Amended Consolidated Class Action Complaint," *In Re Sony PS3 "OtherOS" Litigation*, U.S. District Court for the Northern District of California, Case No. C-10-1811 (YGR), May 29, 2014. The lawsuit was settled in 2016, but then renegotiated in 2017 after Judge Yvonne Gonzalez Rogers found the claims process to be burdensome for some PS3 owners. Under terms of the second settlement agreement, each injured PS3 owner was eligible to receive up to sixty-five dollars for any pain or damage they experienced due to the loss of technical functionality. For the zombies of the ApocalyPSN, however, it was surely cold comfort.

FIVE. We Are Heroes

1. Miller, quoted in Megan Farokhmanesh, "A Tale of Two Cities: How the City of Heroes Community Is Creating a Successor," *Polygon*, May 2, 2013, http://www.polygon.com/features/2013/5/2/4271302/city-of-heroes-community-phoenix-project.

2. Davies, quoted in Robert Purchese, "City of Heroes and Developer Paragon Studios to Be Closed by NCsoft," *Eurogamer*, September 3, 2012, http://www.eurogamer.net/articles/2012-09-03-city-of-heroes-and-developer-paragon-studios-to-be-closed-by-ncsoft.

3. Andy Belford, "Farewell, from All of Us at Paragon Studios," *City of Heroes®: The World's Most Popular Superpowered MMO*, August 31, 2012, http://na.cityofheroes.com/en/news/news_archive/thank_you.php.

4. Andy Belford [a.k.a. Zwilliger], "To All of You . . . ," *City of Heroes* forums, August 31, 2012, http://boards.cityofheroes.com/showthread.php?t=295790.

5. Belford, "Farewell, from All of Us at Paragon Studios."

6. The economist Edward Castronova has described player investments in MMO characters in terms of "avatar capital," accounting for the accrual of both economic and social value; see Castronova, *Synthetic Worlds*.

7. TonyV, "We Are Heroes. This Is What We Do," Titan Network forums, September 2, 2012, http://www.cohtitan.com/forum/index.php/topic,4882.0.html.

8. On the crystallization of superhero narratives in relation to patriotic imagery, see B. Wright, *Comic Book Nation*, and Goodnow and Kimble, *10 Cent War*.

9. For key examples of these diverse efforts, see Meggan Russell, "Keep NCsoft from Shutting Down City of Heroes!," Change.org, 2012, https://www.change.org/p/ncsoft-keep-ncsoft-from-shutting-down-city-of-heroes; Victoria Victrix [Mercedes Lackey], "Call to Action! Team Wildcard Needs You!," *Save City of Heroes*, November 26, 2012, http://www.savecoh.com/2012/11/call-to-action-team-wildcard-needs-you.html;

Matthew Bennet, "The Save City of Heroes Campaign Reveals NCsoft's Firewall of Silence," *EMG Now*, October 24, 2012, https://www.egmnow.com/articles/news/the -save-city-of-heroes-campaign-reveals-ncsofts-firewall-of-silence/; Ryan Day, "NCsoft: Open Source the Code for City of Heroes/Villains," Change.org, 2012, http://www .change.org/petitions/ncsoft-corp-open-source-the-code-for-city-of-heroes-villains; and RoxziJames, "A Hero to Save," *CNN iReport*, December 5, 2012, http://ireport.cnn .com/docs/DOC-891039.

10. Travis Smith, response to Russell, "Keep NCsoft from Shutting Down City of Heroes!"

11. Brad Parton, response to Russell, "Keep NCsoft from Shutting Down City of Heroes!"

12. Mark Moore, response to Russell, "Keep NCsoft from Shutting Down City of Heroes!" As Katherine Isbister argues, "The combination of these features contributed to [*City of Heroes*] players' emotional and social engagement—deep avatar customizability linked integrally to gameplay and framed with a rich and evolving backstory, and a variety of ways to play together and stay connected." See Isbister, *How Games Move Us*, 62. On the processes of community formation in MMOs and the ways in which playing together allows for insights into the technical affordances and constraints of online communities, see Taylor, *Play between Worlds*; Boellstorff, *Coming of Age in Second Life*; Nardi, *My Life as a Night Elf Priest*; Corneliussen and Rettberg, *Digital Culture, Play, and Identity*; and Mark Chen, *Leet Noobs*. In many instances, as we have seen, the end of an online gameworld and the subsequent gamer diaspora into other online spaces is an occasion for rediscovering the meanings and values that were essential to the original social network, fully recognized only in its loss; see Pearce and Artemesia, *Communities of Play*.

13. Courtney Panos, response to Russell, "Keep NCsoft from Shutting Down City of Heroes!"

14. Nathaniel Reardon [a.k.a. RiskoVinsheen], "City of Heroes Documentary: We Are Heroes, This Is What We Do," YouTube, March 8, 2013, http://www.youtube.com /watch?v=pGcFC197rfQ.

15. Fruzsina Eördögh, "A Eulogy for City of Heroes—How a Video Game Saved My Life," *ReadWrite*, December 4, 2012, http://readwrite.com/2012/12/04/a-eulogy-for-city -of-heroes-how-a-video-game-saved-my-life.

16. Daniel Mages, response to Russell, "Keep NCsoft from Shutting Down City of Heroes!"

17. Michele Alexander-Sichelle, response to Russell, "Keep NCsoft from Shutting Down City of Heroes!" For other examples of the rhetoric of vital online community and the idea of *City of Heroes* as a living technological space, see Shelby Reiches, "In Memoriam: City of Heroes," *Cheat Code Central*, December 7, 2012, http://dispatches .cheatcc.com/dispatches/43#.UVfUtqUx_zI; Ardwulf, "MMO Life Expectancy (or, City of Heroes: A Eulogy)," *Ardwulf's Lair: The Universe of RPGs*, September 3, 2012, http:// ardwulfslair.wordpress.com/2012/09/03/mmo-life-expectancy-or-city-of-heroes-a -eulogy/; Rienuaa, "City of Heroes Died Friday Night," *League of Legends Community*,

December 2, 2012, http://na.leagueoflegends.com/board/showthread.php?t=2856930; and The Geebs That Is a Pony, "RIP City of Heroes," *Penny Arcade*, September 2012, http://forums.penny-arcade.com/discussion/166289/rip-city-of-heroes. On the intense emotional connections that some players had to their avatars, investing them with an uncanny life of their own, see Alec Meer, "City of Heroes: A Farewell to Superarms," *Rock, Paper, Shotgun*, December 4, 2012, http://www.rockpapershotgun.com/2012/12/04/city-of-heroes-a-farewell-to-superarms/.

18. Travis Fleury-Lopez, response to Russell, "Keep NCsoft from Shutting Down City of Heroes!"

19. Kaylan Lyndell-Lees, quoted in Farokhmanesh, "Tale of Two Cities."

20. See Real World Hero, 2013, http://realworldhero.com/. On other charity events organized by players of *City of Heroes*, see Omali, "Save CoH Plays for Charity," *MMO Fallout*, October 22, 2012, http://mmofallout.com/?p=8940; and Maressa, "Unity Event: Extra Life Charity Drive and Gameathon," Titan Network forums, September 28, 2012, http://www.cohtitan.com/forum/index.php?topic=5378.0 ("The City of Heroes community has always been known as one of the most charitable of all the MMO communities out there. This is another chance for us to be the heroes").

21. On the (often conflicted) cosmopolitan and countercultural values propagated by superhero fictions, see Fawaz, *New Mutants*. On the ethical codes and political positions advanced by superhero fictions that make the stakes of heroic action legible in historical context, see Kaveney, *Superheroes!*, and DiPaolo, *War, Politics and Superheroes.*

22. See Marshall, "Borders and Bodies in *City of Heroes*." On toxic discourse and antisocial practices in gamer communities, see Nakamura, "Don't Hate the Player, Hate the Game"; Consalvo, "Confronting Toxic Gamer Culture"; and Salter and Blodgett, "Hypermasculinity and Dickwolves."

23. Stephen Hutchison, response to Russell, "Keep NCsoft from Shutting Down City of Heroes!"

24. michael nagy, response to Russell, "Keep NCsoft from Shutting Down City of Heroes!"

25. For examples, see TonyV, "Announcement: Sentinel+ Character Extractor Available!," Titan Network forums, September 6, 2012, https://www.cohtitan.com/forum/index.php?topic=4971.0; Justin Olivetti, "A City of Heroes Memorial, Part 1," The Game Archaeologist, *Massively*, October 20, 2012, http://i.massively.joystiq.com/2012/10/20/the-game-archaeologist-a-city-of-heroes-memorial-part-1/; and The Geebs That Is a Pony, "RIP City of Heroes." On the players' efforts to archive *City of Heroes* as practices of memorialization, reconstructing the past for unknown future contexts, see Sköld, "Documenting Virtual World Cultures."

26. monsoongibby, November 28, 2012, response to Eliot Lefebvre, "The End of the City of Heroes," A Mild-Mannered Reporter, *Massively*, November 28, 2012, http://massively.joystiq.com/2012/11/28/a-mild-mannered-reporter-the-end-of-the-city-of-heroes/.

27. On the function of exodus and immigration narratives in shaping the figure of the superhero and the emergence of the U.S. comic-book industry, see Tye, *Superman.*

28. Virfortis, November 28, 2012, response to Lefebvre, "End of the City of Heroes."

29. RobertPennington, December 2, 2012, response to Lefebvre, "End of the City of Heroes."

30. LocCo, November 28, 2012, response to Lefebvre, "End of the City of Heroes."

31. NeoConzell, November 29, 2012, response to Lefebvre, "End of the City of Heroes."

32. Lefebvre, "End of the City of Heroes." Nonfictional discussion of these issues, including the ramifications of legal versus illegal routes and examples of ongoing efforts in both directions, have taken place on various message boards, including the Titan Network forums. For example, see the discussion thread started by sindyr, "OK, What Now? I Need a Private Server or the Ability to Run My Own," Titan Network forums, December 6, 2012, https://www.cohtitan.com/forum/index.php?topic=6673.20.

33. "About Us," Missing Worlds Media, 2012, http://www.missingworldsmedia.com/.

34. The media scholar Amanda Phillips, in her talk "Game Over: Permadeath, Virtuosity, and the Mechropolitics of Precarious Masculinities," given at the National Women's Studies Association annual conference in November 2015, has analyzed Iron Man mode as a performance of durability that addresses the uncertainties of social change and the fragility of heteronormative manhood. On the extensive ways in which gamers invent alternative modes of play like Iron Man mode, see Boluk and LeMieux, *Metagaming*.

35. Dan Bull, "Iron Man Mode," YouTube, August 18, 2012, https://www.youtube.com/watch?v=w7fl_7noJd8.

36. On the ways in which Iron Man and other cyborg superheroes have informed discourses of human enhancement, see Oehlert, "From Captain America to Wolverine"; Pedersen and Simcoe, "Iron Man Phenomenon"; Milburn, *Mondo Nano*; and Jeffery, *Posthuman Body in Superhero Comics*.

37. Zeke Iddon, "FAQ," October 30, 2011, *Iron Man Mode: The Blog*, http://www.ironmanmode.com/faq.

38. See, for example, Jose Pagliery, "Meet the Vigilante Who Hacks Jihadists," *CNNMoney*, January 16, 2015, http://money.cnn.com/2015/01/16/technology/security/jester-hacker-vigilante/ ("To some, he's an Internet superhero. Think Batman, with all the vengeance-laden moral qualms of vigilantism included."); Jose Pagliery, "American Vigilante Hacker Sends Russia a Warning," *CNNMoney*, October 26, 2016, http://money.cnn.com/2016/10/22/technology/russian-foreign-ministry-hacked/ ("In the past, Jester has taken down jihadist websites, hacking into communication forums, and identifying potential terrorist threats. Ex-FBI agents have called him 'the Batman of the internet'"); Rhett Jones, "The Batman of the Internet Hacks Russian Government Website, Demands Retribution," *Gizmodo*, October 23, 2016, http://gizmodo.com/the-batman-of-the-internet-hacks-russian-government-web-1788119820 ("Holy cyber attack! The man that former FBI agents have dubbed the 'Batman of the Internet' has returned. And this time he's targeting Russia with one simple message: 'I am vengeance!'").

39. Jeff Stone, "Dridex Hacker Latest 'Gray Hat' to Seek Justice; Internet Vigilantes Target ISIS, Botnets, Other Online Threats," *International Business Times*, February 9, 2016, http://www.ibtimes.com/dridex-hacker-latest-gray-hat-seek-justice-internet-vigilantes-target-isis-botnets-2300463. See also Jai Vijayan, "Online 'Batman' Takes

on Dridex Banking Trojan Operators," *Dark Reading*, February 5, 2016, http://
www.darkreading.com/endpoint/online-batman-takes-on-dridex-banking-trojan
-operators/d/d-id/1324214.

40. Dr. Krypt3ia [Scot Terban], "INFOSEC: The Eternal Struggle," *Krypt3ia*, April 5,
2012, https://krypt3ia.wordpress.com/2012/04/05/.

41. Dr. Krypt3ia, "Handwringing, Moralizing, Anonymous, Paedophilia, and Digital
Vigilantism," *Krypt3ia*, October 28, 2011, https://krypt3ia.wordpress.com/2011/10/28
/handwringing-moralizing-anonymous-paedophilia-and-digital-vigilantism/. See
also Dr. Krypt3ia, "Virtual Arkham: Explaining Anonymous, Lulzsec, and Antisec
Animus in Our Digital Gotham City," *Krypt3ia*, August 19, 2011, https://krypt3ia
.wordpress.com/2011/08/19/virtual-arkham-explaining-anonymous-lulzsec-and-antisec
-animus-in-our-digital-gotham-city/.

42. A Guest, "#OpMaryville—Anonymous," Pastebin, October 14, 2013, https://
pastebin.com/3rqoZSrY. The events of the Maryville case are recounted in the
documentary *Audrie & Daisy* (2016, dir. Bonni Cohen and Jon Shenk), which also addresses the 2012 rape and subsequent suicide of Audrie Pott, as well as other cases of
rape involving cyberbullying and the compounding of tragedy through online media.

43. MetaGameTheory, response to BenwithacapitalB, "Hacker Activist Group
Anonymous Set to Target Rural Missouri Town for Not Prosecuting Rapists," Reddit,
October 14, 2013, https://www.reddit.com/r/news/comments/10g2a5/hacker_activist
_group_anonymous_set_to_target/.

44. UnholyDemigod, "The Boston Bombing Debacle," MuseumOfReddit (archived
post), Reddit, July 23, 2013, https://www.reddit.com/r/MuseumOfReddit/comments
/1iv343/the_boston_bombing_debacle/.

45. honestbleeps, reply to pizzatime, "Is Missing Student Sunil Tripathi Marathon
Bomber #2?," Reddit, April 19, 2013, https://www.reddit.com/r/boston/comments
/1cn9ga/is_missing_student_sunil_tripathi_marathon_bomber/.

46. Jay Caspian Kang, "Should Reddit Be Blamed for the Spreading of a Smear?,"
New York Times Magazine, July 25, 2013, http://www.nytimes.com/2013/07/28
/magazine/should-reddit-be-blamed-for-the-spreading-of-a-smear.html. See also
Alexis C. Madrigal, "#BostonBombing: The Anatomy of a Misinformation Disaster,"
Atlantic, April 19, 2013, https://www.theatlantic.com/technology/archive/2013/04/
-bostonbombing-the-anatomy-of-a-misinformation-disaster/275155/. On the gami-
fication of journalism and playable modes of newscasting, see Bogost, Ferrari, and
Schweizer, *Newsgames*.

47. Nicholas White, "Dot Dot Dot: What Starts on the Web Changes the World,"
Daily Dot, December 10, 2015, https://www.dailydot.com/via/web-changes-world-psy
-bitcoin-spam/.

48. *Batman: Arkham Knight* (Rocksteady Studios, 2015). The Joker—or rather, the
haunting figure of the Joker, emerging from a virus in Bruce Wayne's DNA, tinged by
the Scarecrow's fear toxin and Wayne's own growing guilt—refers specifically to the
events of Alan Moore and Brian Bolland's *Batman: The Killing Joke* (1988) and Jim
Starlin and Jim Aparo's *Batman: A Death in the Family* (1988–89), as well as the overall
arc of the Rocksteady "Arkham" games. While there is a self-critical dimension to the

repeated destruction of Batman's allies in *Batman: Arkham Knight*, drawing attention to Batman's share of culpability in a never-ending cycle of violence, the development of this theme disproportionately makes women into sexualized victims to prop up Batman's character development, recalling the notorious "women-in-refrigerators syndrome." See Gail Simone et al., *Women in Refrigerators*, 1999, http://www.lby3 .com/wir/. The game is awkwardly aware of its own reliance on such plot devices—at one point, a captive Catwoman makes a sarcastic quip about serving as Batman's "motivation"—ironizing its own narrative even while raising questions about the effectiveness of irony in subverting recalcitrant tropes.

49. See Alyssa Royse, "Business Lessons from Batman and *The Dark Knight*," *Start Her Up: For Women Entrepreneurs*, SeattlePi, August 2, 2008, http://blog .seattlepi.com/startherup/2008/08/02/business-lessons-from-batman-and-the -dark-knight/. Although *SeattlePi* closed and removed the comments from this blog post, Royse reproduced a selection of the attacks in her follow-up reflections on this incident. See Royse, "My First Death Threats—And They Weren't from Batman," *Start Her Up: For Women Entrepreneurs* blog, *SeattlePi*, August 3, 2008, http://blog.seattlepi.com/startherup/2008/08/03/my-first-death-threats--and-they -werent-from-batman/; and Royse, "Rape and Death and Batman, OH MY!" *Alyssa Royse*, August 8, 2008, https://alyssaroyse.wordpress.com/2008/08/08/batman/. The legal scholar Danielle Keats Citron has analyzed this incident and dozens of others as evidence for the ways in which the internet creates the conditions not simply for new *kinds* but also for new *scales* of hate crime: "The Internet was key to the formation of the anonymous cyber mob that attacked the journalist [Royse]. It is easy to bring large groups of people together online. Gone are the physical and time restraints that make it difficult and expensive for people to meet in real space. All that is needed is an Internet connection. Whereas cost and geography once prevented individuals from finding one another and from meeting, search engines make it happen with little effort. Networked technologies remove practical barriers that once protected society from the creation of antisocial groups." See Citron, *Hate Crimes in Cyberspace*, 61–62.

50. On the history of these attacks in connection to longer controversies about sexism in video games, see Chess and Shaw, "Conspiracy of Fishes"; Chess, *Ready Player Two*; Kocurek, *Coin-Operated Americans*; and Boluk and LeMieux, *Metagaming*, 275–89. On the role of Quinn's *Depression Quest* within GamerGate conspiracy theories and debates over its status as a game, see Jagoda, "Videogame Criticism and Games in the Twenty-First Century," 208–10. Quinn has offered her own perspective on these events; see Quinn, *Crash Override*. For some GamerGate supporters, journalistic critiques of the movement were taken as evidence of a nefarious plan to invalidate gamers as a demographic. For example, shortly after the creation of the #GamerGate hashtag, several journalists and media critics published their reactions to the harassment of prominent feminists in gaming. A few suggested that the harassment was symptomatic of an ongoing identity crisis, an effort to preserve the subcultural status of the "gamer" identity at a moment when video games had become a ubiquitous and even dominant media form. See, for example, Dan Golding, "The End of Gamers," *Dan Golding* Tumblr blog, August 28, 2014, http://dangolding

.tumblr.com/post/95985875943/the-end-of-gamers; Leigh Alexander, "'Gamers' Don't Have to Be Your Audience. 'Gamers' Are Over," *Gamasutra*, August 28, 2014, https://www.gamasutra.com/view/news/224400/Gamers_dont_have_to_be_your_audience_Gamers_are_over.php; and Luke Plunkett, "We Might Be Witnessing The 'Death of An Identity,'" *Kotaku*, August 28, 2014, http://kotaku.com/we-might-be-witnessing-the-death-of-an-identity-1628203079. Nearly a dozen articles addressing similar themes appeared in short succession, leading some GamerGaters to suspect a coordinated assault. Henceforth known to the GamerGate faithful as the "Gamers Are Dead" articles, these publications were flash points of controversy. For further assessment of gamer identity in the contemporary mediascape, see Shaw, *Gaming at the Edge*, and Golding and van Deventer, *Game Changers*.

51. animemoemoney, "A Quick History of 4chan and the Rightists Who Killed It (Guest Post)," *Noahpinion*, May 2, 2015, http://noahpinionblog.blogspot.com/2015/05/a-quick-history-of-4chan-and-online.html. On the transitions of online trolling cultures and the wider implications for political discourse, see W. Phillips, Beyer, and Coleman, "Trolling Scholars Debunk the Idea That the Alt-Right's Shitposters Have Magic Powers," and W. Phillips and Milner, *Ambivalent Internet*. On situating the political tenor of early 4chan discourse and Anonymous—made especially complicated by certain "lulzy" practices on the 4chan /b/ board that have often used the language of misogyny and racism even if allegedly parodying it—see Manivannan, "Tits or GTFO"; Ravetto-Biagioli, "Anonymous"; Mitchell, "'Because None of Us Are as Cruel as All of Us,'" Fuchs, "Anonymous"; and W. Phillips, *This is Why We Can't Have Nice Things*.

52. Commander X [a.k.a. Chris Doyon], quoted in Caitlin Dewey, "Anonymous, Gamergate, and the Impossible Dream of Vigilante Justice," *Washington Post*, October 27, 2014, https://www.washingtonpost.com/news/the-intersect/wp/2014/10/27/anonymous-gamergate-and-the-impossible-dream-of-vigilante-justice/. Commander X, a prominent yet controversial figure in Anonymous, has sometimes framed his own activities in comic-book terms: "The 'Commander X' persona has become a bit like Batman, a sort of cyber-super hero. But like Batman, the impossible persona of 'Commander X' rests upon the shoulders of a simple man. And like all men, I have frailties, weaknesses—and limits." See Commander X, "Farewell Statement from X," Pastebin, August 27, 2013, https://pastebin.com/fEwdTWKo. He has been on the run from the U.S. government since 2012, fleeing an indictment for his role in organizing a DDOS attack against the county website of Santa Cruz, California, in protest of the county's homeless encampment policies. For his own account of hacktivism and his involvement in Anonymous operations, see Commander X, *Behind the Mask*, and Commander X, *Dark Ops*.

53. Operation GamerGate, "So Much Butthurt," Twitter, October 24, 2014, https://twitter.com/OpGamerGate.

54. Anonymous Watcher, "Anonymous Message to #GamerGate," YouTube, October 29, 2014, https://www.youtube.com/watch?v=L37PDk9ipEM. The Anonymous Watcher account on YouTube notes that "anyone can make one of these shitty videos," emphasizing the multiplicities of Anonymous as a performative identity: a collective that is not one.

55. Max Read, "Did I Kill Gawker? Or Was It Nick Denton? Hulk Hogan? Peter Thiel? Or the Internet?," *New York*, August 19, 2016, http://nymag.com/selectall/2016/08/did-i-kill-gawker.html.

56. The posting was widely recopied—and also widely parodied. The first appearance seems to have been Ssilversmith, in response to SellTheSun, "'[Feminists] Did It to Scientists, They Did It to Sports—The Gamers Were the First Group . . . That Really Fought Back . . . They Like to Win . . . They Were Not the Right Group to Pick a Fight With'—Christina Hoff Sommers," KotakuInAction, Reddit, October 10, 2015, https://np.reddit.com/r/KotakuInAction/comments/3068ia/feminists_did_it_to_scientists_they_did_it_to/.

57. Brianna Wu, "I Watched Dark Knight Again Recently," Twitter, December 6, 2014, https://twitter.com/spacekatgal/status/541360951967358976, and subsequent tweets.

58. Kukuruyo, "GamerGate Life 1," *Kukuruyo Comics and Illustration*, December 3, 2014, modified October 3, 2016, http://kukuruyo.com/comic/gamergate-life-1/.

59. Kukuruyo, "GamerGate Life 54 (English)," *Kukuruyo Comics and Illustration*, August 1, 2015, http://kukuruyo.com/comic/gamergate-life-54-english/.

60. TastetheSweet, response to Chewiemuse, "I've Had Enough of Anti [Gamer-Gate] sjw's Comparing Themselves to Batman," KotakuInAction, Reddit, February 15, 2015, https://www.reddit.com/r/KotakuInAction/comments/2vyohh/ive_had_enough_of_anti_sjws_comparing_themselves/.

61. GarytheBum, reply to fearghul, "Showerthought," KotakuInAction, Reddit, April 9, 2016, https://www.reddit.com/r/KotakuInAction/comments/4e155g/showerthought_the_media_is_jj_jameson_and/.

62. fearghul, "Showerthought," KotakuInAction, Reddit, April 9, 2016, https://www.reddit.com/r/KotakuInAction/comments/4e155g/showerthought_the_media_is_jj_jameson_and/; LordRaa, response to Spectral-Ninja, response to Chewiemuse, "I've Had Enough of Anti [GamerGate] sjw's."

63. Spectral-Ninja, response to Chewiemuse, "I've Had Enough of Anti [Gamer-Gate] sjw's."

64. Milo Yiannopoulos, "Unlike Video Game Console Launches," Twitter, February 20, 2013, and Milo Yiannopoulos, "Few Things Are More Embarrassing," Twitter, February 20, 2013, https://twitter.com/Nero/status/304385532367106048. He featured the moniker of the "most fabulous supervillain on the internet" on his Twitter account, https://twitter.com/Nero, as well as his Facebook page, https://www.facebook.com/myiannopoulos/, and other personal media pages. Yiannopoulos's Twitter account was permanently suspended on July 19, 2016, due to his sustained usage of the platform for abusive purposes and for inciting harassment against various people, including the actress Leslie Jones. On Yiannopoulos's remarkably changed opinions about video games, see Xavier Glitch (a.k.a. Pedro Castilho), "The GamerGate-Supporting Journalist Who Hates Gamers," *Storify*, November 2014, https://storify.com/x_glitch/the-gamergate-supporting-journalist-who-hates-game. On the paradoxes and complexities of Yiannopoulos's rise as a star of the alt-right, as well as his spectacular downfall in 2017 due to comments he made in support of pedophilia, see Bob Ostertag, "Silencing Milo," *Huffington Post*, January 6, 2017, http://www.huffingtonpost.com/entry

/silencing-milo_us_586f3975e4b0eb9e49bfba52; and Bob Ostertag, "Milo Yiannopou-los on Pedophilia and 'This Arbitrary and Oppressive Idea of Consent,'" *Huffington Post*, February 20, 2017, http://www.huffingtonpost.com/entry/milo-yiannopoulos-on -pedophilia-and-this-arbitrary_us_58ab52a5e4b029c1d1f88d77. On GamerGate as an element contributing to the rise of the alt-right, see Nagle, *Kill All Normies*.

65. GitGud, "Don't Forget the Words of Bane," Twitter, November 5, 2014, https:// twitter.com/gitgudgg/status/530233883397455872. The Bane quotation is from *The Dark Knight Rises* (2012, dir. Christopher Nolan).

66. MGRourke, "Brianna Wu Is Batman," reply to fearghul, "Showerthought."

67. See Braithwaite, "It's about Ethics in Games Journalism?," and Mortensen, "Anger, Fear, and Games."

SIX. Green Machine

1. See Dyer-Witheford and de Peuter, *Games of Empire*, 222–24, and Maxwell and Miller, "'Warm and Stuffy.'" On the material infrastructures and global supply chains of media technologies that contribute to environmental risk, see Bozak, *Cinematic Footprint*; Cubitt, *Finite Media*; Maxwell and Miller, *Greening the Media*; Parikka, *Geology of Media*; Starosielski and Walker, *Sustainable Media*; and Taffel, "Escaping Attention."

2. See Hari, "Congo's Tragedy"; Lasker, "Inside Africa's PlayStation War"; and Frec-cia, "PlayStation War." Johann Hari first coined the phrase "PlayStation War" in his essay "A Journey into the Most Savage War in the World: My Travels in the Demo-cratic Vacuum of Congo," JohannHari.com, May 7, 2006, http://www.johannhari.com /archive/article.php?id=863. This essay is a slightly different version of his published article "Congo's Tragedy."

3. See Montague, "Stolen Goods"; Jackson, "Making a Killing"; Moyroud and Katunga, "Coltan Exploration in Eastern Democratic Republic of the Congo"; Mantz, "Improvisational Economies"; and Smith, "Tantalus in the Digital Age." In the United States, the 2010 Dodd-Frank Act included a provision requiring electron-ics manufacturers to prove that their supply chains do not support armed conflict in Africa. While it was an important step in trying to address the problem of conflict minerals, the long-term efficacy of this kind of legislation remains unclear, because the global mineral trade often promotes mystery and obfuscation.

4. Oona King, quoted in Hari, "Congo's Tragedy."

5. See Wakabi, "Arms Smugglers"; Lasker, "Inside Africa's PlayStation War"; Dyer-Witheford and de Peuter, *Games of Empire*, 223; and Mantz, "Improvisa-tional Economies." On Sony's own uncertainty about the supply chain mix, see Noah Shachtman, "Inside Africa's 'PlayStation War,'" *Wired*, July 15, 2008, https://www.wired .com/2008/07/the-playstation-2/.

6. See Smith and Mantz, "Do Cellular Phones Dream of Civil War?," and Nest, *Coltan*.

7. Redmond, *Coltan Boom, Gorilla Bust*, 4. For a similar, updated assessment of the situation, see Plumptre et al., *Status of Grauer's Gorilla and Chimpanzees in Eastern Democratic Republic of Congo*. For further context, see Hayes and Burge, *Coltan*

Mining in the Democratic Republic of Congo, and Glew and Hudson, "Gorillas in the Midst."

8. See Gabrys, *Digital Rubbish*; Grossman, *High Tech Trash*; and Parks, "Falling Apart."

9. See Delforge and Horowitz, *Latest-Generation Video Game Consoles*; Webb et al., "Estimating the Energy Use of High Definition Games Consoles"; Desroches et al., "Video Game Console Usage and U.S. National Energy Consumption"; Mills and Mills, "Taming the Energy Use of Gaming Computers"; and Mayers et al., "Carbon Footprint of Games Distribution."

10. On games and playable media as mediating environmental and technological modes of perception, see Chang, "Games as Environmental Texts"; Chang and Parham, "Green Computer and Video Games"; Bealer, "Eco-Performance in the Digital RPG Gamescape"; Heise, *Sense of Place and Sense of Planet*; Kelly and Nardi, "Playing with Sustainability"; Abraham, "Video Game Visions of Climate Futures"; and Swanstrom, *Animal, Vegetable, Digital*.

11. Beck, *World Risk Society*, 9. On the extent to which *risk media* cultivate eco-political perceptions, see Cubitt, *Ecomedia*; Ziser and Sze, "Climate Change, Environmental Aesthetics, and Global Environmental Justice Cultural Studies"; Heise, *Sense of Place and Sense of Planet*; and Mayer and Weik von Mossner, *Anticipation of Catastrophe*.

12. Foucault, *Discipline and Punish*, 202–3. See also Foucault, *Birth of the Clinic* and *Order of Things*. On the history of the carceral function as rendered through narrative fictions and the structures of novelistic discourse, see Bender, *Imagining the Penitentiary*. On ways that video games promote social discipline, see Chess, "Playing the Bad Guy."

13. See Douglas, *Purity and Danger*; Kristeva, *Powers of Horror*.

14. See Agamben, *Homo Sacer*; Agamben, *State of Exception*.

15. Deleuze, "Postscript on the Societies of Control," 3–4.

16. See Wiener, *Cybernetics*; Wiener, *Human Use of Human Beings*.

17. On the history of cybernetics and its impact on scientific and cultural production, see Hayles, *How We Became Posthuman*; Galloway, *Protocol*; Halpern, *Beautiful Data*; Heims, *Constructing a Social Science for Postwar America*; Edwards, *Closed World*; L. Kay, *Who Wrote the Book of Life?*; Pickering, *Cybernetic Brain*; and B. Clarke and Hansen, *Emergence and Embodiment*. On the role of cybernetic models in the ecological sciences, see Bowler, *Earth Encompassed*; Hagen, *Entangled Bank*; Golley, *History of the Ecosystem Concept in Ecology*; Edwards, *Vast Machine*; B. Clarke, "Steps to an Ecology of Systems"; Horton, "Collapsing Scale"; and Schwarz and Jax, *Ecology Revisited*.

18. Galloway, *Gaming*, 106. On games as self-figuring instances of cybernetic systems and the form of control societies, see also Nichols, "Work of Culture in the Age of Cybernetic Systems"; Salen and Zimmerman, *Rules of Play*; Wark, *Gamer Theory*; Dyer-Witheford and de Peuter, *Games of Empire*; and Jagoda, "Gamification and Other Forms of Play." While games often reinforce the experience of cybernetic control, they sometimes work to confound or diminish control, emphasizing elements of uncontrollability and nonsovereign connections in network systems; see Jagoda, *Network Aesthetics*, 143–80.

19. Bang, Torstensson, and Katzeff, "PowerHouse," 128–29.

20. Bang, Gustafsson, and Katzeff, "Promoting New Patterns in Household Energy Consumption with Pervasive Learning Games," 58–59.

21. Deleuze, "Postscript on the Societies of Control," 7.

22. Reeves et al., "Increasing Energy Efficiency with Entertainment Media."

23. Gordon, March 14, 2013, reply to Susie Cagle, "The New *SimCity*: Green Urbanist Dream, Gamer Nightmare," *Grist*, March 12, 2013, http://grist.org/news/the-new-simcity-green-urbanist-dream-gamer-nightmare/. See also James Sinclair, "*SimCity* 5 Arrives to Abysmal Reviews, 1950's Planning," *Stop and Move*, March 8, 2013, http://stopandmove.blogspot.com/2013/03/simcity-5-arrives-to-abysmal-reviews.html.

24. Haraway, *When Species Meet*, 71.

25. On countergaming, see Galloway, *Gaming*; Dyer-Witheford and de Peuter, *Games of Empire*; and Raley, *Tactical Media*.

26. On gray goo and its figurative role in nanotechnology discourse, see Milburn, *Nanovision*.

27. marydell, "Re: Tasty Planet," *Whateveresque*, September 9, 2007, http://whateveresque.com/phpBB3/viewtopic.php?f=14&t=66; Joshalos, lewiss4455 and Pandermatism, comments in "Tasty Planet" thread, *Kongregate*, February 12, 2011, August 24, 2012, and December 22, 2012; and icicie, comment in "Tasty Planet: DinoTime" thread, *Kongregate*, December 7, 2011, http://www.kongregate.com/games/dingogames/tasty-planet-dinotime/comments.

28. santaclaws11, Biddybuddy, BonesJustice7, and armando602, comments in "Tasty Planet" thread, *Kongregate*, February 21, April 29, February 24, and November 3, 2011, http://www.kongregate.com/games/dingogames/tasty-planet/comments; and kouredios, "Tasty Planet," *Whateveresque*, September 3, 2007, http://whateveresque.com/phpBB3/viewtopic.php?f=14&t=66.

29. mysticicedragon3, LittleFanGirl, Brogers44, and kingsnake6666, comments in "Tasty Planet" thread, *Kongregate*, November 19, 2011, December 24, 2011, May 28, 2012, and April 10, 2011, http://www.kongregate.com/games/dingogames/tasty-planet/comments; FANBUSCUS, comment for "Tasty Planet: DinoTime" thread, *Kongregate*, December 8, 2012, http://www.kongregate.com/games/dingogames/tasty-planet-dinotime/comments; and DarkraiPrince and DCervan, comments in "Tasty Planet" thread, *Kongregate*, December 12 and December 11, 2012, http://www.kongregate.com/games/dingogames/tasty-planet/comments.

30. StarProgrammer, comment for "Tasty Planet: DinoTime" thread, *Kongregate*, December 7, 2011, http://www.kongregate.com/games/dingogames/tasty-planet-dinotime/comments; and Merido, comment in "Tasty Planet" thread, *Kongregate*, February 2, 2011, http://www.kongregate.com/games/dingogames/tasty-planet/comments.

31. For discussions of playbor and other forms of immaterial labor that sustain the digital economy, see Kücklich, "Precarious Playbour"; Postigo, "From *Pong* to *Planet Quake*"; Dyer-Witheford and de Peuter, *Games of Empire*; Terranova, *Network Culture*; Castronova, *Synthetic Worlds*; Yee, "Labor of Fun"; Goggin, "Playbour, Farming and Labour"; Scholz, *Digital Labor*; and Jagoda, "Gamification and Other Forms of Play."

32. wquach, "A Tribute to 'Shadow of the Colossus,'" N4G, September 11, 2011, http://n4g.com/user/blogpost/wquach/518464.

33. BlackFeathers, "Shadow of the Colossus. This Game Is Sooo Sad," *GameFAQs*, October 9, 2011, http://www.gamefaqs.com/boards/998181-the-ico-and-shadow-of-the -colossus-collection/60593475.

34. ferdk16, response to BlackFeathers, "Shadow of the Colossus."

35. Henry Phillips, "Games and Love: *Shadow of the Colossus*," *Taufmonster's Log*, February 14, 2012, http://taufmonster.blogspot.com/2012/02/games-and-love-shadow -of-colossus.html.

36. Alex Higgins, "Shadow of the Colossus and the Unique Capabilities of Games for Storytelling," *Beta Fish Mag*, December 20, 2012, http://betafishmag.wordpress .com/2012/12/20/shadow-of-the-colossus-and-the-unique-capabilities-of-games-for -storytelling/. On ways in which transspecies narration in different media forms contributes to a posthumanist ethics, see Wolfe, *What Is Posthumanism?*; McHugh, *Animal Stories*; Vint, *Animal Alterity*.

37. Tornadosaurus Rex, October 11, 2010, response to Sean Beanland, "Shadow of the Colossus—I Feel So Sad," *Alethiometry*, February 5, 2008, http://seanbeanland .blogspot.com/2008/02/shadow-of-colossus-i-feel-so-sad.html.

38. Akshay Mathew, "How Shadow of the Colossus Taught Me Empathy," *How Games Saved My Life*, http://www.gamessavedmylife.com/post/10561678024/how -shadow-of-the-colossus-taught-me-empathy.

SEVEN. **Pwn**

1. Sour Grape, in response to lynm pahcuh, "FFVII vs. FFVIII," *Square Insider*, March 23, 2005, http://www.squareinsider.com/forums/index.php?showtopic=19295.

2. Baka Neko, in response to cosmic999, "Does Anyone Still Play This?," *Neoseeker*, May 25, 2008, http://www.neoseeker.com/forums/1169/t1161488-does-anyone-still -play-this/.

3. Master_Moron, May 12, 2006, in response to ToneDizzle05, "Anything Final Fantasy VII," *Rooster Teeth*, July 1, 2005, http://roosterteeth.com/forum/playstation /topic/2167862?page=140.

4. KylesKingdomHearts, "Final Fantasy VII Frigin Pwns Anyone and Anything!!!" You-Tube, October 10, 2009, https://www.youtube.com/playlist?list=PLE20DDFFD08C15371.

5. Legendary Nick, "Final Fantasy 7," *Urban Dictionary*, May 28, 2005, http://www .urbandictionary.com/define.php?term=Final+Fantasy+7&defid=1285455.

6. For summations of these widespread internet theories, see "Pwned," *Urban Dictionary*, http://www.urbandictionary.com/define.php?term=pwned; and soaps-cum, "Owned (Pwned)," *Know Your Meme*, 2009, http://knowyourmeme.com/memes /owned-pwned.

7. Sora_lion_heart, in response to Bambi, "Birds Nest on Mt Corel," *Final Fantasy Forums*, October 25, 2008, http://www.finalfantasyforums.net/threads/24277-Birds -Nest-on-Mt-Corel; Siara_Sendai, in response to chaosinwriting, "The Treasure in the Baby Bird's Nest on the Mt. Corel Train Tracks," *GameFAQs*, 2012, http://www .gamefaqs.com/boards/130791-final-fantasy-vii/64181986; MadMonkey and poker king46 in response to Bambi, "Birds Nest on Mt Corel."

8. Bambi, "Birds Nest on Mt Corel"; Sohryuden666 and joeyfinalfantasygod, in response to Bambi, "Birds Nest on Mt Corel."

9. Caostotale, in response to Cadtalfryn, "Games with Environmental Themes," *Destructoid*, August 14, 2010, http://forum.destructoid.com/showthread.php?19383 -Games-with-environmental-themes.

10. Heidegger, "Question Concerning Technology."

11. The concept of ludonarrative dissonance was coined by the game designer Clint Hocking. For discussion, see Bissell, *Extra Lives*.

12. See Nixon, *Slow Violence and the Environmentalism of the Poor*.

13. On ways that games compel learning through error, see Juul, *Art of Failure*. On ways that characteristics of game avatars affect perceptions and behaviors of their players, see Yee, *Proteus Paradox*. On Cloud as a self-reflexive avatar of the player, see Burn, "Playing Roles."

14. Pseudonym2, in response to Fightgarr, "Environmentalism and Games," *The Escapist*, January 15, 2009, http://www.escapistmagazine.com/forums/read/9.83914 -Environmentalism-and-Games.

15. LegendofLegaia, in response to Ultima_Terror, *GameFAQs*, 2011, http://www .gamefaqs.com/boards/605802-dissidia-012-duodecim-final-fantasy/61004655.

16. See Heidegger, "Question Concerning Technology." For some players, *Final Fantasy VII* is an introduction to such philosophical issues. As one player attests, "I learned of Heidegger" from playing this game. See DJZen, April 30, 2005, in response to Jojee, "How Has FFVII Changed Your Perception of Life?," *Eyes on Final Fantasy*, April 30, 2005, http://home.eyesonff.com/showthread.php/61134-How-has-FFVII-changed-your -perception-of-life. On the ways in which *Final Fantasy VII* figures the history of environmental destruction as also occasioning a more sustainable relation of nature and technology—affirming convergence, symbiosis, and cultural syncretism over oppositional conflict—see Mitropoulos, "Shinto and Alien Influences in *Final Fantasy VII*."

17. While the ambiguous ending makes it unclear whether the whole of civilization, or instead Midgar alone, was destroyed in the final conflict, the 2005 sequel movie *Final Fantasy VII: Advent Children* retcons in favor of the latter situation, indicating that the remaining human population eventually transitioned away from the Mako economy. Regardless, the thematic implications of the game's coda remain the same, as several players have argued:

> When watching the ending to FF7, you have to remember that the crux of
> the story is based around themes of environmentalism. When you do that,
> then the meaning of the ending becomes entirely clear: No matter how badly
> we mistreat it, the planet will always eventually recover, and it will always
> defend itself. But when it does respond to the pollution and the abuse that
> we have put it to, it may well decide (symbolically of course) that humanity
> is no longer welcome, and in defending itself it may well wipe us out. That
> is what the ruins of Midgar stand for. The planet is still there, and it is still
> alive, but it may well be that while the planet was able to survive, humanity
> was not.

When you look at the impending threat of climate change, the melting of the ice caps and the rising of the sea levels, the increase in drought and famine across the world, then it is easy to see the poignancy of the game's message. It would be the simplest thing for Planet Earth to wipe out humanity in the course of responding to the pollution and stripping of the environment we are responsible for, and such a cataclysm becomes more likely every day that we leave these environmental issues unaddressed. (j-e-f-f-e-r-s, in response to Firefilm, "Worst Videogame Ending Ever," *The Escapist*, April 23, 2012, http://www.escapistmagazine.com /forums/read/6.372664-Worst-Videogame-Ending-Ever?page=1)

18. Some politically conservative players adore the game intensely even while denying the reality of global warming and other environmental problems. See the discussion started by LuvBatenKaitos, "Does Anyone Else Get These Vibes? (Possible Spoilers)," *GameFAQs*, November 11, 2013, http://www.gamefaqs.com/boards /197341-final-fantasy-vii/67872771. Other players find such attitudes to be shocking: "I wondered immediately, 'How can someone who views environmentalism as "annoying hippyism" possibly be a fan of a decade of FF games more or less devoted to that very theme?' . . . I'm still really shocked that someone who'd chalk up one of the major themes of the game as 'annoying hippyism' could possibly finish FF7, having to hear all of this information about the lifestream and how to use it to save the world. . . . I'm still rather mystified as to how people so averse to what I consider to be major themes through the FF series can sit through hundreds of hours of FF gameplay and dialogue." See Paul Goshi, "Conservative Attitudes and Final Fantasy," *RPG Gamer*, 2004, http://www.rpgamer.com/editor/2004/q1/030104pg.html.

19. Jon Hochschartner, "'Final Fantasy,' Capitalism, and the Environment," *People's World*, October 24, 2013, http://peoplesworld.org/final-fantasy-capitalism-and-the -environment.

20. Jiro, "FFVII Preempting Climate Change Movement," *Eyes on Final Fantasy*, December 24, 2013, http://home.eyesonff.com/archive/index.php/t-153624.html.

21. Ender, "A Final Fantasy VII Take on World Issues," *The Final Fantasy VII Citadel*, 2000, http://ff7citadel.com/efiction/viewstory.php?sid=69.

22. Bretth2, "Game Analysis: Final Fantasy VII," *ENG 380*, University at Buffalo, June 21, 2013, http://eng380newmedia.wordpress.com/2013/06/21/game-analysis-final -fantasy-vii.

23. Loveless [a.k.a. Casimir], "What Are You Happy That Video Games Taught You?," *Nerd Fitness Rebellion*, November 26 and November 27, 2013, http://rebellion .nerdfitness.com/index.php?/topic/40752-what-are-you-happy-that-video-games -taught-you; Seraf, KoShiatar, Ravendale, and MercenX, in response to Jojee, "How Has FFVII Changed Your Perception of Life?" *Eyes on Final Fantasy*, April 30, 2005, http://home.eyesonff.com/showthread.php/61134-How-has-FFVII-changed-your -perception-of-life.

24. See Newman, *Best Before*, and Guins, *Game After*. Relatedly, see Sterne, "Out with the Trash"; Parks, "Falling Apart." On the upgrade drives of digital culture, see Harpold, *Ex-Foliations*; Chun, *Updating to Remain the Same*.

25. The Sentient Meat, in response to Jason Schreier, "This *Minecraft* Recreation of *Final Fantasy VII*'s Midgar Is Absurdly Detailed," *Kotaku*, April 17, 2012, http://kotaku.com/5902834/this-minecraft-recreation-of-final-fantasy-viis-midgar-is-absurdly-detailed.

26. Stiegler, "Distrust and the Pharmacology of Transformational Technologies." On the *pharmakon*—and, in particular, the extent to which the history of occidental thought has rendered the technics of writing as *pharmakon*, both poison and remedy—see Derrida, *Dissemination*.

Conclusion

1. Quotation from the box cover of the North American release of *Animal Crossing: Wild World* (Nintendo, 2005).

2. The technical systems underlying the world of *Animal Crossing: Wild World* have become especially pronounced since the discontinuation of the Nintendo wfc service in 2014. Today, players wanting to travel to other villages in this game must either rely on the local multiplayer function of the ds or instead figure out how to connect to rogue servers using illicit software or hardware hacks. The disappearance of Nintendo's official remote networking service for the game has therefore rendered the bucolic narrative frame inextricable from high-tech skills and knowledge. On the ways in which the aesthetics of video games and other forms of twenty-first-century media make visible the cultural imaginaries of computational networks, see Jagoda, *Network Aesthetics*.

3. Chun, *Updating to Remain the Same*, 19.

4. Chun, *Updating to Remain the Same*, 89–90.

5. See the October 2012 discussion between Satoru Iwata (Nintendo's president from 2002 until his death in 2015) and the *Animal Crossing: New Leaf* developers Koji Takahashi, Isao Moro, and Ana Kyogoku, "Iwata Asks—*Animal Crossing: New Leaf*," *Iwata Asks*, Nintendo website, April 2013 (English translation), http://iwataasks.nintendo.com/interviews/#/3ds/animalcrossing-newleaf. Kyogoku reported, "We really weren't sure about [including] Mr. Resetti, as he really divides people. Some people love him, of course, but there are others who don't like being shouted at in his rough accent." Iwata confirmed this anecdotal evidence: "It seems like younger female players, in particular, are scared. I've heard that some of them have even cried." It could be asked whether such rumors, seemingly based on gender stereotypes, might rather imply that some players have understood the deeper meanings of Resetti's philosophical rants— and their legitimately disconcerting implications—more intelligently than others.

6. Doctorow, *For the Win*, 443.

7. Cline, *Ready Player One*, 60.

8. Cline, *Ready Player One*, 364.

9. On the thesis that the foundations of contemporary technoculture were shaped in the 1980s, especially by the decade's pop media, see Sirota, *Back to Our Future*. Cline's *Ready Player One* as well as his 2016 novel *Armada* present more or less the same thesis, albeit in the guise of fiction.

10. *Ready Player One* is narrated retrospectively, written from Wade's first-person perspective as an older man looking back on his youth. He introduces himself at the beginning of the text as a well-known celebrity, composing his memoirs for an imagined audience in the future eager to know all about his exploits as a teenager. However, this fabulated future audience does not seem to know much about the OASIS, because Wade actually has to explain what it meant to him back in the day: "I'd heard of Halliday, of course. Everyone had. He was the videogame designer responsible for creating the OASIS, a massively multiplayer online game that had gradually evolved into the globally networked virtual reality most of humanity now used on a daily basis" (1). Wade's presumption that his readers may not quite remember Halliday or the world-defining impact of the OASIS may imply that that system no longer exists or has significantly changed its nature by the time Wade sits down to write his memoirs.

11. See Haraway, *Staying with the Trouble*; Alaimo, *Exposed*; and Weston, *Animate Planet*. As Haraway suggests, in the midst of trouble, we must not give in to what she calls a "game over" attitude: "In fact, staying with the trouble requires learning to be truly present, not as a vanishing pivot between awful or edenic pasts and apocalyptic or salvific futures, but as mortal critters entwined in myriad unfinished configurations of places, times, matters, meanings" (1).

Aarseth, Espen. *Cybertext: Perspectives on Ergodic Literature.* Baltimore: Johns Hopkins University Press, 1997.

Abraham, Benjamin. "Video Game Visions of Climate Futures: ARMA 3 and Implications for Games and Persuasion." *Games and Culture* 13 (2018): 71–91.

Agamben, Giorgio. *Homo Sacer: Sovereign Power and Bare Life.* Translated by Daniel Heller-Roazen. Stanford, Calif.: Stanford University Press, 1998.

Agamben, Giorgio. *State of Exception.* Translated by Kevin Attell. Chicago: University of Chicago Press, 2005.

Alaimo, Stacy. *Exposed: Environmental Politics and Pleasures in Posthuman Times.* Minneapolis: University of Minnesota Press, 2016.

Allen, Robertson. *America's Digital Army: Games at Work and War.* Lincoln: University of Nebraska Press, 2017.

Altice, Nathan. *I Am Error: The Nintendo Family Computer/Entertainment System Platform.* Cambridge, Mass.: MIT Press, 2015.

Anderson, Tim. "The History of *Zork*—First in a Series." *New Zork Times* 4, no. 1 (Winter 1985): 6–7, 11.

Anthropy, Anna. *Rise of the Videogame Zinesters: How Freaks, Normals, Amateurs, Artists, Dreamers, Dropouts, Queers, Housewives, and People Like You Are Taking Back an Art Form.* New York: Seven Stories Press, 2012.

Asimov, Isaac. "Nightfall." 1941. In *The Science Fiction Hall of Fame*, Vol. 1, *1929–1964*, edited by Robert Silverberg, 113–44. Garden City, N.Y.: Doubleday, 1970. Reprint, New York: Tor, 2003.

Bamford, James. *The Shadow Factory: The Ultra-Secret NSA from 9/11 to the Eavesdropping on America.* New York: Doubleday, 2008.

Bang, Magnus, Anton Gustafsson, and Cecilia Katzeff. "Promoting New Patterns in Household Energy Consumption with Pervasive Learning Games." In *Persuasive Technology: Second International Conference on Persuasive Technology, Persuasive 2007*, edited by Yvonne de Kort, Wijnand IJsselsteijn, Cees J. H. Midden, Berry Eggen, and B. J. Fogg, 55–63. Berlin: Springer-Verlag, 2007.

Bang, Magnus, Carin Torstensson, and Cecilia Katzeff. "The PowerHouse: A Persuasive Computer Game Designed to Raise Awareness of Domestic Energy Consumption." In *Persuasive Technology: First International Conference on Persuasive Technology for Human Well-Being*, edited by Wijnand IJsselsteijn, Yvonne de Kort, Cees J. H. Midden, Berry Eggen, and Elise van den Hoven, 123–32. Berlin: Springer-Verlag, 2006.

Barron, Arthur S. "Why Do Scientists Read Science Fiction?" *Bulletin of the Atomic Scientists* 13, no. 2 (1957): 62–70.

Barry, John A. *Technobabble*. Cambridge, Mass.: MIT Press, 1991.

Barton, Matt, and Bill Loguidice. "The History of *Spacewar!* The Best Waste of Time in the History of the Universe." *Gamasutra*, June 10, 2009, http://www.gamasutra.com /view/feature/132438/the_history_of_spacewar_the_best_.php.

Baudrillard, Jean. *Simulacra and Simulation*. Translated by Sheila Faria Glaser. Ann Arbor: University of Michigan Press, 1994.

Bealer, Adele H. "Eco-Performance in the Digital RPG Gamescape." In *Dungeons, Dragons, and Digital Denizens: The Digital Role-Playing Game*, edited by Gerald Voorhees, Josh Call, and Katie Whitlock, 27–47. New York: Continuum, 2012.

Beardsworth, Richard. *Derrida and the Political*. London: Routledge, 1996.

Beck, Ulrich. *World Risk Society*. Malden, Mass.: Polity, 1999.

Bender, John. *Imagining the Penitentiary: Fiction and the Architecture of Mind in Eighteenth-Century England*. Chicago: University of Chicago Press, 1987.

Bennington, Geoffrey. *Interrupting Derrida*. London: Routledge, 2000.

Beyer, Jessica L. *Expect Us: Online Communities and Political Mobilization*. Oxford: Oxford University Press, 2014.

Bissell, Tom. *Extra Lives: Why Video Games Matter*. New York: Pantheon, 2010.

Boellstorff, Tom. *Coming of Age in Second Life: An Anthropologist Explores the Virtually Human*. Princeton, N.J.: Princeton University Press, 2008.

Bogost, Ian. *How to Do Things with Videogames*. Minneapolis: University of Minnesota Press, 2011.

Bogost, Ian. *Persuasive Games: The Persuasive Power of Videogames*. Cambridge, Mass.: MIT Press, 2007.

Bogost, Ian, Simon Ferrari, and Bobby Schweizer. *Newsgames: Journalism at Play*. Cambridge, Mass.: MIT Press, 2010.

Boluk, Stephanie, and Patrick LeMieux. "Annotating *Adventure*." *Electronic Book Review*, May 31, 2011, http://www.electronicbookreview.com/thread/firstperson /colossalintro.

Boluk, Stephanie, and Patrick LeMieux. *Metagaming: Playing, Competing, Spectating, Cheating, Trading, Making, and Breaking Videogames*. Minneapolis: University of Minnesota Press, 2017.

Bowler, Peter J. *The Earth Encompassed: A History of the Environmental Sciences*. New York: Norton, 2000.

Bozak, Nadia. *The Cinematic Footprint: Lights, Camera, Natural Resources*. New Brunswick, N.J.: Rutgers University Press, 2012.

Braithwaite, Andrea. "It's about Ethics in Games Journalism? Gamergaters and Geek Masculinity." *Social Media and Society* 2, no. 4 (2016), DOI: 10.1177/2056305116672484.

Brake, Mark L., and Neil Hook. *Different Engines: How Science Drives Fiction and Fiction Drives Science*. London: Macmillan, 2008.

Brand, Stewart. "Spacewar: Fantastic Life and Symbolic Death among the Computer Bums." *Rolling Stone*, no. 123 (December 7, 1972): 50–58.

Brunton, Finn. *Spam: A Shadow History of the Internet*. Cambridge, Mass.: MIT Press, 2013.

Bukatman, Scott. *Terminal Identity: The Virtual Subject in Postmodern Science Fiction*. Durham, N.C.: Duke University Press, 1993.

Burak, Asi, and Laura Parker. *Power Play: How Video Games Can Save the World*. New York: St. Martin's, 2017.

Burden, Michael, and Sean Gouglas. "The Algorithmic Experience: *Portal* as Art." *Game Studies* 12, no. 2 (2012), http://gamestudies.org/1202/articles/the_algorithmic _experience.

Burkart, Patrick. *Pirate Politics: The New Information Policy Contests*. Cambridge, Mass.: MIT Press, 2014.

Burn, Andrew. "Playing Roles." In *Computer Games: Text, Narrative and Play*, edited by Diane Carr, David Buckingham, Andrew Burn, and Gareth Schot, 72–87. Cambridge: Polity, 2006.

Burnham, Van. *Supercade: A Visual History of the Videogame Age, 1971–1984*. Cambridge, Mass.: MIT Press, 2003.

Burrill, Derek A. *Die Tryin': Videogames, Masculinity, Culture*. New York: Peter Lang, 2008.

Caillois, Roger. *Man, Play and Games*. Translated by Meyer Barash. Urbana: University of Illinois Press, 2001.

Campbell-Kelly, Martin. *From Airline Reservations to Sonic the Hedgehog: A History of the Software Industry*. Cambridge, Mass.: MIT Press, 2003.

Canaday, John. *The Nuclear Muse: Literature, Physics, and the First Atomic Bombs*. Madison: University of Wisconsin Press, 2000.

Castronova, Edward. *Synthetic Worlds: The Business and Culture of Online Games*. Chicago: University of Chicago Press, 2005.

Chang, Alenda Y. "Games as Environmental Texts." *Qui Parle* 19 (2011): 57–84.

Chang, Alenda, and John Parham, eds. "Green Computer and Video Games." Special section, *Ecozon@* 8, no. 2 (2017): 1–150.

Chen, Mark. *Leet Noobs: The Life and Death of an Expert Player Group in World of Warcraft*. New York: Peter Lang, 2012.

Chen, Mel Y. *Animacies: Biopolitics, Racial Mattering, and Queer Affect*. Durham, N.C.: Duke University Press, 2012.

Chess, Shira. "Playing the Bad Guy: *Grand Theft Auto* in the Panopticon." In *Digital Gameplay: Essays on the Nexus of Game and Gamer*, edited by Nate Garrelts, 80–90. Jefferson, N.C.: McFarland, 2005.

Chess, Shira. *Ready Player Two: Women Gamers and Designed Identity*. Minneapolis: University of Minnesota Press, 2017.

Chess, Shira, and Adrienne Shaw. "A Conspiracy of Fishes, or, How We Learned to Stop Worrying about #GamerGate and Embrace Hegemonic Masculinity." *Journal of Broadcasting and Electronic Media* 59 (2015): 208–20.

Ching, Cynthia Carter, and Brian J. Foley. *Constructing the Self in a Digital World*. Cambridge: Cambridge University Press, 2012.

Choy, Tim. *Ecologies of Comparison: An Ethnography of Endangerment in Hong Kong*. Durham, N.C.: Duke University Press, 2011.

Chun, Wendy Hui Kyong. *Control and Freedom: Power and Paranoia in the Age of Fiber Optics*. Cambridge, Mass.: MIT Press, 2006.

Chun, Wendy Hui Kyong. *Programmed Visions: Software and Memory*. Cambridge, Mass.: MIT Press, 2011.

Chun, Wendy Hui Kyong. *Updating to Remain the Same: Habitual New Media*. Cambridge, Mass.: MIT Press, 2016.

Citron, Danielle Keats. *Hate Crimes in Cyberspace*. Cambridge, Mass.: Harvard University Press, 2014.

Clarke, Arthur C. *Profiles of the Future: An Inquiry into the Limits of the Possible*. 1962. Rev. ed. New York: Harper and Row, 1973.

Clarke, Arthur C. *Report on Planet Three and Other Speculations*. New York: Harper and Row, 1972.

Clarke, Bruce. "From Information to Cognition: The Systems Counterculture, Heinz von Foerster's Pedagogy, and Second-Order Cybernetics." *Constructivist Foundations* 7 (2012): 196–207.

Clarke, Bruce. "Steps to an Ecology of Systems: *Whole Earth* and Systemic Holism." In *Addressing Modernity: Social Systems Theory and U.S. Cultures*, edited by Hannes Bergthaller and Carsten Schinko, 258–88. Amsterdam: Rodopi, 2011.

Clarke, Bruce, and Mark B. N. Hansen, eds. *Emergence and Embodiment: New Essays on Second-Order Systems Theory*. Durham, N.C.: Duke University Press, 2009.

Cline, Ernest. *Ready Player One*. New York: Crown, 2011.

Coleman, Gabriella. *Coding Freedom: The Ethics and Aesthetics of Hacking*. Princeton, N.J.: Princeton University Press, 2013.

Coleman, Gabriella. "From Internet Farming to Weapons of the Geek." *Current Anthropology* 58, no. s15 (2017): s91–s102.

Coleman, Gabriella. *Hacker, Hoaxer, Whistleblower, Spy: The Many Faces of Anonymous*. New York: Verso, 2014.

Coleman, Gabriella. "The Public Interest Hack." In *Hacks, Leaks, and Breaches*, edited by E. Gabriella Coleman and Christopher M. Kelty, *Limn* 8 (2017), http://limn.it /issue/08/.

Coleman, E. Gabriella, and Alex Golub. "Hacker Practice: Moral Genres and the Cultural Articulation of Liberalism." *Anthropological Theory* 8 (2008): 255–77.

Commander X. *Behind the Mask: An Inside Look at Anonymous*. Morrisville, N.C.: Lulu, 2016.

Commander X. *Dark Ops: An Anonymous Story*. Morrisville, N.C.: Lulu, 2017.

Consalvo, Mia. *Cheating: Gaining Advantage in Videogames*. Cambridge, Mass.: MIT Press, 2007.

Consalvo, Mia. "Confronting Toxic Gamer Culture: A Challenge for Feminist Game Studies Scholars." *Ada* 1 (2012), http://adanewmedia.org/2012/11/miaconsalvo/150/.

Consalvo, Mia. "There Is No Magic Circle." *Games and Culture* 4 (2009): 408–17.

Consalvo, Mia. "*Zelda 64* and Video Game Fans: A Walkthrough of Games, Intertextuality, and Narrative." *Television and New Media* 4 (2003): 321–34.

Conway, Erik M. *High-Speed Dreams: NASA and the Technopolitics of Supersonic Transportation, 1945–1999*. Baltimore: Johns Hopkins University Press, 2005.

Cooper, Melinda. *Life as Surplus: Biotechnology and Capitalism in the Neoliberal Era*. Seattle: University of Washington Press, 2008.

Corneliussen, Hilde G., and Jill Walker Rettberg, eds. *Digital Culture, Play, and Identity: A World of Warcraft Reader*. Cambridge, Mass.: MIT Press, 2008.

Crogan, Patrick. *Gameplay Mode: War, Simulation, and Technoculture*. Minneapolis: University of Minnesota Press, 2011.

Cross, Katherine. "'We Will Force Gaming to Be Free': On GamerGate and the License to Inflict Suffering." *First Person Scholar*, October 8, 2014, http://www.firstpersonscholar.com/we-will-force-gaming-to-be-free/.

Csicsery-Ronay, Istvan, Jr. *The Seven Beauties of Science Fiction*. Middletown, Conn.: Wesleyan University Press, 2008.

Cubitt, Sean. *Ecomedia*. Amsterdam: Rodopi, 2005.

Cubitt, Sean. *Finite Media: Environmental Implications of Digital Technologies*. Durham, N.C.: Duke University Press, 2017.

Cusack, Carole M. "Science Fiction as Scripture: Robert A. Heinlein's *Stranger in a Strange Land* and the Church of All Worlds." *Literature and Aesthetics* 19 (2009): 72–91.

da Costa, Beatriz, and Kavita Philip, eds. *Tactical Biopolitics: Art, Activism, and Technoscience*. Cambridge, Mass.: MIT Press, 2008.

D'Andrea, Vincenzo, Stefano De Paoli, and Maurizio Teli. "Open to Grok: How Do Hackers' Practices Produce Hackers?" In *Open Source Development, Communities and Quality*, edited by Barbara Russo, Ernesto Damiani, Scott Hissam, Björn Lundell, and Giancarlo Succi, 121–29. Boston: Springer, 2008.

Davidson, Cathy N. *Now You See It: How the Brain Science of Attention Will Transform the Way We Live, Work, and Learn*. New York: Viking, 2011.

de Certeau, Michel. *The Practice of Everyday Life*. Translated by Steven Rendall. Berkeley: University of California Press, 1984.

Deleuze, Gilles. "Postscript on the Societies of Control." *October* 59 (1992): 3–7.

Delfanti, Alessandro. *Biohackers: The Politics of Open Science*. London: Pluto Press, 2012.

Delforge, Pierre, and Noah Horowitz. *The Latest-Generation Video Game Consoles: How Much Energy Do They Waste When You're Not Playing?* New York: Natural Resources Defense Council, 2014.

DeNardis, Laura. *Protocol Politics: The Globalization of Internet Governance*. Cambridge, Mass.: MIT Press, 2009.

Denson, Shane. *Postnaturalism: Frankenstein, Film, and the Anthropotechnical Interface*. Bielefeld: Transcript-Verlag, 2014.

Der Derian, James. *Virtuous War: Mapping the Military-Industrial-Media-Entertainment-Network*. 2nd ed. New York: Routledge, 2009.

Derrida, Jacques. *The Animal That Therefore I Am*. Translated by David Wills. Edited by Marie-Louise Mallet. New York: Fordham University Press, 2008.

Derrida, Jacques. *Archive Fever: A Freudian Impression*. Translated by Eric Prenowitz. Chicago: University of Chicago Press, 1996.

Derrida, Jacques. *Dissemination*. Translated by Barbara Johnson. Chicago: University of Chicago Press, 1981.

Derrida, Jacques. *Of Grammatology*. Translated by Gayatri Chakravorty Spivak. Baltimore: Johns Hopkins University Press, 1976.

Derrida, Jacques, and Bernard Stiegler. *Echographies of Television: Filmed Interviews*. Translated by Jennifer Bajorek. Cambridge: Polity, 2002.

Deseriis, Marco. *Improper Names: Collective Pseudonyms from the Luddites to Anonymous*. Minneapolis: University of Minnesota Press, 2015.

Desroches, Louis-Benoit, Jeffery B. Greenblatt, Stacy Pratt, Henry Willem, Erin Claybaugh, Bereket Beraki, Mythri Nagaraju, Sarah K. Price, Scott J. Young, Sally M. Donovan, and Mohan Ganeshalingam. "Video Game Console Usage and U.S. National Energy Consumption: Results from a Field-Metering Study." *Energy Efficiency* 8 (2015): 509–26.

Dick, Philip K. *Do Androids Dream of Electric Sheep?* Garden City, N.Y.: Doubleday, 1968. Reprint, New York: Del Rey, 1996.

DiPaolo, Marc. *War, Politics and Superheroes: Ethics and Propaganda in Comics and Film*. Jefferson, N.C.: McFarland, 2011.

Doctorow, Cory. *For the Win*. New York: Tor, 2010.

Douglas, Mary. *Purity and Danger: An Analysis of Concepts of Pollution and Taboo*. London: Routledge, 2005.

Doyle, Richard. *On Beyond Living: Rhetorical Transformations of the Life Sciences*. Stanford, Calif.: Stanford University Press, 1997.

Doyle, Richard. *Wetwares: Experiments in Postvital Living*. Minneapolis: University of Minnesota Press, 2003.

Drury, Paul. "The Making of *Asteroids*." *Retro Gamer*, no. 68 (2009): 24–29.

Dunbar-Hester, Christina. *Low Power to the People: Pirates, Protest, and Politics in FM Radio Activism*. Cambridge, Mass.: MIT Press, 2014.

Dyer-Witheford, Nick, and Greig de Peuter. *Games of Empire: Global Capitalism and Video Games*. Minneapolis: University of Minnesota Press, 2009.

Edwards, Paul N. *The Closed World: Computers and the Politics of Discourse in Cold War America*. Cambridge, Mass.: MIT Press, 1996.

Edwards, Paul N. *A Vast Machine: Computer Models, Climate Data, and the Politics of Global Warming*. Cambridge, Mass.: MIT Press, 2010.

Eglash, Ron, Jennifer L. Croissant, Giovanna Di Chiro, and Rayvon Fouché, eds. *Appropriating Technology: Vernacular Science and Social Power*. Minneapolis: University of Minnesota Press, 2004.

Elliott, Shawn. "Beyond the Box." *Games for Windows*, no. 13 (December 2007): 54–61.

Epstein, Steven. *Impure Science: AIDS, Activism, and the Politics of Knowledge*. Berkeley: University of California Press, 1998.

Fawaz, Ramzi. *The New Mutants: Superheroes and the Radical Imagination of American Comics*. New York: New York University Press, 2016.

Ferro, David L., and Eric G. Swedin, eds. *Science Fiction and Computing: Essays on Interlinked Domains*. Jefferson, N.C.: McFarland, 2011.

Fischer, Michael M. J. *Anthropological Futures*. Durham, N.C.: Duke University Press, 2009.

Fischer, Michael M. J. *Emergent Forms of Life and the Anthropological Voice*. Durham, N.C.: Duke University Press, 2003.

Fleischmann, Kenneth R., and Thomas Clay Templeton. "Past Futures and Technoscientific Innovation: The Mutual Shaping of Science Fiction and Science Fact." *Proceedings of the American Society for Information Science and Technology* 45 (2008), DOI: 10.1002/meet.2008.1450450345.

Follis, Luca, and Adam Fish. "Half-Lives of Hackers and the Shelf Life of Hacks." In *Hacks, Leaks, and Breaches*, edited by E. Gabriella Coleman and Christopher M. Kelty, *Limn* 8 (2017), http://limn.it/issue/08/.

Foster, Thomas. *The Souls of Cyberfolk: Posthumanism as Vernacular Theory*. Minneapolis: University of Minnesota Press, 2005.

Foucault, Michel. *The Birth of the Clinic: An Archaeology of Medical Perception*. Translated by Alan Sheridan. New York: Vintage, 1975.

Foucault, Michel. *Discipline and Punish: The Birth of the Prison*. Translated by Alan Sheridan. New York: Vintage, 1977.

Foucault, Michel. *The Order of Things: An Archaeology of the Human Sciences*. New York: Vintage, 1973.

Freccia, Tim. "The PlayStation War: Battling for Coltan in the Congo." *Chronogram Magazine* 18, no. 5 (2010), https://www.chronogram.com/hudsonvalley/the-playstation-war/Content?oid=2170010.

Frelik, Paweł. "Video Games." In *The Oxford Handbook of Science Fiction*, edited by Rob Latham, 226–38. Oxford: Oxford University Press, 2014.

Friedman, Ted. *Electric Dreams: Computers in American Culture*. New York: New York University Press, 2005.

Fuchs, Christian. "Anonymous: Hacktivism and Contemporary Politics." In *Social Media, Politics and the State: Protests, Revolutions, Riots, Crime and Policing in the Age of Facebook, Twitter and YouTube*, edited by Daniel Trottier and Christian Fuchs, 88–106. London: Routledge, 2014.

Gabrys, Jennifer. *Digital Rubbish: A Natural History of Electronics*. Ann Arbor: University of Michigan Press, 2011.

Galison, Peter. "The Ontology of the Enemy: Norbert Wiener and the Cybernetic Vision." *Critical Inquiry* 21 (1994): 228–66.

Gallagher, Rob. "Intergenerational Tensions: Of Sex and the Hardware Cycle." In *Rated M for Mature: Sex and Sexuality in Video Games*, edited by Matthew Wysocki and Evan W. Lauteria, 13–27. New York: Bloomsbury Academic, 2015.

Galloway, Alexander R. *Gaming: Essays on Algorithmic Culture*. Minneapolis: University of Minnesota Press, 2006.

Galloway, Alexander R. *Protocol: How Control Exists after Decentralization*. Cambridge, Mass.: MIT Press, 2004.

Galloway, Alexander R., and Eugene Thacker. *The Exploit: A Theory of Networks*. Minneapolis: University of Minnesota Press, 2007.

Gee, James Paul. *What Video Games Have to Teach Us about Learning and Literacy*. Rev. and updated ed. New York: Palgrave Macmillan, 2007.

Genosko, Gary. *When Technocultures Collide: Innovation from Below and the Struggle for Autonomy*. Waterloo, Ont.: Wilfred Laurier University Press, 2013.

Get Lamp. Written and directed by Jason Scott. Bovine Ignition Systems, 2010.

Ghosh, Bishnupriya. *Global Icons: Apertures to the Popular*. Durham, N.C.: Duke University Press, 2011.

Glew, L., and M. D. Hudson. "Gorillas in the Midst: The Impact of Armed Conflict on the Conservation of Protected Areas in Sub-Saharan Africa." *Oryx* 41, no. 2 (2007): 140–50.

Goggin, Joyce. "Playbour, Farming and Labour." *Ephemera* 11 (2011): 357–68.

Golding, Dan, and Leena van Deventer. *Game Changers: From Minecraft to Misogyny, the Fight for the Future of Videogames*. Melbourne: Affirm Press, 2016.

Goldstein, Emmanuel. *The Best of 2600: A Hacker Odyssey*. Indianapolis: Wiley, 2008.

Golley, Frank B. *A History of the Ecosystem Concept in Ecology: More Than the Sum of the Parts*. New Haven, Conn.: Yale University Press, 1993.

Golumbia, David. *The Cultural Logic of Computation*. Cambridge, Mass.: Harvard University Press, 2009.

Goodnow, Trischa, and James J. Kimble, eds. *The 10 Cent War: Comic Books, Propaganda, and World War II*. Jackson: University Press of Mississippi, 2017.

Graetz, J. M. "The Origin of *Spacewar!*" *Creative Computing* 7, no. 8 (August 1981): 56–67. Rev. and reprinted in Van Burnham, *Supercade: A Visual History of the Videogame Age, 1971–1984* (Cambridge, Mass.: MIT Press, 2003), 42–48.

Greenberg, Andy. *This Machine Kills Secrets: How WikiLeakers, Cypherpunks, and Hacktivists Aim to Free the World's Information*. New York: Dutton, 2012.

Greenwald, Glenn. *No Place to Hide: Edward Snowden, the NSA, and the U.S. Surveillance State*. New York: Metropolitan, 2014.

Grossman, Elizabeth. *High Tech Trash: Digital Devices, Hidden Toxics, and Human Health*. Washington, D.C.: Island Press / Shearwater Books, 2006.

Guins, Raiford. *Game After: A Cultural Study of Video Game Afterlife*. Cambridge, Mass.: MIT Press, 2014.

Hafner, Katie, and Matthew Lyon. *Where Wizards Stay Up Late: The Origins of the Internet*. New York: Simon and Schuster, 1996.

Hafner, Katie, and John Markoff. *Cyberpunk: Outlaws and Hackers on the Computer Frontier*. Updated ed. New York: Simon and Schuster, 1995.

Hagen, Joel B. *An Entangled Bank: The Origins of Ecosystem Ecology*. New Brunswick, N.J.: Rutgers University Press, 1992.

Hague, James. *Halcyon Days: Interviews with Classic Computer and Video Game Programmers*. Savoy, Ill.: Dadgum Games, 1997. Reprint, online ed., 2002. Available at http://www.dadgum.com/halcyon/.

Halpern, Orit. *Beautiful Data: A History of Vision and Reason since 1945*. Durham, N.C.: Duke University Press, 2014.

Halter, Ed. *From Sun Tzu to Xbox: War and Video Games*. New York: Thunder's Mouth Press, 2006.

Hansen, Mark B. N. *Bodies in Code: Interfaces with Digital Media*. London: Routledge, 2006.

Haraway, Donna J. "A Cyborg Manifesto: Science, Technology, and Socialist-Feminism in the Late Twentieth Century." In *Simians, Cyborgs, and Women: The Reinvention of Nature*, 149–81. New York: Routledge, 1991.

Haraway, Donna J. *Staying with the Trouble: Making Kin in the Chthulucene*. Durham, N.C.: Duke University Press, 2016.

Haraway, Donna J. *When Species Meet*. Minneapolis: University of Minnesota Press, 2008.

Hari, Johann. "Congo's Tragedy: The War the World Forgot." *Independent*, May 5, 2006, 2–4.

Harpold, Terry. *Ex-Foliations: Reading Machines and the Upgrade Path*. Minneapolis: University of Minnesota Press, 2009.

Hassler-Forest, Dan. *Science Fiction, Fantasy and Politics: Transmedia World-Building Beyond Capitalism*. London: Rowman and Littlefield, 2016.

Hayes, Karen, and Richard Burge. *Coltan Mining in the Democratic Republic of Congo: How Tantalum-Using Industries Can Commit to the Reconstruction of the* DRC. Cambridge, U.K.: Fauna and Flora International, 2003.

Hayles, N. Katherine. *How We Became Posthuman: Virtual Bodies in Cybernetics, Literature, and Informatics*. Chicago: University of Chicago Press, 1999.

Hayles, N. Katherine. *How We Think: Digital Media and Contemporary Technogenesis*. Chicago: University of Chicago Press, 2012.

Hayles, N. Katherine. *My Mother Was a Computer: Digital Subjects and Literary Texts*. Chicago: University of Chicago Press, 2005.

Hecht, Gabrielle. *The Radiance of France: Nuclear Power and National Identity after World War II*. Cambridge, Mass.: MIT Press, 1998.

Heidegger, Martin. "The Question Concerning Technology." In *The Question Concerning Technology, and Other Essays*, translated by William Lovitt, 3–35. New York: Garland, 1977.

Heims, Steve Joshua. *Constructing a Social Science for Postwar America: The Cybernetics Group, 1946–1953*. Cambridge, Mass.: MIT Press, 1993.

Heinlein, Robert A. *Rocket Ship Galileo*. New York: Charles Scribner's Sons, 1947.

Heise, Ursula K. *Sense of Place and Sense of Planet: The Environmental Imagination of the Global*. Oxford: Oxford University Press, 2008.

Helmreich, Stefan. *Silicon Second Nature: Culturing Artificial Life in a Digital World.* Updated ed. Berkeley: University of California Press, 1998.

Hilderbrand, Lucas. *Inherent Vice: Bootleg Histories of Videotape and Copyright.* Durham, N.C.: Duke University Press, 2009.

Horowitz, Noah, Riley Neugebauer, Brooke Frazer, Peter May-Ostendorp, and Chris Calwell. *Lowering the Cost of Play: Improving the Energy Efficiency of Video Game Consoles.* New York: National Resources Defense Council, 2008.

Horton, Zach. "Collapsing Scale: Nanotechnology and Geoengineering as Speculative Media." In *Shaping Emerging Technologies: Governance, Innovation, Discourse,* edited by Kornelia Konrad, Christopher Coenen, Anne Dijkstra, Colin Milburn, and Harro van Lente, 203–18. Berlin: AKA-Verlag / IOS Press, 2013.

Huizinga, Johan. *Homo Ludens: A Study of the Play-Element in Culture.* London: Routledge and Kegan Paul, 1949.

Huntemann, Nina, and Matthew Thomas Payne, eds. *Joystick Soldiers: The Politics of Play in Military Video Games.* New York: Routledge, 2010.

Hurley, Kameron. *The Geek Feminist Revolution.* New York: Tor, 2016.

The Internet's Own Boy: The Story of Aaron Swartz. Directed by Brian Knappenberger. Participant Media and FilmBuff, 2014.

Isbister, Katherine. *How Games Move Us: Emotion by Design.* Cambridge, Mass.: MIT Press, 2016.

Ito, Mizuko. *Engineering Play: A Cultural History of Children's Software.* Cambridge, Mass.: MIT Press, 2009.

Jackson, Stephen. "Making a Killing: Criminality and Coping in the Kivu War Economy." *Review of African Political Economy* 29 (2002): 516–36.

Jagoda, Patrick. "Digital Games and Science Fiction." In *The Cambridge Companion to American Science Fiction,* edited by Eric Carl Link and Gerry Canavan, 139–52. New York: Cambridge University Press, 2015.

Jagoda, Patrick. "Gamification and Other Forms of Play." *boundary 2* 40 (2013): 113–44.

Jagoda, Patrick. *Network Aesthetics.* Chicago: University of Chicago Press, 2016.

Jagoda, Patrick. "Videogame Criticism and Games in the Twenty-First Century." *American Literary History* 29 (2017): 205–18.

Jameson, Fredric. *Archaeologies of the Future: The Desire Called Utopia and Other Science Fictions.* New York: Verso, 2005.

Jeffery, Scott. *The Posthuman Body in Superhero Comics: Human, Superhuman, Transhuman, Post/Human.* New York: Palgrave Macmillan, 2016.

Jenkins, Henry. *Convergence Culture: Where Old and New Media Collide.* New York: New York University Press, 2006.

Jenkins, Henry. *Fans, Bloggers, and Gamers: Exploring Participatory Culture.* New York: New York University Press, 2006.

Jenkins, Henry. *Textual Poachers: Television Fans and Participatory Culture.* New York: Routledge, 1992.

Jenkins, Henry, Mizuko Ito, and danah boyd. *Participatory Culture in a Networked Era: A Conversation on Youth, Learning, Commerce, and Politics.* Cambridge: Polity, 2015.

Jenkins, Henry, Sangita Shresthova, Liana Gamber-Thompson, Neta Kligler-Vilenchik, and Arely M. Zimmerman. *By Any Media Necessary: The New Youth Activism*. New York: New York University Press, 2016.

Jerz, Dennis G. "Somewhere Nearby Is Colossal Cave: Examining Will Crowther's Original 'Adventure' in Code and in Kentucky." *Digital Humanities Quarterly* 1, no. 2 (2007), http://www.digitalhumanities.org/dhq/vol/1/2/000009/000009.html.

Johnson, Steven. *Everything Bad Is Good for You: How Today's Popular Culture Is Actually Making Us Smarter*. New York: Riverhead, 2005.

Johnston, John. *The Allure of Machinic Life: Cybernetics, Artificial Life, and the New AI*. Cambridge, Mass.: MIT Press, 2008.

Jones, Steven E. *The Meaning of Video Games: Gaming and Textual Strategies*. New York: Routledge, 2008.

Jordan, Tim, and Paul A. Taylor. *Hacktivism and Cyberwars: Rebels with a Cause?* London: Routledge, 2004.

Juris, Jeffrey S. *Networking Futures: The Movements against Corporate Globalization*. Durham, N.C.: Duke University Press, 2008.

Juul, Jesper. *The Art of Failure: An Essay on the Pain of Playing Video Games*. Cambridge, Mass.: MIT Press, 2013.

Juul, Jesper. *Half-Real: Video Games between Real Rules and Fictional Worlds*. Cambridge, Mass.: MIT Press, 2005.

Kaveney, Roz. *Superheroes! Capes and Crusaders in Comics and Films*. London: I. B. Tauris, 2008.

Kay, Alexx, David Ladyman, Chris McCubbin, and Melissa Tyler. *System Shock 2: Prima's Official Strategy Guide*. Rocklin, Calif.: Prima, 1999.

Kay, Lily E. *Who Wrote the Book of Life? A History of the Genetic Code*. Stanford, Calif.: Stanford University Press, 2000.

Kelly, Shawna, and Bonnie Nardi. "Playing with Sustainability: Using Video Games to Simulate Futures of Scarcity." *First Monday* 19, no. 5 (2014), http://journals.uic.edu/ojs/index.php/fm/article/view/5259/3877.

Kelty, Christopher M. *Two Bits: The Cultural Significance of Free Software*. Durham, N.C.: Duke University Press, 2008.

Kember, Sarah, and Joanna Zylinska. *Life after New Media: Mediation as a Vital Process*. Cambridge, Mass.: MIT Press, 2012.

Kidder, Tracy. *The Soul of a New Machine*. Boston: Little, Brown, 1981.

Kilgore, De Witt Douglas. *Astrofuturism: Science, Race, and Visions of Utopia in Space*. Philadelphia: University of Pennsylvania Press, 2003.

King, Brad, and John Borland. *Dungeons and Dreamers: The Rise of Computer Game Culture from Geek to Chic*. New York: McGraw-Hill / Osborne, 2003.

Kline, Stephen, Nick Dyer-Witheford, and Greig de Peuter. *Digital Play: The Interaction of Technology, Culture, and Marketing*. Montreal: McGill-Queen's University Press, 2003.

Kocurek, Carly A. *Coin-Operated Americans: Rebooting Boyhood at the Video Game Arcade*. Minneapolis: University of Minnesota Press, 2015.

Krapp, Peter. *Noise Channels: Glitch and Error in Digital Culture*. Minneapolis: University of Minnesota Press, 2011.

Kristeva, Julia. *Powers of Horror: An Essay on Abjection*. Translated by Leon S. Roudiez. New York: Columbia University Press, 1982.

Krulos, Tea. *Heroes in the Night: Inside the Real Life Superhero Movement*. Chicago: Chicago Review Press, 2013.

Kücklich, Julian. "Precarious Playbour: Modders and the Digital Games Industry." *Fibreculture* 5 (2005), http://five.fibreculturejournal.org/fcj-025-precarious-playbour-modders-and-the-digital-games-industry/.

Lacan, Jacques. *The Seminar of Jacques Lacan, Book XI: The Four Fundamental Concepts of Psycho-Analysis*. Translated by Alan Sheridan. Edited by Jacques-Alain Miller. New York: Norton, 1998.

Lasker, John. "Inside Africa's PlayStation War." *Toward Freedom*, July 8, 2008, http://towardfreedom.com/home/content/view/1352/1. Archived at https://towardfreedom.com/archives/africa-archives/inside-africas-playstation-war/.

Latham, Rob. *Consuming Youth: Vampires, Cyborgs, and the Culture of Consumption*. Chicago: University of Chicago Press, 2002.

Latour, Bruno. "Give Me a Laboratory and I Will Raise the World." In *The Science Studies Reader*, edited by Mario Biagioli, 258–75. New York: Routledge, 1999.

Latour, Bruno. *An Inquiry into Modes of Existence: An Anthropology of the Moderns*. Translated by Catherine Porter. Cambridge, Mass.: Harvard University Press, 2013.

Latour, Bruno. *We Have Never Been Modern*. Translated by Catherine Porter. Cambridge, Mass.: Harvard University Press, 1993.

Legends of the Knight. Written and directed by Brett Culp. Brett Culp Films, 2013.

Lenoir, Tim, and Luke Caldwell. *The Military-Entertainment Complex*. Cambridge, Mass.: Harvard University Press, 2018.

Lenoir, Timothy. "All but War Is Simulation: The Military-Entertainment Complex." *Configurations* 8 (2000): 289–335.

Lessard, Jonathan. "*Adventure* before Adventure Games: A New Look at Crowther and Woods's Seminal Program." *Games and Culture* 8 (2013): 119–35.

Levy, Steven. *Hackers: Heroes of the Computer Revolution*. Garden City, N.Y.: Anchor Press / Doubleday, 1984.

Loeve, Sacha. "About a Definition of Nano: How to Articulate Nano and Technology?" *Hyle* 16 (2010): 3–18.

Lorge, Greta, and Mike Antonucci. "Game Changers." *Stanford* 41, no. 3 (2012): 46–49.

Losh, Elizabeth. *Virtualpolitik: An Electronic History of Government Media-Making in a Time of War, Scandal, Disaster, Miscommunication, and Mistakes*. Cambridge, Mass.: MIT Press, 2009.

Lovink, Geert. *Dark Fiber: Tracking Critical Internet Culture*. Cambridge, Mass.: MIT Press, 2002.

Lowood, Henry. "Videogames in Computer Space: The Complex History of Pong." *IEEE Annals of the History of Computing* 31, no. 3 (2009): 5–19.

Luttmann, Edgar, Daniel L. Ensign, Vishal Vaidyanathan, Mike Houston, Noam Rimon, Jeppe Øland, Guha Jayachandran, Mark Friedrichs, and Vijay S. Pande. "Accelerating Molecular Dynamic Simulation on the Cell Processor and PlayStation 3." *Journal of Computational Chemistry* 30 (2009): 268–74.

Mackenzie, Adrian. *Transductions: Bodies and Machines at Speed*. London: Continuum, 2002.

MacKinnon, Rebecca. *Consent of the Networked: The Worldwide Struggle for Internet Freedom*. New York: Basic Books, 2012.

Maher, Jimmy. *The Future Was Here: The Commodore Amiga*. Cambridge, Mass.: MIT Press, 2012.

Manivannan, Vyshali. "Tits or GTFO: The Logics of Misogyny on 4chan's Random - /b/." *Fibreculture* 22 (2013): 109–32.

Mantz, Jeffrey W. "Improvisational Economies: Coltan Production in the Eastern Congo." *Social Anthropology* 16 (2008): 34–50.

Markey, Patrick M., and Christopher J. Ferguson. *Moral Combat: Why the War on Violent Video Games Is Wrong*. Dallas: BenBella Books, 2017.

Markley, Robert. *Dying Planet: Mars in Science and the Imagination*. Durham, N.C.: Duke University Press, 2005.

Marshall, Nowell. "Borders and Bodies in *City of Heroes*: (Re)Imaging American Identity Post 9/11." In *Computer Games as a Sociocultural Phenomenon: Games without Frontiers, War without Tears*, edited by Andreas Jahn-Sudmann and Ralf Stockmann, 140–49. Basingstoke, U.K.: Palgrave Macmillan, 2008.

Massingham, Tim, and Nick Goldman. "All Your Base: A Fast and Accurate Probabilistic Approach to Base Calling." *Genome Biology* 13, no. 2 (2012): R13.

Maxwell, Richard, and Toby Miller. *Greening the Media*. New York: Oxford University Press, 2012.

Maxwell, Richard, and Toby Miller. "'Warm and Stuffy': The Ecological Impact of Electronic Games." In *The Video Game Industry: Formation, Present State, and Future*, edited by Peter Zackariasson and Timothy L. Wilson, 179–97. New York: Routledge, 2012.

Mayer, Sylvia, and Alexa Weik von Mossner, eds. *The Anticipation of Catastrophe: Environmental Risk in North American Literature and Culture*. Heidelberg: Universitätsverlag Winter, 2014.

Mayers, Kieren, Jonathan Koomey, Rebecca Hall, Maria Bauer, Chris France, and Amanda Webb. "The Carbon Footprint of Games Distribution." *Journal of Industrial Ecology* 9 (2015): 402–15.

McCarthy, Wil. *Bloom*. New York: Del Rey, 1998. Reprint, 1999.

McDonough, Jerome, Matthew Kirschenbaum, Doug Reside, Neil Fraistat, and Dennis Jerz. "Twisty Little Passages Almost All Alike: Applying the FRBR Model to a Classic Computer Game." *Digital Humanities Quarterly* 4, no. 2 (2010), http://www.digitalhumanities.org/dhq/vol/4/2/000089/000089.html.

McGonigal, Jane. *Reality Is Broken: Why Games Make Us Better and How They Can Change the World*. New York: Penguin, 2011.

McHugh, Susan. *Animal Stories: Narrating across Species Lines*. Minneapolis: University of Minnesota Press, 2011.

Mead, Corey. *War Play: Video Games and the Future of Armed Conflict*. Boston: Houghton Mifflin Harcourt, 2013.

Mejias, Ulises Ali. *Off the Network: Disrupting the Digital World*. Minneapolis: University of Minnesota Press, 2013.

Milburn, Colin. "Ahead of Time: Gerald Feinberg, James Blish, and the Governance of Futurity." In *Histories of the Future*, edited by Erika Milam and Joanna Radin (2015), http://histscifi.com/essays/milburn/time.html.

Milburn, Colin. "Modifiable Futures: Science Fiction at the Bench." *Isis* 101 (2010): 560–69.

Milburn, Colin. *Mondo Nano: Fun and Games in the World of Digital Matter*. Durham, N.C.: Duke University Press, 2015.

Milburn, Colin. *Nanovision: Engineering the Future*. Durham, N.C.: Duke University Press, 2008.

Mills, Nathaniel, and Evan Mills. "Taming the Energy Use of Gaming Computers." *Energy Efficiency* 9 (2016): 321–38.

Milner, Ryan M. *The World Made Meme: Public Conversations and Participatory Media*. Cambridge, Mass.: MIT Press, 2016.

Mitchell, Liam. "'Because None of Us Are as Cruel as All of Us': Anonymity and Subjectivation." *CTheory*, April 4, 2013, http://www.ctheory.net/articles.aspx?id=720.

Mitchell, Syne. *Technogenesis*. New York: Roc, 2002.

Mitchell, Timothy. *Rule of Experts: Egypt, Techno-Politics, Modernity*. Berkeley: University of California Press, 2002.

Mitropoulos, Jonah. "Shinto and Alien Influences in *Final Fantasy VII*." In *Final Fantasy and Philosophy: The Ultimate Walkthrough*, edited by Jason P. Blahuta and Michel S. Beaulieu, 125–41. Hoboken, N.J.: Wiley, 2009.

Montague, Dena. "Stolen Goods: Coltan and Conflict in the Democratic Republic of Congo." *SAIS Review* 22, no. 1 (2002): 103–18.

Montfort, Nick. *Twisty Little Passages: An Approach to Interactive Fiction*. Cambridge, Mass.: MIT Press, 2003.

Montfort, Nick, and Ian Bogost. *Racing the Beam: The Atari Video Computer System*. Cambridge, Mass.: MIT Press, 2009.

Mortensen, Torill Elvira. "Anger, Fear, and Games: The Long Event of #GamerGate." *Games and Culture* (2016), DOI: 10.1177/1555412016640408.

Moyroud, Celine, and John Katunga. "Coltan Exploration in Eastern Democratic Republic of the Congo." In *Scarcity and Surfeit: The Ecology of Africa's Conflicts*, edited by Jeremy Lind and Kathryn Sturman, 157–85. Pretoria: Institute for Security Studies, 2002.

Mueller, Milton. *Ruling the Root: Internet Governance and the Taming of Cyberspace*. Cambridge, Mass.: MIT Press, 2002.

Murray, Janet H. *Hamlet on the Holodeck: The Future of Narrative in Cyberspace*. New York: Free Press, 1997.

Nagle, Angela. *Kill All Normies: Online Culture Wars from 4chan and Tumblr to Trump and the Alt-Right*. Alresford, U.K.: Zero Books, 2017.

Nakamura, Lisa. "Don't Hate the Player, Hate the Game: The Racialization of Labor in World of Warcraft." *Critical Studies in Media Communication* 26 (2009): 128–44.

Nakamura, Lisa. "The Socioalgorithmics of Race: Sorting It out in Jihad Worlds." In *The New Media of Surveillance*, edited by Shoshana Magnet and Kelly Gates, 149–61. London: Routledge, 2009.

Nardi, Bonnie A. *My Life as a Night Elf Priest: An Anthropological Account of World of Warcraft*. Ann Arbor: University of Michigan Press, 2010.

Nest, Michael. *Coltan*. Cambridge: Polity, 2011.

Newman, James. *Best Before: Videogames, Supersession and Obsolescence*. New York: Routledge, 2012.

Newman, Michael Z. *Atari Age: The Emergence of Video Games in America*. Cambridge, Mass.: MIT Press, 2017.

Nguyen, Josef. "*Minecraft* and the Building Blocks of Creative Individuality." *Configurations* 24 (2016): 471–500.

Nichols, Bill. "The Work of Culture in the Age of Cybernetic Systems." *Screen* 21 (1988): 22–46.

Nixon, Rob. *Slow Violence and the Environmentalism of the Poor*. Cambridge, Mass.: Harvard University Press, 2011.

Nooney, Laine. "Let's Begin Again: Sierra On-Line and the Origins of the Graphical Adventure Game." *American Journal of Play* 10 (2017): 71–98.

November, Joseph. *Biomedical Computing: Digitizing Life in the United States*. Baltimore: Johns Hopkins University Press, 2012.

Nunes, Mark. *Error: Glitch, Noise, and Jam in New Media Cultures*. New York: Continuum, 2011.

Oehlert, Mark. "From Captain America to Wolverine: Cyborgs in Comic Books, Alternative Images of Cybernetic Heroes and Villains." In *The Cyborg Handbook*, edited by Chris Hables Gray, Heidi J. Figueroa-Sarriera, and Steven Mentor, 219–32. New York: Routledge, 1995.

Olson, Parmy. *We Are Anonymous: Inside the Hacker World of LulzSec, Anonymous, and the Global Cyber Insurgency*. New York: Little, Brown, 2012.

Parikka, Jussi. *Digital Contagions: A Media Archaeology of Computer Viruses*. 2nd ed. New York: Peter Lang, 2016.

Parikka, Jussi. *A Geology of Media*. Minneapolis: University of Minnesota Press, 2015.

Parikka, Jussi. *Insect Media: An Archaeology of Animals and Technology*. Minneapolis: University of Minnesota Press, 2010.

Parkin, Simon. *Death by Video Game: Danger, Pleasure, and Obsession on the Virtual Frontline*. New York: Melville House, 2016.

Parks, Lisa. "Falling Apart: Electronics Salvaging and the Global Media Economy." In *Residual Media*, edited by Charles R. Acland, 32–47. Minneapolis: University of Minnesota Press, 2007.

Payne, Matthew Thomas. *Playing War: Military Video Games after 9/11*. New York: New York University Press, 2016.

Pearce, Celia, and Artemesia. *Communities of Play: Emergent Cultures in Multiplayer Games and Virtual Worlds*. Cambridge, Mass.: MIT Press, 2009.

Pedersen, Isabel, and Luke Simcoe. "The Iron Man Phenomenon, Participatory Culture, and Future Augmented Reality Technologies." In CHI '12 *Extended*

Abstracts on Human Factors in Computing Systems, 291–300. New York: ACM, 2012.

Penley, Constance. *NASA/Trek: Popular Science and Sex in America*. London: Verso, 1997.

Pesce, Mark. "Magic Mirror: The Novel as a Software Development Platform." *Media in Transition*, December 19, 1999, http://web.mit.edu/m-i-t/articles/index_pesce.html.

Peterson, Dale. *Genesis II: Creation and Recreation with Computers*. Reston, Va.: Reston, 1983.

Phillips, Amanda. "Shooting to Kill: Headshots, Twitch Reflexes, and the Mechropolitics of Video Games." *Games and Culture* 13 (2018): 136–52.

Phillips, Whitney. *This Is Why We Can't Have Nice Things: Mapping the Relationship between Online Trolling and Mainstream Culture*. Cambridge, Mass.: MIT Press, 2015.

Phillips, Whitney, Jessica Beyer, and Gabriella Coleman. "Trolling Scholars Debunk the Idea That the Alt-Right's Shitposters Have Magic Powers." *Motherboard*, March 22, 2017, https://motherboard.vice.com/en_us/article/z4k549/trolling-scholars-debunk-the-idea-that-the-alt-rights-trolls-have-magic-powers.

Phillips, Whitney, and Ryan M. Milner. *The Ambivalent Internet: Mischief, Oddity, and Antagonism Online*. Cambridge, U.K.: Polity, 2017.

Pickering, Andrew. *The Cybernetic Brain: Sketches of Another Future*. Chicago: University of Chicago Press, 2010.

Plumptre, Andrew J., Stuart Nixon, Robert Critchlow, Ghislain Vieilledent, Radar Nishuli, Andrew Kirkby, Elizabeth A. Williamson, Jefferson S. Hall and Deo Kujirakwinja. *Status of Grauer's Gorilla and Chimpanzees in Eastern Democratic Republic of Congo: Historical and Current Distribution and Abundance*. New York: Wildlife Conservation Society, Fauna and Flora International, and Institut Congolais pour la Conservation de la Nature, 2016.

Poster, Mark. *Information Please: Culture and Politics in the Age of Digital Machines*. Durham, N.C.: Duke University Press, 2006.

Postigo, Hector. *The Digital Rights Movement: The Role of Technology in Subverting Digital Copyright*. Cambridge, Mass.: MIT Press, 2012.

Postigo, Hector. "From *Pong* to *Planet Quake*: Post-Industrial Transitions from Leisure to Work." *Information, Communication and Society* 6 (2003): 593–607.

Quinn, Zoë. *Crash Override: How GamerGate (Nearly) Destroyed My Life, and How We Can Win the Fight against Online Hate*. New York: PublicAffairs, 2017.

Raley, Rita. "Dataveillance and Counterveillance." In *"Raw Data" Is an Oxymoron*, edited by Lisa Gitelman, 121–45. Cambridge, Mass.: MIT Press, 2013.

Raley, Rita. *Tactical Media*. Minneapolis: University of Minnesota Press, 2009.

Ravetto-Biagioli, Kriss. "Anonymous: Social as Political." *Leonardo Electronic Almanac* 19 (2013): 178–95.

Raymond, Eric S. *The Cathedral and the Bazaar: Musings on Linux and Open Source by an Accidental Revolutionary*. Rev. ed. Sebastopol, Calif.: O'Reilly, 2001.

Redmond, Ian. *Coltan Boom, Gorilla Bust: The Impact of Coltan Mining on Gorillas and Other Wildlife in Eastern DR Congo*. Stroud, U.K.: Dian Fossey Gorilla Fund and Born Free Foundation, 2001.

Reeves, Byron, James J. Cummings, James K. Scarborough, and Leo Yeykelis. "Increasing Energy Efficiency with Entertainment Media: An Experimental and Field Test of the Influence of a Social Game on Performance of Energy Behaviors." *Environment and Behavior* 47 (2013): 102–15.

Rheingold, Howard. *Virtual Reality*. New York: Summit Books, 1991.

Rieder, John. *Science Fiction and the Mass Cultural Genre System*. Middletown, Conn.: Wesleyan University Press, 2017.

Robinett, Warren. "Adventure as a Video Game: Adventure for the Atari 2600." In *The Game Design Reader: A Rules of Play Anthology*, edited by Katie Salen and Eric Zimmerman, 690–713. Cambridge, Mass.: MIT Press, 2006.

Ross, Andrew. *Strange Weather: Culture, Science, and Technology in the Age of Limits*. New York: Verso, 1991.

Ruberg, Bonnie, and Adrienne Shaw, eds. *Queer Game Studies*. Minneapolis: University of Minnesota Press, 2017.

Russworm, TreaAndrea, and Jennifer Malkowski, eds. *Gaming Representation: Race, Gender, and Sexuality in Video Games*. Bloomington: Indiana University Press, 2017.

St. Jude, R. U. Sirius, and Bart Nagel. *Cyberpunk Handbook: The Real Cyberpunk Fakebook*. New York: Random House, 1995.

Salen, Katie, and Eric Zimmerman. *Rules of Play: Game Design Fundamentals*. Cambridge, Mass.: MIT Press, 2003.

Salter, Anastasia, and Bridget Blodgett. "Hypermasculinity and Dickwolves: The Contentious Role of Women in the New Gaming Public." *Journal of Broadcasting and Electronic Media* 56 (2012): 401–16.

Sarkar, Bhaskar. "Media Piracy and the Terrorist Boogeyman: Speculative Potentiations." *positions* 24 (2016): 343–68.

Sauter, Molly. *The Coming Swarm: DDOS Actions, Hacktivism, and Civil Disobedience on the Internet*. New York: Bloomsbury Academic, 2014.

Schleiner, Anne-Marie. *The Player's Power to Change the Game: Ludic Mutation*. Amsterdam: Amsterdam University Press, 2017.

Scholes, Robert E. *Structural Fabulation: An Essay on Fiction of the Future*. Notre Dame, Ind.: University of Notre Dame Press, 1975.

Scholz, Trebor, ed. *Digital Labor: The Internet as Playground and Factory*. New York: Routledge, 2013.

Schrank, Brian. *Avant-Garde Videogames: Playing with Technoculture*. Cambridge, Mass.: MIT Press, 2014.

Schrier, Karen. *Knowledge Games: How Playing Games Can Solve Problems, Create Insight, and Make Change*. Baltimore: Johns Hopkins University Press, 2016.

Schwarz, Astrid, and Kurt Jax, eds. *Ecology Revisited: Reflecting on Concepts, Advancing Science*. Dordrecht: Springer Netherlands, 2011.

Seegert, Alf. "Doing There vs. Being There: Performing Presence in Interactive Fiction." *Journal of Gaming and Virtual Worlds* 1 (2009): 23–37.

Serres, Michel. *The Parasite*. Translated by Lawrence R. Schehr. With a new introduction by Cary Wolfe. Minneapolis: University of Minnesota Press, 2007.

Shaviro, Steven. *Connected, or, What It Means to Live in the Network Society*. Minneapolis: University of Minnesota Press, 2003.

Shaw, Adrienne. *Gaming at the Edge: Sexuality and Gender at the Margins of Gamer Culture*. Minneapolis: University of Minnesota Press, 2014.

Shifman, Limor. *Memes in Digital Culture*. Cambridge, Mass.: MIT Press, 2014.

Shoch, John F., and Jon A. Hupp. "The 'Worm' Programs—Early Experience with a Distributed Computation." *Communications of the ACM* 25 (1982): 172–80.

Simondon, Gilbert. *On the Mode of Existence of Technical Objects*. 1958. Translated by Cecile Malaspina and John Rogove. Minneapolis: Univocal, 2017.

Sirota, David. *Back to Our Future: How the 1980s Explain the World We Live in Now—Our Culture, Our Politics, Our Everything*. New York: Ballantine, 2011.

Sköld, Olle. "Documenting Virtual World Cultures: Memory-Making and Documentary Practices in the *City of Heroes* Community." *Journal of Documentation* 71 (2015): 294–316.

Slatalla, Michelle, and Joshua Quittner. *Masters of Deception: The Gang That Ruled Cyberspace*. New York: HarperCollins, 1995.

Smith, James H. "Tantalus in the Digital Age: Coltan Ore, Temporal Dispossession, and 'Movement' in the Eastern Democratic Republic of the Congo." *American Ethnologist* 38 (2011): 17–35.

Smith, James H., and Jeffrey W. Mantz. "Do Cellular Phones Dream of Civil War? The Mystification of Production and the Consequences of Technology Fetishism in the Eastern Congo." In *Inclusion and Exclusion in the Global Arena*, edited by Max Kirsch and June Nash, 71–94. New York: Routledge, 2006.

Standage, Tom, ed. *The Future of Technology*. London: Economist / Profile Books, 2005.

Stanton, Richard. *A Brief History of Video Games: The Evolution of a Global Industry*. Philadelphia: Running Press, 2015.

Starosielski, Nicole, and Janet Walker, eds. *Sustainable Media: Critical Approaches to Media and Environment*. New York: Routledge, 2016.

Steele, Guy L., Donald R. Woods, Raphael A. Finkel, Mark R. Crispin, Richard M. Stallman, and Geoffrey S. Goodfellow. *The Hacker's Dictionary: A Guide to the World of Computer Wizards*. New York: Harper and Row, 1983.

Sterling, Bruce. *The Hacker Crackdown: Law and Disorder on the Electronic Frontier*. New York: Bantam, 1992.

Sterne, Jonathan. "Out with the Trash: On the Future of New Media." In *Residual Media*, edited by Charles R. Acland, 16–31. Minneapolis: University of Minnesota Press, 2007.

Stevens, Hallam. *Life out of Sequence: A Data-Driven History of Bioinformatics*. Chicago: University of Chicago Press, 2013.

Stiegler, Bernard. "Distrust and the Pharmacology of Transformational Technologies." In *Quantum Engagements: Social Reflections of Nanoscience and Emerging Technologies*, edited by Torben B. Zülsdorf, Christopher Coenen, Ulrich Fiedeler, Arianna Ferrari, Colin Milburn, and Matthias Wienroth, 27–39. Heidelberg: IOS Press / AKA-Verlag, 2011.

Stiegler, Bernard. *Technics and Time, 1: The Fault of Epimetheus*. Translated by Richard Beardsworth and George Collins. Stanford, Calif.: Stanford University Press, 1998.

Stiegler, Bernard. *Technics and Time, 2: Disorientation*. Translated by Stephen Barker. Stanford, Calif.: Stanford University Press, 2009.

Stokes, Benjamin, and Dmitri Williams. "Gamers Who Protest: Small-Group Play and Social Resources for Civic Action." *Games and Culture* (2015), DOI: 10.1177/1555412015615770.

Stryker, Cole. *Epic Win for Anonymous: How 4chan's Army Conquered the Web*. New York: Overlook Duckworth, 2011.

Stuhlinger, Ernst, and Frederick I. Ordway. *Wernher von Braun, Crusader for Space: A Biographical Memoir*. Malabar, Fla.: Krieger, 1994.

Suits, Bernard. *The Grasshopper: Games, Life and Utopia*. Peterborough, Ont.: Broadview, 2005.

Sunder Rajan, Kaushik. *Biocapital: The Constitution of Postgenomic Life*. Durham, N.C.: Duke University Press, 2006.

Superheroes. Directed by Mike Barnett. Written by Mike Barnett and Theodore James. SuperFilms, 2011.

Suvin, Darko. *Metamorphoses of Science Fiction: On the Poetics and History of a Literary Genre*. New Haven, Conn.: Yale University Press, 1979.

Swanstrom, Elizabeth. *Animal, Vegetable, Digital: Experiments in New Media Aesthetics and Environmental Poetics*. Tuscaloosa: University of Alabama Press, 2016.

Taffel, Sy. "Escaping Attention: Digital Media Hardware, Materiality and Ecological Cost." *Culture Machine* 13 (2012), http://www.culturemachine.net/index.php/cm/article/view/468.

Taylor, T. L. *Play between Worlds: Exploring Online Game Culture*. Cambridge, Mass.: MIT Press, 2006.

Taylor, T. L. "Pushing the Borders: Player Participation and Game Culture." In *Structures of Participation in Digital Culture*, edited by Joe Karaganis, 112–32. New York: Social Science Research Council, 2007.

Terranova, Tiziana. *Network Culture: Politics for the Information Age*. London: Pluto, 2004.

Thacker, Eugene. *Biomedia*. Minneapolis: University of Minnesota Press, 2004.

Thacker, Eugene. *The Global Genome: Biotechnology, Politics, and Culture*. Cambridge, Mass.: MIT Press, 2005.

Thomas, Douglas. *Hacker Culture*. Minneapolis: University of Minnesota Press, 2002.

Toumey, Christopher P. *Conjuring Science: Scientific Symbols and Cultural Meanings in American Life*. New Brunswick, N.J.: Rutgers University Press, 1996.

Trekkies. Directed by Roger Nygard. Paramount, 1997.

Trekkies 2. Directed by Roger Nygard Paramount, 2004.

Tringham, Neal Roger. *Science Fiction Video Games*. Boca Raton, Fla.: Taylor and Francis, 2015.

Turkle, Sherry. *The Second Self: Computers and the Human Spirit*. 20th anniversary ed. Cambridge, Mass.: MIT Press, 2005.

Turner, Fred. *From Counterculture to Cyberculture: Stewart Brand, the Whole Earth Network, and the Rise of Digital Utopianism*. Chicago: University of Chicago Press, 2006.

Tye, Larry. *Superman: The High-Flying History of America's Most Enduring Hero*. New York: Random House, 2012.

uncertain commons. *Speculate This!* Durham, N.C.: Duke University Press, 2013.

van Der Walt, Charl. "The Impact of Nation-State Hacking on Commercial Cyber-Security." *Computer Fraud and Security* 22, no. 4 (2017): 5–10.

Vint, Sherryl. *Animal Alterity: Science Fiction and the Question of the Animal*. Liverpool: Liverpool University Press, 2010.

Vint, Sherryl. *Science Fiction: A Guide for the Perplexed*. London: Bloomsbury Academic, 2014.

Wakabi, Wairagala. "The Arms Smugglers." *New Internationalist* 367 (2004): 20–21.

Waldby, Catherine. *The Visible Human Project: Informatic Bodies and Posthuman Medicine*. London: Routledge, 2000.

Walz, Steffen P., and Sebastian Deterding, eds. *The Gameful World: Approaches, Issues, Applications*. Cambridge, Mass.: MIT Press, 2015.

Wark, McKenzie. *Gamer Theory*. Cambridge, Mass.: Harvard University Press, 2007.

We Are Legion: The Story of the Hacktivists. Written and directed by Brian Knappenberger. Luminant Media, 2012.

Webb, Amanda, Kieren Mayers, Chris France, and Jonathan Koomey. "Estimating the Energy Use of High Definition Games Consoles." *Energy Policy* 61 (2013): 1412–21.

Wegner, Phillip E. *Shockwaves of Possibility: Essays on Science Fiction, Globalization, and Utopia*. Oxford: Peter Lang, 2014.

Weis, Martin. "*Assassin's Creed* and the Fantasy of Repetition." In *Early Modernity and Video Games*, edited by Florian Kerschbaumer and Tobias Winnerling, 201–11. Newcastle upon Tyne, U.K.: Cambridge Scholars, 2014.

Weis, Martin. "Bio-Gaming: The Real Biopolitics of Virtual Bodies." PhD diss., University of California, Davis, 2015.

Wells, Matthew. "The Programmer as Player: Uncovering Latent Forms of Digital Play Using Structuration and Actor-Network Theory." *Loading . . . 7* (2013): 59–80.

Welsh, Timothy J. *Mixed Realism: Videogames and the Violence of Fiction*. Minneapolis: University of Minnesota Press, 2016.

Wesch, Michael, and the Digital Ethnography Class of Spring 2009. "Anonymous, Anonymity, and the End(s) of Identity and Groups Online: Lessons from the 'First Internet-Based Superconsciousness.'" In *Human No More: Digital Subjectivities, Unhuman Subjects, and the End of Anthropology*, edited by Neil L. Whitehead and Michael Wesch, 89–104. Boulder: University Press of Colorado, 2012.

Weston, Kath. *Animate Planet: Making Visceral Sense of Living in a High-Tech, Ecologically Damaged World*. Durham, N.C.: Duke University Press, 2017.

Wiener, Norbert. *Cybernetics: Or, Control and Communication in the Animal and the Machine*. 1948. 2nd ed. Cambridge, Mass.: MIT Press, 1961.

Wiener, Norbert. *The Human Use of Human Beings: Cybernetics and Society*. Boston: Houghton Mifflin, 1954.

Wills, Melissa A. "Corporate Agriculture and the Exploitation of Life in *Portal 2*." *Games and Culture* (2016), DOI: 10.1177/1555412016679771.

Wolf, Mark J. P. "Genre Profile: Adventure Games." In *The Video Game Explosion: A History from Pong to PlayStation and Beyond*, edited by Mark J. P. Wolf, 81–90. Westport, Conn.: Greenwood, 2008.

Wolfe, Cary. *What Is Posthumanism?* Minneapolis: University of Minnesota Press, 2010.

Wright, Bradford W. *Comic Book Nation: The Transformation of Youth Culture in America*. Baltimore: Johns Hopkins University Press, 2001.

Wright, J. Talmadge, David G. Embrick, and András Lukács, eds. *Utopic Dreams and Apocalyptic Fantasies: Critical Approaches to Researching Video Game Play*. Lanham, Md.: Lexington Books, 2010.

Wysocki, Matthew, and Evan W. Lauteria, eds. *Rated M for Mature: Sex and Sexuality in Video Games*. New York: Bloomsbury Academic, 2015.

Yee, Nick. "The Labor of Fun: How Video Games Blur the Boundaries of Work and Play." *Games and Culture* 1 (2006): 68–71.

Yee, Nick. *The Proteus Paradox: How Online Games and Virtual Worlds Change Us— and How They Don't*. New Haven, Conn.: Yale University Press, 2014.

Ziser, Michael, and Julie Sze. "Climate Change, Environmental Aesthetics, and Global Environmental Justice Cultural Studies." *Discourse* 29 (2007): 384–410.

CPSIA information can be obtained
at www.ICGtesting.com
Printed in the USA
FSHW021701061120
75497FS

9 781478 002925